The Twentieth-Century American Fiction Handbook

Blackwell Literature Handbooks

This new series offers the student thorough and lively introductions to literary periods, movements, and, in some instances, authors and genres, from Anglo-Saxon to the Postmodern. Each volume is written by a leading specialist to be invitingly accessible and informative. Chapters are devoted to the coverage of cultural context, the provision of brief but detailed biographical essays on the authors concerned, critical coverage of key works, and surveys of themes and topics, together with bibliographies of selected further reading. Students new to a period of study or to a period genre will discover all they need to know to orientate and ground themselves in their studies, in volumes that are as stimulating to read as they are convenient to use.

Published

The Science Fiction Handbook
M. Keith Booker and Anne-Marie Thomas

The Seventeenth-Century Literature Handbook
Marshall Grossman

The Twentieth-Century American Fiction Handbook
Christopher MacGowan

The Twentieth-Century American Fiction Handbook

Christopher MacGowan

WILEY-BLACKWELL

A John Wiley & Sons, Ltd., Publication

This edition first published 2011
© 2011 Christopher MacGowan

Blackwell Publishing was acquired by John Wiley & Sons in February 2007. Blackwell's publishing program has been merged with Wiley's global Scientific, Technical, and Medical business to form Wiley-Blackwell.

Registered Office
John Wiley & Sons Ltd, The Atrium, Southern Gate, Chichester, West Sussex, PO19 8SQ, United Kingdom

Editorial Offices
350 Main Street, Malden, MA 02148-5020, USA
9600 Garsington Road, Oxford, OX4 2DQ, UK
The Atrium, Southern Gate, Chichester, West Sussex, PO19 8SQ, UK

For details of our global editorial offices, for customer services, and for information about how to apply for permission to reuse the copyright material in this book please see our website at www.wiley.com/wiley-blackwell.

The right of Christopher MacGowan to be identified as the author of this work has been asserted in accordance with the UK Copyright, Designs and Patents Act 1988.

Wiley also publishes its books in a variety of electronic formats. Some content that appears in print may not be available in electronic books.

Designations used by companies to distinguish their products are often claimed as trademarks. All brand names and product names used in this book are trade names, service marks, trademarks or registered trademarks of their respective owners. The publisher is not associated with any product or vendor mentioned in this book. This publication is designed to provide accurate and authoritative information in regard to the subject matter covered. It is sold on the understanding that the publisher is not engaged in rendering professional services. If professional advice or other expert assistance is required, the services of a competent professional should be sought.

Library of Congress Cataloging-in-Publication Data

MacGowan, Christopher J. (Christopher John)
  The twentieth-century American fiction handbook / Christopher MacGowan.
     p. cm. – (Blackwell literature handbooks)
  Includes bibliographical references and index.
  ISBN 978-1-4051-6023-0 (hardcover: alk. paper) – ISBN 978-1-4051-6024-7 (pbk.: alk. paper)
  1. American fiction – 20th century – History and criticism – Handbooks, manuals, etc. I. Title.
  PS379.M255 2011
  813'.509–dc22   2010035340

A catalogue record for this book is available from the British Library.

Set in 10/13 pt Sabon by Thomson Digital, Noida, India
Printed in Malaysia by Ho Printing (M) Sdn Bhd

1   2011

Contents

Acknowledgments

I would like to thank Emma Bennett for giving me the opportunity to write this book, and I am grateful to the patient editorial staff at Wiley-Blackwell, especially Isobel Bainton, Ben Thatcher, and Caroline Clamp, and Caroline Richards. I received helpful suggestions from a number of my colleagues at the College of William and Mary, including Susan Donaldson, Colleen Kennedy, and Elsa Nettles, and also from John Gamber of Columbia University and Glen MacLeod of the University of Connecticut, Waterbury. I am always grateful to have had as my earliest teachers of American literature Tony Tanner, Emory Elliott, and A. Walton Litz.

How to Use This Book

This book is one of a series of Blackwell Literature Handbooks and consistent with the design of the series is intended as a guide both for the independent reader who wishes for an introduction to the major writers, texts, and issues of twentieth-century American fiction, and also for graduate students and upper-level undergraduates taking courses that focus upon this subject area. The book should also be helpful to students studying twentieth-century American literature more generally, as well as students of modern or contemporary fiction written in English.

After reading this book the reader will be aware of the major figures in twentieth-century American fiction and some of its central texts and themes. The book discusses some of the characteristics that distinguish the fiction of the century's early decades from the writing impacted by the rise of international modernism. There are also essays outlining the fiction of the Depression years, the fiction that emerged after World War II, and more recent fiction that explores the complexities of ethnic and national identity. Separate essays discuss the central importance of race in twentieth-century American fiction, the cultural assumptions that often limited the possibilities afforded women writers, the influence of Hollywood on the careers and subject matter of a number of major authors, and the notable achievements of American writers in the short story form.

As the reader will see from the Contents page, the information within the book is organized in a number of ways. A Chronology sets out some of the major social, technological, political, and literary events of the century as they provide a broad context for the fiction. In the Introduction I set out the thinking behind the choice of writers and texts for individual treatment, and discuss the scope of the more general historical and thematic essays. The reader who has little familiarity with the subject would do best starting with the general Introduction and the chronological essays. The four thematically focused essays are designed for a reader more familiar with the general subject of the volume, but may be read as individual, self-contained introductions to their topics.

The individual essays on writers and texts offer two perspectives upon the same story. The reader might choose to switch between individual writers and texts, to juxtapose larger groupings based upon chronology or shared formal or thematic concerns, or to read each section as a separate narrative. Not all writers who are the subject of an individual essay are represented by an essay in the section on texts. Note that where quotations are given, the page references are always from the edition listed first in the Bibliography at the end of the chapter.

Finally, the Guide to Further Reading is designed to point the way to further discussion of a century of writing which this one volume cannot hope to fully represent, but about which – if this book has achieved one of its primary aims – the reader will wish to know more.

Chronology: Significant Dates and Events, 1900–2000

1900	US population around 75 million, 14 times greater than in 1800; death of Stephen Crane
1901	First transatlantic radio transmissions; President McKinley assassinated, Theodore Roosevelt at 42 becomes the youngest President in the nation's history; first Nobel Prize for Literature Awarded (to French poet Sully Prudhomme)
1903	Wright Brothers make the first successful airplane flight; Leo and Gertrude Stein settle in Paris and begin to collect modern art; W. E. B. Du Bois publishes *The Souls of Black Folk*
1904	Pacific cable completed
1909	National Association for the Advancement of Colored People (NAACP) founded; Henry Ford begins production of Model "T" automobile
1910	Death of Mark Twain
1911	The Nestor Company opens the first film studio in Hollywood
1914	Panama Canal opens
1916	Death of Henry James
1917	US enters World War I

1918	First Pulitzer Prize for the Novel awarded, to *His Family* by Ernest Poole
1919	Alcock and Brown make the first non-stop flight in an aircraft across the Atlantic; O. Henry Awards begin for best short story: winners include William Faulkner (1939, 1949), Eudora Welty (1942, 1943, 1968), John Cheever (1956, 1964), Flannery O'Connor (1959, 1963, 1965), John Updike (1966), Joyce Carol Oates (1967, 1973), Saul Bellow (1978), Raymond Carver (1983, 1988), Alice Walker (1986)
1920	18th Amendment to the US Constitution prohibits the manufacture, sale, and transportation of alcoholic beverages ("Prohibition"); 19th Amendment grants the vote to women
1925	*The New Negro*, edited by Alain Locke, published
1926	Sinclair Lewis declines a Pulitzer Prize for *Arrowsmith* on the grounds that with the award's criterion that a winning novel "'present the wholesome atmosphere of American life' ... every compulsion is put upon writers to become safe, polite, obedient, and sterile"
1927	Transatlantic telephone service begins; Warner Brothers releases *The Jazz Singer*, the first successful sound film
1929	Stock market crash, beginning of the Great Depression; New York's Museum of Modern Art opens
1930	Sinclair Lewis becomes the first American to win the Nobel Prize in Literature; over four million unemployed
1933	"Prohibition" repealed; James Joyce's *Ulysses* allowed to be published in the United States; Screen Writers Guild formed in Hollywood; Franklin Roosevelt's first "New Deal" legislation; worst year for jobless rate in the Depression, 24.9%, 13 million unemployed
1935	Robert Penn Warren and Cleanth Brooks start the *Southern Review*; Federal Writers Project established as part of the Works Progress Administration
1936	Spanish Civil War (1936–1939) begins

1938	Pearl S. Buck becomes the first American women writer awarded the Nobel Prize in Literature
1939	John Crowe Ransom founds *The Kenyon Review*, a major literary journal of the 1940s and 1950s; regular transatlantic air service begins; mass-market paperbacks introduced in United States
1940	Richard Wright's *Native Son* is the first book by an African American writer to become a Book-of-the-Month Club selection. The novel sold 315 000 copies in the first three months of publication; Scott Fitzgerald dies owing Scribners $5456.92, his 1939 royalties total $33
1941	US enters World War II following Japanese attack upon Pearl Harbor
1944	US Supreme Court rules that no citizen may be denied the vote on grounds of color
1947	House Un-American Activities Committee begins investigation of alleged communist influence in Hollywood studios: nine screenwriters and one director who refuse to answer questions receive jail terms; Richard Wright leaves the United States and settles in France
1948	Invention of the transistor; *Literary History of the United States* published, 54 male editors listed, one female
1949	Network television starts in the United States
1950	US population 150 million; Korean War (1950–1953) begins; the first National Book Award for Fiction awarded to Nelson Algren's *The Man With the Golden Arm*
1954	US Supreme Court rules that racial segregation in schools is unconstitutional
1956	Martin Luther King Jr. leads bus boycott in Montgomery, Alabama
1958	Chester Carlson invents the photocopier for Xerox

1960	Beginning of the Civil Rights movement with a sit-in at the Woolworth's lunch counter, Greensboro, North Carolina; Zora Neale Hurston dies in a welfare nursing home, buried in an unmarked grave
1961	Suicide of Ernest Hemingway
1963	Civil Rights March on Washington; assassination of President Kennedy
1964	Race riots in Harlem and Philadelphia
1965	Vietnam War (1965–1973); Malcolm X assassinated; Congress establishes the National Endowment for the Arts
1966	National Organization for Women founded; Massachusetts Supreme Judicial Court declares William Burrough's *Naked Lunch* not obscene, ending the last major literary censorship battle in the United States
1967	Protest against Vietnam War grows; March on the Pentagon, October 21, Norman Mailer arrested; race riots in major cities continue
1968	Martin Luther King and Robert Kennedy assassinated
1969	Stonewall riots in New York City lead to beginning of Gay Liberation Movement; Apollo moon landing; Native American writer N. Scott Momaday's *House Made of Dawn* wins Pulitzer Prize for Fiction
1970	Native American Rights Fund established, non-profit law firm dedicated to asserting and defending the rights of Indian tribes, organizations, and individuals nationwide; first important black feminist anthology, *The Black Woman: An Anthology*, edited by Toni Cade Bambara
1972	Watergate break-in, President Nixon resigns in 1974
1976	US Bicentennial
1982	First Library of America volumes published, Jack London is the first twentieth-century writer included

1985	First year the National Award of Arts presented, Ralph Ellison among the recipients
1989	US invades Panama, first use of American military force since 1945 unrelated to the Cold War; fall of the Berlin Wall, collapse of the Soviet Union
1990	Oscar Hijuelos is the first Hispanic writer to receive a Pulitzer Prize for Fiction, for *The Mambo Kings Play Songs of Love*
1991	Iraq invades Kuwait, leading to Gulf War; World Wide Web introduced; Sandra Cisneros is the first Chicana writer to receive a contract from a major publishing house
1992	End of the Cold War (1945–1992); US intervention in Somalia
1993	Toni Morrison becomes the first African American to win the Nobel Prize in Literature
1994	US intervention in Haiti
1998	Eudora Welty is the first living author included in the Library of America series
1999	US part of NATO-backed military intervention in former Yugoslavia
2000	2000 census shows US population 281 million: 69.1% white, 12.5% Hispanic, 12.1% Black, 3.7% Asian and Pacific Islander, 0.7% American Indian; Hispanic population the fastest-growing group

Introduction

The block of five essays in this book that precede those treating individual writers and texts is broadly chronological in its arrangement. While the calendar provides neat boundaries to decades and centuries, history, of course, including the history of a century's literature, is never so tidy. Many of the prevailing ideas of the nineteenth century spill over into the twentieth in the history of American fiction, just as a few of the earlier century's major writers lived on into the new century. Both the writers and the prevailing ideas can be seen influencing the early history of the American Institute of Arts and Letters. The Institute was created in 1898, originally limited to 150 members (250 after 1907). In 1904 the members of the Institute elected the first seven members of an eventual fifty to the more elite American Academy of Arts and Letters (this two-tier system was eventually dropped in 1993). Of the four who represented literature in the 1904 election, John Hay was best known for his political and diplomatic career and for his biography of Lincoln, whom he had served as private secretary. Edmund Clarence Stedman was a respected poet and anthologist. The other two members elected are central to any history of American literature: William Dean Howells and Mark Twain. When the Academy expanded its membership the following year Henry James and Henry Adams were elected.

Howells, Twain, James, and Adams are major figures, yet arguably all but Adams had his best work behind him by 1905, and at least three of them, including Adams, had misgivings about what the new century would bring. Twain's work had become darker in his last years, and when he died in 1910 he left an unfinished novel, *The Mysterious Stranger*, which, while it is a celebration of imagination and the power of print, is deeply nostalgic about a lost innocence somewhat ambivalently associated with the antebellum South

The Twentieth-Century American Fiction Handbook   By Christopher MacGowan
© 2011 Christopher MacGowan

of his youth, an innocence that is both national and personal. James, elected to the Academy a year after beginning his first visit to the United States for 22 years, was deeply disturbed by many of the changes he witnessed, as he records in *The American Scene* (1907). Henry Adams, in *The Education of Henry Adams* (published in 1918 but written a dozen years earlier), saw himself as ill prepared for the twentieth century by his nineteenth-century education and experience. For Adams there seemed little place for the literary or the literary imagination in a new century dominated by the powerful and ever-growing world of science. Howells, elected the first President of the Academy in 1904, and outliving Twain, James, and Adams, had a forum for his views on literature – the "Editor's Easy Chair" column in *Harper's Monthly* – right up to his death in 1920. While Howells's views remained relatively conservative, he supported the writing of a number of emerging poets and novelists, recognizing the talents of Robert Frost and Edwin Arlington Robinson, but silent on Ezra Pound; including in his edition of *Great Modern American Short Stories* (1920) work by James, Twain, Charlotte Perkins Gilman, Sarah Orne Jewett, Theodore Dreiser, and Edith Wharton, but not Sherwood Anderson.

Although Julia Ward Howe was not a particularly adventurous choice as the first woman to be elected to the Academy in 1908 (she wrote the lyric to "The Battle Hymn of the Republic" in 1861 and was in her late eighties), more significant in literary terms was the election of Edith Wharton to the Institute in 1926 and to the Academy in 1930 (she had originally been nominated in 1908 along with Howe). The first black writer, however, W. E. B. Du Bois, was not elected to the Institute until 1944.

In the 1920s Ford Madox Ford, writing from Paris in the *transatlantic review*, where Hemingway was his assistant editor, more than once insisted that the most interesting work coming into the journal came from Americans. But a more prominent sign that American literature had received interna-tional recognition 110 years after Washington Irving had become its first internationally known author was the award to Sinclair Lewis in 1930 of the Nobel Prize in Literature. In his speech to the Swedish Academy Lewis surveyed the field of contemporary American literature, and in the process took to task the American Academy of Arts and Letters for still harboring the genteel ideas of late nineteenth-century Boston, and he particularly singled out its deceased first president.

Lewis regretted Howells's continuing influence "down even to 1914," and what Lewis saw as the timid gentility of Howells's realism. For Lewis, "Mr. Howells was one of the gentlest, sweetest, and most honest of men, but he had the code of a pious old maid whose greatest delight was to have tea at the vicarage," and he sought "to guide America into becoming a pale edition of an

English cathedral town." Howells had, for Lewis, presided over an Academy which even 10 years after his death could not find a place in its ranks for Theodore Dreiser, Willa Cather, Sherwood Anderson, Eugene O'Neill, Ernest Hemingway, John Dos Passos, William Faulkner, or Thomas Wolfe. Ironically, as Lewis half-recognized in his speech, he was naming some of the figures who would succeed him in the decade to become America's most important writers. By 1935 Lewis was willing to have his name on the ballot for the Institute, feeling that it had become a "much more vital" body since 1930, and most members were willing to forgive him. He was duly elected to the Institute, and admitted to the Academy in 1937. Of those on Lewis's Nobel list, Dreiser and Hemingway declined to be nominated, and were apparently not sufficiently moved by the changes that impressed Lewis to regret their exclusion.

The early history of the Institute of Arts and Letters is a useful touchstone to academic ideas of the canon in the first decades of the century, and a reminder of the marginalization of women's and minority voices in the circles of official culture at the time. Dreiser himself, in 1900, had encountered such conservative forces when he published *Sister Carrie*. Dreiser's novel refused to reward its heroine's immoral actions with ruin, pictured the streets of Chicago and New York as little more than urban jungles, and saw biological determinism as much more a force in human behavior than any kind of innate goodness. Dreiser had to revise his manuscript to make it even remotely publishable. And then, when Doubleday, Page accepted the novel – after further toning down – they tried to renege on the contract and refused to market the book, which eventually sold only 456 copies. Dreiser took matters into his own hands in 1907 and arranged for a reprint, and the novel was eventually picked up by Harper in 1912, even though they had originally rejected the novel in 1900 on the grounds that it would bring "offense to the reader." Dreiser's experience made him a hero for writers whose ideas of realism clashed with those of the more genteel tradition, and who demanded that serious writing be free from censorship. Sherwood Anderson dedicated his short story collection *Horses and Men* (1923) to Dreiser, adding "Because of him, those who follow will never have to face the road through the wilderness of Puritan denial, the road that Dreiser faced alone;" while for Lewis, in his Nobel Speech, *Sister Carrie* "came to housebound and airless America like a great free Western wind, and to our stuffy domesticity gave us the first fresh air since Mark Twain and Whitman."

The censorship of serious literature was not finally settled in the United States, however, until the mid-1960s, and the courts and government agencies were the opposition rather than the publishers. There were landmark cases along the way involving such high-profile texts as James Joyce's *Ulysses* and

Erskine Caldwell's *God's Little Acre*, but two later court decisions settled the matter. In 1964 the Supreme Court overruled earlier State Court decisions and declared Henry Miller's *Tropic of Cancer* not obscene. The book had been published in Paris in 1934 was banned in the United States until Grove Press published it in 1961. Two years later, in 1966, the Massachusetts Supreme Judicial Court lifted a Boston ban on William Burrough's *Naked Lunch*, which Grove had published in 1962, and which had also first been published in Paris. (Curiously, what is arguably the most famous work of American fiction first published in Paris, Vladimir Nabokov's *Lolita*, was not banned in the United States but in France. Nevertheless Orville Prescott, reviewing the novel in the *New York Times* upon its US publication in 1958 found it "repulsive" and "disgusting.")

In his Nobel speech Lewis expressed confidence that American literature was "coming out" of its "incredibly dull provincialism." The charge is unfair to the international scope of American writing going back to Benjamin Franklin, Fennimore Cooper, Herman Melville, Nathaniel Hawthorne, and Margaret Fuller, and of course to the international themes of Henry James; and Lewis could only have been thinking of fiction, since 15 years earlier Pound, Eliot, and H.D., working out of London, had turned American poetry in a direction anything but provincial. But as far as fiction was concerned, the 1920s had seen further achievements that justified Ford Madox Ford's claims and Lewis's assertion. The centers of American writing moved out from New England to include New York, Chicago, and New Orleans, and the setting of the novels reflected the diversity of the country's regions, whether New York, the Midwest, the South or the Southwest.

The international scope of American literature was continued, particularly in the 1920s, by those writers who felt that the United States was a country and a culture to observe from a distance. The essay "Expatriates: 1920s and Beyond" looks at the decade famously associated with the "lost generation," and at some of the writers who chose exile in subsequent decades. Hemingway's *The Sun Also Rises* and *A Farewell to Arms* are both set in Europe, as is his novel of the Spanish Civil War, *For Whom the Bell Tolls*, and many of his short stories. Many of the characters, particularly in his earlier works, are suffering from a displacement, partly that of exile and partly that of a cultural shift associated with the Great War, a displacement that finally cannot be ameliorated by alcohol, money, aimless travel, or nostalgia for the old moral, emotional, and gender certainties. A kind of cultural homelessness is also central to Fitzgerald's *Tender is the Night*, and to Djuna Barnes's *Nightwood*. In these expatriate novels the United States looms large as a presence, shaping from a distance both desire and loss. The same might be said of two later novels set in Europe, Burrough's *Naked Lunch* and Joseph Heller's *Catch 22*, novels in which the protagonists are caught in a dangerous world from which escape seems a promise as dangerous as it is desired.

In novels by black writers a protagonist may be exiled within his or her own culture, as happens with Bigger Thomas in *Native Son*, the unnamed narrator of *Invisible Man*, and Sethe of *Beloved*. Alienation is also the condition of white antagonists in *The Catcher in the Rye*, *The Crying of Lot 49*, *The Sound and the Fury*, *Wise Blood*, the novels of Raymond Chandler and Nathanael West, and the stories of Raymond Carver. But there are major works about what kind of community *is* achievable too, whether in the fragmentary moments of *Winesburg, Ohio*, or the more celebratory possibilities of *Their Eyes Were Watching God*.

While exile is a major theme of some writers, emigration to the United States, the expectations and the realities, is a theme of others. *My Ántonia*, *The House on Mango Street*, and *The Joy Luck Club* are all stories of the immigrant experience across more than one generation, and arguably *Herzog* and *Portnoy's Complaint* too – and even *Lolita*. And a theme associated with both exile and immigrants is travel, another way in which the century's American fiction avoids the provincial. Jack Kerouac's title *On the Road* could sum up such novels of travel as *The Grapes of Wrath*, *Neuromancer*, *All the Pretty Horses*, and *Ceremony*.

The growing wealth of the nation as it entered the new century, and the impact of that wealth upon those who share in it, or crave it, is also a major theme of twentieth-century American fiction – from the vulnerable heiresses of Henry James, to the consumption-oriented suburbias of Sinclair Lewis, John Cheever, John Updike, and Don DeLillo. The story of what wealth can and cannot buy is told in novels as complex as *The Wings of the Dove* and *The Great Gatsby*, and in stories as pared down as Hemingway's "Cat in the Rain." The heroines in four of the first six novels treated in the individual essays each have to make a choice between money and moral integrity, and in each case there are important consequences.

Money not as fictional theme but as a practical necessity has contributed to the impact of Hollywood, and to the role of the short story, in the history of twentieth-century American fiction – and these are the focus of two of the later essays in this book. Hollywood could be a source of riches for an author fortunate enough to sell a novel to the studios, or a last resort for an author whose novels weren't selling and needed an income. Employment could be very short term, and even lucrative contracts, as Scott Fitzgerald discovered, might not be renewed. Somewhere between the extremes of a large check in the mail and working on an assembly line churning out screenplays was the possibility for some – Raymond Chandler and William Faulkner are examples – of working on particular projects for a fixed period, using

Hollywood as something of a convenient supplement. Most novelists who worked in Hollywood held jaundiced views about the film industry or the individuals who controlled it, and their fiction about Hollywood reflected those views, although in the best-known of such novels, Fitzgerald's unfinished *The Last Tycoon*, the central figure, Monroe Stahr, is more sympathetically treated and at one point teaches a patronizing novelist a lesson about writing for film. There were always major novelists who had little success writing screenplays. Norman Mailer had an unproductive stint in Hollywood, and Stanley Kubrick preferred his own screenplay of *Lolita* to Nabokov's, even while giving the novelist the screen credit.

The large number of magazines and newspapers in the United States – and the circulation of some in the millions – meant that for twentieth-century fiction writers, at least until the advent of television, there was a well-paying market for short stories and even – in the earliest part of the century – for serialized novels. Short stories could help a new writer gain attention, as in the case of Hemingway, Flannery O'Connor, Eudora Welty, J. D. Salinger, and Sherman Alexie, or provide income between the appearance of novels, as happened with Fitzgerald and Thomas Wolfe. The reputation of some writers stems entirely, or mostly, from their short stories, as with O. Henry, Katherine Anne Porter, and Raymond Carver, or from the short story cycle, as with Sarah Orne Jewett and Sherwood Anderson. The commercial incentives and the nationwide circulation of the magazines contributed to make the short story genre an important component of the century's American fiction.

Developments in the 1930s are treated in the essay "Charting the Depression: The 1930s." The writers who could command high prices from Hollywood or from what became a diminished magazine market were spared the financial hardships of a decade that made others thankful to be employed in the Federal Writers Program – a branch of Franklin Roosevelt's New Deal. Modernist experiment continued to produce important texts – 1936 was the year of Faulkner's *Absalom, Absalom!*, and 1937 Djuna Barnes's *Nightwood* – but much of the fiction turned to individuals and families struggling to survive, and to the social and labor unrest brought on by the financial crisis. Of the two most prominent novels, Steinbeck's *The Grapes of Wrath* focused on the farmers displaced by the Dust Bowl in the Southwest and their exploitation in California, while Erskine Caldwell's *God's Little Acre* was set among the mill workers of North Carolina and their attempts to unionize. Steinbeck eventually won the Nobel Prize, and Caldwell's book became one of the best-selling novels ever published in the United States, its sales helped by the racy scenes that had the book prosecuted in New York for obscenity. The productions of the

Federal Writers Project were less prominent but have proven historically valuable, particularly the series of state guides, the research into black history, and the documentary photographs. Among the writers, Eudora Welty was one of the figures involved with the photography projects, Zora Neale Hurston's anthropological work received important support, Richard Wright worked on his first book while working at the Project's offices in Chicago and New York, and Ralph Ellison, only in his twenties, served a valuable writing apprenticeship.

Any selection of writers and texts to receive individual treatment can only be representative in a book with a century of fiction as its scope. My principle of selection has been to include among the writers some figures once more prominent than they now are but who have an importance that is more than just historical. The reputations of Sinclair Lewis, Thomas Wolfe, and John Barth, for example, are not what they were at the peak of their careers, but they remain important writers. Not every list of important texts might include *Nightwood*, *Naked Lunch*, or *The Color Purple*, while *Winesburg, Ohio* and *Portnoy's Complaint* do not shock as they once did, but all these texts add significantly to the story that this book has to tell. *Neuromancer* may stand out for some as an odd choice, yet Gibson's novel is the one science fiction text most likely to be included in Contemporary American Fiction courses and as such represents a breakthrough for a genre often unfairly dismissed. No writer is represented by an essay on more than one individual text since I was able to discuss the wider range of his or her career in the essays on individual writers. But clearly Henry James, Edith Wharton, William Faulkner, Thomas Pynchon, and Toni Morrison, perhaps others, could have been represented by more than one text. The novels by these writers that I selected for individual treatment seem to me important in various ways both in themselves and to the writer's career, but arguments could be made in every case for a different selection, with the exception perhaps of Morrison's *Beloved*. The dates assigned to individual texts are those of the first United States publication.

The thematic essays that accompany those on Hollywood and the short story take up the successful struggle undertaken by black writers and women writers over the century for the freedom to write and publish, and on subjects of their own choice. Sometimes this freedom could only be achieved at a distance from a culture viewed as hostile, and sometimes, understandably, that hostility was the subject of the fiction. Charlotte Perkins Gilman had complained early in the century that women were being limited in their fiction to a few repetitive subjects, but by the end of the century any genre and any subject – even westerns or boxing – was open to a writer who happened to be a woman.

My hope is that the reader interested in pursuing further some of the issues raised in the historical and thematic essays, and in the essays on individual writers and texts, will find helpful the Guide to Further Reading that concludes this book. This list, too, can only be representative, but I have tried to suggest some of the ways in which the careers, achievements, and issues that make up the subject of this book can be more fully explored.

Part 1

Historical Contexts

The American Scene, *c.*1900

When Henry James visited his home country in 1904 for the first time in 21 years, a visit partially recorded in his 1907 *The American Scene*, he was disappointed with the changes that he saw. He was disturbed by the evidence of massive immigration, and also by what he viewed as the country's rampant materialism. James's account is colored, of course, by his own career-long ambivalence toward the United States. His earliest novels, such as *The American* (1877) and *Daisy Miller* (1878), had portrayed their central American characters as naïve, as victims – each in their way wealthy without social sophistication, and each driven by a misguided self-reliance. Yet these characters are arguably morally superior to most of the Europeans with whom they interact. While James's later novels are considerably more complex, his overall view is little changed. In his early book-length study of Hawthorne (1879) James had regretted what he saw as the provincial limitations of the earlier writer, and his relatively late experience of European travel.

James was one of a number of prominent Americans, including painters James McNeill Whistler, John Singer Sargent, and Mary Cassatt, and novelist Edith Wharton, who chose to base themselves in Europe rather than staying in the United States. For some other writers disturbed by the vast changes in the United States in the last decades of the nineteenth century the changes provided new material for their fiction – raising questions about the ideals of democracy, about the degree and even the possibility of freedom of will, and about the quality of life produced by the hazardous working conditions and overcrowded housing that governed the existence of so many in the rapidly growing cities. Mark Twain, the opposite of James in so many ways in his subject matter and concept of fictional form, provided a bleak view of human

The Twentieth-Century American Fiction Handbook   By Christopher MacGowan
© 2011 Christopher MacGowan

nature in his final, unfinished novel *The Mysterious Stranger*, published posthumously in 1916. Set in 1490, two years before Columbus's landing, the book makes clear through its antagonist's trips into the future that the discovery of America will bring no fundamental changes to the human condition or to its ultimate fate.

By the turn of the century the United States had shifted from the largely agrarian economy in place at the end of the Civil War in 1865 to an economy that was fast making the country one of the world's major industrial powers. The opening of the transcontinental railroad meant that after 1880 the United States could be one vast, interconnected manufacturing center, the railroads linking the centers of raw materials, manufacturing, and distribution. This growth and new power was highlighted in two major international events, the 1893 World's Columbian Exposition in Chicago, celebrating the 400th anniversary of Columbus's arrival in the New World, and the 1904 St. Louis World's Fair celebrating the centennial of the Louisiana Purchase. The 1904 Fair also hosted the first Summer Olympic Games to be held in the United States.

Henry Adams, related to the second and sixth Presidents, his father a Congressman and US ambassador to Britain, and himself a Harvard graduate and eminent historian, used the Paris World's Fair of 1900 as the setting for his account of feeling confronted by a world of force for which his education and experience had little prepared him. "Historians undertake to arrange sequences ... assuming in silence a relation of cause and effect," but for Adams such sequences were broken by the scientific advances that he saw around him in the Great Exposition. He needed a scientist to guide him through the great hall of dynamos, but even so "found himself lying in the Gallery of Machines at the Great Exposition of 1900, his historical neck broken by the sudden irruption of forces totally new." Adams's recognition of the challenge posed to conventional arrangements of cause and effect anticipates the complexities of modernist form in a writer such as Faulkner, or in much modernist poetry, where continuities are dissolved and juxtaposition suggests the multiple possible relationships between events.

The new wealth and power of the United States was also projected abroad, and not just through the trips abroad that became a regular part of a wealthy family's experience. The Spanish American War of 1898 brought the United States – following Spain's defeat – Puerto Rico, the Philippines, and Guam, making the United States for the first time one of the colonial powers. In the same year the United States annexed the island of Hawaii, which would eventually become the fiftieth state in 1959.

The total population of the United States in 1870 was 38.5 million. By 1890 the population had doubled and by 1920 the figure was 123 million.

The largest cities by 1920 were New York, Philadelphia, and Chicago, which as well as being major industrial centers became central literary and publishing centers too, displacing the role formerly held by Boston. In these centers the influx of immigrants, mainly from Europe, together with a migration from small towns into the cities, made for a surplus of labor and kept wages low and living conditions poor. These poor living conditions were exacerbated by the boom-and-bust business cycles that came with the largely unregulated economic activity, a situation that also produced such immense fortunes as those of Andrew Carnegie, John D. Rockefeller, and J. Pierpont Morgan. Businessmen became the central figures of such realist novels as William Dean Howells's *The Rise of Silas Lapham* (1885), and later the trilogy by Theodore Dreiser, *The Financier* (1912), *The Titan* (1914), and *The Stoic* (1947). Novels by Upton Sinclair and Frank Norris also took up the world of business, merchandising, and labor, most notably in Sinclair's *The Jungle* (1906) and Norris's *The Octopus* (1901). The Jewish immigrant experience was captured by Abraham Cahan's *The Rise of David Levinsky* (1917).

This largely unregulated capitalism – attempts by workers to unionize and strike were likely to be countered by violence – was seen by some novelists in terms of the theories of competition laid out in the works of Charles Darwin and Herbert Spenser. Initially these conditions produced a call for greater realism in fiction, including contemporary settings and dialogue that reflected the speech of the day. But when such realism produced mainly accounts of middle-class urban life, naturalists such as Norris, Dreiser, and Stephen Crane – influenced by the writings of Émile Zola in France – presented a picture of conditions in which human will could do little to influence the forces of nature that determined individual fates. The realism of Howells appeared sentimental alongside such novels.

Henry James noticed on his 1904 visit the new freedoms allowed to American women, but this freedom did not extend to voting rights, which were not granted to women until 1920. Nevertheless, a number of important colleges for women had been established in the second half of the century, including Vassar (1861), Wellesley, Bryn Mawr, and Smith (all 1865), Barnard (1889), and Radcliffe (1894). The tensions between this move to greater independence and the moral and social expectations of female behavior remained very present. Edith Wharton's *The House of Mirth* (1905) illustrates the problems that lack of financial independence, the need to appear morally pure, and lack of the power that is available to men could bring to a young woman whose social world could ostracize as easily as it could protect her. One of Wharton's last short stories, "Roman Fever" (1936), shows how far women still had to come for social freedom at the turn of the century. As Grace Ansley and Alida Slade, in "ripe but well-cared for middle age," sit on a terrace in Rome while their daughters disappear for the day with two aviators, they reflect upon the generations of mothers who have sought to protect their young daughters on visits to the city: the dangers shifting from the "Roman Fever" that worried their grandmothers to "the spice of disobedience" that concerned their mothers, to the lack of concern felt by the two contemporary middle-aged ladies sitting on the terrace at their lunch table. James's unprotected Daisy Miller is a victim of "Roman Fever," while a generation later Kate Chopin's "disobedience" in publishing the story of Edna Pontellier's rebellion against a stifling marriage in *The Awakening* (1899) sharply curtailed Chopin's future writing career, and her heroine found no alternative to suicide. Little wonder that Dreiser had trouble publishing *Sister Carrie* (1900), where his Carrie Meeber goes largely un-punished for her ruthless independence – a novel which Sinclair Lewis, upon accepting the Nobel Prize (in 1930 the first American writer so honored), declared "came to housebound and airless America like a great free Western wind."

Frank Norris tried to help Dreiser get his novel published, and later Dreiser in turn helped Sherwood Anderson. Anderson rejected realism as merely the reporting of surface differences, and instead was interested in the inner, subconscious and often sexual, forces that drove his characters. His *Wines-burg, Ohio* (1919) is set in the last years of the century. Its "backward view" illustrates the impact of the growth of cities upon small-town life, the struggles of women to find a voice and an independent role in a world still largely dominated by men and male assumptions, the warping of imagination that Anderson felt commercial standards in writing and publishing had brought to literature, and the over-investment in empty rhetoric and facile idealism that he thought had taken both literature and the country itself in the wrong direction at a moment when both might have finally begun to fulfill their potential. Anderson's resistance to the plot-shaped short story and his interest in the inner life of his characters were features explored further by Ernest Hemingway and William Faulkner, two writers who received help and advice from Anderson early in their careers.

Willa Cather, in a series of novels, also looked back at the end of the nineteenth century from the perspective of the 1920s. In *A Lost Lady* (1923) and *The Professor's House* (1925) both title characters live into a century at odds with the era that shaped their identities and values. Marion Forrester is a survivor, but finds only in the frontier culture of South America a place in which she can still – now wearing heavy makeup – feel at ease. Professor Godfrey St. Peter opts for isolation, as the goals of his family and the college administrators change around him. Cather eventually abandoned the juxtaposition of historical periods that shape these and some of her other novels, and turned completely to the past. In Cather's *Death Comes for the Archbishop* (1927), set in nineteenth-century New Mexico, the aged, now retired Bishop and his Navajo friend and former guide reflect upon the changes and innovations that have come to the Southwest in the decades since they first traveled together across the vast distances of the new diocese. "Men travel faster now," reflects the guide, "but I do not know if they go to better things."

For America's black population, in some ways there had been too little change. The Thirteenth Amendment to the constitution abolished slavery in 1865 following the end of the Civil War, and during the period known as Reconstruction the federal government attempted to rebuild the South and enforce a degree of equality. But after 1877, when federal intervention in the South ceased, the southern states began to enact restrictions upon black voting rights, and to enforce the segregation in public transport and public schools that would last into the middle of the next century. The *Plessy vs. Ferguson* Supreme Court decision of 1896 affirmed the legality of racial segregation, a decision not overturned until the Supreme Court ruled in 1954 with *Brown vs. Board of Education* that such inequality was unconstitutional. A difference arose between the two black leaders Booker T. Washington and W.E. B. Du Bois over the degree of compromise that should be made with white racism and the segregation laws. Washington's "Atlanta Compromise" speech of 1895 and his autobiography *Up from Slavery* (1901) argued for a more incremental approach. Du Bois, co-founder of the influential National Association for the Advancement of Colored People in 1909, and author of *The Souls of Black Folk* (1903), argued for a more radical challenge to racial inequality. Washington became the first head of the Tuskegee Institute (now Tuskegee University) at the age of 25, and Du Bois was the first African American to receive a doctorate from Harvard University. Despite their different approaches, the legacy of both leaders was important to the later civil rights campaigns of the mid-century. Washington's views were treated scathingly, however, by Ralph Ellison in his novel *Invisible Man* (1952), where a thinly disguised version of Tuskegee is presented as making too much of a compromise with its white patrons.

The end of the Indian Wars came in 1890 with the Battle of Wounded Knee, which involved remnants of the Sioux Nation. The most famous Apache, Geronimo, had surrendered in 1886, and in 1905 rode in President Theodore Roosevelt's inaugural parade. The Native American population had been the victims of a federal policy of forced removal from their native lands – westward and into poverty-stricken reservations. Then the General Allotment Act of 1887 went against Indian cultural tradition by giving individual plots to individual Indians, and dissolved collective tribal claims to the land. But the land was often of too poor a quality to farm successfully, and the Indians lacked the resources and skills for modern agricultural methods. Indian children attended schools away from the reservations where the education sought to remove them from attachment to their tribal heritage and customs as part of a plan to assimilate them into mainstream culture. A number of Native American writers sought to keep their cultural heritage alive in the early decades of the century, along with describing the dislocation that resulted from such government policies. Most notable among these writers was Zitkala-Sa, an important activist and reformer. The poverty, isolation, and alienation that characterized reservation life through to the end of the twentieth century, despite the Allotment Act being repealed in 1934, are recorded powerfully in the works of such later Native American writers as N. Scott Momaday, Leslie Marmon Silko, and Sherman Alexie.

Expatriates: 1920s and Beyond

American writers had been writing about Americans in Europe long before Henry James. Most of Washington Irving's essays in *The Sketch Book of Geoffrey Crayon* (1819–1820) describe his impressions of England. Following the Civil War, as the wealthy upper middle class increased in number, and improvements in transportation made the Atlantic crossing easier, more and more Americans visited Europe, motivated by fashion, curiosity, and an interest in Europe's cultural heritage – an interest sometimes so worshipful as to reveal insecurities about the newness of their own country. A number of travelers wrote accounts of their trips and impressions, including James Fenimore Cooper, Frederick Douglass, Ralph Waldo Emerson, Margaret Fuller, and Herman Melville. These accounts are serious reflections upon cultural differences, but Mark Twain satirized the tendency of less thoughtful tourists to defer to all things European and old in a number of his books, most notably *The Innocents Abroad* (1869) and *A Connecticut Yankee in King Arthur's Court* (1889).

But some Americans in Europe were not tourists but exiles. Hawthorne's *The Marble Faun* (1860) and the many Henry James novels with an international setting feature colonies of American expatriates who for artistic, cultural, or personal reasons prefer to live in Europe. Sometimes these expatriates are like the American society ladies living in Rome in *Daisy Miller* (1878), whose study of the natives, inflexibility concerning social mores, and concern about how they themselves are judged leaves them with a framework of social values alien to both their homeland and their adopted land.

James himself lived in England for the last 40 years of his life, but it was left to two later expatriates, Ezra Pound and T. S. Eliot, to be among the first to

The Twentieth-Century American Fiction Handbook   By Christopher MacGowan
© 2011 Christopher MacGowan

recognize the importance of his achievement. Pound's essays in particular reveal that James's attitude to the United States speaks to the poet's own sense of alienation. Fellow exile Edith Wharton, once she had separated from her husband in 1911, lived in France for the rest of her life. As well as setting some of her novels in Europe, and publishing accounts of her travels, she was honored by the French government after World War I for her work with war orphans and refugees. Her final, unfinished, novel, *The Buccaneers* (1938), brings to England a group of five rich American girls whose money is too new for acceptance into New York Society. In England they look to marry into the aristocracy.

However, a number of events at the end of World War I combined to make the 1920s the most prominent decade of expatriate life in twentieth-century American fiction, both in terms of subject matter and the decision by individual writers to live in exile. Paris was usually the city of choice. Just a few years earlier New York had started to become an important center of international avant-garde artistic activity. With the 1913 Armory Show, the citizens of New York, Chicago and Boston were introduced to the work of such European artists as Cézanne, Matisse, Brancusi, Gleizes, and Marcel Duchamp. During the war Duchamp – whose work was one of the sensations of the exhibition – made New York his base, as did a number of other modernist artists. When the war finished, the European artists returned home, mostly to Paris, and were soon followed by many Americans. This exodus led William Carlos Williams, who had joined in the hopes for a post-war United States to become the major center of modernist experiment, to express his disappointment by titling his next book of poems *Sour Grapes* (1921).

The United States' involvement in the war further increased that international presence which had begun at the end of the previous century. The consequences of its intervention and its role in the founding of the League of Nations left the United States a global power by the beginning of the 1920s. A few American writers had been part of the US forces in Europe, but two of the most prominent, e. e. cummings and Ernest Hemingway, had been volunteers for the Red Cross Ambulance services. Cummings's autobiographical novel *The Enormous Room* (1922) describes his temporary imprisonment by the French authorities in 1917. Hemingway's war experiences are central to the narrative of his *A Farewell to Arms* (1929). Both Cummings and Hemingway spent much of the 1920s in Paris, where the strength of the dollar against the currencies of an economically weakened Europe offered many American writers and artists the chance to live cheaply and write – or, in the case of not a few, to talk about writing and being a writer. Paris also offered an escape from Prohibition, enacted in the United States in 1920 and not repealed until 1933. Prominent among the Americans spending a substantial amount of time in

Europe in the 1920s – joining such exiles from their European homelands as James Joyce, Ford Madox Ford, and Pablo Picasso – were Man Ray, Charles Demuth, F. Scott Fitzgerald, Djuna Barnes, H.D., Ezra Pound, Henry Miller, and John Dos Passos. Paris was also the center of the most famous expatriate salon, run by Gertrude Stein and her companion Alice B. Toklas. Stein and Toklas's apartment at 27 rue de Fleurus was a place to see the work of such painters as Matisse, Picasso, Braque, and Juan Gris, to meet writers and to discuss writing – including Stein's own experiments. Also living in Paris were Natalie Barney, Peggy Guggenheim, and the English-born Nancy Cunard, three of the most visible expatriate patrons, and they too were the center of much artistic activity.

Paris, along with a number of other European capitals, was an inexpensive place to put out a limited circulation magazine publishing experimental writing. *The Little Review*, which had published Joyce's *Ulysses* serially when the magazine was still based in the United States, moved to Paris, along with its editors Margaret Anderson and Jane Heap. Robert McAlmon started his Contact Editions, publishing Hemingway, William Carlos Williams, Ezra Pound, and Gertrude Stein, among others, while other important small presses included William Bird's Three Mountains Press and the Black Sun Press run by Harry and Caresse Crosby. Influential expatriate magazines included Ford Madox Ford's *transatlantic review* (where Hemingway worked as assistant editor), *transition*, *Broom*, and *This Quarter*. These books and magazines could be read, borrowed, or purchased at the fabled Shakespeare and Company bookshop at 12 rue de l'Odéon, run by Sylvia Beach, while another gathering place was the bookstore across the road run by French-born Adrienne Monnier. Sylvia Beach wrote her own memoir of these years, *Shakespeare and Company* (1956), as did McAlmon in his *Being Geniuses Together* (1938). McAlmon's account was reissued in 1968, with supplementary chapters by Kay Boyle adding her own account of the decade.

Hemingway and Fitzgerald are two of the American writers most prominently associated with the decade. Many of Hemingway's early short stories concern Americans attracted to Europe who find that whatever sense of emptiness or rootlessness took them away from the United States cannot be remedied merely by having money. Money might allow the aimless drifting of the Elliots in "Mr. and Mrs. Elliot," or buy excellent service from a hotel keeper in "Cat in the Rain," but cannot solve the barren marriages of the couples in these stories. In the two novels that established Hemingway's reputation, *The Sun Also Rises* (1926) and *A Farewell to Arms* (1929), both central characters are expatriates suffering a painful loss, both tortured by a romantic longing made impossible to fulfill by events over which they have no control. In a later novel, *For Whom the Bell Tolls* (1940), which is set in the

Spanish Civil War, the central American character comes more fully to terms with these limitations, but at the cost of his life.

Hemingway's posthumously published memoir of his Paris years, *A Moveable Feast* (1964, newly edited 2009), is openly nostalgic, but is unsympathetic in its treatment of a number of the most famous expatriates, including Ford Madox Ford, Gertrude Stein, and Scott and Zelda Fitzgerald. Fitzgerald himself looks back on the decade in his often-anthologized story "Babylon Revisited," first published in the *Saturday Evening Post* in February 1931. This thinly disguised autobiographical account that takes in the Wall Street crash of 1929, Zelda's mental deterioration, and the couple's excessive drinking, examines the cost to the writer and his family of early success and self-indulgence. Like Fitzgerald himself in the early 1930s, Charlie Wales is trying to put the years of his Paris excesses behind him in order to begin a life with his young daughter, but as often happens in Fitzgerald's fiction the impact of the past can never be fully escaped. Fitzgerald's major work to come out of his expatriate years is his 1934 *Tender Is the Night*, a novel which shares some of the same autobiographical background as Zelda Fitzgerald's only novel, *Save Me the Waltz*, which had appeared two years earlier. The composition of Fitzgerald's novel was slow, delayed in part by his having to publish commercial short stories to help cover the cost of Zelda's treatment. When the book eventually appeared, its story of wealthy expatriates and its Riviera setting in the 1920s marked this novel for some as belonging to another, now largely irrelevant, world.

Although most of the American expatriates returned home following the Wall Street crash in 1929, one writer who had arrived in 1921 and stayed for 20 years was Djuna Barnes, whose novel of the more sexually diverse side of expatriate life, *Nightwood*, did not appear until 1936 but is set in the 1920s. The novel's impressionistic style has been seen as anticipating the work of a number of later post-modern writers, and it is generally considered one of the first books by a major novelist to openly depict homosexuality. Another writer who broke some of the boundaries of writing about sex, Henry Miller, spent the 1930s in Paris. Gertrude Stein and Sylvia Beach were also two figures who stayed in the city, although their lives were eventually disrupted by the Nazi occupation, and Beach's bookstore had suffered economically in the 1930s.

In the year that Gertrude Stein died, 1946, she met Richard Wright in Paris, and the following year he took up residence in the city permanently – part of a second wave of expatriates in the city that reached its height in the 1950s. Despite Wright's success as the author of *Native Son* (1940) and *Black Boy* (1945), books which won him transatlantic fame, he felt constrained as a writer by the racial climate within the United States. Wright's major novel written in exile, *The Outsider* (1953), is strongly influenced by European concepts of existentialism. James Baldwin also found in Europe relief from American racism, and also from prejudice against homosexuals. His book of essays, *Notes of a Native Son* (1955), includes several essays that examine aspects of expatriate life, whether finding himself the only black person in an Alpine village, or looking at the numbers of ex-GIs who stayed on in Europe after the war and speculating on their awareness of their homeland's racial history. Baldwin set his second novel, *Giovanni's Room* (1956), in France, its central, white, American character ambivalent about his own and others' homosexuality.

It was racial and sexual prejudice that led Wright and Baldwin into exile, but the McCarthy witch hunts drove some other writers and artists to leave the United States in the 1950s, particularly writers and directors based in Hollywood. Some, like Joseph Losey and Stanley Kubrick, stayed in Europe, feeling that they could enjoy greater creative freedom in Europe without the commercial constraints of Hollywood financing. Kubrick came to this conclusion while filming *Lolita* (1962) in England. Yet with the publication of that famous book, author Vladimir Nabokov, previously an exile from Russia in Germany, and later an exile who became an American citizen, joined the ranks of American exiles himself when he moved to Switzerland. Although the country lost this particular author, Nabokov's international journeys foreshadow not only the blurring of national identities and boundaries to come in the second half of the century, but also the ability of the United States to attract major writers and artists with its financial opportunities and more tolerant cultural climate – rather than, as in its previous decades, to alienate them.

Charting the Depression: The 1930s

The stock market crash of October 24, 1929 is usually seen as marking the beginning of the Great Depression in the United States. By the middle of November about $30 billion had been wiped from stock values, and by March unemployment had doubled to affect 3.2 million workers. By 1932 the figure stood at 12 million. In 1931 food riots broke out in a number of cities, there was a growing resentment of foreign workers, and at the end of the year the biggest bank failure up to that date occurred with the collapse of New York's Bank of the United States. The newly formed Reconstruction Finance Corporation offered some support to banks, and also to the individual states, but it was left to President Roosevelt's administration once he took office in 1933 to initiate fuller and more creative government intervention. This intervention included the wholesale reform of the banking system, and a number of large-scale employment programs – including the support of writers. High unemployment continued into the late years of the decade, and was only relieved by the focus on the war effort that came with US entry into World War II in 1941.

With the onset of the Depression opportunities for writers to publish their work began to diminish as fewer books were published or reprinted. Publishers' revenues halved between 1929 and 1934, and writers' royalty incomes plummeted. Some of the better-paying magazines went out of business, and newspapers laid off staff. For some writers Hollywood offered an alternative source of income, but while contracts could be lucrative, often employment might be ended unpredictably as the needs of a producer or studio boss changed. Some of the best-known novels of the century appeared in the

The Twentieth-Century American Fiction Handbook   By Christopher MacGowan
© 2011 Christopher MacGowan

1930s, and sold very well for their authors, including Erskine Caldwell's *God's Little Acre* (1933), James T. Farrell's *Studs Lonigan Trilogy* (1932–1935), the *U.S.A.* trilogy of John Dos Passos (1930–1936), and, most famous of all, John Steinbeck's *The Grapes of Wrath* (1939).

Much of the fiction of the decade reflected the leftward political shift taken by many of the writers. Democracy and capitalism seemed to have failed, or at least to be in crisis. The boundaries between fiction, journalism, and documentary became blurred in the detailed accounts of suffering working-class families on the farms or in cities. Socialist and communist remedies were often part of the aesthetic within the decade's proletarian novels, although, as Walter B. Rideout has shown in his *The Radical Novel in the United States, 1900–1954* (1956), there were disputes among different writers about what the necessary politics and subject matter of a proletarian novel should be. The social and political concerns of many writers became even more acute with the rise of fascism in Italy and Germany through the decade.

Fiction writers who had established successful careers in the 1920s responded to the changed conditions in different ways. Sherwood Anderson became more involved in labor politics and wrote more non-fiction. Sinclair Lewis produced his anti-utopian novel *It Can't Happen Here* in 1935, a reflection on the danger of a government elected on a wave of populism turning into a dictatorship. The changed conditions less directly affected the fiction of Willa Cather, F. Scott Fitzgerald, Ernest Hemingway, William Faulkner, and Thomas Wolfe. Cather turned her attention to novels with an historical setting. Although one of Fitzgerald's finest short stories, "Babylon Revisited," is a post-Depression narrative, the central character, Charlie Wales – as he tells the barman at the Ritz at the end of the story – suffered his losses in the boom, not in the crash. Much of Hemingway's 1930s fiction is set abroad, and he was particularly active in support for the Republican cause in the Spanish Civil War. The South of Faulkner's fiction is haunted by events more sweeping and more rooted in the past than the Wall Street Crash. Thomas Wolfe's writing continued the multi-novel autobiographical narrative that he had begun with *Look Homeward, Angel* (which had been published just 11 days before the stock market crash). Wolfe did begin to be disturbed, on his travels to Germany in the mid-1930s, by what he could see of the activities of Hitler's government.

For those writers who weren't already established, didn't author a best-seller, or pick up a lucrative contract in Hollywood, the best chance of a reliable income lay with working for a government-supported program – usually the Federal Writers Project. The federal government recognized that unemployed writers, as well as unemployed farmers and factory workers, desperately needed assistance, and therefore the Writers Project was set up in

1935. Among the Project's tasks was employing writers to work on guides to each of the states, as part of a proposed multi-volume guidebook of the whole country. One drawback to the plan was that most writers congregated in the country's large urban areas, and in some more rural states few professional writers could be found. The individual guidebooks as they appeared varied greatly in quality and approach, despite the efforts of the Project's coordinating office in Washington, but they nevertheless remain an invaluable account of the landscape, culture, and attitudes of the time. On average the Federal Writers Project had about 5000 people annually on its regular payroll during the four years of its existence. Among the fiction writers employed by the agency were John Cheever on the New York State project, Nelson Algren – who in 1950 would publish *The Man With the Golden Arm* – in Chicago, and Tillie Olson – whose novel of the 1920s working poor, *Yonnondio: From the Thirties*, would not be published for 40 years – in California. Novelist Dorothy Canfield Fisher wrote the introduction to the Vermont volume. Studs Terkel worked in the Chicago office and in later life would undertake a number of valuable oral histories, including *Hard Times: An Oral History of the Great Depression* (1970). For one of the auxiliary projects Philip Rahv and Nathan Asch helped translate articles on Jewish life in America from Yiddish into English. In 1939 the Federal Writers Project came under increasing attack for what were seen as its socialist politics, and it began to be phased out, to be replaced in 1941, the year that the last of the state guides appeared, by a pared-down Writers Program.

Black writers were very underrepresented on the Federal Writers Project payrolls, but among those employed were Claude McKay and Ralph Ellison in New York, Arna Bontemps in Chicago, and Richard Wright – who worked at different times in both cities. With the help of this support Wright began work on the short stories of *Uncle Tom's Children* (1938) and the novel *Native Son* (1940). The Project also supported Zora Neale Hurston's anthropological work in Florida. Generally the Project's recognition of the importance of recording African American history and folklore helped to offset some of the underrepresentation and prevailing stereotypes of blacks and black history that found its way into some of the state guidebooks.

The book containing the best-known documentary work of the era, James Agee and photographer Walker Evans's *Let Us Now Praise Famous Men*, was not a Federal Writer's Project publication. The book appeared in 1941, but had its beginnings in an article commissioned in 1936 by *Fortune* magazine to explore the lives of tenant farmers in Alabama. The article never appeared, having grown beyond the bounds of its original commission, and the 400-page book initially received little attention upon publication. But since its republication in 1960 it has been widely praised both for its documentary value and for the way in which it mixes journalism, essays, and fiction in order to get closer to the lives of the sharecropper families it records – as well as to convey the experience of undertaking the assignment itself.

The focus in much 1930s fiction on contemporary events, the often overt political positions behind its social protest, and its sometimes schematic narratives, lead to its comparative neglect in the decades that immediately followed. The political and social issues for many readers were dated, and the novels seen as of more historical than creative interest. Even the work of Steinbeck and Dos Passos suffered somewhat from this view, a situation not helped by both authors' later work being seen as adding little to their reputations. But the recent renewal of interest in the decade, together with a more sympathetic examination of the interplay of history, fiction, and non-fiction, has brought new attention to some neglected writers. One writer whose reputation suffered far more than Steinbeck's or Dos Passos's was Josephine Herbst. Herbst worked as a correspondent for many of the most prominent left-wing journals of the decade, such as *New Masses* and *Partisan Review*, covering such events as the Iowa farm strikes, the auto-workers' protests, the General Strike in Cuba, and the rise of fascism. She had already published two novels and many short stories when she began her Depression-era trilogy *Pity Is Not Enough* (1933), *Executioner Waits* (1934), and *Rope of Gold* (1939). The novels chart American history from the Civil War to 1937, focusing on one family's successive generations as they move across the continent.

Two other writers whose Depression-era work fared better in later years than Herbst's are Erskine Caldwell and James T. Farrell. Caldwell published 25 novels during his career, but his two novels from the early 1930s remain his best known. *Tobacco Road* (1932) centers upon extreme rural poverty in the South, while *God's Little Acre* (1933) focuses on the South's industrial problems, particularly among workers in the textile mills. The latter is often cited as one of the best-selling American novels of the century. It played an important early role in establishing First Amendment freedom of expression rights for authors when the New York Society for the Suppression of Vice lost a court case that accused the book of being pornographic in its explicit scenes of sexuality. *Tobacco Road*, dramatized by Jack Kirkland, opened on Broadway in 1933, and when it closed in 1941 it had set a record for the longest run by a play on Broadway at that time. The film version was less successful. The same Twentieth Century Fox team of director John Ford and writer Nunnally Johnson, who had produced the much-admired film version of *The Grapes of Wrath*, were behind the production. But the studio interfered to such an extent that the film sentimentalizes Caldwell's characters in a way that the novel refuses to do, as well as turning the subtleties of Caldwell's comedy into burlesque humor.

Like so many of the novelists, James T. Farrell was a central figure in left-wing politics in the 1930s, although his best-known trio of novels, the *Lonigan* trilogy, is set in the decades just before the Depression. As with Dos Passos's *U.S.A.* trilogy, which also ends with the 1920s, the accounts of the earlier decades are infused with the politics and aesthetics of the 1930s. As told in *Young Lonigan* (1932), *The Young Manhood of Studs Lonigan* (1934), and *Judgment Day* (1935), Studs grows up to live a brutal life on the streets of Chicago's Catholic South Side. Farrell's stark realism in these novels and in his other writing influenced many social protest writers in later decades, including novelist Norman Mailer and oral historian Studs Terkel, who apparently adopted his first name after Farrell's famous character.

Post-war Alienation, Experiment, and Alternatives

World War II left the United States economically powerful, in contrast to the devastated economies of Europe and the Soviet Union. But new enemies arose, either external – the Soviet Union and later China – or internal – the communist infiltrators and sympathizers seen everywhere by Joseph McCarthy's Senate hearings and the investigations of the House Committee on Un-American Activities. One effect of seeing such pervasive threats was a tendency toward cultural uniformity in the 1950s, reinforced by growing middle-class wealth, the mobility offered by the newly built national inter-state highway system, the explosive growth of television ownership and the stations' increasingly homogenized programming, and the growth of city suburbs quickly and uniformly laid out across the country. Poet Robert Lowell described the decade in his book *Life Studies* (1959) as "the tran-quillized fifties," and in declaring his own alienation he saw President Dwight Eisenhower, elected in 1952, as an appropriately bland leader.

Television situation comedies, light entertainment, and the popular press often stressed this uniformity, but the tranquility was only on the surface and the 1960s would bring discontent, violence, and challenges to many cultural and political assumptions. This discontent was already making itself felt in the 1950s through the Civil Rights movements. Some of the racial segregation barriers that had returned, particularly to the South, began to be dismantled by the federal government. The US armed services were integrated in 1948, the Supreme Court found segregation in public schools unconstitutional in 1954, and a bus boycott in 1956, organized by Martin Luther King in Montgomery, Alabama, ended the practice of making black passengers sit

The Twentieth-Century American Fiction Handbook   By Christopher MacGowan
© 2011 Christopher MacGowan

in the back of a bus. In the 1960s the Kennedy and Johnson administrations involved the federal government even more fully in enforcing the law, for example forcing the integration of the University of Mississippi in 1962. Martin Luther King famously demanded full equality in the August 1963 March on Washington for Civil Rights, where in front of some 200,000 protesters he delivered his "I Have a Dream" speech. The Civil Rights Act of 1964 and the Voting Rights Act of 1965 were important later milestones. The fiction of America's major black writers reflected the sense of discontent behind the protests in their different ways. Richard Wright's Bigger Thomas in *Native Son* (1940) had been defeated by whiteness and Wright himself went into exile. James Baldwin also became an exile, but argued for a more conciliatory position, calling for a broader understanding of racial history as a way for whites and blacks to understand their shared heritage. Ralph Ellison, who did not choose exile, depicted in his *Invisible Man* (1952) the unnamed central figure turning his invisibility into a way to survive an oppressive system, living underground, preparing his plans to re-emerge.

Award-winning poet and playwright LeRoi Jones changed his name to Imamu Amiri Baraka in the mid-1960s and began to write exclusively for a black audience. Jones had originally been associated with the Beat writers in New York's Greenwich Village but concluded that their work was finally more self-absorbed than radical. But the works of the Beats, most famously Allen Ginsberg's poem *Howl* (1956) and *On the Road* (1957) by one of *Howl*'s dedicatees, Jack Kerouac, were rebellious enough to indicate that not all was quiet among America's youth in the 1950s. The depictions of a frustrated raw energy translated into the excesses of sex, travel, drugs, and finally self-destruction predicted the larger spread of a counterculture in the decade to come. To various degrees the central characters in some of the key novels of the decade are alienated from mainstream culture. In addition to *On the Road* the list includes William Burroughs's *Naked Lunch* (1959/1962) and J. D. Salinger's *The Catcher in the Rye* (1951), while Flannery O'Connor in her novels and stories showed characters so caught up in the self-satisfied materialism of this world that they alienated themselves from the spiritual needs of the next. Her narratives used comic understatement, images of sudden cruelty, and the intrusion of violence in an attempt to shatter these materialistic values.

Illusions of 1950s tranquility became impossible to carry into the next decade, which was marked by a series of shattering events, including the assassinations of President Kennedy, his brother Robert, Malcolm X, and Martin Luther King, the Civil Rights marches and urban race riots, and the polarizing war in Vietnam. Some writers began to question whether creating fictions was an adequate or even responsible way to take account of such events, while others raised questions about the nature of fiction itself and its relationship – if any – to the world outside of its own constructions.

Some writers continued to write fine realistic fiction, and John Updike was one of its leading proponents. Saul Bellow's novels also remained realistic, his central characters arguably even more isolated, confused, and insecure than Updike's. But others emphasized that literature should do what they argued literature does best: bring reader and author together on what Vladimir Nabokov called in *Lolita* (1958) an "island of entranced time" within which one can realize "aesthetic bliss." Nabokov insisted that he was neither a reader nor a writer of moral fiction, and such novels as *Lolita* and *Pale Fire* (1962) determinedly call attention to themselves as constructed texts (although arguably the theme of exile at the center of both reflects Nabokov's own status). The two points of view can be summed up in a 1970s exchange between John Gardner, defending the moral role of fiction and the possibilities of realism, and William Gass, an admirer of Nabokov and himself author of a number of game-playing works which circle back to reflect on their own textuality. For Gardner, writers like Gass and Nabokov emphasized texture and process at the expense of the social contributions that the novel could make, the novel being particularly well suited to explore and reflect the psychology and social values of its time. "The difference," Gardner argued in a 1978 debate with Gass at the University of Cincinnati, "is that my 707 will fly and his is too encrusted with gold to get off the ground." To which Gass replied, "There is always that danger. But what I really want is to have it sit there solid as a rock and have everybody *think* it is flying." Later prominent novelists whose narratives reflect upon their own fictionality include John Barth, Philip Roth, and Don DeLillo.

Two of the responses to anxiety about fiction's relevance to a turbulent decade can be illustrated in the work of Thomas Pynchon and Norman Mailer. Few American writers have been as reclusive as Pynchon, and few have been as visible, sometimes notoriously so, as Mailer. In Pynchon's *The Crying of Lot 49* (1966) the heroine Oedipa Maas suspects the possibility of an America that offers an alternative to the bland world of Tupperware parties, the superficial products of the media, and the ubiquitous manufacturers of weapons systems. This alternative America might offer another way to communicate, where imaginative expression is valued, and the alienated invited to be part of a community. In short, it might be an America in which the central values of imaginative literature can play a major part. On the other hand, this alternative world might just be only a fantasy, a way to escape a deadening culture. It could be a self-indulgent and possibly self-destructive delusion – the very kind of delusion that literature encourages through its increasing divorce from a world it once engaged with. Pynchon provides no definitive answers, but in exploring the question the novel itself offers, via the reading experience, an alternative world. But the novel also expresses the anxiety that comes from needing to address the question. In this novel the communication system that may be merely fiction uses for its distribution network W.A.S.T.E. bins, and these receptacles may be where the writer and the writer's works are assigned by a society too passive and too comfortable to look for alternatives to the world of Tupperware parties. The multiple and exaggerated plots in this and Pynchon's other novels call further attention to the anxious issue – for the writer – of the relationship between fictional narrative and the world as experienced outside of a printed text.

In 1967, the year after *The Crying of Lot 49* appeared, a crowd variously estimated at between 50 000 and 200 000 gathered at the Lincoln Memorial in Washington to protest the war in Vietnam and march to the nearby Pentagon. Norman Mailer's account of the event, and of his involvement in it, appeared the following year as *The Armies of the Night* and went on to win a Pulitzer Prize and a National Book Award. Mailer records that he became involved in the weekend of protests – he would be arrested and spend a night in prison – because he was unable to convince himself that his fiction writing was sufficient response to the war in Vietnam. He had recently published a novel, *Why Are We in Vietnam?* (1967), but he concluded that to have any kind of significant impact a writer needed to act as well as write. Thus a third-person "Mailer" became the central figure for the first part of a book that the author divided into "History as the Novel" and "The Novel as History."

"As the power of communication grew larger," Mailer reflects on the bus taking him and some fellow prisoners into detention, "so the responsibility to educate a nation lapped at the feet, new tide of a new responsibility, and one had become a writer after all to find a warm place where one was safe ... writers were born to discover wine." For Mailer that "safe" and "warm place" was no longer an option for a responsible novelist. In *The Armies of the Night* he wants to bring together the techniques of the novel, history, and journalism to restore the relevance of the novelist's craft to contemporary issues. In the first two-thirds of the book the history of the event is told through the personal experience of the character "Mailer," shaped and narrated using various novelistic techniques by the author Norman Mailer.

As Mailer illustrates a number of times in the book, the author who becomes involved in public, particularly controversial, activities becomes subject to the media's editorializing and interpretations. This in turn can influence a writer's ability to communicate with his or her audience. By the 1960s television and newspaper reporting had appropriated some of the relevance and immediacy that had arguably once been associated with fictional treatments of contemporary events. Mailer's blend of journalism, history, and the novel is an attempt to bring some of the media's new status to bear upon his craft. The resulting genre, which came to be termed "new journalism," was also practiced notably by Truman Capote, Tom Wolfe, and Joan Didion. In a related response, as Mailer explains in his book, he had begun experiments making an improvisatory film. And as he reveals at the moment of his arrest at the Pentagon, many of the actions that his novelistic personal history describes are themselves being filmed for a BBC documentary.

Any heroic associations that might gather around Mailer's arrest for the cause are compromised in his own account in a number of ways, most of them illustrative of the tensions between the public and private roles that he is trying to balance. Mailer and fellow demonstrator poet Robert Lowell engage in more than one comical but anxious exchange about their individual status as writers, and in the march itself both are irritated when the "notables" in the front line – who include Mailer and Lowell – are in danger of being supplanted in the pushing and shoving by a second line of notables less notable than themselves. To these anxieties about public and literary stature are added the hope that Mailer's act of breaking the law will be viewed by the authorities as largely symbolic – a quick arrest matched by a quick release. Both writers have invitations to a party in New York that evening which promises to be fun, even wicked, and might well provide material for subsequent writing. Mailer's public act is complicated further by the compromises he makes with the enemy itself to avoid a prison sentence – pleading as the government insists, and allowing his lawyer to misrepresent his attitude as one of contrition. That "warm place" where a writer "was safe" is not prison.

Mailer describes two orchestrated boycotts that illustrate the limitations of the writer as public actor. At a National Book Awards ceremony Bernard Malamud accepted his award gratefully even though agreeing with the anti-war motives of the boycott. And Robert Lowell's gesture of refusing President Johnson's invitation to a White House garden party was canceled out by Saul Bellow's attending. Understandably, writers are much happier to receive prizes and to have experiences that will subsequently produce material for profitable writing than to be hit on the head by a federal marshal. *The Armies of the Night* does not pretend to offer answers, but with this book Mailer won his prizes, lived the experience, and even managed to avoid the crack on the head.

Multicultural America: Borders, Tradition, and Identity

The American literature canon was a largely white male listing in the first half of the century, with a nod to the achievements of Edith Wharton, Willa Cather, and the Harlem Renaissance. With the work of, in particular, Langston Hughes, Richard Wright, Ralph Ellison, and James Baldwin black writers slowly found publication opportunities among the major commercial presses. But it was not until the 1960s and 1970s that such opportunities opened up for Native American, Asian American, and Mexican American writers. However, over the last four decades of the century the contributions of America's ethnic minority writers greatly enriched the range and perspectives offered by the nation's fiction. These writers brought their own traditions to storytelling, adapting them to a greater or lesser degree to more mainstream, conventional modes. The degree of adaptation and the fact of writing in English were sometimes contentious issues in themselves, consequences of different attitudes between generations toward heritage and assimilation, and of identities shaped sometimes by conflicting cultures. In the first wave of newly prominent minority writing the pressing concern was to assert ethnic identity, to bring to the center voices previously marginalized. But then interest shifted more to what is shared as well as what is different – that borders, whether geographical or cultural, are shared, are often crossed, and have been too often arbitrarily imposed.

Native American literature is often concerned with trying to recover something of a past almost obliterated by wars, forced cultural assimilation, and the dying out of the last generations that remember the important myths, traditions, and stories. This search often takes place alongside the

The Twentieth-Century American Fiction Handbook   By Christopher MacGowan
© 2011 Christopher MacGowan

alcoholism, violence, and chronic unemployment characterizing life on the reservations. The novel usually acknowledged as first bringing Native American literature into prominence is N. Scott Momaday's *House Made of Dawn*, published in 1968 and winner of the Pulitzer Prize for Fiction the following year. In the novel Momaday, born of a Kiowa father and a mother part Cherokee, describes Abel's alienation from his tribe and its traditions after returning from World War II. Only after years of violence, drunkenness, and drifting can Abel rediscover his tribal roots through the help of his dying grandfather. Momaday has published in a number of genres, and his subsequent books include *The Way to Rainy Mountain* (1976), a memoir that retells a number of Kiowa myths, and *The Ancient Child: A Novel* (1989), centered upon the Kiowa myth of a boy who turns into a bear.

Leslie Marmon Silko acknowledged the important influence of *House Made of Dawn* for her novel, *Ceremony* (1977). Silko is of mixed Laguna, white, Mexican and Plains descent, and most of her fiction is set, like *Ceremony*, in the Laguna area in New Mexico. *Ceremony* focuses upon the importance of bringing the power of traditional healing ceremonies back to the area's Native American people, to their fragmented culture and their scarred landscape. Silko's wide-ranging and challenging second novel, *Almanac of the Dead* (1991), focuses on 500 years of racial conflict, spanning the United States, Mexico, and Africa. Landscape is always important in Silko's fiction, but gardens and plants play a particularly central role in her third novel, *Gardens in the Dunes* (1999). Set at the end of the nineteenth century, the novel follows the stories of two sisters who are among the last of the Sand Lizard Indians.

Gerald Vizenor, of mixed French and Chippewa descent, mixed Native American themes with post-modern techniques in some of his novels. For example, the trickster figures of some of his novels perform a familiar post-modern role of challenging fixed assumptions about identity and narrative, while at the same time arising out of the novels' treatment of tribal heritage and customs. Two of Vizenor's major novels are his first, *Darkness in Saint Louis Bearheart* (1977), which uses elements of the science fiction genre, and *Fools Crow* (1986), the story of a young Blackfoot Indian just after the Civil War who witnesses the destruction of his tribe's traditional way of life. The latter won Vizenor an American Book Award. Two prominent younger Native American writers are Louise Erdrich, whose focus upon one region and experiments with crossing between generations in her narratives has brought comparison to the work of Faulkner, and Sherman Alexie. In addition to their achievements as fiction writers, both have also forged important reputations as poets.

"Chicano" was originally a pejorative term for working-class Mexican Americans, but developed, along with "Chicana," to describe writing that comes out of the mixed Spanish, Mexican, and American heritage of its authors. A major foundation text for Chicano/a writing is Gloria E. Anzaldúa's *Borderlands/La Frontera: The New Mestiza* (1987), a memoir that uses historical narrative and poetry to analyze the role of "borderlands" in sexual and cultural identity as well as geography.

Sandra Cisneros's *The House on Mango Street* (1984) appeared three years before Anzaldúa's influential text. Cisneros, born in Chicago of Mexican parentage, tells the story of a young girl's growing awareness of prejudice and of her own sexuality. The novel was originally published by the specialist Latino/a press Arte Publico, and slowly began to receive a good deal of attention. It was reissued by mainstream publisher Random House in 1991. Cisneros's association with Random House is usually identified as the first publishing contract for a Chicana writer with a major publisher. A break-through had come a year earlier when Cuban American writer Oscar Hijuelos's second novel, *The Mambo Kings Play Songs of Love* (1989), had been awarded the Pulitzer Prize for Fiction, the first time that the award had gone to an Hispanic-American writer. In the next few years a number of Chicano/a and Latino/a writers moved from small, specialist presses to mainstream publishers, the reward of wider distribution offset sometimes by a sense of having abandoned a core readership. Hijuelos meanwhile has gone on to publish a number of novels focused upon the immigrant experience, while Cisneros has produced two volumes of poetry, a collection of stories, and a well-received novel, *Caramello* (2002), that chronicles three generations of a Mexican American family.

Latina writer Julia Alvarez's novels blend autobiography, history, and fiction. She grew up in the Dominican Republic and New York City, and the double identity of immigrant life is the subject of her *How the Garcia Girls Lost Their Accents* (1991), sometimes referred to as a novel, sometimes as related short stories. The narrative follows four sisters and their parents through 15 interconnected stories in reverse chronological order. *In the Time of Butterflies* (1994) is a fictional retelling of the story of the three Mirabal sisters murdered by agents of then Dominican dictator Rafael Trujillo. Yolanda, one of the Garcia sisters from the 1991 book, is the subject of *¡Yo!* (1997), where in each chapter a different character offers a view of her. In Alvarez's *In the Name of Salome* (2000) history comes more to the fore, telling the story of Dominican poet Salome Urea and her daughter, Camila. *Saving the World* (2006) juxtaposes two stories that are two centuries apart – one concerning smallpox and the other involving AIDS – in order, as Alvarez has put it, to have them "speak" to each other.

When playwright and novelist Frank Chin – whose *Chickencoop Chinaman* became in 1972 one of the first plays by an Asian American to be produced on a major Broadway stage – co-edited an anthology of Chinese American and Japanese American literature in 1991, two writers missing from the selection were Maxine Hong Kingston and Amy Tan. The editors charged in their introduction that these writers had compromised the original material behind their narratives to make their writing more acceptable to a white readership. The omission and the charge produced some controversy, for in most accounts Kingston and Tan were two of the most important and influential of all Asian American writers.

Kingston, whose parents had emigrated from China, won the National Book Critics Circle award for general non-fiction for her first book, *The Woman Warrior* (1976). The book combines Chinese legends, family stories, and autobiography to describe the difficulties that Chinese American women have experienced in the past and still experience in the present, in large part through the demeaning attitude toward women in traditional Chinese culture, and the racism encountered in America. *China Men* (1980) complements the earlier book by looking at the experiences of male Chinese immigrants, many of whom in the earlier years of the century provided the labor for building railroads, working on sugar plantations, and clearing land for farming. *China Men* won the National Book Award for non-fiction, but although both books won non-fiction awards there has recently been fuller discussion of how they use some of the resources of fiction, particularly in the case of *The Woman Warrior*. *Tripmaster Monkey* (1989) is a multi-layered novel recounting the adventures of fifth-generation Wittman Ah Sing in the 1960s, alongside allusions to a traditional Chinese-American story of the King of the Monkeys – a trickster figure associated with bringing Buddhism to China. *The Fifth Book of Peace* (2003) again mixes fiction and autobiography in a book whose five sections deal in various ways with loss and with attempts to find peace.

Amy Tan's best-known novel, *The Joy Luck Club* (1989), and her second, *The Kitchen God's Wife* (1991), concern the relationships of mothers and daughters when they are complicated by different attitudes to assimilation and to traditional culture, values, and rituals. *The Hundred Secret Senses* (1995) focuses on the relationship of two half-sisters, one Chinese-born and one Chinese American. *The Bonesetter's Daughter* (2001) returns to exploring the relationship between a Chinese American daughter and her mother's past in China, while *Saving Fish from Drowning* (2005) follows a group of American tourists on their travels in Burma and marks a more comic turn in Tan's writing.

The work and ethnic identity of Jessica Hagedorn represents in many ways the multiplicity of racial, cultural, gender, and genre categories that so much multicultural writing has set out to explore. Hagedorn was born in the Philippines, and moved to the United States with her family when she was 14. By one biographical account her mother's background is Scottish-Irish-French-Filipino and her father is considered Filipino-Spanish, although his great-grandmother was Chinese. Hagedorn considers herself primarily a Filipino writer. Although she has published three novels, she has also published short stories and poetry, performed with and written songs for a rock group, written multimedia plays, and been involved in performance art, film making, photography, and an animation project. She is also the editor of the first major anthology of contemporary Asian American writing, *Charlie Chan Is Dead: An Anthology of Contemporary Asian American Fiction* (1991), and a revised and updated selection, *Charlie Chan 2: At Home in the World* (2004). Hagedorn's first novel, *Dogeaters* (1990), uses multiple perspectives and collage techniques to follow the stories of a number of characters in the Philippines during Ferdinand Marcos's dictatorship, examining the influence of American culture upon a country whose own had already been fragmented by a history of colonial oppression. The novel was a National Book Award finalist. In her second novel, *The Gangster of Love* (1997), a group travels from Manila to the creative communities of San Francisco and New York. *Dream Jungle* (2004), set in the 1970s, returns to the Philippines to explore further the impact of colonization upon the country's history as well as its contemporary life.

Part 2

Major Writers

Henry James (1843–1916)

Henry James argued for the importance of fiction at a time when poetry could still lay claim to being the major literary genre, and in his own work he took the short story and novel to a level of complexity and sophistication that itself provided evidence for his assertion. James was born in New York City to an independently wealthy family, one that included his brother the future philosopher William James, and his sister Alice, who became a diarist of some note. James had been to Europe twice by the time he was 12, and had attended schools in England, Switzerland, and France by the time he was 15. He briefly attended Harvard Law School in 1862–1863, and the following year began to publish reviews and stories. Although James's family had settled in Boston, he spent the years 1869–1876 traveling between the United States and Europe, then settled first in Paris, before finally deciding to live permanently in England.

James published a study of Hawthorne in 1879, which, while recognizing Hawthorne's achievements, listed a series of handicaps that, in James's view, the older writer labored under in writing about his native culture. These included, most importantly, the absence of an established social hierarchy and all the institutions, manners, and traditions that went along with it. The writer could avail himself of these features when setting narratives within the older, more established culture of Europe. Hawthorne's *The Marble Faun* (1860) takes place in Italy, and its theme of Americans in Europe is one that James went on to explore in many novels, particularly in the early and late years of his career. But for James, Hawthorne had discovered Europe too late.

In James's earlier novels the complexities of social and cultural convention are often faced by a morally decent American, one innocent of European complexity, naïve, and well-intentioned, but lacking the experience and knowledge to avoid mistakes. Self-made millionaire Christopher Newman in *The American* (1877) finds the attractions of a copy greater than the real thing when visiting the Louvre. He asks of copyist Noemie's Madonna, "I am not a Catholic, but I want to buy it. *Combien?*" but is later forced to discover the limitations of what money can buy. These limitations exclude him from association with the aristocratic, Catholic family who control the marriage possibilities of the woman he falls in love with.

Wealth as well as naïveté makes American women vulnerable in James's fiction. The title character of his first international success, *Daisy Miller* (1878), is unable to recognize the difference between a real and an imitation gentleman, and possibly may not care. In Rome she becomes a victim of her absent American father (who hires a courier as substitute while he remains behind making money), of an Italian fortune hunter, and of American women more concerned with what Europeans will think of their expatriate group than in practicing the kind of tolerance and forgiveness associated with the beautiful but ruined city and the Catholicism of which it is the center. James soon went on to develop these themes more fully in *The Portrait of a Lady* (1881). The Jamesian narrator in these early novels is the "discriminating observer" that James imagines watching Christopher Newman as he nurses his "aesthetic headache" in the Louvre, a narrator who is perceptive but at times has limited knowledge. James's subsequent fiction showed later writers many ways to exploit the possibilities of such a flexible range of perspective.

The success of *Daisy Miller* made James for a while a popular writer, but he had less success with the more political novels that he wrote between 1885 and 1890, of which *The Bostonians* (1886) is the best known. Over the next five years he tried to write for the theater, but with little success. However, the stories and novels that he wrote in this period, usually with English characters and settings, are generally considered amongst his finest works. "The Real Thing" (1892) and "The Turn of the Screw" (1896) explore what becomes a major theme in the late fiction: that concepts of what is real lie in the perception of the beholder. In "The Real Thing" the issue is presented in aesthetic terms – as depending on the expectations and transformations wrought by model, artist, and audience. In "The Turn of the Screw" the status of what may or may not actually be there, and the state of mind of the observer, are crucial issues in the questions that the story raises about the supernatural. *What Maisie Knew* (1897) is something of a tour de force in its examination of what a young child might understand of adult frivolity and immorality as she grows into her teenage years. James is always a moral writer, but here his condemnation of irresponsible and selfish parenthood is particularly overt.

F. O. Matthiessen in an early influential study of James termed the author's three late novels published between 1901 and 1904 works of "the Major Phase." This assessment is still shared by many commentators. *The Wings of the Dove* (1902), *The Ambassadors* (1903), and *The Golden Bowl* (1904) return to the international theme. In these novels the drama is as likely to be internal as external. Sometimes even seasoned James scholars have been known to find the subtleties of the prose impenetrable, albeit rarely. The triumph of these late novels is that the complex psychological and moral issues are matched by a prose style nuanced and delicately balanced, and by a narrator who all but disappears, leaving events and actions to speak for themselves. Maggie Verver's determination to save her marriage in *The Golden Bowl*, and the moral dilemma of Merton Densher in *The Wings of the Dove* faced with the schemes of Kate Croy and his admiration of Milly Theale, are just two examples of the detailed psychological dramas in these novels. Such works looked forward to the moral and formal complexity that modernist admirers Ezra Pound and T. S. Eliot would shortly explore, and that fellow novelists (and neighbors of James) Joseph Conrad and Ford Madox Ford would develop. James lived long enough to meet Pound and to make more than one appearance in *The Cantos*. In the years immediately following James's death Pound and Eliot argued forcefully in a series of essays for the importance of the work and achievement of their fellow exile. For Eliot, the American novel would make no further advances until Scott Fitzgerald's *The Great Gatsby* in the mid-1920s.

When James travelled to the United States in 1904–1905 for a visit and lecture tour that took him down the east coast, across the Midwest, and out to San Francisco and Washington State, he had not visited his native country for 21 years. Calling himself the "restless analyst," he recorded his mixed impressions, ranging from the exhilarated to the appalled, in *The American Scene* (1907). This book covers the first part of his journey, but a planned second volume covering his trip to the West was never written.

In his last years James turned to autobiography, travel writing – which had been a career-long interest – and to revising many of his novels and tales for the New York Edition of his work, which was published from 1907 to 1909. For this edition he wrote 18 prefaces. In this remarkable series of essays James tells the origins of many of the stories and novels, describes his composition methods, and offers a frank assessment of his fiction. He is harsher on his earlier work than are most critics, arguing, for example, that he now sees that he was writing romances rather than what he intended to be narratives built around plausible motives and events. He brought to his revisions of these earlier novels his later interest in the fuller development of a character's thoughts and motivations, but editors generally prefer to print the earlier versions of these novels.

In 1915 James became a British subject, in protest at the US reluctance to enter World War I. James received the Order of Merit in 1916, a rare honor that is bestowed by the sovereign; by then he was seriously ill. Although he died and was cremated in London, Mrs. William James brought his ashes back to the United States, where he was buried in Cambridge, Massachusetts, beside the graves of his mother and sister. The creator of some of the most memorable female characters in fiction had never married.

Bibliography

There are many contemporary editions available of James's major works, including paperback versions published by Oxford, Penguin, and Norton.

Henry James, *The New York Edition*, 24 vols. (New York, 1907–1909).

F. W. Dupee, *Henry James* (New York, 1951).

Leon Edel, *Henry James: The Master: 1901–1916* (Philadelphia, 1972).

Ross Posnock, *The Trial of Curiosity: Henry James, William James, and the Challenge of Modernity* (New York, 1991).

Adeline R. Tintner, *The Twentieth Century World of Henry James: Changes in His Work After 1900* (Baton Rouge, 2000).

Edith Wharton (1862–1937)

Edith Wharton was born Edith Newbold Jones in New York City, and grew up in a cultivated but conventional wealthy family. The family traveled between Europe, New York City, and Newport, Rhode Island, and Edith was educated and prepared for the conventional role of becoming a decorous extension of a wealthy husband. She married Edward Wharton in 1885, but the marriage had been an unsuccessful one for many years before their divorce in 1913. When she separated from Edward in 1911 she took up residence in France, where she would live for the rest of her life, traveling to the United States only once more, in 1923. Her many friends included some of the most important writers and critics of the time, among them Henry James, William Dean Howells, Sinclair Lewis (who dedicated *Babbitt* to her), Aldous Huxley, and art critics Bernard Berenson and Kenneth Clark. In 1923 Wharton became the first woman awarded an honorary Doctor of Letters degree from Yale University. She was elected to the National Institute of Arts and Letters in 1926, and received the Gold Medal of the American Academy of Arts and Letters in 1929. In addition to her fiction, Wharton published poems, accounts of her travels, essays on art, and, in 1934, a somewhat restrained autobiography, *A Backward Glance*.

Wharton published a handful of poems, essays, and stories in the 1880s, but fully committed herself to a writing career only in the next decade. She began the first novel that brought her wide recognition, *The House of Mirth*, in 1903, and published it two years later, when it became a bestseller. This story of Lily Bart's social decline incorporates many of the major themes of Wharton's fiction to come, particularly the role of money, and the clash of private passions with rigid social rules – rules that often credit appearance and social influence above the truth. Lily's own social and romantic misjudgments make her particularly vulnerable. For all her social sophistication, she fails to recognize the lasting value of genuine affection, and does not fully comprehend the importance of avoiding situations that could be – either willfully or accidentally – misunderstood. Lily's fate raises a question central to all of Wharton's fiction: the degree to which characters are shaped by heredity and upbringing, and the degree to which they have a genuine freedom of choice. The balance between these two in her narratives usually keeps them from being clearly determinist, although there is a sense in which such characters as Lily Bart are at bottom victims. Brought up to present herself as a decorative object, but without the money or influence to permit mistakes, or the ruthlessness to inflict social ruin upon those who would ruin her to save themselves, Lily's fall may be inevitable. Lawrence Selden manages, with a small income, to be both a part of the aristocratic world, and apart from it – but then the freedom granted a man in the world that Wharton's fiction depicts is much greater than that allowed women.

The rural New England setting of *Ethan Frome* (1911) is quite different from the glittering world of New York and Newport that is the background of *The House of Mirth*. The name of the town, Starkfield, in which Ethan has spent "too many winters," sums up the bleakness of the surroundings. Nature governs the lives and opportunities of the inhabitants, especially of the old man and two women whose story the engineer narrator discovers. Ethan lost his chance to escape when as a young man he had to abandon his studies in science to care for his aging parents. Emotional and domestic needs drive him to marry Zeena. But when he later falls in love with Matte Silver the conflicting obligations of husband and lover cause him to fail in both roles. The moral punishment meted out is an ironic but appropriate one, since Ethan's duty becomes his obligation to stay with both women. This short, carefully composed novel is often read as reflecting the unhappiness of Wharton's own marriage, and the joy and guilt she felt in her affair with American journalist Morton Fullerton at the time she was writing it.

Wharton had begun *The Custom of the Country* (1913) some years before *Ethan Frome* but set it aside until 1912. The central character, Undine Spragg, is a ruthless, manipulative social climber whose actions are aimed at gaining wealth for the kind of lifestyle she craves. Nevertheless she remains always unsatisfied despite her material success. With none of Lily Bart's qualms, Undine marries and divorces without regard for the feelings of those she leaves in her wake. Pregnancy is an inconvenience, and emotional commitment a weakness. In this novel, the old New York of social manners is giving way to the more ruthless amorality of the robber barons, but Wharton's sympathies, for some readers, are not entirely with the passing age. The powerful new capitalist operators at least have an energy and vitality that has been lost in the increasingly moribund social aristocracy.

The last of Wharton's major novels, *The Age of Innocence*, was published in 1920 and returns to the clash of social obligations and love. In this case, self-sacrifice leads Newland Archer back to the responsibilities of his loveless marriage. But the novel complicates the motives of Newland's passion for the Countess Elena Olenska. Newland's love may be largely because she represents an escape from the responsibilities of his social obligations to his wife and child – obligations that Wharton never completely denies the importance of in her fiction. At the end of the novel, when he assigns the Countess to his store of memories rather than see her again, he may have made, in the novel's terms, the right as well as the conventionally moral decision. The novel won Wharton a Pulitzer Prize, although the jury had voted to make the award to Sinclair Lewis for *Main Street*.

The highly regulated social world of the Old New York aristocracy usually closes ranks in Wharton's novels against outsiders who threaten change or open scandal. But following World War I, that society had itself become history, a transition which is the central subject of *The Custom of the Country*. Wharton herself, who continued publishing novels, poems, and stories up to her death, became increasingly seen as old-fashioned, and her defense of the novel of manners against modernist experiment seemed to further mark her as from another age. Her work following *The Age of Innocence* is usually regarded as marking a decline in her writing, but the use to which she could put the perspective of her long career is illustrated in a late story that is one of her finest, "Roman Fever," from the 1936 collection *The World Over*. The story reflects on the differing degrees of protection deemed necessary to three generations of young American ladies visiting Rome. As Mrs. Slade observes: "To our grandmothers, Roman fever; to our mothers, sentimental dangers ... to our daughters, no more dangers than the middle of Main Street." In this story's modern Rome of pilots and unchaperoned daughters, the needs of illicit passion and social order are both served – although the rewards greatly favor the consequences of the illicit passion.

Wharton's reputation suffered a further decline after her death, and for some years she was seen as a student of the Jamesian novel who was never quite able to match James. But in more recent years her fiction has come to be appreciated on its own terms, with a fuller recognition of the nuance, passion, and social critique out of which her finest novels are composed.

Bibliography

Edith Wharton: Novels, ed. R. W. B. Lewis (New York, 1985). Library of America edition includes *The House of Mirth, The Custom of the Country,* and *The Age of Innocence.*

Shari Benstock, *No Gifts from Chance: A Biography of Edith Wharton* (New York, 1994).
Kathy Fedorko, *Gender and the Gothic in the Fiction of Edith Wharton* (Tuscaloosa, 1995).
Hermione Lee, *Edith Wharton* (New York, 2007).

Theodore Dreiser (1871–1945)

In 1930 Theodore Dreiser was close to becoming the first American to win the Nobel Prize for Literature, although in the end the honor went to Sinclair Lewis, who was himself one of Dreiser's literary admirers. Always controversial, Dreiser's recognition from the National Institute of Arts and Letters came at the end of his life, in 1944, when he received its Gold Medal and Award of Merit. When he received that recognition in 1944 Dreiser had not published a novel since the critical and commercial success of *An American Tragedy* 19 years earlier.

Dreiser was born Herman Theodore Dreiser, in Terra Haute, Indiana. His father was a Catholic German immigrant, and while initially Johann Dreiser was able to support his large family comfortably – there were 10 surviving children – financial setbacks brought poverty and frequent moves. Dreiser's sisters escaped this poverty by taking up with men who could support them, and Dreiser's older brother Paul, as Paul Dresser, went on to a very successful career in New York City as a songwriter. He died penniless in 1906, however, having given away or mismanaged much of his money. Dreiser's parents and siblings later supplied models and narratives for a number of Theodore's novels, and Paul provided support at a crucial period when his brother moved to New York. In addition to the fictional portraits in his novels, Dreiser wrote of his family and his early career in two autobiographies, *A Book About Myself* (1922), republished as *Newspaper Days* in 1931, and *Dawn* (1931) – which was actually written many years earlier.

Dreiser moved to Chicago once he reached 16, taking a series of odd jobs to support himself. Then one of his former high-school teachers paid for him to spend a year at Indiana University, from 1889 to 1890. This would be

The Twentieth-Century American Fiction Handbook   By Christopher MacGowan
© 2011 Christopher MacGowan

Dreiser's only experience of higher education. Back in Chicago, Dreiser drifted from job to job until in 1892 he obtained his first work at a newspaper, on the *Chicago Globe*. From there he went on to work at newspapers in St. Louis, Toledo, and Pittsburgh. This journalism experience was invaluable for the kind of fiction Dreiser would go on to write, fiction that claimed to be more a report on actual events than prose conforming to the conventions of a well-shaped narrative. Following this newspaper experience, he took on, in 1895, the editorship of a new magazine associated with his brother's New York music business. In 1898 he married Sara White, who was a great help to her husband in the editing and revising of his early work. The two began living separately in 1910, and she had no direct contact with him after 1926, but was still legally married to Dreiser when she died in 1942.

In Pittsburgh and New York Dreiser began the reading that would provide the philosophical underpinning of much of his writing. In the fiction of Balzac and the philosophical writings of Herbert Spencer and Thomas Huxley he found confirmation of the ruthless competitiveness and struggle for survival that he had witnessed in his newspaper reporting. Dreiser's fictional characters live in a world harsh and competitive, a world offering rewards to the ruthless and the lucky, and ruin to those too weak, idealistic, or unfortunate to prosper or even survive. A character's fate is largely out of his or her hands, being determined by chance, and by such basic biological drives as sex and the instinct for survival. There are no supernatural moral codes that bring inevitable retribution to those violating them. In Dreiser's finest work he counters the danger that such a position will produce merely formulaic narratives through complicating the motives and emotional needs of his characters.

Dreiser had written some unpublished short fiction before he began his first novel, *Sister Carrie* (1900). Using his own early experiences in Chicago, and the details of his sister Emma's affair and flight with a Chicago saloon manager, Dreiser tells the story of Carrie Meeber's rise to fame and success, thanks to good luck and the crucial help of two men who become her lovers and whom she subsequently abandons. Dreiser's title is a glance at similar titles by Balzac, and suggests the mix of biological and social forces operating in Carrie's fate. For many readers the characterization of Hurstwood, the man who gives up his marriage, reputation, and career in Chicago for her, is the major triumph of this novel. His decline becomes the chief focus of much of the later part of the novel, a shift seen as an important narrative counterpart to the story of Carrie's success by some critics, and as a structural flaw in the novel by others.

Sister Carrie was accepted for publication by Doubleday, Page, after an enthusiastic recommendation by novelist Frank Norris, serving as a reader for the firm. But the publisher began to have qualms about the commitment and released the book with very little publicity or distribution. The narrative of an immoral woman who is apparently rewarded rather than punished for her actions was certain to shock much of the American reading public of the time. Dreiser's frankness in this novel, and his standing up to threats of censorship to this and to some of his subsequent books, later led Sherwood Anderson and Sinclair Lewis, among others, to acknowledge that Dreiser opened up opportunities for subsequent American writers to explore more explicitly in their fiction issues that had too often been suppressed and excluded.

Although Dreiser suffered from periods of depression in the years immediately following his first novel's almost non-existent publication, by the middle of the decade he had resumed his successful career writing for and editing magazines in New York. But this steady work ended when he was fired as editor of the *Delineator* in 1910 because of his infatuation with the young daughter of one of assistant editors. Dreiser turned to finishing a manuscript he had begun earlier in the decade, his confidence in his fiction helped by the successful reissue of *Sister Carrie* by the B. W. Dodge Company in 1907. He had also gained a prominent supporter in the iconoclastic critic H. L. Mencken. *Jennie Gerhardt* (1911), the novel that resulted from the manuscript, is the story of a figure much more passive than Carrie Meeber, one who lacks the ruthlessness, and luck, to fulfill her hopes, but who finds at length a degree of contentment. Less of a challenge to conventional social mores than *Sister Carrie*, and more sentimental, the book was well received.

Dreiser's next novels, *The Financier* (1912) and *The Titan* (1914), are the first two of a trilogy based on the real-life robber baron Charles T. Yerkes (1837–1905), a major figure in the development of the Chicago and London subway systems. These first two volumes follow the sexual and financial fortunes of Frank Cowperwood in Philadelphia and Chicago. Dreiser did not complete the final volume, *The Stoic*, until the last months of his life, and when it was published posthumously in 1947 it was generally seen as the weakest of the trilogy.

The Genius (1915) is the most autobiographical of Dreiser's novels and was the subject of some hostile criticism for its sexual themes, themes which had also disturbed some cultural conservatives in response to the Cowperwood novels. The book was defended by Mencken and others, as much for the cause of artistic freedom as for the quality of a novel often seen as hampered by its detailed fidelity to actual events. These events include the tensions within, and eventual break-up of, his marriage to Sara White. Following these three novels Dreiser began work on *The Bulwark* (1946), another book that he would not finish until the end of his life and that would be published posthumously. Based on the story that one of Dreiser's assistants had told him earlier in the decade of her father's life, the novel traces the despair of devout Quaker Solon Barnes as his family and his business associates succumb to the temptations of materialism. Barnes dies bewildered and isolated in a world to which the religious principles he holds so dear appear irrelevant and ineffectual.

Dreiser's fiction is often based on real-life events and characters. In the case of his only full-length play, *The Hand of the Potter* (1919), the event was a sex crime committed in New York in 1912. The play's sympathetic treatment of the criminal Isadore Berchansky as a victim of aberrant biological drives over which he could have little control prepared the way for Dreiser's most famous adaptation of a real-life event, *An American Tragedy* (1925). In this sweeping novel Dreiser examines the social and biological forces operating on Clyde Griffiths, caught between the marriage demands of a working girl he has made pregnant, and the social opportunities represented by the strong romantic interest shown him by the daughter of a wealthy local manufacturer.

As Dreiser's title indicates, he saw Clyde's story as a quintessentially American one, inevitable in a capitalist culture in which, from Dreiser's perspective, the rewards of wealth and privilege are achieved only by the few who survive the fight for them. The novel is based upon the story of Chester Gillette, executed in 1908 for the murder two years previously of a local farmer's daughter, Grace Brown. But Dreiser complicated the nature of his protagonist's guilt by having Clyde lose his nerve at a crucial moment, after he has successfully lured his planned victim Roberta onto a rowboat in the middle of the lake. Roberta, seeing – but not comprehending – his distress tries to comfort him, tips the boat over, and drowns – and Clyde swims away rather than helping her. Chance thus plays much more of a part in the murder than was the case in the Gillette crime, but as far as those judging Clyde's guilt are concerned, Roberta is on the lake through the premeditated plans of a murderer.

Chance is just one of the complex set of forces behind Clyde's fate. Clyde rejects the lifestyle and values of his evangelist parents and yearns for the material possessions and glamour that he imagines lie beyond the streets where they proselytize. Working at the Green-Davidson Hotel as a bellhop, he sees that world of glamour from the outside, but he lacks the determination and cunning of a Cowperwood or Carrie to fight for what he wants. He is essentially passive, reacting to circumstances, the forces behind which he barely understands. Dreiser emphasized his conception of Clyde when he objected to some aspects of the 1931 film of the novel. He argued that the story "is an indictment of our social system under which individuals are overwhelmed by forces outside themselves, react in certain ways which are due largely to their background and environment, and individually pay the penalty." The novel's focus on Clyde and its close account of his state of mind while facing execution has the effect, as in the later studies of murderers in Truman Capote's *In Cold Blood* and Norman Mailer's *The Executioner's Song*, of eliciting sympathy for the condemned man without denying any of the horror of his actions.

Following the success of *An American Tragedy*, Dreiser published his second collection of short stories, *Chains*, in 1927, the same year that he visited the Soviet Union for several months. He also published a volume of poems and two volumes of essays, but much of his subsequent writing, in the 1930s and into the 1940s, was directed toward supporting the activist role he now took in social and political causes. In the late 1930s he moved to Hollywood with Helen Richardson, a distant cousin who had become his companion in 1919, and whom he married in 1944. Their relationship had survived Dreiser's many casual affairs, and she later published an account of their years together, *My Life with Dreiser* (1951).

In the final year of his life, and following the recognition from the National Institute of Arts and Letters, Dreiser returned to his two unfinished novels, and had completed *The Bulwark* and almost completed *The Stoic* before he died. In their final pages both novels reflect the increased interest in religion and mysticism that Dreiser showed at the end of his life. The novels' posthumous publication did not help the decline that Dreiser's reputation suffered for some years after his death. His deterministic literary philosophy, his inelegant prose, the formal awkwardness of some of his plotting, and the sometimes intrusive authorial comment of philosophical and psychological generalities did not appeal to New Critics, who looked more to the psychological and stylistic complexities of Henry James for a standard. But the attention of scholars interested in how a serious writer portrays the central issues of his time, coupled with the ability of Dreiser's best fiction to engage generation upon generation of new readers, has brought him renewed recognition as one of the important American novelists of the century.

Since 1981 Dreiser's works have been appearing in scholarly editions in *The Pennsylvania Dreiser Edition* (after 2002 *The Dreiser Edition*), one aim of which is to return to the novels passages that the editors argue Dreiser was pressured to omit from the published versions. The results have sometimes been controversial, but the editions certainly provide a wealth of new information about the composition and publishing histories of the individual texts. The Library of America published a volume of Dreiser's work in 1987 that includes *Sister Carrie* and *Jennie Gerhardt*, and that is based on the more familiar first editions.

Bibliography

Thomas P. Riggio, ed., *The Pennsylvania Dreiser Edition* (Philadelphia, Urbana, and Chicago, 1981 –), multiple volumes.

Leonard Cassuto and Clare Virginia Eby, eds., *The Cambridge Companion to Theodore Dreiser* (Cambridge, 2004).

Richard Lingeman, *Theodore Dreiser: An American Journey, 1908–1945* (New York, 1990).

Jerome Loving, *The Last Titan: A Life of Theodore Dreiser* (Berkeley, 2005).

Willa Cather (1873–1947)

Willa Cather served a long apprenticeship as a journalist and editor before heeding the advice of friends, including writer Sara Orne Jewett, to devote herself full-time to a writing career. She began her journalism work to support herself while still a student at the University of Nebraska, Cather's family having moved to the state from Virginia when she was nine. She pursued a magazine editing and newspaper writing career in Pittsburgh after graduating, before going on to teach high school Latin and English in the city. During this period of teaching, 1901–1906, Cather published her first two books. *April Twilights* (1903), a book of verse, and *The Troll Garden* (1905), a collection of seven short stories, four of which she later revised and reprinted.

Cather's stories drew her to the attention of S. S. McClure, owner of the prominent magazine *McClure's*, and in 1906 she moved to New York to serve as staff writer and managing editor. She lived in New York for the rest of her life, for much of the time sharing an apartment with her companion Edith Lewis. Her editorial position put Cather at the center of a – largely male – literary world that included New York, Boston, and London. The position at *McClure's* took up much of Cather's time and energy, and she wrote only a few stories in her years at the magazine. These stories were heavily influenced by the work of Henry James, as was her first novel, *Alexander's Bridge* (1912), published once she left *McClure's* to take up a full-time writing career.

With her next novel, *O Pioneers!*, Cather found her own voice and subject, recalling her Nebraska childhood, where she knew the newly arrived immigrant farmers, as well as the families in the frontier town of Red Cloud where her father had moved after a year of farming on the plains. The novel combines what Cather had originally intended as two separate stories: that of Alexandra Bergson, the daughter of Swedish immigrants, who takes up the challenge to tame the harsh, undeveloped land, and the story of Alexandra's younger brother Emil, who is murdered as the result of his affair with the wife of a neighboring farmer. The affection and nostalgia that Cather brings to this and her later novels set in Nebraska is accompanied by her recognition of the starkness of pioneer life, and its human tragedies. An important difference in the treatment of the plains in Cather's earlier and later fiction, however, is that whereas in the earlier work the pioneer world limits opportunity and dulls imagination in its relentless demands for hard, physical work, later Cather conveys more of the rewards that come from such a commitment: the beauty of the landscape, and the comfort that family and community can bring at times of tragedy and triumph.

After a novel generally considered one of her less successful, *The Song of the Lark* (1915) – although it introduced the other region that would feature a number of times in Cather's fiction, the Southwest – she published what for many readers is her major work, *My Ántonia* (1918). This novel greatly expands the scope of *O Pioneers!* in telling the story of Ántonia Shimerda, who survives loss and betrayal to find in plains life her own rich rewards, and of Jim Burden, who, like Cather, makes his life on the east coast, but, again like Cather, never loses the memories of his Nebraska childhood. Jim is particularly drawn to his memories of the charismatic Ántonia. The novel also encompasses the stories of some its characters before they came to Nebraska, including the memorable tale of an ill-fated wedding party chased by wolves, and the story of Mr. Shimerda's earlier days that explains why the immigrant life in Nebraska is finally impossible for him to bear. Jim, narrating as an older figure, gives the novel the tone and perspective of affectionate nostalgia, while also keeping the narrative vivid with the recollected detail and intense emotions of childhood memory.

In writing *One of Ours* (1922) Cather went outside her own experience to describe the scenes of World War I in which Claude Wheeler, a Nebraska farm boy, goes off to fight. Although the novel won Cather the Pulitzer Prize for Fiction, and was a bestseller, its critical reception was mixed and it is now seen as something of a failure. However, with *A Lost Lady* (1923) she produced one of her finest novels, one that illustrates her concept of the "unfurnished novel," pared down to essentials of narrative, character, and setting. This short but rich work is based upon Cather's memories of an ex-Governor and his young wife who lived in Red Cloud, transformed in the novel into Captain Forrester and his wife Marian. Making Captain Forrester a railroad pioneer, and linking him to the image of the mountains that the railroad builders must conquer, makes clear that the heroic achievements for which Forrester is admired and respected cannot be repeated in the next generation. Niel Herbert romanticizes this pioneer age, bringing his own unresolved sexual anxieties and unrealized love for Marian Forrester to his later condemnation of her as, now widowed, she attempts to survive in the modern world. Ivy Peters' exploitative dealings are finally of more use to her than Niel's romantic nostalgia. The story is told mostly through Niel's point of view, but not entirely, which allows the novel a more complex view of the pioneer age than Niel holds, and invites a less judgmental view of Marian.

If *My Ántonia* is about people displaced across continents, *A Lost Lady*, like two of the novels that follow, is about characters displaced across time. Marian Forrester makes the compromises that she needs to make in order to resume her pioneer role, although her stage must now be outside the United States. In *The Professor's House* (1925) Godfrey St. Peter's solution to living in a modern world whose values he deplores remains hidden from his family, whose materialist preoccupations, he suspects, will keep them from guessing or even being interested. One of the notable features of this novel is the insertion, two-thirds of the way into the book, of "Tom Outland's Story," the narrative of St. Peter's best student and his discovery of a mesa cliff village. In this novel, rather than the past being romanticized, as it is by Niel Herbert, it is considered merely irrelevant to the material and practical values held by St. Peter's family, by the college where St. Peter teaches, and by the administrators of the Smithsonian Institution whom Tom unsuccessfully tries to interest in his find.

My Mortal Enemy (1926) produces a mixed response from Cather scholars, some seeing it as reflecting a bitterness in Cather's own life that carries over from *The Professor's House*, others as a novel like *A Lost Lady*, showing the limitations of one who tries to categorize another, in this case the central character, Myra Henshawe, as described by first-person narrator Nellie Birdseye. However that is, Myra dies alone and disappointed, resentful of her caring husband, Oswald, and regretting that she married for love rather than material success.

The attitude toward the modern world in *A Lost Lady*, *The Professor's House*, and *My Mortal Enemy* is often linked to Cather's famous remark in the introduction to her collection of essays *Not Under Forty* (1936) that "the world broke in two in 1922 or thereabouts." The remark has often proven convenient in assessing Cather's career in light of such milestones of modernism as *The Waste Land* and *Ulysses*, both published in 1922, but also as a way to consider the temporal and cultural displacement that characters such as Marian Forrester and Godfrey St. Peter confront. For some commentators Cather avoids the issue altogether in the historical fictions that followed *My Mortal Enemy*.

At the end of *Death Comes for the Archbishop* (1927) the old Navajo, Eusabio, remarks to the retired Archbishop Latour, "Men travel faster now, but I do not know if they go to better things." This novel is set in the nineteenth century, in the Southwest that was the background to "Tom Outland's Story." But Latour and Eusabio do not have to confront the twentieth century, only its foreshadowing. Largely fictional but based on the lives of Archbishop Jean Baptiste Lamy and Father Joseph Machebeuf, the novel covers the two priests' work building the Catholic diocese of New Mexico. After a brief prologue set in the Sabine Hills overlooking Rome, the novel proceeds through linked but separate episodes rather than a continuous narrative. The form resembles accounts of saints' lives, a series of sketches capturing the important moments of a long and full life of service. Often together, but sometimes separately, Latour and Vaillant raise money for their missionary work, restore the rituals of the Catholic faith, oust the popular Spanish priests who exploit their positions of power for personal gain, obtain the trust of the Native Americans, and build a foundation for the future – literally, in Latour's case, when he builds the Cathedral in Santa Fe in which he is eventually buried. Cather presents the priests as men with integrity and genuine faith, although they are very human in their occasional material weaknesses or, in Latour's case, his occasional crises of faith. At times they are forced to make compromises for what they see as the greater good of the church. These compromises run from getting an aging beauty to admit her age publicly, to Latour recognizing the limitations of his power to rescue a woman beaten and kept in virtual slavery, and to the inability of the church to affect the government's mistreatment of the Indians.

Latour elects to die in New Mexico rather than France. This is a measure of his commitment to the people and the land of the New World, although some readings of the novel suggest that in successfully following the orders of the cardinals in Rome he has imposed a European culture upon the native landscape; that the faith spread by the two priests is one foreign to the Indians, and even to the rituals and understandings practiced by the Mexicans. Such a reading would emphasize the cultivated landscape surrounding the Cardinal's villa above the Sabine Hills where Latour is selected for the mission, and Latour's disorientation in the "geometrical nightmare" of New Mexico when he first arrives – until he sees a juniper in the shape of a cross. Important to such a reading, too, would be the Santa Fe cathedral, built of native rock but in the Romanesque style, its setting enjoyed only by Latour and the French architect who designed it. But the novel makes no explicit judgments in telling its story of two brave men of faith who try as best they can to improve the lives of those they are charged to serve. Latour's last thoughts as he is dying are of his decision as a young man, along with Vaillant, to join the priesthood. Unlike Myra Henshawe, his memory is not one of regrets.

Shadows on the Rock (1931) moves further back in history, to late seventeenth-century Quebec, and follows the round of seasons in the lives of the French community. Cather always had an affection for France and French culture, having first visited the country in 1902, a trip she had used as background in *One of Ours*. A collection of short stories, *Obscure Destinies* (1932) contains one of her most frequently anthologized pieces, "Neighbor Rosicky," a story that returns to her Nebraska childhood. *Lucy Gayheart* (1935) sold well, although is not considered up to her best work, and *Sapphira and the Slave Girl* (1940) is set in Virginia before and following the Civil War and takes Cather back to the scenes of her earliest years.

Some early assessments of Cather's career categorized her as a regionalist because of the powerful role of landscape in her novels. But more recent discussions recognize the integrated role of the many other features of her fiction too, and recent biographical work has illustrated ways in which Cather's homosexuality – something she did not make an overt subject of her work – sheds further light on the quietly complex work of this writer.

Bibliography

The University of Nebraska Press has published many of Cather's works in scholarly editions, each volume including useful historical essays and explanatory notes.

Hermione Lee, *Willa Cather: Double Lives* (New York, 1989); published as *Willa Cather: A Life Saved Up* (London, 1989).
Marilee Lindemann, *The Cambridge Companion to Willa Cather* (New York, 2005).
Susan J. Rosowski, *The Voyage Perilous: Willa Cather's Romanticism* (Lincoln, 1986).
Joseph R. Urgo, *Willa Cather and the Myth of American Migration* (Urbana, 1995).

Gertrude Stein (1874–1946)

Gertrude Stein was one of the most experimental of American literary modernists, although her more radical work has only begun to receive serious attention in recent years. Her interest in philosophy, and examination of identity, gender, and the nature of consciousness, led her to literary experiments that use repetition, syntactical disruption, and patterning to produce works defying conventional categories of genre. In her lifetime Stein was a well-known figure among avant-garde painters and writers, both for her own work and for the salon she kept with Alice B. Toklas at 27 rue de Fleurus in Paris. She came to wider notice in 1933 with her best-selling *The Autobiography of Alice B. Toklas*, a book that is actually Stein's own autobiography from the point of view of her long-time companion and lover.

Gertrude Stein was born in Allegheny, Pennsylvania, into a family affluent enough to leave her the means to live on a private income. The family traveled in Europe for five years soon after she was born, settling in California by the time she was six. In 1893 when her brother Leo transferred from the University of California, Berkeley, to Harvard, Gertrude followed, and enrolled at the Harvard Annex (a year later renamed Radcliffe). Here she had the opportunity to study with William James, whose theories of psychology had a large impact upon her own ideas. She graduated in 1898 and subsequently followed Leo to Johns Hopkins, where she studied medicine but did not graduate, and again followed him to Paris in 1901, where the two began to purchase impressionist and contemporary art. These purchases included works by Matisse, Picasso, and Cezanne and would form the collection of the famous salon in the years to come. In 1906 Picasso painted the well-known portrait of Gertrude that now hangs in the Metropolitan Museum of Art in New York. Leo, however, did not share his sister's enthusiasm for cubist painting, had little sympathy for her writing, and was disapproving of her lesbianism. In 1913 the collection was split between brother and sister, and Leo moved to Italy. By this time Alice Toklas had become Gertrude's companion and shared the apartment with her in the rue de Fleurus. In 1912 she published two pieces on Matisse and Picasso in Alfred Stieglitz's influential avant-garde journal *Camera Work*. In the years after World War I Stein and Toklas's apartment became a center for such visiting writers and expatriates as Ernest Hemingway, Mina Loy, Thornton Wilder, Ezra Pound, and Sherwood Anderson, as well as for the painters whose work she had early supported.

Three Lives (1909) is based upon her experiences while studying in Baltimore. Unable to find a publisher for the book, Stein paid for its publication herself. She tells the story of three working-class women, two of them German immigrants, the third the daughter of a black father and a mixed-race mother. Stein commented that her use of repetition and restricted vocabulary in this book was a method that she discovered through studying the painting of Cezanne; that every element of a composition was important and made an equal contribution to the whole. Through repetition with slight variation – of word order or of a particular word – Stein forces attention upon word and syntax at every stage of the composition. In this way Stein illustrates her view that consciousness creates meaning through accumulation. Of the three stories, "The Good Anna," "The Gentle Lena," and "Melanctha," the last named is the most ambitious. The story is radical not only in its language and structure but also in putting a sexually liberated black woman at its center. More the record of an emotional journey than a set of narrative actions, the story's treatment of race, sex, and gender has produced much critical discussion.

Tender Buttons, published in 1914, continues Stein's radical experiments with language and signals the kind of prose poetry that characterized her work into the mid-1920s. These experiments are often "portraits" of objects or persons removed from a conventional literary and cultural context and presented in terms of the kind of multiple perspectives that characterize analytical cubist painting. *Geography and Plays* appeared in 1922. A number of the stories in this collection concern lesbian relationships, often based on Stein's life with Toklas.

The Making of Americans was not published until 1925 – following the appearance of extracts in the expatriate journal *transatlantic review* – but Stein had composed this massive work in the years just before and after writing *Three Lives*, and had completed the manuscript in 1911. At more than 900 pages, the book is as much about the act of its writing, and its author's feelings about the task, as it is the story of the Dehning and Hersland families who are its ostensible subject. Gradually, concern with the past disappears from the book and, like much of Stein's later writing, the text becomes focused on the present. In Stein's own day it was probably more admired than read, although it has been recognized in more recent years as the text in which Stein discovered many of the experimental techniques that she went on to develop in her later work. As one commentator, Richard Bridgeman, observes, "If it is regarded as a novel rather than as a psychological and stylistic daybook, _The Making of Americans_ is a disaster." But for Bridgeman the book is "a drama of self education." Stein herself warns the reader early on that the book "is not just an ordinary kind of novel with a plot and conversations to amuse you."

A measure of Stein's prominence in the mid-1920s was her invitation to speak at Oxford and Cambridge Universities in 1926. Virginia and Leonard Woolf published the lectures, titled _Composition as Explanation_, at their Hogarth Press. This text and the later _Lectures in America_ (1935) are useful introductions for readers interested in Stein's own comments on her work.

In an effort to bring more of her writings into print, Stein and Toklas started their own publishing concern, Plain Editions, in 1930, and the novel _Lucy Church Amiably_ was its first book. The novel is set in the landscape of Bilignin in eastern France, where Stein and Toklas had begun to spend their summers. The title refers both to the central character and to a church in the nearby village of Lucey. Stein's "advertisement" at the beginning of the book comments, "This altogether makes a return to romantic nature that is it makes a landscape look like an engraving in which there are some people ..." While for some readers this approach makes for rather a static narrative, the book has also been more sympathetically read as a modernist pastoral romance.

Following the success of _The Autobiography of Alice B. Toklas_, which marked the first time that Stein had reached a wider audience, Stein and Toklas embarked on an extensive speaking tour of the United States, her first visit to her native country for more than 30 years, and her last. Details of the trip are recorded in her 1937 _Everybody's Autobiography_. With the outbreak of war in 1939 Stein and Toklas closed their Paris apartment at rue Christine – having moved from the rue de Fleurus apartment in 1938 – and settled in Bilignin before moving on to Culoz. Despite the dangers of being Jewish, lesbian, and citizens of an enemy combatant, the two survived the war relatively untroubled and returned to Paris in 1944 upon the city's liberation. Stein died of intestinal cancer in 1946 and Toklas lived on in Paris until her death in 1967. A late novel, _Ida_, was published by Random House in 1941.

The appearance of Stein's unpublished writings in the posthumously published Yale University Press editions contributed to the reassessments of her work in the years following her death. Stein has since become a particularly important writer for critics interested in semiotics and in the postmodern subversion of genre. Gay and Feminist Studies have also contributed to perceptive readings of her texts, while cultural critics interested in the history of modernism cannot ignore the remarkable meeting place of persons and ideas that was the salon at 27 rue de Fleurus.

Bibliography

The Yale Edition of the Unpublished Writings of Gertrude Stein, ed. Carl Van Vechten, 8 vols. (New Haven, 1951–1958).

Gertrude Stein, *Writings, 1903–1932* and *Writings, 1932–1946* were published by the Library of America in 1998.

Richard Bridgeman, *Gertrude Stein in Pieces* (New York, 1970).
Ulla E. Dydo, *Gertrude Stein: The Language That Rises, 1923–1934* (Evanston, 2003).
Bruce Kellner, ed., *A Gertrude Stein Companion* (New York, 1988).

Sinclair Lewis (1885–1951)

When in 1930 Sinclair Lewis became the first American to be awarded the Nobel Prize in Literature, he had just completed a decade of remarkable success, having published five novels any one of which would have made him famous. But when he died in Rome in 1951, increasingly isolated, having continued writing and publishing novels almost to the end, he had produced nothing to equal his work of the 1920s. His critical reputation was such that Harold Bloom observed in 1987, "Lewis is of very nearly no interest whatsoever to American literary critics of my own generation and younger, so that it seems likely his decline in renown will continue." However, more recently Lewis's treatment of minorities, gender, and social issues in his fiction has led to some renewed interest in his work.

Harry Sinclair Lewis was born in the town of Sauk Center, Minnesota, and attended the local public schools. In his teenage years he worked for some local publications as a writer and typesetter. In 1903 he entered Yale University, and while there served as editor of the *Literary Magazine*, also working part-time on a couple of New Haven newspapers. His graduation was delayed a year when he left Yale to spend some weeks at Upton Sinclair's utopian colony Helicon Hall in New Jersey, followed by a period living in New York City, and then a voyage to Panama – where he had hoped to find work on construction of the canal. Following his delayed graduation in 1908, he traveled around the United States, returning to New York City where he held various short-lived jobs on city publications. By 1915 he was married, had published three novels that garnered no particular attention, and decided to devote himself full-time to writing. Three more unnoticed novels followed. Then in 1920 Lewis came to national attention with the publication of *Main Street*, a satire upon small-town America. Lewis's publishers could barely keep up with demand for the novel, and it was nominated by the Pulitzer jury for the 1921 Pulitzer Prize in Fiction, although the trustees of Columbia University overruled them to give the award to Edith Wharton's *The Age of Innocence*.

The efforts of *Main Street*'s female protagonist, Carol Milford, to bring change to the dull, provincial town of Gopher Prairie, Minnesota, are largely unsuccessful and are similar to the kind of rebellion and eventual compromise that many of Lewis's central characters make in the novels that follow. Gopher Prairie is based upon Sauk Center, but Lewis's foreword to the novel makes clear that the story is about "Main Streets everywhere." The novel's picture of the self-satisfied insularity of the town and the small-mindedness of its citizens challenged decades of popular fiction that presented communities like Gopher Prairie as centers of home-spun wisdom and moral righteousness. "Main Street is the climax of civilization," declares the foreword. "That this Ford car might stand in front of the Bon Ton Store, Hannibal invaded Rome and Erasmus wrote in Oxford cloisters." In *Main Street* and his other satirical novels of the 1920s Lewis added a sharp eye for detail, and a keen ear for everyday speech (there are many accounts of his gift for mimicry). But this mixture of realism and satire has been posited as the cause of some of Lewis's problems in his later work – that despite his initial successes the two sit together uncomfortably, and that Lewis never could decide on his main focus.

Lewis often undertook extensive research for his novels, and his next book, *Babbitt* (1922) is no exception. The novel is set in the midwestern city of Zenith, and satirizes the shallow commercial and material values of its business community. The story of George F. Babbitt, Lewis wrote in the planning stages of the novel, was to be "the story of the Tired Business Man, of the man in the Pullman smoker, of our American ruler." Babbitt's rebellion against the restrictions of his business routine and his marriage is stifled finally by group pressure: the individual must conform, or at any rate appear to conform, or be excluded from the world of commerce and its material benefits. Any alternatives must remain in the realm of private fantasy, the only outlet that the business community in Zenith allows for imagination. "Babbitt" and "Babbittry" entered the dictionary as terms for the kind of middle-class narrowness and self-satisfaction that Babbitt himself found stifling. The novel is sometimes acknowledged, even by its admirers, as more a series of set pieces, each with its particular target, than a unified narrative. But once again Lewis had written a book that was bought and discussed nationwide. *Babbitt* was the novel that the Swedish Academy had most in mind when awarding Lewis the Nobel Prize.

Arrowsmith (1925) explores the world of medicine and medical ethics, and Lewis had a good deal of assistance from a young medical researcher he met at

New York's Rockefeller Institute, Paul de Kruif. The work of a medical research scientist was virtually a new subject for American fiction. Martin Arrowsmith has a highly successful research and administrative career, although material rewards at times sidetrack him from his important exploration of bacteria-eating viruses. The same narrow-mindedness, materialism, and hypocrisy exposed in the previous two novels are shown here to operate in the medical profession. But, unlike the central characters in *Main Street* and *Babbitt*, Martin Arrowsmith is a figure intended to be admired. He finally returns to his work as an independent researcher, putting marriage to a wealthy woman and a prestigious directorship behind him. The novel was another critical and commercial success for Lewis, but without the controversy of the previous two novels. This time Lewis was awarded the Pulitzer Prize, but he declined to accept it, objecting to the moral principles on which the books were judged rather than only on literary merit.

Mantrap (1926), the story of Lewis's trip on the Mantrap River in Saskatchewan with his brother Claude, added little to his reputation, although it became one of the more than 20 films made from Lewis's work, being released in New York only weeks after the book's publication. But in 1927 came *Elmer Gantry*, and controversy returned. In this novel Lewis presents a ruthless, cynical preacher who is interested only in the money, sexual conquests, and social standing that the profession can bring him. He is increasingly successful despite more than once being exposed as a fraud. Lewis biographer Mark Schorer terms him "one of the great beasts of all literature" and the book "the noisiest novel in American literature." Elmer Gantry is described in the novel itself as one without "any longing whatever for decency and kindness and reason." Not surprisingly, the book was denounced in pulpits nationwide. Once again Lewis had undertaken his research thoroughly, in this case mostly in Kansas City where, along with Boston and a number of other cities, the novel was soon banned – much to the benefit of its sales.

By the late 1920s Lewis's first marriage had failed, and he went on to marry a well-known American journalist then based in Europe, Dorothy Thompson, although that marriage, too, would fail 10 years later. Lewis had written much of *Babbitt* and *Arrowsmith* in Europe, as he did his next novel, *The Man Who Knew Coolidge* (1928), but he returned to the United States to complete the more significant *Dodsworth*, published the following year. Some of the narrative in the novel follows Lewis's own circumstances. Samuel Dodsworth, in retirement and touring Europe after selling his successful automobile company, gradually grows apart from his wife Fran and meets the independent, self-assured Edith Cortright, with whom he hopes for a life more emotionally fulfilling than any satisfaction he has had from business.

Fran's snobbishness and vanity are the targets of the novel, while the central character is clearly a figure who invites approval. Then followed the Nobel Prize, where Lewis used the opportunity of his Prize Address to laud serious American literature while condemning conservative academics and literary juries whom he felt were still rooted in nineteenth-century pieties.

Lewis had planned for some time to write a novel on the American labor movement, but abandoned the project to publish *Ann Vickers* (1933), again to commercial and critical success. Yet in his personal life there were serious troubles, an increasing addiction to alcohol, and tensions in his second marriage. The novel itself is now seen as marking a more nostalgic than satirical Lewis, and flawed by Lewis's moral uncertainty about the actions of his heroine. However, the novel's indictment of the prison system still carries signs of his finer work.

The conservatism in *Ann Vickers* became even more pronounced in Lewis's subsequent novels, where he appeared accepting of values and attitudes that his fiction had once scorned. His critical reputation went into a steep decline, although his new novels continued to sell in good numbers. *It Can't Happen Here* (1935) had a timely success, exploring what might happen if the United States became a fascist dictatorship. Hollywood continued to be interested in filming his novels but his own attempts at writing plays and screenplays did not meet with much success. Reviewers often found Lewis's later novels tired or "out of date," although in recent years there has been some renewed interest in *Cass Tamberlane* (1945) and *Kingsblood Royal* (1947), the latter a novel about the injustice of racial prejudice. Lewis died in Rome of heart disease exacerbated by his heavy drinking. He spent his last months in Europe traveling, increasingly isolated, and writing the posthumously published *World So Wide* (1951), another of the late novels that added little to his reputation.

A number of reasons for the decline of Lewis's writing after 1930 have been advanced by critics and biographers. These include his failure to develop as a writer once he had found his mark, and the suggestion that his later work abandons satire for narratives whose values his finest work had scorned. He had little interest in literary style and none in modernist experiment, and his characters arguably are more often the vehicles for a series of set satirical pieces than fully developed figures – as memorable as some of those characters are. His Nobel Prize, to unsympathetic critics, was due in part to his novels presenting the Swedish Academy, and Europe generally, with the critical view of America that it wanted to hear. Some critics argue that there was a gap that needed to be filled between the genteel tradition of William Dean Howells and the modernist generation that followed Lewis, and that Lewis filled that gap but only as long as it lasted. However this may be, there is no denying that for a decade or so in his fiction Lewis captured some of the key concerns of American life, and while those concerns are inevitably dated in some respects, some of Lewis's targets continue to flourish in ways that have not fundamentally changed.

Bibliography

The Library of America has published a volume containing *Main Street* and *Babbitt* (1992) and a further volume including *Arrowsmith, Elmer Gantry,* and *Dodsworth* (2002).

James M. Hutchisson, ed., *Sinclair Lewis: New Essays in Criticism* (Troy, NY, 1997).

James M. Hutchisson, *The Rise of Sinclair Lewis, 1920–1930* (University Park, PA, 1996).

Richard Lingeman, *Sinclair Lewis: Rebel from Main Street* (New York, 2002).

Raymond Chandler (1888–1959)

For much of his writing career Raymond Chandler was categorized as a mystery writer, albeit one of the best practitioners of the genre. Although some well-known literary figures, including W. H. Auden, J. B. Priestley, and Somerset Maugham, argued that Chandler's work transcended the usual limitations of mystery and detective fiction, and although Chandler himself had such ambitions for his writing, the kind of scholarly and critical discussion that gives serious attention to those ambitions did not come until the 1970s, more than a decade after his death.

This novelist so associated with southern California, particularly Los Angeles and its surroundings, was born in Chicago, received an education at a prestigious English private school, and became a naturalized British citizen in 1907. Chandler's Irish mother took him to England in 1895 following her divorce from his father, Maurice Chandler. He finished attending Dulwich College in 1904, and in 1907 was employed for six months in the British Admiralty. Following this brief career as a civil servant, Chandler worked as a literary journalist in London, publishing poetry, essays, and reviews. In 1912 he returned to the United States, moving around from job to job in California, until in 1917 he enlisted in the Canadian Army and saw combat in France. Following this war experience he returned to Los Angeles, where he fell in love with Cissy Pascal, who was about 20 years his elder. They married in 1924 following the death of his mother, who had disapproved of the relationship. By 1932 Chandler was a well-paid executive in the oil business, which he had entered as a clerk in the early 1920s, but when in 1932 he was fired for excessive drinking and increasingly erratic behavior, he began to think about returning to writing as a career.

The Twentieth-Century American Fiction Handbook   By Christopher MacGowan
© 2011 Christopher MacGowan

Living on an allowance from friends, Chandler studied the successful hard-boiled detective fiction of Erle Stanley Gardner and Dashiell Hammett, and after some false starts, a story he had worked on for five months, "Blackmailers Don't Shoot," was accepted by a leading magazine of the genre, *Black Mask*, in 1933. Chandler then published stories in the magazine regularly until 1941, and after 1937 began to place his stories in other leading detective magazines too.

Chandler's famous private eye, Philip Marlowe, did not make an appearance until the first of his novels, *The Big Sleep*, in 1939, which he had developed from his 1935 story "Killer in the Rain." In the earlier story Chandler had used first-person narration, which when he brought it to the Marlowe novels allowed for greater immediacy and a more complex central character. The narrator was not merely a vehicle on which to hang the unwinding of the mystery. When Marlowe describes his sometimes shifting assessments of the people he encounters, he does so within a world where the wrong judgment could be very dangerous or indeed fatal. Marlowe's vocabulary, similes, and wisecracks became part of the characteristic Chandler style, and furthered the narrative's impression of verisimilitude. In "Killer in the Rain" Chandler also began his practice of using weather and colors symbolically, sometimes to indicate mood, and sometimes to indicate the moral status of a character or a setting.

Chandler's method of taking his earlier stories and "cannibalizing" – as he called it – their plots in order to reuse them for his novels is unusual for a major writer. Commentators have discovered three other previously published Chandler stories behind the narrative of *The Big Sleep* in addition to "Killer in the Rain," and for some critics this explains some of the apparent inconsistencies in the complex plot. But Chandler succeeds in unifying his material through the strong characterization of Marlowe, a figure dogged, isolated, independent, and holding firmly to a moral code. He has to survive in a world of moral corruption, rife with drugs, pornography, blackmail, sexual jealousies, and murder. The old world of order and hierarchy, where money brought unquestioned power but also a sense of duty and responsibility that could be passed on to the next generation, has broken down – reduced in the novel to the ailing General Sternwood, a prisoner in the artificially heated world that keeps him alive, and his two hedonistic daughters. Marlowe is the good man in a corrupt world, getting little material or emotional reward for holding on to an integrity which is sometimes threatened, usually by women. He is an intelligent man surviving through instincts that come from experience, some of which he would just as soon not have experienced. Chandler was 50 when he began writing *The Big Sleep*, a late start for a novelist. But the book sold fairly well, and Chandler was recognized as a major new voice in the genre. Over the next 18 years he published six more novels, all featuring Marlowe.

Farewell My Lovely appeared the year after *The Big Sleep*, in 1940, again including plots borrowed from earlier short stories. Chandler considered this his finest novel, as do a number of commentators. The story fills out more details of Marlowe's background and business routine, and involves him in the narrative in ways that further deepen his character. The novel is something of an anti-romance; to commit oneself emotionally is to become vulnerable, and the price for survival – isolation – is one Marlowe has to pay. The corruption is more extensive than in the previous novel, extending to the handful of rich men who run Bay City, the novel's stand-in for Santa Monica, and even to the police.

Chandler worked on *The High Window* (1942) and *The Lady in the Lake* (1943) at the same time, but completed the former much more quickly. Critics have noticed that Chandler gives more attention to the mystery aspects of the plots in these two novels than in his two previous books, and that the corruption of wealth becomes even more of a theme. Marlowe himself is always scrupulous about money. Although both books continue to push the parameters of the genre, *The Lady in the Lake* is generally considered the more successful of the two and became Chandler's best-selling novel up to that point. But although Chandler was gaining readers and some critical respect, his income from the novels had not been large. In the early 1940s, while writing *The High Window* and *The Lady in the Lake*, he continued to turn out pulp fiction short stories to supplement his income; the money and visibility that working in Hollywood and the movies of his novels was to bring had not yet happened.

But in 1943 Chandler's life and financial situation began to change. His novels were reissued as paperbacks and sold well, and the popular films based on his novels began to appear. He also began working on Hollywood screenplays, a task that was lucrative but that he didn't particularly enjoy. With Billy Wilder he co-scripted *Double Indemnity* (1944), based on a story by James M. Cain. The film was highly successful and the screenplay was nominated for an Academy Award.

The film work delayed Chandler's plans for his next novel, but in 1944 he published his well-known essay "The Simple Art of Murder" in the *Atlantic Monthly*. In the essay he criticized what he saw as the artificiality and limitations of the conventional detective story, with its stereotypical cast of characters and familiar, well-manicured setting. He praised Dashiell Hammett, saying that he "took murder out of the Venetian vase and dropped it into the alley." Chandler also addresses the criticism sometimes made of his work that it does not address the social and political realities of its time. He points out the artificiality of the world in which the classic detective story is set, suggesting that if the setting were realistic it would expose the artificiality of the detective as well as the main characters connected with the mystery. By contrast, he argues, "the realist in murder" must deal with the criminal world as it actually is, a world peopled with gangsters and crooked politicians. His account of the kind of detective who would best figure in such a book lists the very qualities that characterize Marlowe: "the best man in his world and a good enough man for any world."

The film version of *The Big Sleep* reached cinemas in 1946, with a screenplay co-written by William Faulkner and Leigh Brackett, and was a big success. In the same year Chandler and his wife left Los Angeles to live in La Jolla, California, the town that would be his base for the rest of his life. In 1947 he wrote the screenplay *Playback* for Universal Studios, but it remained unproduced due to the studio's financial troubles. The commission further delayed his next novel, but *The Little Sister* finally appeared in 1949. As with a number of Chandler's other novels, the book sold better in England than in the United States. The plot has some scenes set in Hollywood that expand Marlowe's world, but Chandler himself recognized that this time he had not sufficiently integrated setting, characters, and narrative. Marlowe offers some sour views of Los Angeles at various points in the book, comments which have been read as the author incorporating contemporary social conditions into his work, or as a reflection of Chandler's disenchantment with the changing city. In 1950 a collection of Chandler's earlier stories appeared as *The Simple Art of Murder*, and in the same year he agreed to work with Alfred Hitchcock on the screenplay of *Strangers on a Train* (1951). The collaboration was tense and strained, however, and Hitchcock later had enough of the script rewritten that Chandler considered not asking for screen credit. Eventually he shared it.

Under difficult circumstances, isolated and his wife seriously ill, Chandler wrote what many consider his most ambitious and successful novel, *The Long Goodbye* (1954). The book is less fast-paced than the earlier novels, but well plotted, with the social commentary more carefully linked to characterization. Marlowe remains independent, scrupulous about money, and true to the bonds of friendship. The novel was first published a year earlier, in England, where Chandler had traveled in 1952 with his ailing wife, and to which he made a number of extended visits in the 1950s both before and after her death in 1954.

In the mid-1950s, following Cissy Chandler's death, Chandler's periods of depression increased along with his heavy drinking, and he did little serious writing. Eventually he returned to the unfinished novel that he had planned to adapt from the unproduced *Playback* screenplay. This last in the Marlowe series, published in 1958, is generally considered the weakest, although it has its admirers. Marlowe violates some central tenets of his code, some of the writing is stilted, and the plot contains some rather glaring implausibilities. The novel ends with Marlowe accepting a marriage proposal from Linda Loring, a character from *The Long Goodbye*. Chandler wrote a few chapters of a planned next novel recording their turbulent marriage, but got no further.

Chandler cared about the quality of his prose in a genre where plot and the unraveling of the mystery are usually the paramount concern. Chandler wrote of his use of slang, "I'm an intellectual snob who happens to have a fondness for the American vernacular, largely because I grew up on Latin and Greek." Biographer Frank MacShane suggests that Chandler's style derives from "a standard British English sentence structure" and "a predominantly American vocabulary." Whatever the particular ingredients, the result is a prose at once lively, inventive, and entertaining – a stylistic achievement on which rests a good part of Chandler's claim to be treated as a major American novelist.

Bibliography

Chandler's seven novels are included in The Library of America's *Stories and Early Novels* (1995) and *Later Novels and Other Writings* (1995).

Tom Hiney, *Raymond Chandler: A Biography* (New York, 1997).
Gene D. Phillips, *Creatures of Darkness: Raymond Chandler, Detective Fiction, and Film Noir* (Lexington, KY, 2000).
J. K. Van Dover, ed., *The Critical Response to Raymond Chandler* (Westport, CT, 1995).

Zora Neale Hurston (1891–1960)

Alice Walker describes in her essay "Looking for Zora" traveling to Fort Pierce, Florida, in 1973 to learn what she could of the last years of Hurston, a figure who had been prominent in the Harlem Renaissance, and had appeared in the 1937 volume of *Who's Who in America*. Hurston had attended Barnard College, studied folklore with a leading anthropologist, and had been awarded a Guggenheim Fellowship. She had published two studies of her researches, an autobiography, and four novels – one of them a novel that has come to be recognized as a major work of American fiction. Yet she died in poverty, largely forgotten, and, as Walker discovered, was buried in an unmarked grave.

Hurston was born in Alabama, but her family moved to Eatonville, Florida, when she was three. Eatonville was one of the first African American towns to be formed after the Civil War, and in 1887 the first to be incorporated. The town is the setting for a number of Hurston's stories, novels, and folklore collections. Her novel *Their Eyes Were Watching God* tells the story of its founding.

Hurston was awarded an Associates degree by Howard University in 1920, and in 1925 went on to study at Barnard College in New York City, on a scholarship. By this time Hurston had published a handful of stories and had come to the attention of *Opportunity*, the new magazine published by the National Urban League. She came second in their 1925 short story competition for her story "Spunk," and the story was included in Alain Locke's important anthology *The New Negro: An Interpretation* the same year. At Barnard Hurston studied anthropology with Franz Boas, considered the father of American anthropology and the teacher of – among many other notable figures – Margaret Mead. Boas argued for the importance of fieldwork within the discipline of cultural anthropology, and in that spirit Hurston undertook researches in Alabama, Louisiana, and her native Eatonville. This work was later supported financially by Charlotte Mason, the white patroness who also supported the work of Langston Hughes. The price of this support was Mason's ownership of the folklore material that Hurston collected, and control of any publication, but these restrictions led Hurston to end the arrangement in 1932. The first of Hurston's two short-lived marriages – the second was in 1939 – preceded her graduation from Barnard in 1928.

Hurston's writing after Barnard included short stories and plays. On one of the plays, *Mule Bone*, she collaborated with Langston Hughes, but creative disagreements broke up their friendship. Her literary activity also included the often-anthologized short story "The Gilded Six-Bits," notable for its use of slang and folk expressions both in dialogue and narrative style. The story caught the attention of publisher Bertram Lippincott when it appeared in 1933, and led to the publication of her first novel, *Jonah's Gourd Vine*, in 1934, in which the main characters are based on her parents. The novel continues Hurston's practice of reproducing closely the dialect and customs of her African American characters. The rise and fall of John Person's fortunes in the novel are strictly his own responsibility, stemming from his weakness for women, and his subsequent anger and guilt. But such an account of black experience ran counter to the more confrontational writing of Richard Wright, and later of James Baldwin and Ralph Ellison, writing that emphasized the black struggle against racism and exploitation.

Hurston articulated her own attitude toward race in her 1928 essay "How It Feels to Be Colored Me." There she wrote, "I am not tragically colored . . . I do not belong to the sobbing school of Negrohood who hold that nature somehow has given them a lowdown dirty deal and whose feelings are all hurt about it . . . I have no separate feeling about being an American citizen and colored." In this essay she says of her childhood in Eatonville that white people differed only in that they "never lived there." Hurston's approach came out of her experiences in Eatonville, as well as her perspective as an anthropologist. But it put her out of the mainstream of black writing in the 1930s and 1940s, and contributed to her lack of fuller recognition and her eventual neglect.

Mules and Men (1935) is the record of Hurston's folklore collecting in Eatonville, New Orleans, and Florida. Hurston invents a persona for herself in describing her travels, and reshapes the actual time frame to make for a more unified narrative. Franz Boas's introduction emphasizes the closeness that Hurston is able to get to the cultural contexts of the folktales and songs that she records. *Mules and Men* blurs the boundary between anthropology and fiction, just as in her fiction Hurston wanted to record dialect and behavior as she had seen it in her fieldwork. This aim produced the remarkable *Their Eyes Were Watching God* (1937), with its rich use of oral culture and performance rituals. According to Hurston's autobiography the novel was written in seven weeks, while she was living and working in Haiti on a Guggenheim Fellowship to study West Indian folklore. The novel is the story of Janie Crawford and her long struggle to live a life defined by her own choices and emotional needs, and not those of others. Comments by white reviewers were generally positive, but the novel was criticized by Richard Wright and Alain Locke for what they saw as the oversimplification of its characters and narrative events, and, in Wright's case, for its lack of militancy.

Tell My Horse, an account of Hurston's researches in Jamaica and Haiti, appeared in 1938, and a novel, *Moses, Man of the Mountain*, in 1939. Hurston had been working on the novel for five years. The biblical figure of Moses from Exodus is combined in the novel with images of Moses from black folklore, while the story of the Israelites suggests the history of America's Negroes. The novel is usually considered an ambitious failure, its elements of satire, folklore, humor, and serious intent sitting rather uneasily together. Hurston's autobiography, *Dust Tracks in the Road* (1942), revealed the conservative side of her thinking that would increase in the next two decades. The book sold well to a mostly white readership, and won a $1000 prize from the *Saturday Review*, but it was again condemned by some black writers and critics for ignoring what they saw as the central issues shaping black experience in the United States.

Hurston's association with publisher Lippincott ended with his rejection of her next two planned projects, but with the help of novelist Marjorie Kinnan Rawlings she published *Seraph on the Suwanee* in 1948 with Scribner's. This novel of life in Florida centers upon a white family, reflecting Hurston's reluctance to limit herself to writing only of black life. The story of Arvay Henson's troubled marriage to Jim Meserve is more explicit in its treatment of sex and gender roles than Hurston's previous books. Sales were initially promising, but were hurt by the publicity stemming from an accusation, later withdrawn, that Hurston had molested a young boy. This would be the last novel that Hurston published.

The 1950s saw Hurston holding various jobs, as a maid, a teacher, a librarian, and a reporter. Her work appeared occasionally in magazines, but by the time of her death, from heart disease on January 28, 1960, Hurston was largely forgotten as a writer. The manuscript that she was working on in her last years, *Herod the Great*, was partially burned after her death by a janitor at the St. Lucie County Welfare Home, where she spent her last illness.

A deputy sheriff saved the manuscript, thinking that it might contribute something toward paying off Hurston's debts.

The rediscovery of Hurston was helped by the recognition that to write about race was not necessarily to have to write overtly about politics or white oppression, and by the renewed interest among black writers and scholars particularly in the folk and cultural roots of black experience. The writings and attention of Alice Walker, Toni Morrison, and others, together with Robert Hemenway's important biography of Hurston published in 1977, began the reassessment of a writer who is now the frequent subject of articles and books. Both Hurston's writings and the cultural issues that shaped their reception are now recognized as a vital part of the history of twentieth-century American fiction.

Bibliography

The seven books that Hurston published in her lifetime are all available in reprint editions, and the Library of America has published two volumes, *Folklore, Memoirs, & Other Writings* (1995) and *Novels and Stories* (1995).

Valerie Boyd, *Wrapped in Rainbows: The Life of Zora Neale Hurston* (New York, 2003).

John Lowe, *Jump at the Sun: Zora Neale Hurston's Cosmic Comedy* (Urbana, 1994).

Alice Walker, *In Search of Our Mothers' Gardens: Womanist Prose* (New York, 1983).

Genevieve M. West, *Zora Neale Hurston and American Literary Culture* (Gainesville, FL, 2005).

F. Scott Fitzgerald (1896–1940)

Scott Fitzgerald's literary career can be broadly divided between the 1920s, a period of literary fame and commercial success, and the 1930s, by the end of which, working freelance in Hollywood, he died something of a forgotten figure, one who seemed to belong to another age, having squandered his talent and lost his audience. But since the early 1950s Fitzgerald's writings have achieved a sustained popular and critical success that he never enjoyed in his lifetime. From annual royalties amounting to $13.13, the figure on the last royalty statement he received before his death, his books have gone on to sell around half a million copies or more a year. This revival began with the posthumous publication of his unfinished Hollywood novel *The Last Tycoon*, and a rediscovery of *The Great Gatsby* – now recognized as one of the major American novels of the century.

Fitzgerald was among the most autobiographical of writers, using his own life as subject matter both in his fiction and his non-fiction. The settings of his novels follow his own movements across 25 years – the Princeton of his undergraduate days, the parties of the East Coast elite, the world of the expatriates in 1920s France, and the Hollywood of the 1930s. This close relationship of Fitzgerald's life to his work, and the dramatic nature of that life itself, has led to an interest in his biography far greater than that usually shown to novelists.

Fitzgerald was, like Nick Carraway, the narrator of *The Great Gatsby*, from the Midwest, born in St. Paul, Minnesota. Both in high school and at Princeton University, to which he was admitted in 1913, Fitzgerald was writing stories, plays, reviews, and poems. His literary activities came at the expense of his studies, however, and he withdrew for a time from Princeton because of low grades. Despite returning later, he did not graduate. In 1917

The Twentieth-Century American Fiction Handbook   By Christopher MacGowan
© 2011 Christopher MacGowan

he was appointed a second lieutenant in the US Army, although in his 15 months of service his postings were never overseas. During this period Fitzgerald completed a draft of what was to be his first novel. In addition, while stationed near Montgomery, Alabama, he met and fell in love with Zelda Sayre, the popular and attractive daughter of a judge of the Alabama Supreme Court. The two would be married in 1920, but not before the manuscript, "The Romantic Egoist," had been sent to Scribner's and returned – along with a constructive and thoughtful list of suggested revisions from editor Maxwell Perkins – resubmitted, and published as *This Side of Paradise*.

The novel was an enormous commercial success. Fitzgerald was heralded, and condemned, for so successfully bringing into post-war fiction the spirit of the rebellious young generation. The book's central character, Amory Blaine, has a series of adventures that match many of Fitzgerald's own, told through a variety of genres that amount, as some critics have suggested, to the hitherto unpublished collected works of its young author. Amory Blaine is a determined optimist despite his failures, which include losing the girl he loves to the rich Dawson Ryder. The elements of much of Fitzgerald's fiction in the years to come are in this novel: the love of an unattainable girl, the power and glamour of the rich, and the clash of ideals and reality. This early success established Fitzgerald as the foremost chronicler of the Jazz Age, an identity which became a burden in the following decade when it blinded many readers and reviewers to the increased range of his writing.

Fitzgerald soon became a popular and highly paid short-story writer, the stories paying for much of the extravagant lifestyle that he and Zelda kept up for the next decade. Even so, the couple were always in debt. By the end of the 1920s he was receiving more than $3000 a story from the *Saturday Evening Post*. Despite the financial imperative to keep churning out short fiction, and his habit of taking out particularly effective sentences he thought better used in novels, Fitzgerald published many fine short stories. With *This Side of Paradise* Scribner's began the practice of publishing a volume of the stories following the appearance of a novel, and the first of these collections, *Flappers and Philosophers*, appeared later in 1920.

Fitzgerald's second novel, *The Beautiful and Damned* (1922), is a much bleaker tale, recording the marital breakdown and general decline of the once glamorous and attractive Anthony Patch and his wife Gloria Gilbert. This novel received mixed reviews, and the following year a play for which Fitzgerald had high hopes, *The Vegetable*, failed in Atlantic City before it reached Broadway. However, the collection of stories published in 1922, *Tales of the Jazz Age*, indicated more the advances in his fiction, particularly in "May Day," and "The Diamond as Big as the Ritz."

The Fitzgeralds spent much of the first half of the 1920s living in the New York area, but most of Fitzgerald's next novel, *The Great Gatsby* (1925), was written during a stay in Europe in 1924. This book demonstrated a remarkable advance in structure and narrative control over the previous two novels. Nick Carraway narrates the events that lead Jay Gatsby to his doom, a victim of his own romanticism, and of the careless, ruthless behavior of Tom and Daisy Buchanan. "I was within and without," Nick says of his relationship to events, a narrative perspective many critics have suggested that Fitzgerald learned from the Marlow novels of Joseph Conrad. Nick is distantly related to Daisy, knows Tom from their Ivy League college days, finds himself Gatsby's neighbor, and, like Gatsby, is an outsider to Tom and Daisy's world of old money. Gatsby's dreams bear affinities to Fitzgerald's passion for the apparently unobtainable Zelda Sayre, but the novel moves beyond youthful romance and disappointment to include a vision of America itself – a place always ready to discount the lessons of the past, or to romanticize them, in its optimistic vision of the future. Fitzgerald was usually written off by the modernists as a commercial writer, but T. S. Eliot wrote to the author that the book was "the first step American fiction has taken since Henry James." The novel did not match the commercial success of Fitzgerald's earlier books, however, and it would be 25 years before it achieved its now canonical status.

Some of the events from the Fitzgeralds' 1924 trip to Europe, as well as incidents from the second half of the decade – when the couple spent much of their time in France – found their way into Fitzgerald's last completed novel, *Tender Is the Night* (1933). His work on the novel was delayed by false starts, his worsening alcoholism, the financial necessity of keeping up the supply of stories to the well-paying magazines, and the increasing mental instability of Zelda. Zelda would be institutionalized for much of the 1930s, and was one of the patients who died when a fire engulfed Ashville North Carolina's Highland Hospital in 1948.

Fitzgerald began work in earnest on *Tender Is the Night* in 1932, and in the same year Zelda published her own novel broadly based, Fitzgerald protested, on the same experiences. When Zelda's *Save Me the Waltz* appeared it was apparently with much of that material removed under pressure from Scott. *Tender Is the Night* sets the decline of psychiatrist Dick Diver against the background of wealthy expatriates on the French Riviera in the 1920s. The novel is far more expansive in narrative and character development than *The Great Gatsby,* and in that sense is a return to the structure of his earlier novels, but with a maturity of both style and theme which those earlier novels lack. But by 1933 the public's mood was far different from that of the optimistic 1920s, and the book was neither a critical nor a commercial success. In the nine years since *The Great Gatsby* Fitzgerald had lost many of his readers. He fretted with the organization of the book, and suggested a change to Scribner's in 1938 that would move the delayed introduction of Dick Diver's earlier life to the beginning of the book. In 1951 Scribner's published a revised version incorporating these changes, but the general preference has been for the 1934 version, and this is the version currently in print from the publisher.

Taps at Reveille, a collection of short stories that Fitzgerald published in 1935, was barely noticed. And he seemed to write his own epitaph as a writer in a series of essays for *Esquire* the following year, titled *The Crack-Up*. These retrospective essays revealed even more clearly than his fiction that Fitzgerald could see the consequences of his self-destructive behavior with clarity, while being quite unable to stop it. Nevertheless, Fitzgerald's drinking abated somewhat and he moved to Hollywood, initially on a contract from MGM, and when that was not renewed he worked freelance for different studios. He was still short of money, struggling to meet his daughter's college costs and Zelda's medical bills. One source of income was a series of ironically self-mocking stories about Pat Hobby, a scriptwriter who had been much in demand in the days of silent film but now was reduced to freelance hack work at the same studios that had once paid him so handsomely. The $200 that Fitzgerald received for each story from *Esquire* was a long way short of what the *Saturday Evening Post* had paid him.

A long-term relationship with Hollywood gossip columnist Shelia Graham brought some emotional stability to Fitzgerald's life, as well as a source of insider Hollywood stories. This useful source of gossip, his own experience with studios (he had also worked in Hollywood in 1927 and 1931 for brief spells, and two of his novels and a number of his stories had been filmed), and his recollection of MGM producer Irving Thalberg came together in his unfinished novel *The Last Tycoon* and its central character, studio head Monroe Stahr. (The novel was reissued with Fitzgerald's original title, *The Love of the Last Tycoon*, when edited by Matthew Bruccoli in 1993.) Stahr is haunted by the death of his wife, and beset by enemies at the studio and by changing conditions in the movie business itself. The story was to be told, as with *The Great Gatsby*, by a narrator on the margins of the story, Celia Brady. Fitzgerald left an outline of his plans for the novel and extensive notes, and these were included when the manuscript was edited for publication the year after Fitzgerald's death by his Princeton friend Edmund Wilson. Publication in a volume that included *The Great Gatsby* along with selected stories began the reassessment of Fitzgerald's work, a reassessment continued with the 1945 publication, also compiled by Wilson, of "The Crack-Up" and some other essays. Also included were positive evaluations of Fitzgerald's work by such authors as T. S. Eliot, John Dos Passos, and Thomas Wolfe. By the beginning of the 1950s interest in Fitzgerald's writing, and in his legend, was firmly established.

Bibliography

The Cambridge Edition of the Works of F. Scott Fitzgerald (Cambridge, 1991–), is a scholarly edition which includes all the writer's novels and books of short stories.

Matthew Bruccoli, *Some Sort of Epic Grandeur: The Life of F. Scott Fitzgerald*, 2nd edn (Columbia, SC, 2002).

Jackson R. Bryer, Ruth Prigozy, and Milton R. Stern, eds., *F. Scott Fitzgerald in the Twenty-First Century* (Tuscaloosa, 2003).

Ruth Prigozy, ed., *The Cambridge Companion to F. Scott Fitzgerald* (Cambridge, 2002).

Mary Jo Tate, *Critical Companion to F. Scott Fitzgerald* (New York, 2007).

John Dos Passos (1896–1970)

John Dos Passos wrote prolifically on politics, American history, and travel, but is best known for his trilogy *U.S.A.*, which combines fiction, real persons, and experimental narrative techniques into a broad narrative of the first three decades of the century. Over the course of his career Dos Passos's political views moved from voting for the Communist Party candidate in the 1932 presidential election to writing in support of Republican Party nominee Barry Goldwater in 1964. But Dos Passos's view is consistently a pessimistic one. The individual in his novels is usually crushed by forces larger than himself, whether communist or capitalist. Dos Passos is often categorized as a naturalist writer, albeit one whose naturalism in his more important work is grounded in cultural and political history. He was innovative enough for Sinclair Lewis to declare Dos Passos's novel *Manhattan Transfer* "the foundation of a whole new school of novel-writing."

Dos Passos was the illegitimate son of Lucy Madison and John Randolph Dos Passos. His father, a self-made man, the son of Portuguese immigrants, was a prominent corporation lawyer in New York City, and the author of several books on corporation law. Lucy Madison spent a good part of her son's early years dividing her time between Europe and the United States, with the result that at various times Dos Passos attended schools in Washington, DC, London, and Connecticut. His parents married in 1910, upon the death of his father's wife, and the following year Dos Passos adopted his father's surname. He entered Harvard University in 1912, where he was active in college publications and became very interested in modernist art movements. After graduating in 1916 he traveled in Spain, returned to the United States, and began training for a Red Cross volunteer ambulance unit. His subsequent experiences on the European battlefields confirmed his critical view of the war

The Twentieth-Century American Fiction Handbook   By Christopher MacGowan
© 2011 Christopher MacGowan

and the leftward direction of his early politics. The war finished, he spent most of the next few years in Europe. Early publications included political articles, and inclusion in the anthology *Eight Harvard Poets* (1917). In 1920 his first novel, *One Man's Initiation – 1917*, was published in England. *Three Soldiers* appeared the following year, both novels based upon the author's wartime experiences. *Three Soldiers* is one of the key anti-war novels to come out of World War I, and is blunt in its treatment of the conflict, and the war's effect upon its three central characters. Dos Passos's approach in this book of placing his characters within a broad background accompanied by social commentary, rather than engaging in detailed psychological exploration, would remain the method of his subsequent fiction.

Dos Passos continued to spend much of the 1920s traveling: in Europe, the Middle East, North Africa, and the Soviet Union, with occasional trips back to the United States. In his travels he formed friendships with a number of writers and painters, including a close friendship with Ernest Hemingway. His next major work, *Manhattan Transfer*, appeared in 1925. In telling the story of the unsuccessful marriage of Jimmy Herf and Ellen Thatcher – of the compromises Ellen makes for financial security, and of Jimmy's aimless wandering – Dos Passos fills the background with multiple characters and vignettes of the city, sometimes only two or three pages long, sometimes shifting rapidly between one story or group and another. The method develops further the technique of *Three Soldiers*, taking it toward the ambitious scope of the trilogy to come.

In the mid-1920s, despite his travels, Dos Passos became increasingly involved in the New York City literary world. In 1925 he joined the executive board of the left-wing journal *New Masses*, and the following year became associated with the New Playwrights Theatre. The group produced his play *Airways, Inc.* in 1929, although the four-week run was unsuccessful. Shortly thereafter he resigned from the group, disgusted with its infighting. In August of that year Dos Passos married Katharine Smith, a childhood friend of Ernest Hemingway's whom he had met when visiting Hemingway in Key West.

In 1927 Dos Passos began work on the first novel of the *U.S.A.* trilogy. *The 42nd Parallel* was published in 1930, *1919* followed in 1932, and *The Big Money* in 1936. The first book begins in 1900, taking the narrative through the years leading up to World War I, and into the beginning of the war itself. The second book takes the story through the years of America's involvement in the war and the immediate aftermath, and the third is set in the boom years of the 1920s that lead to the Wall Street crash of 1929. Dos Passos uses four recurring narrative techniques throughout the trilogy. The first follows the lives of 12 fictional characters, each character brought into the foreground in one of the volumes. These narratives are accompanied by short biographies of prominent historical figures, such as Andrew Carnegie and William Jennings Bryan. (This feature of the trilogy caused Harper's, publishers of the first volume, to refuse to publish the second because of its treatment of J. P. Morgan.) The "Newsreel" sections print newspaper headlines and song lyrics of the day, while a fourth narrative strand, the "Camera Eye," consists of subjective, impressionistic accounts written in a stream-of-consciousness mode. Recent biographies of the author have identified much of this "Camera Eye" prose as autobiographical.

When the three novels were published together in 1938, Dos Passos added a short prologue and epilogue. The prologue declares in its final paragraph, "U.S.A. is the slice of a continent" and, following a representative catalogue of institutions, places, and situations, it concludes, "But mostly U.S.A. is the speech of the people." Throughout the trilogy that "speech" is manipulated by institutions, businessmen, and politicians, degrading the words of promise that for Dos Passos had once defined what the United States could become. Toward the end of *The Big Money*, when anarchists Sacco and Vanzetti are executed for a crime that Dos Passos, along with many other writers and activists, was convinced they had not committed, the "Camera Eye" records: "America our nation has been beaten by strangers who have turned our language inside out who have taken the clean words our fathers spoke and made them slimy and foul."

The major fictional characters of the first two novels include Fenian McCreary ("Mac"), who has a somewhat ambivalent role in radical labor politics, exploitive capitalist J. Ward Moorehouse, and the morally irresponsible Richard Ellsworth Savage. In these first two books of the trilogy the female characters tend to play roles subservient to the men. In *The Big Money*, however, two of the three protagonists are female and more prominent – the silent screen star Margo Dowling, and political activist Mary French. The trilogy ends with an image of a continent divided: a businessman flies in comfort from the Atlantic to the Pacific coast, and the plane's route crosses the path of a solitary hungry and tired hitchhiker, a man who has benefited from none of the promises proclaimed by the rhetoric of the schools, radio, cinema, and big business.

The story of Mary French in *The Big Money* illustrates the disillusionment that Dos Passos had come to feel about the Communist Party and left-wing politics generally by the late 1930s. This shift in his political position was reinforced by what he saw of the Spanish Civil War when in Spain in 1937, particularly what he viewed as communist betrayals of the Republic's cause. In a number of books and essays on political themes over the next 30 years Dos Passos charted his move toward the right.

During 1942–1943 Dos Passos traveled around the United States covering the effects of World War II on the home front, and then journeyed to the Pacific to write a series of articles on the Pacific War. Later he covered post-war conditions in Europe and the Nuremberg Trials, becoming increasingly pessimistic about the ability of the West to deal with what he saw as the threat of communist domination. Personal tragedy struck in 1947 when his wife Katy was killed in an automobile accident on a Connecticut road, where Dos Passos himself lost his right eye. In 1949 he married Elizabeth Holdridge and the couple settled in Spence's Point, Virginia.

A number of honors had come Dos Passos's way following his work in the 1930s. In 1937 he was elected to the National Institute of Arts and Letters, and in 1947 to the American Academy of Arts and Letters. In 1957 he would win the Institute's Gold Medal for Fiction. But in the 1940s Dos Passos's literary reputation was not helped by three novels, *Adventures of a Young Man* (1939), *Number One* (1943), and *The Grand Design* (1949), which together make up a trilogy much looser and less experimental than *U.S.A.* Titled *District of Columbia*, the three books cover the period from the Spanish Civil War to the late years of Franklin Roosevelt's administration. The trilogy's theme is the power of politicians and the media to oppress and manipulate the individual – a familiar Dos Passos concern, but in this case too often descending into polemics. More ambitious and successful is *Midcentury* (1961), which brings the techniques of *U.S.A.* to the post-war period. The novel is an indictment of labor unions and financiers alike, and is deeply pessimistic in its assessment of the ability of the individual to resist the power of large organizations and institutions.

Much of Dos Passos's published work in his last decade centered upon travel and political writing. This work included two books on Thomas Jefferson, and an unfinished novel, *Century's Ebb*, which looks at the political and racial unrest of the 1960s using a mixture of biography and fiction. The novel was published posthumously in 1975.

Bibliography

The Library of America has published *U.S.A.* in a single volume (1997) as well as *Travel Books and Other Writings, 1916–1941* (2003) and *Novels, 1920–1925* (2003).

Townsend Ludington, *John Dos Passos: A Twentieth Century Odyssey* (New York, 1980).
Lisa Nanney, *John Dos Passos* (New York, 1998).
Donald Pizer, ed., *John Dos Passos's U.S.A.: A Documentary Volume* (Detroit, 2003).

William Faulkner (1897–1962)

William Faulkner invented a richly detailed world, Yoknapatawpha County, within which much of his major fiction takes place. The details of this fictional county owe much to Faulkner's knowledge of northern Mississippi, where he lived much of his life, and critics have often noted the resemblance between Yoknapatawpha's county seat of Jefferson and the town of Oxford, in Lafayette County, Mississippi, where Faulkner's parents made their home in 1902.

Faulkner was the oldest of four brothers in a family that had originally made its money in the railroad business, although Faulkner's father went on to become secretary, then business manager, of the University of Mississippi in Oxford. Faulkner himself attended high school sporadically after eleventh grade, and by early 1916 was working in his grandfather's bank. At this time he formed an important early friendship with Phil Stone, a Yale graduate and native of Oxford, who contributed importantly to Faulkner's early literary education and to whom Faulkner dedicated his late trilogy, *The Hamlet* (1940), *The Town* (1957), and *The Mansion* (1959). In 1918 Faulkner enlisted in the Canadian division of the British Royal Air Force, but too late to see active service. His long interest in flying would find expression in his 1935 novel *Pylon*.

Back at Oxford after the war, Faulkner enrolled in classes at the University of Mississippi, began appearing in campus publications, and had a poem published in the *New Republic*. He withdrew from the university in 1920 to join another early literary mentor, Stark Young, in New York City for a few months. By the end of 1921 he was back in Oxford working as postmaster for the university post office, writing fiction and poetry, and getting to know some of the writers working in New Orleans. In 1924 he was fired from the

The Twentieth-Century American Fiction Handbook   By Christopher MacGowan
© 2011 Christopher MacGowan

post office job, evidently for paying too little attention to his mailing duties. In this same year his first book appeared. *The Marble Faun*, a volume of poems, borrowed its title from Hawthorne's 1860 novel. The publication costs of the book were subsidized by Phil Stone.

Toward the end of 1924 Faulkner met Sherwood Anderson in New Orleans and the two became close for a few months, during which time Anderson convinced Faulkner that his talents and interests were better served by prose, and also that he should write about the region and people he knew best. Anderson had followed his own advice in setting much of his fiction in his boyhood Ohio. Anderson further helped the younger writer by recommending Faulkner's manuscript "Mayday" to publishers Boni and Liveright, where the novel was published in 1926 as *Soldiers' Pay*.

Faulkner spent the second half of 1925 in Europe. On his return to the United States he lived most of the following year in New Orleans, where he completed the manuscript of his second novel, *Mosquitoes*, published by Boni and Liveright in 1927. But Horace Liveright rejected the next manuscript that Faulkner sent him, *Flags in the Dust*, and it was eventually published in a shorter version, as *Sartoris*, by Harcourt, Brace in 1929 (the longer version under the original title was not published until 1973). Faulkner dedicated this first of the novels set in Yoknapatawpha County to Sherwood Anderson. The Sartoris family, aristocratic slaveholders before the Civil War, are in the background of a number of the later novels, and are principal characters again in *The Unvanquished* (1938).

According to Faulkner's own account, after the difficulties he encountered in getting *Sartoris* published he decided to write only for himself and to give little thought to whatever might be a publisher's opinion. The resulting novel, *The Sound and the Fury* (1929), is generally considered the first of Faulkner's major works, and the beginning of what was to be a remarkable period of creativity. The first three sections present the story of the Compson family's decline via the narration of three brothers: the mentally retarded Benjie, the eldest son Quentin – who is oppressed by the debased heritage of his family and his own desperate sense of the need to protect his sister's honor – and the selfish, embittered, manipulative Jason, as much a victim of the past as his siblings, despite his claims to be a realist and to be free of Compson history. The actions and emotional energy of all three brothers are conditioned to a large extent by their responses to their sister Caddy, pregnant outside marriage, rejected by her husband, exiled from the home, and cheated by Jason. Caddy thus functions as a central figure in the novel despite not giving voice to a section. Each chapter told by the brothers reflects in its structure, rhythm, and vocabulary the limitations and obsessions of its narrator through the stream-of-consciousness narration that Faulkner had learned from the work of James Joyce and others. The fourth and last section is objective narration centered, in its first half, on the overburdened black servant Dilsey. Dilsey had tried to serve as something of a mother to the Compson children, Mrs. Compson having retreated into a whining, self-indulgent passivity. The novel's final pages follow Jason's furious chase after Caddy's daughter, Quentin, who has stolen the money that he in turn had stolen from Caddy. The novel's present is Easter Weekend 1928, but its first three narratives move through multiple scenes of the past, sometimes only indicated through fragmentary references. Together the different perspectives tell the history behind Quentin's suicide, Caddy's exile, and Dilsey's painstaking endurance.

The Sound and the Fury was published by a new firm that had been co-founded by Harrison Smith, Faulkner's editor at Harcourt. The novel appeared to warm reviews, but, as with Faulkner's previous books, sales were not high. In 1929 Faulkner married, and now had two stepchildren to support as well as his wife; thus he began work on a tale sensational enough, he hoped, to generate sales and attention. This novel, *Sanctuary*, appeared in 1931, but the manuscript had given enough pause to Harrison Smith that *As I Lay Dying* (1930) appeared first. *As I Lay Dying* records the efforts of the Bundren family to take their dead mother's body to Jefferson, where her family are buried, and their battle against nature to get her there. The forces of both flood and fire delay them, and the body is decaying rapidly inside the coffin – a coffin made lovingly and carefully by eldest son Cash. Each member of the Bundren family has his or her own reasons for wanting to get to Jefferson, or, in the case of Darl, of not wanting to get there. Darl, rejected by his mother but desperately wanting the connection with her that would ground his identity, tells more of the narrative than any other character. When he is seized and taken to the mental hospital in Jackson his incarceration is as much because his father would be liable for his actions in burning Gillespie's barn as for his condition itself. Yet none of the poor farmers of Yoknapatawpha County can afford such loss, and in that sense Darl is a threat to their fragile livelihood. His prescience is also a threat to the pregnant Dewey Dell, and he alone of the surviving members of the family recognizes the truth of his brother Jewel's paternity. The narratives supplied by the various members of the Bundren family are supplemented by the accounts of neighbors, and by the comments of the farmers whom the family encounter on their journey. The indomitable survivor in this novel is the stubbornly narrow and selfish father, Anse, although one could make the case for Addie herself, whose determined will even allows her to speak after death.

When *Sanctuary* appeared the book certainly gained the attention intended by its sensational rape plot, although the attention was not always favorable. Faulkner tended to disparage the book in later interviews, as did earlier critical studies of the author, although *Sanctuary* has since come in for some more extended attention. But neither this novel, nor *Light in August*, published in 1932, solved Faulkner's financial problems, and this year saw the beginning of his work in Hollywood, where he came to have a close professional relationship with director Howard Hawks. Faulkner would go on to co-write the screenplays for two of Hawks's best-known films, *To Have and Have Not* (from Hemingway's novel) and *The Big Sleep* (from the novel by Raymond Chandler).

Faulkner shocked many readers again with his story of barnstorming fliers, *Pylon* (1935), a novel set in New Orleans rather than Yoknapatawpha County. The novel is usually considered more successful in some of its powerful individual passages than as a whole, and Faulkner evidently thought the 1958 film version, *The Tarnished Angels*, directed by Douglas Sirk, not only the best screen adaptation of his work, but an improvement upon the novel itself.

Absalom, Absalom! (1936) is for some readers Faulkner's greatest achievement. The doomed Quentin from *The Sound and the Fury* returns along with his Harvard roommate, the Canadian Shreve McCannon. The two of them try to puzzle out the events behind the story of Thomas Sutpen, with additional narration, sometimes equally speculative, from Quentin's father and Rosa Coldfield. The story of Sutpen's failed attempts to found a dynasty at Sutpen's Hundred examines, among other issues, race, the status of historical record, degrees of knowledge, and the act of storytelling – for much of the narrative necessitates informed guesswork, speculation, and imaginative reconstruction. As with *The Sound and the Fury*, details are revealed through overlapping flashbacks, in this novel with sometimes contradictory accounts. The book was published by Random House, whom Smith and his partner had joined, and Random House would remain Faulkner's publishers for the rest of his life.

In addition to his novels, Faulkner wrote more conventional short stories intended for magazine publication. Sometimes the stories are the precursors of novels; "Twilight," for example, paved the way for *The Sound and the Fury*. In the late 1930s and early 1940s he published three books that brought together a number of these stories. He reshaped *The Unvanquished* (1938) into a novel, while *The Wild Palms* (1939) is structured around two counterpointed stories, "Old Man" and the title story, that together offer different perspectives on the book's central themes of love, hardship, and loss. But critical debate continues over the genre to be ascribed to *Go Down, Moses* (1942). First published as *Go Down, Moses and Other Stories*, Faulkner was evidently not consulted on the title of a book that he regarded as a novel. For some critics the difference is crucial to the interpretation of particular events in the stories, especially in the case of the most famous story in the book, "The Bear." *Go Down, Moses* is arguably the best introduction to Faulkner for a reader new to his work.

Six years elapsed between *Go Down, Moses* and *Intruder in the Dust* (1948), the two works in which Faulkner explores as fully as anywhere in his writing the issue of race relations in the South. In 1940 he had published the first novel, *The Hamlet*, of the trilogy that centers upon the Snopes family, although the second and third volumes appeared much later, *The Town* in 1957 and *The Mansion* in 1959. The Snopes family, particularly Flem Snopes, who is at the center of the trilogy, are ruthless and upwardly mobile, taking over from the fading aristocratic families that ruled the region before the Civil War.

To suggest just something of the way that characters appear and reappear in Faulkner's fiction: various members of the Snopes family appear in a number of earlier novels prior to the trilogy that puts them at the center. Gavin Stevens, the lawyer in the title story of *Go Down, Moses*, also appears in *Intruder in the Dust* as one of those who save Lucas Beauchamp from a murder charge, as well as appearing in a number of Faulkner's subsequent stories. Stevens is the uncle of Charles Mallison, who is also in *Intruder in the Dust*, and uncle and nephew are two of the three narrators of the Snopes trilogy.

The second half of the 1940s saw Faulkner achieve national and international recognition. Malcolm Cowley's *The Portable Faulkner* (1946) brought the scope of Faulkner's work before a larger readership. In 1948 he was elected to the American Academy of Arts and Letters, and he was awarded the 1949 Nobel Prize for Literature. He continued to be productive in the 1950s, although the later works have until recently generally received less attention. Temple Drake of *Sanctuary* returns in *Requiem for a Nun* (1951), which Faulkner subsequently co-adapted for the stage. *A Fable* (1954), a moral tale of World War I, won a National Book Award and Pulitzer Prize. He published the two late additions to the Snopes trilogy, and in 1962 *The Reivers*. Set in Yoknapatawpha County in 1905, the novel appeared a month before Faulkner's death, becoming the final installment of the most sustained and fully imagined fictional real estate in American fiction; real estate of which, as he wrote on a map of Yoknapatawpha County prepared for one of his publishers, the author was the "sole owner and proprietor."

Bibliography

The Library of America has published all of Faulkner's novels in five volumes (New York, 1985–2006), with authoritative texts and helpful notes.

Joseph L. Blotner, *Faulkner: A Biography* (New York, 1984).

Michael Millgate, The Achievement of William Faulkner (New York, 1966).

Charles A. Peek and Robert W. Hamblin, eds., *A Companion to Faulkner Studies* (Westport, CT, 2004).

Eric J. Sunquist, *Faulkner: The House Divided* (Baltimore, 1983).

Ernest Hemingway (1899–1961)

Ernest Hemingway was once almost as well known for his lifestyle as for his writing; a life style of hard drinking, courage – whether as big game hunter or war correspondent – and an aggressively masculine individualism. In his non-fiction, the laconic style of what appeared to be autobiographical prose, and in his fiction the centrality of a particular kind of hero, helped the author's life take on something of the quality of myth. But since his suicide, and the subsequent availability of Hemingway's papers – including earlier drafts of his novels and stories, and manuscripts of uncompleted projects – along with new biographical information, there has emerged a figure more insecure and generally much more complex than the image that the author liked to project. These new perspectives upon Hemingway's work have led to some fresh interpretations of his stories and novels, particularly concerning their treatment of gender. Such discussions are accompanied by the continuing analysis of a quality always recognized in his work, his important and influential achievement as a stylist.

Hemingway was born in Oak Park, Illinois, a suburban town near Chicago. Hemingway's father, Clarence Hemingway, was a doctor, and figures in a number of stories in various guises, including the early Nick Adams stories "Indian Camp" and "The Doctor and the Doctor's Wife." Ill with diabetes, Clarence Hemingway committed suicide in 1928. The shot was overheard by Hemingway's younger brother Leicester, later the writer of a well-received biography of Ernest, and himself a suicide in 1982.

Hemingway's apprenticeship as a writer came through experience as a journalist. After graduating from Oak Park High School in 1917 he worked for the *Kansas City Star* as a cub reporter, and in 1920 began filing stories for the *Toronto Star*, initially in Toronto and subsequently in Paris. In between

The Twentieth-Century American Fiction Handbook   By Christopher MacGowan
© 2011 Christopher MacGowan

these two newspaper jobs Hemingway volunteered for the Red Cross Ambulance service on World War I's Italian front, was wounded after only a few weeks, and following recuperation in a Milan hospital returned to Oak Park. The experience of war, and his romantic relationship in the hospital with nurse Agnes von Kurowsky, would be central to the narrative of *A Farewell to Arms* 10 years later.

In 1921 Hemingway married Hadley Richardson and in November of that year, armed with letters of introduction from Sherwood Anderson, the two sailed for Europe and took up residence in Paris. Anderson's letters helped Hemingway contact the expatriate writers congregating in the city, while an arrangement with the *Toronto Star* to file stories helped to provide an income. These years before the break-up of his marriage to Hadley – they were divorced in 1927 – are described in Hemingway's posthumous memoir *A Moveable Feast* (1964).

Establishing himself among the expatriates in Paris, Hemingway began writing stories and poems, publishing his first book, *Three Stories and Ten Poems*, with Robert McAlmon's Contact Press in 1923. Like all of McAlmon's publications the book had a limited circulation, only 300 copies being printed. Another of the expatriate presses, Three Mountains Press, published the first version of *in our time* in 1924. This book had a run of just 170 copies. The following year Hemingway found a New York publisher, Boni and Liveright, for an enlarged version of *In Our Time*. This version added a number of stories, now considered among Hemingway's finest, to the brief sketches that had appeared in the Three Mountains volume.

However, the Boni and Liveright association was soon to end as a result of the next manuscript that Hemingway sent them. Some of Hemingway's earliest stories are heavily influenced by Sherwood Anderson, then a Liveright author, particularly the first-person narrator in "My Old Man" who has affinities with the naïve narrators of such Anderson stories as "The Triumph of the Egg" and "Death in the Woods." There are other similarities: the adolescent Nick Adams in Hemingway's stories bears some relationship to the George Willard of *Winesburg, Ohio*, and both writers see the commercial, religious, and political manipulation of language as systematic of a culture in crisis. Both also stressed the importance of immediate experience, but emphasized the danger of sentimentalizing the past or projecting assumptions about the future based upon the experience of the present moment. As if Hemingway needed to exorcise the influence of Anderson as part of discovering his own style, he wrote a parody of Anderson's novel *Dark Laughter*, titling it *The Torrents of Spring*, and this was the manuscript that he sent to Horace Liveright. With the manuscript inevitably rejected and the contract between author and publisher broken, Hemingway moved to the much more visible and better-paying Scribner's, who published Hemingway's first major novel, *The Sun Also Rises*, in 1926, and all his subsequent books.

The Sun Also Rises develops many of the features of Hemingway's shorter fiction. Jake Barnes is impotent from a war wound, an injury that makes impossible a sexual relationship with the woman that he loves, Brett Ashley. Jake is usually capable of a kind of stoic discipline, recognizing that the post-war world is one of limitations, and that dreams possible to hold in an earlier age have been exposed as naïvely sentimental. At times, however, he descends into self-pity or bitterness. He finds, like many Hemingway characters in the stories and novels that follow, some relief in the discipline of sports, in the rituals of meals, and in drinking – drinking sufficient to heighten, but not blur, sensation. In sports, particularly fishing, hunting, or bullfighting, a series of ordered steps lead to a defined goal. In addition the sports take place in a largely masculine world, limiting the emotional complications brought by the presence of women in Hemingway's fiction. In *The Sun Also Rises* a group of British and American expatriates who travel from France to Spain to witness the bullfights at Pamplona fail to uphold the necessary discipline when they are tested by the associated fiesta. Their failings are exposed, but there are no solutions for the future discovered by the characters, or offered by the author.

Hemingway's prose in this novel, and in his best work generally, parallels the discipline that his central figures struggle to maintain. The sentences describe objects observed, with little notice of emotional response. A paragraph might be a list of declarative sentences, or a string of phrases describing a series of sensations, each phrase set off only by commas or neutral conjunctions. The result is an economical prose characterized by understatement and emotional detachment. In his 1932 non-fiction treatise on bullfighting, *Death in the Afternoon*, a book also very much about writing, Hemingway described the challenge that he felt he faced in shaping his prose during the early years in Paris:

> I was trying to write then and I found the greatest difficulty, aside from knowing truly what you really felt, rather than what you were supposed to feel, and had been taught to feel, was to put down what really happened in action; what the actual things were which produced the emotion that you experienced . . . the real thing, the sequence of motion and fact which made the emotion and which would be as valid in a year or in ten years or, with luck and if you stated it purely enough, always, was beyond me and I was working very hard to try to get it.

The positive critical response to *The Sun Also Rises*, together with another volume of well-received short stories, *Men Without Women* (1927), and the commercial success of *A Farewell to Arms* (1929), established Hemingway by the end of the 1920s as a major figure in American fiction. His marriage to

Hadley Richardson had crumbled, however, and in 1927 he married Pauline Pfeiffer. The two moved to Key West, Florida, in 1928. This marriage would itself end in divorce in 1940.

As well as his literary success, Hemingway was also becoming a well-known public figure. The 1930s saw the beginning of the legend that, years after his death, remains a part of his reputation. But he increasingly felt misgivings about the time he was spending with the very rich as a result of his fame, and he became concerned that this lifestyle might affect his integrity as a writer. These fears come out in one of his best-known stories, "The Snows of Kilimanjaro" (1936), in which the dying writer Harry reflects upon the promising material that he has failed to turn into good stories, instead making lazy compromises with commercial taste, and giving in to the seductive, wealthy lifestyle that has led him to abandon discipline in both writing and living.

In the 10 years following *A Farewell to Arms* Hemingway published, in addition to *Death in the Afternoon*, *Green Hills of Africa* (1935) – using his hunting experiences on safari – another collection of stories, *Winner Take Nothing* (1933), and what is generally regarded as one of his weakest novels, *To Have and Have Not* (1937).

By the end of the decade Hemingway was supporting the Republican cause in the Spanish Civil War, and writing some distinguished journalism in his role as war correspondent. His novel *For Whom the Bell Tolls* (1940) uses the Civil War as its setting and marked for many readers his finest writing since the 1920s. The novel centers upon Robert Jordan, an American explosives expert, and the Republican guerrilla band he is helping. Death is a constant threat, and the courage of Jordan and other individuals in the group is strongly tested over the critical weekend covered by the story. Hemingway's narrative perspective is less rigorously limited in this novel than in his first two novels, with the result that the picture of Robert Jordan is both richer but also more conventional. In the novel's dialogue Hemingway tries to suggest English that has been translated from Spanish, an experiment that for some critics works well, although for others produces at times some rather labored prose.

Following his divorce from Pauline Pfeiffer, Hemingway married the well-known journalist Martha Gellhorn, although this marriage too ended in divorce. Hemingway continued his war reporting during World War II, and in 1946 he moved to Cuba where in the same year he married Mary Welsh, also a journalist. Hemingway struggled with his fiction projects following the war, and the novel that he eventually published, *Across the River and Into the Trees* (1950), is generally considered his weakest. Two posthumously published novels, *Islands in the Stream* (1970) and *The Garden of Eden* (1986), had their source in the manuscript material that he worked on at this period. *The Garden of Eden* in particular helped to generate a new look at the role of gender in Hemingway's work.

Hemingway had a triumphant commercial and artistic success with the short novel *The Old Man and the Sea* (1952), which won the Pulitzer Prize for Fiction. In 1954 he was awarded the Nobel Prize in Literature, cited by the Swedish Academy "for his powerful, style-forming mastery of the art of modern narration." In his last years Hemingway worked on a memoir of the 1920s in Paris, *A Moveable Feast*, an account that mixes nostalgia with lively anecdote. The book is regretful about the end of his marriage to Hadley, and contains a number of portraits, some scathing (Gertrude Stein, Scott and Zelda Fitzgerald, Ford Madox Ford) and some respectful (Ezra Pound), of the writers Hemingway had known and sometimes worked with. Ford had been particularly helpful to Hemingway in these years, taking him on as assistant editor of the important expatriate journal *transatlantic review*. The book was published posthumously in 1964.

In the late 1950s Hemingway became increasingly ill and depressed. He moved to Ketchum, Idaho, when Fidel Castro came to power in Cuba, and in his Ketchum home on July 2, 1961, he committed suicide – like his father more than 30 years earlier, by shooting himself.

Bibliography

Hemingway's writings are generally available in paperback form. There is no standard edition.

Nancy R. Comley and Robert Scholes, *Hemingway's Genders: Rereading the Hemingway Text* (New Haven, 1994).
Kenneth S. Lynn, *Hemingway* (New York, 1987).
Jeffrey Meyers, *Hemingway: A Biography* (New York, 1985).
Charles M. Oliver, *Ernest Hemingway: A Literary Guide to His Life and Work* (New York, 2007).

Vladimir Nabokov (1899–1977)

The author of one of the most famous books in twentieth-century American literature was born in Russia, attended an English university, began his early writing career in Germany, escaped to the United States in May 1940 (just three weeks before Paris fell to the Germans), and lived the last years of his life in the opulent Montreux Palace Hotel in Switzerland. Not surprisingly, Nabokov's fiction often takes place against a broad international background and is usually peopled by cosmopolitan figures with complex international identities. Sometimes they are striving to reach a place other than the one that they find themselves in, a place either actual or imagined, or even something of both. And sometimes Nabokov's narrators seem to become aware of their existence within the fiction that the author is creating around them – and sometimes not.

Nabokov was born in St. Petersburg. His father was a liberal politician who served in the Provisional Government that followed the abdication of the Tsar in 1917. He served the next year in the Crimean Regional Government, before being forced to flee with his family ahead of the Bolshevik forces. Left behind was the family's recently inherited 2000-acre estate and a substantial fortune. The family spent time in England, and Nabokov began his studies at Cambridge University. He began his publishing career while at college, publishing poems in England and poems and prose in the Berlin newspaper that his father edited once the family settled in the German capital. In 1922, in the spring that Nabokov graduated, his father was killed trying to protect a fellow member of the former Provisional Government from assassination, an event that critics have noticed is echoed in various forms in Nabokov's fiction.

Settled in Berlin following his graduation, Nabokov published two volumes of poetry, and a Russian translation of *Alice in Wonderland*, using the pen name V. Sirin (allusions to Lewis Carroll's famous work crop up in a number of Nabokov's later novels, most centrally in *Lolita*). Nabokov earned an income from teaching and journalism, and increasingly from short stories that appeared in Russian expatriate journals. He married Vera Slonim, formerly of St. Petersburg, in 1925, and the following year published his first novel, translated as *Mary* when it appeared in English in 1970. The novel has much in common with a central theme in Nabokov's later fiction, the power of memory to evoke the past, but the importance of not becoming trapped in that past. In 1928 appeared the novel titled in its 1968 English translation *King, Queen, Knave*; *The Defense*, as it was translated in 1964, appeared in 1930. In the later novel, chess, and in both more generally, game playing, are central features, as they continue to be in Nabokov's later fiction. By this time Nabokov had established himself as one of the leading Russian émigré writers, a position confirmed by the series of novels, all first published in Russian, that followed: *The Eye* (1930, English translation 1965); *Glory* (1932, 1971); *Laughter in the Dark* (1933, first translated as *Camera Obscura*, 1936, retranslated in 1938); *Despair* (1936, 1937); *Invitation to a Beheading* (1938, 1959), and *The Gift* (1952, 1963).

These novels develop in increasingly complex ways the themes introduced in Nabokov's earliest work. Autobiographical details might slide into fantasy. For example, the protagonist of *Glory*, Martin Edelweis, has a number of experiences that parallel his creator's, including attending Cambridge University and returning to Berlin. Some of the passages in the novel later reappeared in Nabokov's autobiography. But unlike his creator, Martin is determined to undertake what is probably a doomed quest to return to a land half Soviet Russia and half fantasy, a goal that is part romantic gesture to impress a lady, and part a childhood dream associated with a painting that hung on his bedroom wall. Dmitri Nabokov, Nabokov's son, born in 1934, translated *Glory* when it appeared in English, but Nabokov himself translated some of the Russian novels.

The first novel that Nabokov actually wrote in English, as part of an attempt to expand his audience, was *The Real Life of Sebastian Knight* – written in the late 1930s, but not published until 1941, the year after the Nabokovs arrived in the United States. His autobiography, *Conclusive Evidence: A Memoir*, was also written in English, and published in 1951. Nabokov revised and translated the work into Russian in 1954, and revised it again as *Speak Memory: An Autobiography Revisited* in 1967. The book covers Nabokov's life up to the point where he and his family are about to depart for the United States.

Nabokov had been looking for an opportunity to leave Germany as early as 1932, and this finally occurred in 1937. By 1938 the family was in Paris, where Nabokov was writing in French as well as English. He explored the possibilities of an academic position in England, but a teaching offer brought him to the United States in 1940. Subsequently he lectured at Stanford and Wellesley before accepting a permanent position at Cornell, where, starting in 1948, he taught Russian and European literature. His sometimes quirky but always entertaining lectures have been published as *Lectures on Literature* (1980), and include discussion of, among others, Dickens, Austen, Flaubert, Joyce, and Proust.

Writer and critic Edmund Wilson was an important supporter in Nabokov's first years in the United States, among other things helping him to obtain the Guggenheim Fellowship that he was awarded in 1943, and opening up connections to publishers and magazine editors, although the friendship would sour in the 1960s. Along with *The Real Life of Sebastian Knight*, and poems and stories that appeared in such magazines as *The New Yorker*, Nabokov published the novel *Bend Sinister* in 1947 and a collection of short fiction, *Nine Stories*, the same year. In 1945 he became an American citizen.

Nabokov began writing *Lolita* in 1950, although he did not finish the novel until 1953, delayed by his teaching duties and his work on other manuscripts, including his autobiography and a four-volume translation with commentary of Pushkin's *Eugene Onegin* (1964). Just as Lolita has a precursor, Annabel Lee, in narrator Humbert Humbert's confessions, so too does the narrative of *Lolita*. In 1939 Nabokov wrote a story in Russian in which a man schemes to marry a woman in order to become stepfather to her daughter, the actual object of his desires. This early version of the famous novel was eventually published in English in 1986 as *The Enchanter*, while the Russian original appeared in 1991.

The narrator of *Lolita*, Humbert Humbert, manipulates his readers just as he manipulates the young girl whom he abuses. Both text and 12-year-old victim are constructions. Lolita is both the object of Humbert's projected fantasy, and the girl created out his, and ultimately of course Nabokov's, engagement with the world of language and reading. Reminders that this is a book about language and the ways in which it constructs its own particular reality begin with the first page. A dead protagonist's narrative about a young girl, one whose death is announced at the beginning of the novel using her married name so that it obscures the very information supposedly being conveyed, is introduced by an editor whose double name, John Ray, Jr., suggests that he belongs in the narrative itself – so peppered with double names, mirrors, and coincidences – rather than outside it. This editor, furthermore, proclaims that he has changed the names of most of the "real" people in this fictional narrative, although whether this includes "Annabel

Lee" and the associated Poe references is unclear. Ray does claim that he has not changed Lolita's first name, the middle syllable of which only complicates the source and status of the tragic young figure of Lee in Poe's famous poem. Of course the source is finally Nabokov himself, who takes a bow at one point in the novel as the anagrammatical Vivian Darkbloom.

The provocative subject matter of *Lolita* caused many US publishers to be wary of publishing the manuscript, and when it eventually appeared in 1955 it was put out by the somewhat disreputable Olympia Press in Paris. But then English novelist Graham Greene plucked the book from possible obscurity by naming the novel one of the three best books of 1955 in the London *Sunday Times*. The resulting debate in the London and New York newspapers led to offers from a number of US publishers. When *Lolita* was eventually published in the United States in 1958 it found an immediate and wide readership, although some customers may have been under a misapprehension about the kind of book they were buying. Sales were the fastest for an American novel since *Gone with the Wind*. By the mid-1980s, according to biographer Brian Boyd, *Lolita* had sold 14 million copies around the world. Financially secure thanks to the commercial success of the novel, Nabokov resigned from Cornell in 1959 and he and wife Vera subsequently made their home in Europe. Nabokov wrote a screenplay for Stanley Kubrick's film version of *Lolita* (1962), but Kubrick made enough changes for Nabokov to be dissatisfied with the result. Nabokov's screenplay was published in 1974.

While *Lolita* was taking some time to find an American publisher, *Pnin*, about a mishap-prone Russian émigré professor teaching in the United States, appeared in 1957, and was nominated for a National Book Award. More complex is *Pale Fire*, which appeared in 1962. The book purports to be an edition by Charles Kinbote of a poem by his deceased neighbor John Shade, although the main result of Kinbote's interpretation and commentary is to reveal Kinbote's own projections into the poem. The degree to which Kinbote and Shade have any identity independent of each other, and the role of Shade's dead daughter Hazel in both poem and commentary, has produced a number of different interpretations of the novel.

Ada or Ardor: A Family Chronicle (1969) is a long, complex novel that met with a mixed reception, and is variously a love story, a treatise on the nature of time and memory, and a parody of various linguistic, narrative, and genre conventions. Memory is also a central feature of *Transparent Things* (1972), a much shorter novel, the status of whose narrator remains an issue for much of the book. Nabokov completed one further novel before his death, *Look at the Harlequins!* (1974), in which the narrator Vadim Vadimovich has written a number of books with similar titles to Nabokov's, and whose life, as many critics have noted, parallels his creator's in details that are the opposite of

Nabokov's own. Many commentators have suggested that the novel is Nabokov's reaction to the biography by Andrew Field, *Nabokov: His Life in Art*, which appeared in 1967. Nabokov initially cooperated in the project, but became disappointed by the errors in Field's scholarship, and by what he regarded as misrepresentations of his work and personal and literary relationships.

In his last years Nabokov was recognized as one of the most important living writers, although his English novels following *Pale Fire* had met with mixed reactions from readers and critics. In addition to writing his new fictions he worked with his son Dmitri on translations, and sometimes revisions, of the books from his Berlin years, revised his autobiography, and also undertook a revision of his *Eugene Onegin* translation. The new edition appeared in 1975. Illness and various publishing commitments meant that *The Original of Laura*, a novel with dying as one of its central themes and which Nabokov had mapped out in his head as early as 1974, would remain unfinished at his death. Nabokov requested that the extant manuscript, on 138 index cards, be burned. But Dmitri Nabokov, more than 30 years after his father's death, allowed publication in 2009 – just one of the many indications of the wide and continuing interest in Nabokov's work.

Bibliography

Nabokov's American novels have been published in three volumes by the Library of America (1996), from *The Real Life of Sebastian Knight* to *Look at the Harlequins!*, including his Lolita screenplay. His and Dmitri Nabokov's translations of the Russian novels are generally available in paperback format.

Brian Boyd, *Vladimir Nabokov: The Russian Years* (Princeton, 1990); *Vladimir Nabokov: The American Years* (Princeton, 1991).
Julian W. Connolly, ed., *The Cambridge Companion to Nabokov* (Cambridge, 2005).
Neil Cornwell, *Vladimir Nabokov* (Plymouth, UK, 1999).
Stacy Schiff, *Vera (Mrs Vladimir Nabokov)* (New York, 1999).

Thomas Wolfe (1900–1938)

Thomas Wolfe is one of the most autobiographical of major American novelists. The four books for which he is best known correspond to four stages in the life of Thomas Wolfe, although there is evidence in the writing of the last years in his aborted career that he was trying to write with more objectivity, a broader social perspective – to move beyond the lyrical celebration of youthful experience which had contributed so much to the power of his earlier novels. Whether Wolfe could have achieved this aim, or completed all or any of the sweeping plans that he harbored for future novels, remains a question for critical speculation.

Wolfe was born in Asheville, North Carolina, a city that features in his novels first as Altamont, and later as Libya Hill. North Carolina in the novels is "Old Catawba." Wolfe's father was a stonecutter, and his mother owned and ran a boarding house, spending much of her time speculating in real estate. By the time Wolfe was six his mother and father were living apart. Thomas was the last of the couple's eight children. Two of his brothers were twins, both dying young in circumstances recorded movingly in Wolfe's fiction. Grover died before reaching his teens, while the family was visiting the St. Louis World's Fair in 1904. His death forms the narrative of one of Wolfe's most admired short stories, "The Lost Boy." Grover's twin, Benjamin, was particularly close to Wolfe and was only in his mid-twenties when he died of pneumonia. The death of Ben Gant, as Benjamin is called in *Look Homeward, Angel*, is generally considered one of the most effective scenes in all of Wolfe's fiction.

Wolfe was something of a precocious student and entered the University of North Carolina at the age of 15. His early ambition as a writer was to be a playwright, and one of his plays was performed at the university in 1919. The following year Wolfe began graduate work at Harvard University,

The Twentieth-Century American Fiction Handbook   By Christopher MacGowan
© 2011 Christopher MacGowan

studying with George Pierce Baker, whose famous 47 Workshop gave students an opportunity to have their plays produced. Two of Wolfe's plays were put on locally through the workshop, but he was unsuccessful in getting any New York theater producers interested in his work.

Needing an income, Wolfe began teaching at New York University's Washington Square campus in early 1924, and would teach there as an instructor of composition intermittently until 1930. In the fall of 1924 he took the first of his seven trips to Europe, traveling in France and Germany, before returning in 1926 to New York City. At the end of the voyage he met the much older, well-connected – and married – set designer Aline Bernstein, and the two began what would turn out to be a passionate and turbulent affair over the next few years. She accompanied Wolfe, and supported him, on his second trip to Europe later that year, and continued to support him when they returned. Since he continued to have no success in getting his plays produced, he turned to prose fiction, and used the time off from teaching that Bernstein's financial support brought him to begin the manuscript that would eventually become *Look Homeward, Angel*. Wolfe dedicated the novel to Bernstein when it was published. She would subsequently appear as Esther Jack in *The Web and the Rock*.

Wolfe finished the manuscript in March 1928, but "O Lost" – as *Look Homeward, Angel* was titled at that point – was rejected by at least three publishers. Following one of his quarrels with Bernstein, and bitterly disappointed at his inability to find a publisher, Wolfe escaped to Europe. The trip led to some excessive drinking and some self-destructive behavior, although somehow Wolfe managed to begin work on another novel. Finally, while still abroad, he received word that Maxwell Perkins, the editor at Scribner's who worked closely with Hemingway and Fitzgerald, was interested in his manuscript.

Wolfe met with Perkins in New York in early January 1929, and in light of the editor's suggestions began the process of revising, cutting, and shaping the manuscript, with Perkins occasionally taking a more active role in the cutting, the two working to bring the 294 000-word manuscript down to what Perkins regarded as publishable length. The original "O Lost" manuscript has been published by the University of South Carolina Press, edited by Arlyn and Matthew J. Bruccoli (2000) and its judicious introduction dispels a number of myths that have arisen in earlier Wolfe scholarship about the length of the original manuscript and the nature of Wolfe and Perkins's collaboration.

In August of 1929 *Scribner's Magazine* prepared the way for the novel by publishing a story originally written to be part of *Look Homeward, Angel*, "An Angel on the Porch," and in October – within a week of the Wall Street crash – the novel itself appeared. The novel tells the story of Eugene Gant, a surrogate for the author, and the journey of self-discovery that eventually leads him to take up graduate study at Harvard. The first of the novel's three parts concentrates on Eugene's family, with Wolfe's father represented by the outgoing, dynamic, sometimes drunken W. O. Gant, and his mother by the frugal Eliza Gant. In the second part, Eugene discovers his love of language, and the third part sees Eugene go to college, covers the death of his brother Ben, and leaves Eugene standing on his father's porch looking toward the future, "his eyes upon the distant soaring ranges." Critics have noticed the influence of Sherwood Anderson in the book's rhapsodic prose, of James Joyce's Stephen Dedalus in some aspects of the treatment of Eugene, and of Sinclair Lewis in the satire on the town of Altamont.

The citizens of Asheville were generally outraged by the book's treatment of the town, while some members of Wolfe's own family were hurt by the intimate details that he presented in the novel. Reviewers were impressed by the language and power of individual scenes, but noted what has become a staple in discussion of Wolfe's novels, what they saw as the lack of any controlling form.

Look Homeward, Angel was not a bestseller but sold steadily, was considered for the Pulitzer Prize, and brought Wolfe a good deal of attention in literary and social circles. Sinclair Lewis, for example, praised the novel in his Nobel Prize speech in December 1930. Royalties from the novel, along with the award of a Guggenheim Fellowship, allowed Wolfe to give up his intermittent teaching at New York University. He also began the difficult process of breaking away from his relationship with Aline Bernstein.

At the beginning of the summer in 1930 Wolfe made his fifth journey to Europe, visiting France, Germany, Switzerland, and England. On this trip he met Scott Fitzgerald and Sinclair Lewis, feeling much more at home with the latter, and continued work on his second novel. When he returned to the United States the following year he took an apartment in Brooklyn, and, committing himself to a disciplined and somewhat solitary life, continued working on the manuscript, although with increasing anxiety and self-doubt. When he published the extended novella "A Portrait of Bascom Hawke," based upon his uncle Henry Westall, in *Scribner's Magazine* that year it was the first fiction he had published in over two years. Meanwhile his manuscript, he had come to realize, contained material for more than half a dozen books, and this realization, along with various false starts, meant the novel continued to be delayed.

Perkins turned down the first manuscript that Wolfe put before him. Titled "K-19," the manuscript centered upon the stories of various characters all traveling on a train bound from New York to Asheville. Parts of this rejected manuscript would appear in *Of Time and the River*, and other parts in *You Can't Go Home Again*. Meanwhile Wolfe lived on the occasional sale of short stories culled from his various manuscripts, and on advances from Scribner's. He was interested in writing narratives organized more by thematic connections than by linear plot, but Perkins, judging that Wolfe was floundering in this attempt, persuaded him to make the novel a chronological continuation of Eugene Gant's story. Upon receiving this version, in a manuscript evidently close to a million words, Perkins further persuaded Wolfe to end the narrative at the point when Eugene sees his future lover, the Aline Bernstein character. The story of their affair would be matter for a subsequent novel. The resulting somewhat perfunctory ending to *Of Time and the River* is just one example of the general formlessness that resulted from the cuts and hastily written new transitions that writer and editor worked on in preparing the manuscript for publication.

The day that *Of Time and the River* was published in the United States, March 8, 1935, Wolfe was in Paris, nervous and apprehensive about a book that he felt Perkins had published before it was ready. But the reviews were generally warm and appreciative, even celebratory, despite complaints about its episodic structure and what some saw as its lyrical verbosity. The book became Wolfe's only bestseller. In as much as the novel continues the story of Eugene Gant, it is a sequel to *Look Homeward, Angel*, tracing the death of W. O. Gant, Eugene's study of playwriting, his aspirations as an artist, and recording his adventures in Europe before he sails home and glimpses the woman who would become his lover. But Wolfe also tried to universalize Eugene's experience, as suggested by the titles of the book's eight parts (for example, the first two sections are titled "Orestes: Flight Before Fury," and "Young Faustus").

Wolfe was back in the United States by mid-summer, to find that he was now a literary celebrity. The second novel had confirmed his status as a major American writer. On his first trip west he gave a highly successful talk at the Colorado Writers' Conference, and visited Hollywood – where he turned down a lucrative offer to write for one of the studios.

Wolfe's next book for Scribner's, following a book of short stories that did not sell particularly well, was *The Story of a Novel* (1936), a polished version of his talk at the Colorado conference. In its candid account of the help that Perkins gave him in getting *Of Time and the River* into publishable condition, the book detailed some of Wolfe's problems in organizing his manuscripts. Inevitably it invited the kind of charges leveled at him later that year in an essay by Bernard De Voto in the *Saturday Review of Literature*: that Wolfe was a limited writer because of his need for editorial intervention from what De Voto termed "the Scribner's assembly line." De Voto's attack was just one contribution to the deteriorating relations with Perkins that finally led Wolfe to leave Scribner's. Among other problems were Perkins's lack of enthusiasm for most of Wolfe's plans for a third novel, including the editor's wariness about the Aline Bernstein material, disputes about the printer's bill for the many changes to *Of Time and the River* on the proof sheets, and Wolfe's plans to write about a publishing company that was obviously Scribner's and characters employed there who were clearly identifiable. The outcome of a long and difficult period of uncertainty for Wolfe, complicated by his continuing affection for Perkins, was that in 1937 Wolfe signed up with Harper and Brothers and began work with a relatively inexperienced editor there, Edward C. Aswell.

In the middle 1930s Wolfe aimed for a leaner, less prolix style. At the same time his writing showed a broader, keener social awareness than had been the case in the two novels, focused as they were on their central protagonist. One measure of this change is that in Wolfe's final visit to Europe in 1936 he was disturbed that Germany, a country he had always enjoyed visiting, had so changed under the oppressive policies of the Nazis. Back in the United States, Wolfe was still at work on a novel for his new publishers when in July 1938 he traveled west for what was supposed to be something of a break. But he subjected himself to an exhausting routine and in Seattle became seriously ill. Moved on medical advice to Johns Hopkins in Baltimore, his doctors discovered that an old tubercular lesion in his lung had spread to his brain. He died on September 15, a few days short of his thirty-eighth birthday.

Wolfe left behind so much unpublished material that his story does not taper to an end with his death. Before traveling west he had arranged to store his manuscripts at Harper's. This material included the current version of his new novel, various short novels in different states of completion, many different versions of scenes related and unrelated to his current project, and various outlines and notes. Out of this material Aswell extracted three novels: *The Web and the Rock* (1939), and when that sold quite well, *You Can't Go Home Again* (1940), and a third, shorter, novel, *The Hills Beyond* (1941).

For *The Web and the Rock* Wolfe had changed the name of his protagonist from Eugene Gant to George Webber. Webber is less youthfully naïve than Gant, but the narrative remains broadly autobiographical. The first chapters trace Webber's earlier life in Libya Hill, the new name for Asheville. The book then picks up where *Of Time and the River* left off, recounting the turbulent affair with Esther Jack, and Webber's attempts to find a publisher for his long novel, corresponding to the details of Wolfe's life from 1925 to 1928. *You Can't Go Home Again*, as arranged by Aswell, takes Webber through his literary fame, his break with Esther, his disillusionment with Germany, and in general his move toward a greater maturity and social awareness. *The Hills Beyond* includes a number of previously published stories as well as new material that draws on the Westalls, the family of Wolfe's mother.

The nature and degree of Aswell's editing received some comment in contemporary reviews, and in recent Wolfe scholarship has become a controversial issue. By any standard it was quite radical. Some transitional passages in the 1939 and 1940 novels, for example, were written by Aswell himself, a fact only acknowledged later in a note published with *The Hills Beyond*. Aswell consolidated versions of scenes written over different years, sometimes dropping characters for consistency; he omitted some of Wolfe's more lyrical passages, and in *You Can't Go Home Again* invented a character who was in none of Wolfe's material. Harper's published a misleading "Publisher's Note" at the front of *The Web and the Rock*, claiming that it was "the first of two novels which Thomas Wolfe completed and delivered to his publishers a few months before his untimely death." On the other hand, scholars note that Wolfe's manuscripts were far from being in publishable shape when Aswell inherited the task of dealing with them, and that if they were to be published in any form other than as sketches and notebooks they required a good deal of editorial shaping of some kind.

The textual history of Wolfe's posthumous novels has complicated assessments of the direction that Wolfe's work was taking in his last years, since the published versions combine material written over a number of years. For some critics Wolfe remained a writer limited to autobiography and to recording adolescent emotions, while others see a more mature, disciplined, and objective approach in his later work. And while Wolfe may have been unable to put his large projects into publishable shape without the editorial supervision of first Perkins and then Aswell, he clearly was able to master the short novel genre. The case has been made that Wolfe's own tendency to think of his narratives on a grand scale, combined with the particular demands of 1930s commercial publishing, may have denied him the chance to pursue the form that showed his powerful gifts at their best.

Bibliography

Wolfe's four major novels are available in paperback editions, and much of the manuscript and notebook material behind them has been edited for university presses. C. Hugh Holman edited *Short Novels* (New York, 1961).

David Herbert Donald, *Look Homeward: A Life of Thomas Wolfe* (Cambridge, 1987).
John Lane Idol, Jr., *A Thomas Wolfe Companion* (Westport, CT, 1987).
Joanne Marshall Mauldin, *Thomas Wolfe: When Do the Atrocities Begin?* (Knoxville, TN, 2007).
Ted Mitchell, ed., *Thomas Wolfe: A Documentary Volume* (Detroit, 2001).

John Steinbeck (1902–1968)

John Steinbeck won the Nobel Prize for Literature late in his career, only six years before his death. The general consensus was that he had received the award for his achievements some 25 years earlier. Nevertheless, Steinbeck had a long career in which he produced some distinguished work in a variety of genres, including travel writing, short stories, scientific accounts, and screenplays, as well as the novel. He continues to be widely read, although he has never been the subject of as much academic discussion as some of his equally famous contemporaries.

Steinbeck was born in Salinas, on the Central California coast, near Monterey Bay. This is the region in which most of his notable books are set. He entered Stanford University in 1919, where he published some stories in the campus literary magazine. He was asked to leave because of poor grades in 1920, and spent some time working with a dredging crew. Although he returned to Stanford, he left in 1925 without having graduated. He then worked at various jobs, including a stint as a reporter in New York City, and at the same time tried to interest magazines in his stories, but had little success. In 1927, while serving as caretaker of a log cabin on Lake Tahoe, Steinbeck wrote what would be his first published novel, *Cup of Gold* (1929). The narrative is based on the life of the famous seventeenth-century pirate Henry Morgan, and although Steinbeck soon confessed himself embarrassed by the book, it contains a number of themes and interests that appear in his later fiction. Two in particular are the search for happiness as a version of the Grail quest, and a fascination with the stories and characters of Malory's *Morte d'Arthur*.

Steinbeck's next novel, *The Pastures of Heaven*, appeared in October 1932. Although these stories, set in the Las Pasturas del Ceilo valley in California, are, for some commentators, rather heavy-handedly grafted onto the story of

Genesis, the book also contains examples of human interaction with the land that Steinbeck makes so powerful in his subsequent work. In 1933 Steinbeck began to have more success with placing his short stories, including some of the stories later to appear in *The Red Pony* (1937) and *The Long Valley* (1938). He published his third novel, *To a God Unknown*, in 1933, a book strongly influenced by the ideas of mythology being developed by Joseph Campbell, whom Steinbeck had met in Monterey.

All three publishers of Steinbeck's first books went out of business, but in December 1934 he became associated with Pascal Covici, who as publisher and later editor would work with him until Covici's death in 1964. The first book to appear under this new relationship was *Tortilla Flat* (1935), Steinbeck's first bestseller, and something of an introduction to the three major labor novels that followed. The stories of the ethnically mixed shantytown dwellers living just outside Monterey are loosely associated with the stories of King Arthur, but far more than in Steinbeck's earlier novels the stories are grounded in the world and the people that he knew. The novel has many humorous incidents, which made Steinbeck's attitude toward the characters difficult for early reviewers to fathom, and some, while admiring the novel, nevertheless judged it lightweight.

Steinbeck published the first of his labor novels, *In Dubious Battle*, in 1936. In this book he depicts the plight of the migrant workers drawn to California in the Depression, their exploitation by the large farming conglomerates, and the workers' attempts at organized action to improve their working conditions. Steinbeck does not present the confrontation between the companies and strikers in a one-sided way. Labor leader Mac, for example, has an amoral side, and is quick to treat any incident, even the death of his disciple Jim, as material for his larger causes. The events are accompanied by a commentary from "Doc Burton," who serves as a Greek-chorus-like neutral observer; he stands outside the violence of the group activities and is in consequence something of an isolated figure.

Of Mice and Men followed in 1937 and was much more successful commercially. Steinbeck wrote the book with the intention that it be converted into a play. In November the play duly opened on Broadway and ran for more than 200 performances. The story again concerns migrant farm workers, but this time focuses upon George and his doomed companion Lennie, whose inability to control his physical strength and emotional needs brings about his tragedy. The two try to mitigate the harsh demands of their itinerant work by sharing a dream of buying land and starting their own farm, but the book is clear from the first about the impossibility of those dreams ever being achieved. Sharing the dream is one way that George shows his affection and concern for his friend, whose disability always threatens to put him in danger, and whose eventual fate George can make more humane, but cannot prevent.

Steinbeck visited a number of the California migrant labor camps, and was assisted by Tom Collins, the administrator of the Arvin Sanitary Camp that would provide the model for the Weedpatch Camp in *The Grapes of Wrath*. He met Collins in 1936 while researching a series of newspaper articles on migrant labor for the *San Francisco News*. The essays appeared as "The Harvest Gypsies" in 1936, and were reprinted as a pamphlet titled "Their Blood Is Strong" in 1938. *The Grapes of Wrath*, co-dedicated to Collins, along with Steinbeck's first wife, was published in 1939 by Viking, since Pascal Covici's own publishing firm had gone bankrupt at the end of 1937. At Viking Covici continued his editing relationship with Steinbeck, while his new employer went on to enjoy the huge commercial success of the novel when it appeared in April 1939. Half a million copies were sold within a year of publication. In this novel the kind of objective observations provided by Doc Burton in *In Dubious Battle* are now supplied by periodic summaries of the depressed labor and economic conditions, summaries that contextualize the central narrative of the Joad family's determined migration from Oklahoma to California. The juxtaposition produces a complex picture of the novel's action, driven by a combination of individual will, the group dynamics and mutual support that Steinbeck had explored in his previous two novels, and the presence of larger forces outside the control of individuals and even of groups. The courage and generosity of individuals such as Jim Rawley, administrator of the Weedpatch Camp, the ex-preacher Jim Casey, and Rose of Sharon are celebrated in the book, without any sentimental claims that their actions can do more than make the suffering somewhat more tolerable, and sometimes even survivable. The novel established Steinbeck as a major figure in American writing. In 1939 he was elected to the National Institute of Arts and Letters, and in 1940 *The Grapes of Wrath* won the Pulitzer Prize for Fiction.

Steinbeck's important friendship with marine biologist Edward Ricketts began when the two met in 1930, and continued until Ricketts's death in 1948. Ricketts contributed to Steinbeck's ideas of group unity, and to his thinking about will power and biological motivation. A version of Ricketts appears in a number of Steinbeck's fictions, for example Doc Burton in *In Dubious Battle*, and Slim in *Of Mice and Men*. Ricketts's Pacific Biological Laboratories became a place where Steinbeck pursued his own interest in science, and its location in the district of sardine canneries known as Cannery Row gave him the locale and title for his ninth novel in 1945. Steinbeck's major record of this friendship is *Sea of Cortez* (1941), a jointly authored account of an expedition that Steinbeck and Ricketts undertook in the Gulf of

California in the spring of the previous year. The book sold little in comparison to Steinbeck's novels, but is regarded by many scholars as an important source for Steinbeck's views on the human condition.

In the early 1940s Steinbeck's first marriage ended in divorce. He began to work more with film scripts, including a rather unhappy period collaborating with Alfred Hitchcock on *Lifeboat* (1944). In 1943, the year he remarried, he reported on the war in Europe and North Africa for the *New York Herald Tribune*. When *Cannery Row* appeared in 1945, early reviewers noted the humor of the derelicts and prostitutes inhabiting the rundown waterfront, but caught little of the satire on the world of commerce and competitiveness behind the sympathetic treatment of Cannery Row's residents. Another character based upon Ed Ricketts plays an important role in the novel, Doc, the owner and operator of the Western Biological Laboratory.

Steinbeck continued to publish prolifically, as well as continuing his association with Hollywood (between 1944 and 1952 he received three Academy Award nominations). The short novel *The Pearl* (1947) was his seventeenth book. This parable of a young man discovering a valuable pearl only to find it causing him so much trouble and grief that he throws it back into the sea has been interpreted a number of ways, most often as a rejection of materialism. Steinbeck had first heard the story on his travels with Ricketts. For some critics the novel marks the beginning of a decline in Steinbeck's writings, although it has received praise from others and continues to be one of his most widely read works.

In 1948, the year that Steinbeck was elected to membership in the American Academy of Arts and Letters, he was divorced from his second wife. He met his third wife, Elaine, the following year through one of his Hollywood friends, Ann Sothern. For the next few years Steinbeck focused much of his time on writing *East of Eden*, which was eventually published in 1952. Steinbeck's books continued to sell well through the 1950s and 1960s, but *East of Eden* is for some critics his last significant work. The novel is based in part on the history of Steinbeck's maternal ancestors, and follows the history of this family, the Hamiltons, as well as the fictional Trasks, from the middle of the nineteenth century up to World War II. The personal nature of the book is reinforced by Steinbeck himself serving as narrator. The notable film based on the novel, directed by Elia Kazan and starring James Dean, is probably as well known as the book.

Sweet Thursday (1954), *The Short Reign of Pippin IV: A Fabrication* (1957), and *The Winter of Our Discontent* (1961) were Steinbeck's final three novels. All three illustrate the more conservative politics that Steinbeck held in his later years, and his greater concern with individual morality rather than with the broader social issues that marked his work of the 1930s. All three books were greeted by reviewers with more respect than enthusiasm upon publication, but have more recently come in for scholarly discussion.

Sweet Thursday is a lighthearted sequel to *Cannery Row*. Some of the characters from the 1945 book have died, and the waterfront has fallen on even harder times. Much of the action again centers upon the now aging and lonely Doc. Steinbeck wrote the novel in conjunction with plans for a musical adaptation, *Pipe Dream*, with music and lyrics by Rodgers and Hammerstein. *Pipe Dream* opened on Broadway in November 1955 and despite lukewarm reviews managed a run of 246 performances. *The Short Reign of Pippin IV: A Fabrication* is a fantasy set in the near future about the restoration of the monarchy in France. The general assessment is that the satire does not support the serious concerns that Steinbeck tries to impose on the narrative. Steinbeck's final novel, *The Winter of Our Discontent*, his only novel set in an eastern seacoast town, appeared the year before the author was awarded the Nobel Prize. The novel's selection as a Book of the Month Club choice attests to Steinbeck's continuing popularity with readers.

Although Steinbeck did not publish another novel after winning the Nobel Prize in 1962, he continued to produce newspaper and magazine articles and to publish his travel writing. In the winter of 1966 he covered the Vietnam War as a correspondent for *Newsday*. He also worked extensively on a modern translation of Malory's *Morte d'Arthur*, a project that was published posthumously in 1976 as *The Acts of King Arthur and His Noble Knights*. Two other significant posthumous publications were *The Journal of a Novel* (1969), an account through letters of the daily writing of *East of Eden*, and in 1989 *John Steinbeck's Working Days: The Journal of The Grapes of Wrath, 1938–1941*.

Bibliography

The Library of America has published Steinbeck's major novels and stories in four volumes, *Novels and Stories, 1932–1937* (1994), *The Grapes of Wrath and Other Writings* (1996), *Novels 1942–1952* (2002), and *Travels with Charley and Later Novels, 1947–1962* (2007).

Jackson J. Benson, *The True Adventures of John Steinbeck, Writer* (New York, 1984).
John Ditsky, *John Steinbeck and the Critics* (Rochester, NY, 2000).
Brian Railsback and Michael J. Meyer, *A John Steinbeck Encyclopedia* (Westport, CT, 2006).
Susan Shillinglaw and Kevin Hearle, *Beyond Boundaries: Rereading John Steinbeck* (Tuscaloosa, 2002).

Nathanael West (1903–1940)

Nathanael West published just four novels in his lifetime, and all four were commercially unsuccessful. But he has been recognized as an important influence on a number of post-war writers, including Flannery O'Connor, Joseph Heller, and Thomas Pynchon. The only steady income West managed from writing was his work as a screenwriter in Hollywood, and while his screenplays were generally for minor films and second-rung studios, the experience gave him the background for one of the most important novels published about Hollywood, and the sometimes desperate characters that live on its margins.

West was born Nathan Weinstein, in New York City. His parents had emigrated from Russia. Early on West was ambivalent about his Jewish heritage, eventually changing his name legally to Nathanael West on August 16, 1926. His fiction is consistently anti-Jewish, and anti-Catholic too. Some commentators argue that the parade of characters in his fiction who are lonely, tormented, and desperate are a result of his sense of being treated as an outcast because of his Jewish background.

West was a poor student in high school. He managed to enroll into Tufts College, now Tufts University, in 1921 on a forged transcript, but was asked to leave after two months because of failing to attend classes. He then transferred to Brown University on the strength of the transcript of a different Nathan Weinstein. At Brown he edited and contributed to the college literary magazine and became interested in such modernist writers as Pound, Eliot, Stevens, and Joyce. Upon graduation in 1924 West resisted pressures to join his father's construction business, instead persuading his family to support him in Paris, where he lived for three months in the winter of 1926. Back in

New York, his family's fortune eroding, he began work as night manager at a second-rate hotel in Manhattan.

Between 1927 and 1929 West tried selling short fiction but with little success. However, during this time he wrote his first novel, *The Dream Life of Balso Snell* (1931), and eventually found a publisher in Contact Editions. Martin Kamin and David Moss had purchased the press from Robert McAlmon, who had run it in France. One of McAlmon's friends who had previously published with the press, William Carlos Williams, recommended the manuscript to the new owners and later West and Williams revived for a few issues the magazine *Contact* that McAlmon and Williams had edited in the early 1920s. Like all Contact Editions (this would turn out to be the last publication of the series) the book had a small print run, just 500 copies, and was largely ignored by reviewers. Many copies remained unsold for years.

The Dream Life of Balso Snell is something of a mock-epic voyage, in this case into the alimentary canal of the wooden Trojan Horse. The narrative is a series of sketches describing Balso Snell's journey, during which he encounters various guides, discovers letters, and hears stories, and stories within stories. The novel is rich in the kind of comic virtuosity that West would make more incisive in his later novels. The narrative is frequently scatological, appropriately perhaps for a journey that begins at the horse's anus, and for some readers the book suggests that the whole of Western tradition is similar to a pile of excrement. A list of the characters Balso meets on his journey gives some indication of the narrative's range of targets and its always-surprising turns. He first meets a Jewish guide, whom Balso has trouble escaping; then Maloney the Areopagite, who tells the story of a flea who lives and dies on the flesh of Christ; then John Gilson, an eighth-grade schoolboy whose pastiches of Dostoevsky are intended to woo his English teacher; and finally the teacher herself, Miss McGeeney, whom, after hearing several stories from her, Balso seduces. The narrative blurs the distinctions between dreams, fantasy, and fiction, while at times almost returning to conventional storytelling. In this and all of West's novels the role of dreams, their place in contemporary culture, and the manipulation of them by the media are central themes.

While trying to place *The Dream Life of Balso Snell* with a publisher, West began writing *Miss Lonelyhearts*, having conceived of the idea when he met a columnist who wrote a lonely hearts column for the *Brooklyn Eagle*. West finished the book in late 1932, and it was published by Horace Liveright in 1933.

For many readers *Miss Lonelyhearts* is West's finest novel. In an essay, "Some Notes on Miss L.," that West published in May 1933 he called the book "a novel in the form of a comic strip." The various short chapters jump from scene to scene as the desperate central character searches for a way to live in the world revealed to him by the suffering of the letter writers, and the cynicism of his boss, Shrike. In the same essay West declares that one model for Miss Lonelyheart's experience is William James's *Varieties of Religious Experience*, and while some critics suggest that West's comment is tongue-in-cheek, there are some suggestive parallels. Miss Lonelyhearts, confronted with the suffering revealed by a position that he had initially treated as a joke, and taunted by Shrike, sinks into lethargy, revives with a conversion experience, and thinks that he can perform miracles. Appropriately for this novel's chaotic world, chance determines his fate as soon as he steps outside his room, in a scene suggesting that violence, religion, and sexuality are forces that will always undo any kind of order that the individual might project, or any fantasy that the media might try to sell.

The novel received excellent reviews but they did not translate into sales, for the Liveright company declared bankruptcy with most copies of the book still at the printer's, and unfortunately for West the printer held on to them in lieu of payment. By the time Harcourt, Brace took over the book two months later the attention brought by the reviews had passed. West did manage to sell the rights for a movie version, however, released as *Advice to the Lovelorn* at the end of 1933 (bearing little resemblance to the novel), and as a result of the attention was offered and accepted a writing position with Columbia Pictures.

West had little success with screenwriting, and before the end of the year had returned east where he began work on *A Cool Million*. The novel, published in 1934, is a satire on Horatio Alger success stories. Confidence in the myth of success drives hero Lemuel Pitkin off on a journey to New York to save his family home. He is cheated and wrongly arrested before he gets there, and this is just the first of a series of misadventures that gradually take away parts of Pitkin's body. He saves a bank president's daughter from death or serious injury, but instead of a rich reward receives abuse. Corrupt, inhuman, and misinformed officials, along with a revengeful brothel owner, and two vaudevillians who use him as a comic stooge, gradually deprive him of his teeth, an eye, his thumb, his scalp, and part of his leg. He forfeits his life in confused service to banker and ex-President Whipple's fascist National Revolutionary Party. And Pitkin continues to be used by others after death; his martyrdom is celebrated in song by the triumphant Party much as the Nazis celebrated Horst Wessel. Reviews were mixed and generally argued that the novel did not match *Miss Lonelyhearts*. The book was remaindered the following year, and West was still unable to support himself by his writing. He was able to sell the novel to Hollywood, but such a ruthless satire had little chance of being filmed, and no production resulted.

West was very disheartened by his lack of success. One admirer, F. Scott Fitzgerald, mentioned West in his 1934 Preface to a reissue of *The Great Gatsby*, noting that West was a writer "being harmed ... for lack of a public." In the spring of 1935 West returned to Hollywood, the idea for *The Day of the Locust* already in his mind. With little money and no job, he lived on the Hollywood margins alongside the kinds of characters who would people his novel. Eventually he found work with Republic Productions, one of Hollywood's minor studios, where a number of his screenplays were turned into films. He was successful enough that by 1938 he was working at the more important RKO. But a further disappointment in that year was when an anti-war play he had co-authored failed on Broadway after only two performances.

West found a major New York publisher, Random House, for *The Day of the Locust*, which was published in May 1939. The role of the church and the media in offering fantasies that attract and then frustrate is even more central here than in *Miss Lonelyhearts*. California, and particularly Hollywood, attracts the dispossessed and disappointed from elsewhere in the nation, but almost everything in the culture is a copy of something else. The houses are a mixture of clashing ethnic and historical styles; the "Old West" is represented by a Trading Post, outside of which stands an Indian with a sandwich board; the cowboys who gravitate toward it at one point camp in a garage; and the film studios reduce important episodes in history to costume drama and scenic flats. Violence, whether subjugated into a cockfight, or released in the hysteria of the mob scene at the film premiere, is ever-present. The novel's central characters respond variously to this chaotic world. The disappointed Homer Simpson tries to return to the Midwest but his frustration finally finds violent expression and he disappears into the hostile and uncontrollable crowd. Faye Greener, whose relationship with her actor/salesman father does not distinguish between a long familiar script and genuine attempts at communication, survives through movie fantasies and a crude sexual power. And scenic designer Todd Hackett, who thinks that he can capture the hysteria of the culture in his painting "The Burning of Los Angeles," has to be rescued from a scene in which painting and subject combine to almost consume him. Despite some positive reviews, the book sold only half of its 3000 print run.

West married Eileen McKenney in April 1940. Working with other writers he began to have some success selling individual screenplays to studios, and he also had a contract with Random House for another novel. But on December 22, the day after his friend Scott Fitzgerald's death by heart attack, and by some accounts on his way back for the funeral, West ran a stop sign at an intersection in El Centro, California, collided with another car, and both he and his wife were killed.

Bibliography

West's four novels, some of his other writings, and a selection of his letters have been published in a single volume by the Library of America, *Novels and Other Writings* (1997).

Robert Emmet Long, *Nathanael West* (New York, 1985).

Jay Martin, *Nathanael West: The Art of His Life* (New York, 1970).

Jonathan Veitch, *American Superrealism: Nathanael West and the Politics of Representation in the 1930s* (Madison, WI, 1997).

Kingsley Widmer, *Nathanael West* (Boston, 1982).

Richard Wright (1908–1960)

Richard Wright's career can be usefully divided into two parts. In the years up to 1946 he lived and wrote in the United States, concerned in his fiction with the racial injustice accorded America's black population both in the South and in such major urban centers as Chicago. After visiting France in 1946 Wright moved there the following year, and remained resident in France until his death. In France he became interested in the existentialist ideas of Jean Paul Sartre and Simone de Beauvoir, and also, in the 1950s, in the future of the former European colonies in Africa just receiving independence. What unites these various aspects of Wright's career is the theme of alienation, whether through racial oppression, or more generally the modern condition; and also the exposure of what he regarded as the archaic and superstitious rituals holding the individual back from achieving freedom.

Wright was born into rural surroundings in Roxie, on a farm just over 20 miles east of Natchez, Tennessee. When he was three the family moved to Memphis in what would be the first of a series of moves and disruptions that seriously disrupted Wright's formal education. His barely literate father, Nathan Wright, abandoned the family when Richard was seven, and the boy lived at various times with aunts and uncles in Mississippi and Arkansas, and at one point in an orphanage. His intermittent schooling finished by 1925, when he returned to Memphis for two years, working as a messenger, and reading voraciously. His discovery of the writings of social and literary critic H. L. Mencken provided him with a reading list of European and American literature. As Wright describes in his autobiography, *Black Boy*, because of his color he had to use subterfuge to obtain the books he wanted to read from the public library.

Wright continued his self-directed reading when he moved to Chicago in 1927, where he worked as a postal clerk before being laid off. He began attending meetings of a communist literary organization, and later formally joined the Communist Party. He went on to publish a number of radical poems in left-wing journals, and by 1935 had completed a first novel, "Cesspool" (published posthumously as *Lawd Today* in 1963), as well as a number of short stories. In 1936 he had a story published in the prominent anthology *The New Caravan*, the first time that Wright was paid for his writing. By the time Wright moved to New York in 1937 he was a nationally known figure in left-wing circles, although he was beginning to have the differences with the Communist Party over its race policies that would lead to his withdrawing from party activities in the early 1940s and publicly breaking with it in 1944 when he published his essay "I Tried to Be a Communist."

In New York Wright worked as Harlem editor of the communist paper *Daily Worker*, and wrote the short stories that would form his first book publication, *Uncle Tom's Children* (1938). One of these stories, "Fire and Cloud," had won a *Story* magazine prize, and this led to Harper's offering to publish all four of the stories that Wright had submitted to the competition. The protagonists of the stories in this first book, like those of his books to come, fight for survival and freedom in a world of violence and prejudice. Sales were relatively modest, but the book gained significant attention. An essay and an additional story were added when the book was reprinted in 1940.

When Wright began writing *Native Son* (1940) he was determined to produce a book which did not invite what he felt had been the sentimental response of too many readers to the central figures in *Uncle Tom's Children*. Bigger Thomas is a confused, violent, selfish, and angry young man. The first murder that he commits is ambiguously presented; it is accidental, but equally a product of the misunderstandings and confusion between black and white – between well-intentioned white liberals, and the fear, anger, and cunning produced in Bigger by his sense of being excluded from so many possibilities because of his color. The second murder is ruthless and premeditated. Bigger rejects the spiritual comforts of religion, and also the arguments that his communist lawyer Boris Max makes to the court, that Bigger is a victim of racist, capitalist oppression. Bigger exults instead in his freedom to have chosen an act that was not determined for him by whites.

The book is universally recognized as a pioneer work in black American writing for its frank, uncompromising indictment of the effects of racial oppression, and for preparing the way for such writers as Ralph Ellison and James Baldwin. But for some critics the book has some crucial flaws. The powerful narrative thrust of the book's first two parts comes to a halt with Bigger's trial, where the arguments within the court scenes function as a commentary upon the earlier narrative – but this commentary is excessive for some critics. There is also, for some readers, a possible contradiction in Wright's view of Bigger. Wright wants, the argument runs, to have Bigger be a victim of determinist racial forces, but at the same time the novel celebrates Bigger's discovery of the freedom to choose. Put another way, the book is grounded in the naturalism that Wright discovered in his Mencken-directed reading of Dreiser and Crane, but points toward the ideas of Sartre and Simone de Beauvoir that would interest him in the second part of his career.

Native Son's influence and success was assisted by its being a Book of the Month Club selection, the first time its panel had selected a book by a black author. However the Club's editors insisted upon some revisions, the toning down of sexual scenes in particular, and Wright agreed. The reviews of the novel were almost all full of praise, and after three weeks the book had sold almost a quarter of a million copies. The sales made Wright the first best-selling black writer in American literary history.

Wright remained active writing reviews and working on other literary projects. He collaborated on a well-received Works Projects Administration book on black history, *12 Million Black Voices* (1941), and also worked on two new novels. Neither novel was at this time published, although excerpts of one, "The Man Who Lived Underground," were published in 1942, and the novel would appear in full in 1961.

Wright eventually turned to autobiography for his next book, *Black Boy* (1945). This narrative of his childhood and youth in the South, up to his departure for Chicago, was only the first part of the book that Wright originally intended. An excerpt of the second part, concerning his life in Chicago, was published in Wright's lifetime, but it was not published in full until 1977, as *American Hunger*. Once again pressure had come from the Book of the Month Club, who were interested in distributing just the first part. The result, as one of Wright's biographers argues, is that while *Black Boy* is usually read as a success story, as the writer having overcome the handicaps of his background, Wright's original plan had intended the opposite. The Chicago and Communist Party episodes in the planned second part were to provide further evidence of the oppressive, exploitative treat-ment of America's black population. With the Club's help the book was an even larger commercial and critical success for Wright, selling twice as many copies as *Native Son*.

A successful second book behind him, Wright used his name and influence to help such younger black writers as James Baldwin, Chester Himes, and Gwendolyn Brooks. In May 1946 Wright and his family – he had remarried in

1941 after a short-lived first marriage in 1939 – left the United States to visit France. Wright was encouraged to make the trip by Gertrude Stein, and was treated as an official guest of the French government. In January the following year the family returned to New York, but Wright now had experience of a culture where he did not always have to be wary of walking with his white wife in public, and where he did not have to tolerate racial insults – insults all the more frequent because of his fame. In July 1947 the family returned to France, which would be Wright's home base until his death.

The disruption of the move as well as work on various other projects kept Wright from completing his next novel. These projects included filming *Native Son* in Argentina, improving his French and his understanding of existentialism, and completing various essays and reviews. Another distraction was his argument with James Baldwin, who claimed in his 1949 essay "Everybody's Protest Novel" that Wright's *Native Son* was as limited a narrative as *Uncle Tom's Cabin* in its views of race.

When *The Outsider* was published in 1953 reviews were mixed, and stronger in Europe than in the United States. The symbolically named Cross Damon takes advantage of an accident in which he is thought to have died to escape from his commitments both to his family and to his pregnant mistress. He takes on a new identity, but his attempts to retain it lead him into murder and deceit, and finally toward his own violent death. The novel mixes detective story and philosophy in a way that is successful for some readers, but with a plot too contrived and melodramatic for some others.

Savage Holiday (1954) is more Freudian in its treatment of character and motive. All of the major characters are white. Wright could only find a paperback publisher for the novel in the United States, where it was little reviewed, but again it was generally well received in Europe. While working on this novel Wright visited the Gold Coast, the British colony in Africa later renamed Ghana. With the account that came out of that trip, *Black Power: A Record of Reactions in a Land of Pathos* (1954), Wright began his writing on the emerging Third World colonies. In *Black Power* he suggests that tribal heritage and rituals handicap the newly emerging nations in their vital need to learn from Western technology. This view is repeated in a book that focuses upon Asia, *The Color Curtain: A Report on the Bandung Conference* (France 1955, United States 1956). In *Pagan Spain: A Report of a Journey into the Past* (1957), Wright is particularly critical of the hold of religion upon Spain. *White Man, Listen!* (1957) is a collection of lectures that Wright gave in various countries across Europe; it includes many of his ideas on Christianity, on Black Literature in the United States, on Africa, and on the future of the West.

The last novel that Wright published in his lifetime, *The Long Dream* (1958), returns to his early Mississippi background. The narrative centers upon the exploitation of his fellow blacks by black mortician and brothel owner Tyree Tucker, and the corruption of white police chief Gerald Cantley. When threatened with exposure Cantley arranges to have Tucker murdered. The novel ends with Fishbelly, Tucker's son, boarding a plane for Paris having served his prison time on a false charge instigated by Cantley. The novel was intended to be the first in a trilogy, and in "Island of Hallucinations" Wright had written a substantial further portion before his death. But only part of this planned continuation, tracing Fishbelly's life in France, was published ("Five Episodes" in *Soon, One Morning*, edited by Herbert Hill [1963]). Wright became ill in 1960 and died of a heart attack while in a medical center for diagnostic tests. He had been working on *Eight Men*, a volume of stories, some of them previously published. The book appeared posthumously in 1961, and includes two stories often discussed, "The Man Who Lived Underground" and "The Man Who Was Almost a Man." Wright was also working on a collection of haiku poems; these appeared in 1998 as *Haiku: This Other World*, edited by Yoshinobu Hakatuni and Robert L. Tener. On the centenary of Wright's birth, 2008, Harper's published an unfinished novel that he had also been working on in the last months of his life, *A Father's Law*, with an introduction by his daughter, Julia Wright.

A number of the reviews of *The Long Dream* argued that Wright had been away too long from the South that was the setting of the novel; that many changes had occurred which the novel failed to recognize. The protest novel was, in addition, out of fashion in the late 1950s, and so assessments of the novel tended to become assessments of Wright's career, with the conclusion that he was no longer the important figure that he had been in the 1940s. The discussions of *Eight Men*, despite the recognition accorded "The Man Who Lived Underground" in particular, generally repeated these assessments in reviews that had become obituaries. There was no argument, however, about Wright's contribution to black American writing. He had shown that a black writer could become a major American novelist with a worldwide reputation, and need not compromise with the expectations of white readers. This achievement, rather than any purely literary influence, was seen as his main legacy.

However, the Black protest movements of the 1960s renewed interest in Wright's work, and brought the posthumous publication or republication of much of his fiction. He has since regularly been the subject of scholarly books and articles. There have been calls for a reassessment of the books written in exile, and for a more broadly conceived discussion of Wright's attempt in his later work to combine philosophical inquiry with the resources of fiction.

Bibliography

Since the 1990s Harper's have printed unexpurgated versions of *Native Son* and *Black Boy*. The two Library of America volumes of Wright's work (1991) also print the unexpurgated texts, and include *Lawd Today!* and *American Hunger*.

Yoshinobu Hakutani, *Richard Wright and Racial Discourse* (Columbia, MO, 1996).
Keneth Kinnamon, *Richard Wright: An Annotated Bibliography of Criticism and Commentary, 1983–2003* (Jefferson, NC, 2006).
Hazel Rowley, *Richard Wright: The Life and Times* (New York, 2001).
Virginia Whatley Smith, ed., *Richard Wright's Travel Writings* (Jackson, MS, 2001).

William S. Burroughs (1914–1997)

William Seward Burroughs was the oldest of the major figures associated with the Beat Generation in the 1950s, and when he died aged 83 he was the longest lived. He published his first book at the age of 39, and by one biographer's account he eventually published 20 novels, as well as hundreds of short pieces and essays. The radical structure of his novels, along with their frank subject matter and language, contributed to making him a major icon to the counterculture movements of three decades.

Burroughs was born in St. Louis, Missouri. His paternal grandfather was the inventor of the first successfully marketed adding machine, and the founder of the Burroughs Adding Machine Company, later the Burroughs Corporation. Burroughs's father sold his share in the company in 1929, three months before the stock market crash. Burroughs was certainly helped by the checks that arrived regularly thanks to his grandfather's patent, but he was not the rich legatee that he complained Jack Kerouac's novels made him out to be. Burroughs graduated from Harvard in 1936 having majored in English, and thinking little of the university or of his education there. In 1938 while studying medicine in Vienna he married the Jewish Ilse Klapper to help her escape from Germany, although the two always lived apart.

Burroughs returned to Harvard for graduate work in anthropology, and began writing stories in collaboration with a St. Louis friend, Kells Elvins, who was studying psychology. They tried publishing their 1938 collaboration, a satire on the sinking of the *Titanic* titled "Twilight's Last Gleamings," but received only rejections. The story introduces the sinister Dr. Benway, a recurring character in Burroughs's later fiction. Burroughs recalls in an essay collected in *The Adding Machine* (1986) that he then lost interest in writing until he met Allen Ginsberg and Jack Kerouac in the mid-1940s, when he took it up once more. One result was a collaboration with Jack Kerouac, unpublished until 2008, titled "And the Hippos Were Boiled in Their Tanks." He lost interest again until 1949, when he began to set down the record of his heroin addiction. "Twilight's Last Gleamings" would appear with revisions as part of Burroughs's 1964 novel *Nova Express*.

In 1946 Burroughs settled in Texas with Joan Vollmer, his common-law wife, and her infant daughter. In 1948 they moved to Algiers, across the river from New Orleans, following the birth of their son. One section of Jack Kerouac's *On the Road* describes his visit to the Burroughs family while they lived in Algiers. The family fled to Mexico in 1949 when Burroughs was charged with possession of illegal drugs and firearms. But this period of Burroughs's life ended when, on September 6, 1951, he accidentally killed Joan in the course of a "William Tell" game, trying to shoot a glass balanced on the top of her head. The children went to their grandparents, and Burroughs himself left Mexico, traveled in Central and South America, and eventually, in 1953, settled in Tangier, Morocco, where the drugs he needed for his addiction could be had without too many complications.

Burroughs had begun writing *Junkie* while in Mexico, its original title being "Confessions of an Unredeemed Drug Addict." He sent chapters to Ginsberg, who through personal connections was able to get an expurgated version of the book published in 1953 by paperback publisher Ace Books. Burroughs's novel was bound with *Narcotic Agent* by Maurice Helbrant as a double-decker paperback. Largely autobiographical, it tells the story of William Lee (the name under which Burroughs published the novel) and his addiction to morphine, his various attempted cures, and his journeys further and further south to evade the law. The narrative is interspersed with factual information about drugs, and the book ends with Lee searching for new drugs to feed his addiction. The 1953 publication was little noticed by reviewers. In 1977 Penguin published the complete original text, now titled *Junky*, with an introduction by Ginsberg.

In Tangier Burroughs set about writing *Naked Lunch*, helped in his typing and arrangement of the manuscript by Kerouac and Ginsberg when they visited, and by Brion Gysin, who would became an important collaborator on some later projects. The book was published in Paris in 1959 as *The Naked Lunch* and is the work for which Burroughs is best known, introducing the radical disjunctions of character, mood, and geography which characterize his later books. The novel ranges between four regions: South America, the United States, Interzone/Tangier, and Freeland; the Interzone has four parties, Liquefactionists, Conferents/Senders, Divisionists, and Factualists.

But as many have observed, the book is more a display of the mind that created its narrative than a coherent story. Its episodes, termed "skits" and "routines" by Burroughs, often concern attempts by those in power to manipulate and control others. The sudden narrative shifts are part of the aim to resist systems of control, while the shock tactics are similarly part of a determination to break conventional habits of thought in language, narrative form, and fiction. In as much as there is a frame story, William Lee, the name imported from *Junky*, flees from the US police into Mexico. The series of events that follow – among them violent orgies, and scenes centered around drugs, hangings, abortion, and sickness – return to Lee and the police at the end, although without any narrative closure. The novel was published by Grove Press in 1962, and became the last major literary work in the United States to be subjected to a censorship trial. The book was declared not obscene by the Massachusetts Supreme Court in 1966 after testimony to its merits from writers including Ginsberg and Norman Mailer. Grove Press put out a "restored text" in 2001, edited by James Grauerholz and Barry Miles, containing some previously unpublished drafts and some different versions of scenes.

Naked Lunch raised a literary as well as legal controversy upon its publication, and the publicity ensured that it was widely reviewed. Burroughs meanwhile began writing and organizing material for his *Nova* trilogy: *The Soft Machine*, *The Ticket that Exploded*, and *Nova Express*. The first two were initially published in Paris, and all three were available in the United States by 1967. For this trilogy Burroughs introduced his "cut-up" methods, an idea that came from Gysin's work on newspaper collages. For Burroughs such a technique – the casual, non-narrative juxtaposition of his own and other writings within the trilogy – opened up new possible associations and a broader perspective. The novels once published did not remain fixed texts; Burroughs rearranged them as the books appeared at different times, in different countries, with different publishers. The novels were reviewed in far fewer mainstream publications than had been the case with *Naked Lunch*.

Some of the characters in the trilogy return from *Naked Lunch* and others are new, including the members of the Nova Mob and the Nova Police. In *The Soft Machine* and *The Ticket that Exploded* agent Lee tries to subvert the methods of the Nova Mob, the intergalactic criminals who are attempting to destroy the planet Earth. *The Ticket that Exploded* incorporates an interest that Burroughs developed when he was living at one point in London, of looking at the relationships between the "cut-up" technique and spliced tape and photomontage constructions. Collaboration remained an important feature of Burroughs's writing. The book's "Acknowledgment" notes that the sections *in a strange bed* and *the black fruit* are collaborations with Michael Portman and Ian Sommerville, while the book's "film experiments" are suggested by Anthony Balch. The novel originally ended with a page of calligraphy by Brion Gysin, although in a revised edition Burroughs added a concluding essay, "the invisible generation," that suggests the reader try various experiments with tape recorders as part of "breaking obsessional association tracks." For Burroughs "a tape recorder is an externalized section of the human nervous system" and he argues that by recording the voices of those trying to control thought and life patterns, and then cutting and cutting the tape, their power can be diminished and eventually vanish "into air into thin air." The verbal equivalents of such techniques complicate the account in *Nova Express* of the continuing conflict between the Nova Mob and the Nova Police.

The Wild Boys: A Book of the Dead (1971) continues the theme of global warfare, with the gang of the title trying to battle free from control systems in a narrative that continues to reflect Burroughs's interest in film techniques. The novel introduces the character of Audrey Carsons, who appears in a number of Burroughs's subsequent novels, and who in the 1973 *Port of Saints* joins the Wild Boys.

The 1970s saw the first major academic discussions of Burroughs's work and attempts to evaluate its place in contemporary American literature. Burroughs's role as culture hero for a younger generation had begun in the 1960s; he appears on the cover of the Beatles' *Sergeant Pepper's Lonelyhearts Club Band*, for example, and numerous bands and songs take their names from his work.

In the 1960s Burroughs lived at various times in London, Paris, and Tangier, but in the mid-1970s he moved to the United States, where he began to be in demand as a reader of his work. The 1980s saw Burroughs inducted into the American Academy and Institute of Arts and Letters; a film biography, *Burroughs: The Movie*; and an important book-length study of his work by Jennie Skerl. He published *Cities of the Red Night* in 1981, a book more linear than the earlier cut-up novels, and a novel that has been seen as a precursor to cyberpunk science fiction. *Cities of the Red Night* began a trilogy that continued with *The Place of Dead Roads* (1984) and *The Western Lands* (1987).

Burroughs's 1995 collection, *My Education: A Book of Dreams* (1995), was his last book. When he died aged 83 he had spent the last 16 years of his life based in Lawrence, Kansas, but by no means isolated from artistic events. Still pushing boundaries in his writing, he lived to see himself acknowledged as one of the most influential American fiction writers of the second half of the century.

Bibliography

Burroughs's major novels are available from Grove Press in paperback form.

Sylvere Lotringer, ed., *Burroughs Live: The Collected Interviews of William S. Burroughs* (Los Angeles, 2001).

Barry Miles, *William S. Burroughs, El Hombre Invisible: A Portrait* (New York, 1993).

Davis Schneiderman and Philip Walsh, *Retaking the Universe: William S. Burroughs in the Age of Globalization* (London, 2004).

Jennie Skerl, *William S. Burroughs* (Boston, 1985).

Saul Bellow (1915–2005)

Saul Bellow was born Solomon Bellow in Lachine, Quebec. His parents, of Orthodox Jewish background, had recently emigrated from Russia. A typical Bellow novel is one centered upon ideas rather than plot. His protagonists are often fumbling and uncertain, sometimes comically so. But they have enough leisure and concern to worry about the conditions and direction of modern life. Jewish life and identity is often an important part of the novels, but Bellow strongly resisted being categorized as a Jewish writer.

When he was awarded the Nobel Prize in Literature in 1976, Bellow argued that "the value of literature lies" in the "intermittent 'true impressions'" that can take us beyond "the world of objects, of actions, of appearances." Bellow's novels record that world of objects, actions, and appearances carefully and lyrically, but also the other side of experience, the "true impressions," which for Bellow's characters offer some promise of purpose, some promise of possible redemption. Poet Von Humboldt Fleischer in *Humboldt's Gift* reminds writer Charles Citrine in a farewell letter to remember that "we are not natural beings but supernatural beings."

Bellow's family moved to Chicago when he was nine, a city that would later be associated with many of his novels. He attended the University of Chicago before transferring to Northwestern University, and graduated in 1937 having majored in sociology and anthropology. He spent a few months on graduate work in anthropology, but at the end of 1937 he married (the first of what would be five marriages) and left the program, determined to be a writer, finding employment with the Federal Writers Project. He had his first publishing success when two of his stories appeared in the *Partisan Review* in the early 1940s.

Bellow's first novel, *Dangling Man*, was published in 1944. The title sums up the predicament in which many of Bellow's central characters find themselves in later novels: dangling between decisions, dangling between marriages, or dangling between the material world and an elusive metaphysical world which they are certain is there. Joseph, the central character of *Dangling Man*, is waiting to hear from his Draft Board (as Bellow was too, at the time), and awaits the news in a self-imposed isolation – hoping in vain that meditation might bring some form of enlightenment. The call coming, he rejoins the world, and marches in line with his fellow draftees. The book was extensively reviewed for a first novel, and some reviewers saw an author of great promise. Commentators were divided, however, on Joseph's attitude to his defeat – whether he saw it as a welcome release, or whether he just resigned himself to his fate. Bellow's own attitude toward his protagonist even appeared problematic.

The Victim (1947), Bellow's next novel, explores the profound effect upon Asa Leventhal of the accusations by Kirby Allbee that Leventhal's thoughtless actions had cost Allbee his job and marriage. These pressures confront Leventhal at a period when his wife is away and his brother Max is neglecting his family. Leventhal is prompted to consider his degree of responsibility toward others, and the extent to which his own behavior is selfish. Allbee's fortunes eventually improve, and Leventhal learns much from the experience, but his weeks alone, the victim of what might well be another's paranoia, are difficult for him. For some readers Allbee's attempt to scapegoat the Jewish Leventhal is a mirror of the scapegoating behind the Holocaust, although others see the novel as more concerned with the modernist angst and alienation shared by the two central characters.

Bellow had been teaching at the University of Minnesota in the two years leading up to the publication of *The Victim*. The novel helped him to win a Guggenheim Fellowship, with time and funds to travel to Paris and Rome. *The Adventures of Augie March* (1953) won Bellow his first National Book Award the following year. Rich and detailed in its description of South Side Chicago and its immigrant neighborhoods, the novel describes the coming-of-age adventures of the optimistic Augie, and his relationship with his more cynical brother, Simon. The novel is usually seen as Bellow's rejection of the more existentialist tenor of his two earlier novels, as well as a rejection of the stress-filled and misanthropic worldview of their main protagonists. Nevertheless the world in which Augie grows into middle age is still one that leaves him scarred and less optimistic.

Bellow continued his nomadic teaching, at Bard College and then back again at Minnesota, before settling in Tivoli, New York, with his second wife. His next book consisted of a number of short works including the novella

Seize the Day (1956) which gives the collection its title. The narrative covers a day in the life of unemployed, middle-aged Tommy Wilhelm. Tommy lives in a run-down hotel, is refused assistance by his father, and is estranged from wife and children. He suffers the nihilist jargon of charlatan psychologist Tamkin, who manages to lose all of Tommy's savings by speculating on the corn market. Defeated, rejected by his father, Tommy wanders the streets but finds expression for his grief, and a sense of shared sorrow, weeping over the funeral casket and corpse of a man he does not know. A degree of social contact, qualified as it is, mitigates Tommy's despair, and illustrates the qualities of decency and fellow feeling that might help him survive.

Henderson the Rain King (1959) is the novel from which Bellow himself dated his maturity. Eugene Henderson's initials suggest a parody of the persona projected by Bellow's fellow Midwesterner Ernest Hemingway. Henderson's journey into Africa, having alienated his family and having caused the death of his housekeeper, is also a journey into his own mind. Driven by a modernist fantasy that the spiritual power of primitivism can redeem a cursed land and time, he journeys further and further into the wilderness before he finds a more authentic kind of spiritual equilibrium.

In fall 1961, now married for a third time, Bellow accepted what eventually turned into a permanent position at the University of Chicago. A number of the scenes in his next novel, *Herzog* (1964), are set in the city, and some of its events are based on details of Bellow's second marriage. The novel brought Bellow his second National Book Award, and its bestseller status gave him for the first time a degree of financial freedom. The title character is in emotional turmoil: feeling furious and betrayed by the discovery that his wife had been having an affair with his best friend; worried about his young daughter's life in the hands of the two lovers; musing on the failure of his academic career; and facing the vindictive maneuvers of the now estranged wife. Herzog moves from place to place restlessly, writes – mostly unsent – letters to famous public figures living and dead, as well as letters to family, friends, and enemies, and finally settles down alone in his house in the Berkshires. The letters help him work out his attitude both to his own despair, and to the modernist, materialist views which see such despair as the central condition of modern man.

Mosby's Memoirs (1968) is a book of short stories. Two years later Bellow's next novel, *Mr Sammler's Planet* (1970), won him his third National Book Award. Artur Sammler is a Holocaust survivor living into the rebellious youth culture of 1960s New York. He has become bitter, misanthropic, and misogynistic, and the novel explores the possibilities of his getting beyond this self-imposed withdrawal. Whether Sammler's critical views of women, his racist stereotypes, and his general condemnation of youth culture in this novel also represent Bellow's own views has been the subject of some critical debate, but many critics see Bellow's work taking a more conservative direction with *Herzog* and the novels that follow.

For his seventh novel, *Humboldt's Gift* (1975), Bellow was awarded the Pulitzer Prize. Narrator Charles Citrine explores what characteristics in modern America would lead to the destruction of a poet with such talent as his one-time friend Von Humboldt Fleischer. Citrine also examines his own sense of alienation from the contemporary world, even though his compromises with that world have brought him a great deal of money. While Citrine meditates on these matters, the problems of his daily life intrude, as he is pursued by gangsters, lawyers, and a number of women. The central question posed by both narratives is how to preserve the integrity of an inner imaginative life, while living in the kind of modern culture in which we are obliged to exist day to day. The character of Humboldt is based on two gifted and troubled poets whom Bellow had known personally, John Berryman and Delmore Schwartz.

In 1976, the same year that Bellow was awarded the Nobel Prize, he published *To Jerusalem and Back: A Personal Account*. The book resulted from Bellow's three-month stay in Israel the previous year and comes to the conclusion that finding any lasting solution to the area's conflicts is a near-impossibility. For some commentators on his next novel, *The Dean's December* (1982), Dean of Students Albert Corde is too obviously a spokesman for Bellow's own views on the failure of modern culture. That failure is illustrated in this novel not only by the grim communist capital, Bucharest, but also by the city of Chicago, ruthlessly materialist, and economically and bureaucratically mismanaged.

More Die of Heartbreak (1987) followed Bellow's third collection of stories, *Him with His Foot in His Mouth and Other Stories* (1984). *More Die of Heartbreak* has a farcical plot in which Assistant Professor of Russian Literature Kenneth Trachtenberg and botanist Benn Crader exchange misogynist views on women, seeing women as obstacles to their own enlightenment and best avoided or even fled. The novel received a mixed, somewhat puzzled reaction from reviewers and is still the subject of differing assessments. For some commentators this is Bellow's weakest novel. More generally, critics noted the increasingly discursive nature of Bellow's narratives, with views expounded upon rather than dramatized, and some repetition of themes. This tendency continued in the series of novellas that Bellow published in the following years. *A Theft* and *The Bellarosa Connection* both appeared in 1989, and *The Actual* in 1997.

Bellow's last novel, *Ravelstein* (2000), published when he was 85, is a portrait of Allan Bloom, the conservative author of the best-selling *The*

Closing of the American Mind (1987). Bloom, who had died in 1992, had been a close friend and colleague of Bellow at the University of Chicago. The novel is largely an account of the conversations between Ravelstein and the novel's Bellow surrogate, Chick, and for the most part is set in Ravelstein's apartment. The portrait of Ravelstein is affectionate, but apparently frank. The book created something of a stir in its revelation that Bloom was homosexual, and that, according to the novel, he had died of Aids.

Bellow had left Chicago and his university position there in 1993 and moved to New England, where he continued to teach, this time at Boston University. The obituaries upon his death at age 89 were not merely respectful memorials of a figure belonging to the past, but acknowledgments of a distinguished career that had received recognition at the highest levels. There were, within the assessments, some dissenting comments, particularly upon what some saw as the misogynistic views behind his portrayal of women. Vladimir Nabokov, years earlier in a private letter, had referred to Bellow as a "miserable mediocrity," but Bellow, who was, in some important ways, resolutely old-fashioned in his views and an admirer of the nineteenth-century realist novel, would have been an unlikely favorite of one whose work took an entirely different direction.

Bibliography

Bellow's novels from *Dangling Man* to *Herzog* have been published in two volumes by Library of America, and Bellow's fiction is generally available in paperback format from Penguin.

James Atlas, *Bellow* (New York, 2000).
Gerhard Bach and Gloria L. Cronin, eds., *Small Planets: Saul Bellow and the Art of Short Fiction* (East Lansing, MI, 2000).
Gloria L. Cronin, *A Room of His Own: In Search of the Feminine in the Novels of Saul Bellow* (Syracuse, 2001).
Ellen Pifer, *Saul Bellow Against the Grain* (Philadelphia, 1990).

Norman Mailer (1923–2007)

Norman Mailer found himself a literary celebrity at the age of 25 with the critical and commercial success of his first book, *The Naked and the Dead.* But there was little chance that Mailer would suffer the fate that sometimes descends on a writer who achieves such early fame: either to repeat himself in the same vein until readers lose interest, or always to have his later books compared to his first. For Mailer's instincts were usually to try something different. There are critics who, while recognizing Mailer's willingness to take such risks, conclude that he never fulfilled his early promise; and Mailer contributed to such conclusions by hints of a long-planned, sometimes multi-volume, masterpiece to come, as if such a book were necessary to complement the more than 40 books that he did publish. Mailer's combative role as a public figure, both literary, political, and on at least two occasions criminal, also contributed to some mixed assessments of his work, while financial necessity – Mailer was married six times and had nine children – caused him sometimes to publish hurriedly, and to turn out books that were close to being potboilers. But Mailer's risks brought him, among other honors, two Pulitzer Prizes, a National Book Award, and fame (on occasions, notoriety) that went well beyond that accorded many equally important writers.

Mailer was born in Long Branch, New Jersey, although the family moved to Brooklyn while he was still a child. He attended Harvard University from 1939 to 1943, where he studied aeronautical engineering. He moved in the direction of his future career by winning *Story* magazine's annual college contest, working on the university's *Advocate* literary magazine, and completing at least one apprentice novel.

Mailer was drafted into the army in 1944, the year of his marriage to Bea Silverman. His posting was to the Pacific island of Luzon. Although he saw relatively little action, the setting and experience gave him material for *The Naked and the Dead* (1948), which went on to sell nearly 200 000 copies in its first year and always remained Mailer's biggest commercial success. The action of the novel takes place on the fictional island of Anopopei in the South Pacific, and centers around the differences between the totalitarian-minded General Cummings, commander of the unit, and his more liberal aide, Lieutenant Hearn. Set alongside this conflict is the account of the enlisted men and the story of a failed patrol led by the violent Sergeant Croft. Mailer adapted techniques from John Dos Passos and James T. Farrell in his organization of the narrative. Subsections titled "Chorus," and "The Time Machine" provide additional perspectives upon the unit and fill in biographical details of its central characters. The picture of the military in the novel is a critical one, with incompetent officers and petty conflicts adding to the ever-present danger represented by the Japanese enemy. In a short introduction to the Fiftieth Anniversary edition, Mailer commented that prior to writing the book he had "already written more than a quarter of a million words in college," and that the novel was the work of "a hard working amateur who loved writing."

While his first novel was being prepared for publication Mailer studied in Paris on the GI Bill, where he became interested in the left-wing politics and existentialist ideas that he would adapt to his own purposes in his future writing. Mailer's second book, *Barbary Shore* (1951), emerged from this experience, and Mailer has called it his most autobiographical novel. But the book received poor reviews, seen as more a political tract than a fully realized narrative. The central action, set in a Brooklyn rooming house, concerns the attempt by socialist McLeod to win over narrator and amnesiac war veteran Mikey Lovett to his views, views that are symbolized by the "little object" that, just before being killed by a government agent, McLeod manages to pass on to Lovett. The political events are complicated by romantic subplots, but the narrative has little of the inventiveness of the first novel.

The world of Hollywood and McCarthyism are the setting for Mailer's third novel, *The Deer Park* (1955), which was better received than *Barbary Shore* but still with a good deal of qualification. Mailer and his first wife had been in Hollywood in 1949 when Mailer was trying to get *The Naked and the Dead* filmed, and also trying his hand at screenplays. A central theme of this novel is the clash of commercial interests with artistic integrity, particularly the ability of corporations to corrupt the moral values of those who work within them. Mailer experienced difficulties getting this novel published because of its frank language, the manuscript passing through eight publishers before being picked up by G. P. Putnam's.

In 1959 Mailer collected many of his shorter fiction and non-fiction pieces for the volume *Advertisements for Myself*. These included some columns that he had written for *The Village Voice*, the influential weekly based in Greenwich Village, New York City, that he helped to found in 1955. Also included is an account of Mailer's troubles writing *The Deer Park* and discussion of the revisions that he made to the novel just before its publication. The best-known piece in the book is "The White Negro," originally published in 1957. In this influential essay Mailer argues that America's Negroes have "been living on the margin between totalitarianism and democracy for two centuries," thus in a state of alienation, and with an ever-present sense of danger. He contends that some post-war white youth, through music, especially jazz, have felt an affinity with this condition and that the attitude is caught in the terms "hip" and "hipster." A key idea in the essay is that violence can be redemptive, if its causes are understood and its results liberating. The ideas in "The White Negro" appear in many of Mailer's later works, although he uses the term "existentialist" rather than "hip." *The Presidential Papers* (1963) was another collection of shorter pieces, presented as advice for the new President, John F. Kennedy, who had been elected in 1960. Mailer saw Kennedy as possibly the first "Hipster as Presidential Candidate."

An American Dream (1965) was Mailer's first novel in 10 years. Stephen Rojack feels confined and oppressed by the manipulations and values of his wife and her ruthless father. He sees his murder of her as his only opportunity to escape this trap, to have a chance to find his authentic self. Following the murder, presented to some extent as a self-defense of his physical as well as his psychic manhood, he undergoes a series of further challenges that he manages to surmount, but at the cost of isolation. The book has been praised for its exuberant mix of realism and hyperbole. But some readers were disturbed by the parallels between the narrative and Mailer's much-publicized stabbing of his second wife, in November 1960, at a campaign gathering when he was running for mayor of New York City. Novel and stabbing, together with Mailer's view that the decade's rising tide of feminism was another version of totalitarianism, made him a target of feminist writers and activists over the next few years. He published a defense of his views in *The Prisoner of Sex* (1971).

Why Are We in Vietnam? (1967) recounts narrator D.J.'s thoughts on the night before he is to leave to serve in the Vietnam War. Through the narrative of an Alaska hunting trip two years earlier, the novel explores the ways in which violence can be regenerative, as against the unfair slaughter in the hunting techniques used by D.J.'s father. *Why Are We in Vietnam?* was nominated for a National Book Award. Mailer's next book, *The Armies of the Night* (1968), an account of the March on the Pentagon to protest the war in October 1967, won both that award and a Pulitzer Prize. The book is a key text in the genre of New Journalism, mixing non-fiction with various fictional techniques, a genre also explored by such writers as Truman Capote, Tom Wolfe, and Joan Didion. Mailer divides his account into "History as a Novel," which contains the account of his own experience over the weekend as the protagonist "Mailer," and "The Novel as History," which provides a broader picture of the events that Mailer did not personally experience. Mailer's participation, as he recounts it in the book, was the result of recognizing that a novelist must play an active part in opposing the war. Mailer marched at the front of the column, along with such figures as iconic pediatrician Dr. Spock and poet Robert Lowell, the plan being that all three would get themselves arrested. As a measure of Mailer's tarnished public image, the police promptly arrested Mailer and ignored the other two.

The success of *The Armies of the Night* led Mailer to write a number of non-fiction books that blended novelistic devices. These included *Miami and the Siege of Chicago* (1968), an account of the political conventions of that year; *Of a Fire on the Moon* (1971), on the Apollo 11 Moon landing; and, most successfully, *The Executioner's Song* (1979), the story of Gary Gilmore, whose execution on January 17, 1977 ended the US moratorium on the death penalty. Mailer manages to make Gilmore a figure demanding some sympathy from the reader, but without softening in any way Gilmore's heartless and unthinking violence. This book brought Mailer his second Pulitzer Prize.

Before the publication of his next novel, *Ancient Evenings* (1983), Mailer was in the news again for his role in the paroling of murderer Jack Abbott. The two had been corresponding since 1978. Mailer was impressed by Abbott's writing talent, and by Abbott's ability to help him better understand Gilmore. Helped by Mailer's advocacy, Abbott was released in June 1981, at the same time that his letters to Mailer were published as *In the Belly of the Beast*. Mailer contributed an introduction and the book received excellent reviews. But within a month of his release Abbott murdered a waiter at a New York restaurant during a trivial dispute. Mailer acknowledged being blinded by his enthusiasm for Abbott's writing, and came in for a good deal of public criticism.

Ancient Evenings, set in the Egypt of the Pharaohs, had taken Mailer a good deal of research and 11 years to write. He planned at one point that it be the first of a trilogy, with the final volume to end in modern times. The novel received mixed, mostly negative, reviews, many critics puzzling over its mix of history, reincarnation, and myth, and what they saw as the awkward intrusion into the novel's historical context of Mailer's familiar ideas on sex and violence. The book was seen generally as a failed experiment by a writer who by this stage of his career was respected for his literary risks, and whose reputation could withstand a novel that didn't work. Nevertheless *Ancient Evenings* had its important admirers. Harold Bloom in *The New York Review of Books* found it to be "not the historical novel that it masks itself as being," but a book containing much that is relevant to "current reality in America." Anthony Burgess included the book in his *Ninety-nine Novels: The Best in English Since 1939* (1984). In years to come, Mailer himself often cited it as his best book.

Rushing to complete a novel owed to publishers Little, Brown, before moving to Random House, Mailer published *Tough Guys Don't Dance* in 1984. The book is often compared to *An American Dream* since both explore the effect of a woman's murder upon a male protagonist. Critics note the confident celebration of released masculinity in the earlier novel, and the much more circumscribed conditions facing Tim Madden in the later book. Although the novel's events are generally implausible, the book was enjoyed as a mystery novel by enough readers to make the bestseller lists. Two years later Mailer directed an unsuccessful film version that has become something of a cult classic.

In 1984 Mailer began a controversial tenure as President of the American Center of PEN, the international writers' association. But otherwise he kept a lower public profile in the 1980s, working on a 1300-page novel about the CIA, *Harlot's Ghost*, which appeared in 1991. The narrator, Harry Hubbard, following the death of his mentor Hugh Montague, the Harlot of the title, and discovering that his wife Kittredge, once also married to Harlot, had been unfaithful to him, flees to Moscow where he starts to recall his own long career at the CIA. Again, reviews were mixed, some noting the uneven quality of the writing and what was seen as the book's excessive length. There was general agreement that in Kittredge Mailer had created his most successful female heroine, and that the opening of the novel is particularly effective. Historical figures such as Allen Dulles and E. Howard Hunt enter the narrative alongside fictional characters. Mailer records in an "Author's Note" at the end of the novel: "The events described are either real, or able to respect the proportions of the factual events." The CIA of *Harlot's Ghost*, he hopes, moves "in parallel orbit to the real one." The novel concludes with "TO BE CONTINUED," for Mailer intended to take the history into the 1980s, but this sequel never appeared.

Following *Harlot's Ghost*, Mailer published a book on Lee Harvey Oswald, and another on Pablo Picasso, but his next novel was a generally straightforward life of Christ, *The Gospel According to the Son* (1997), with the details taken in most part from the four gospels. Ten years later Mailer received some of the best reviews of his career for *The Castle in the Forest* (2007), an account of the early childhood of Adolf Hitler as recounted by a devil who is living in the body of an SS man named Dieter. Mailer was writing a sequel to this novel when he died, of acute renal failure, at the age of 84. In a writing career covering 60 years Mailer was the chronicler of some of the major events of his times. A writer uneven in his publications, embarrassing at times in his public activities, but never one to be ignored or written off as finished, twentieth-century American literature has no other figure like him.

Bibliography

Norman Mailer's fiction and the collections of his shorter fiction and non-fiction are generally available in paperback format from his various publishers.

Mary V. Dearborn, *Mailer: A Biography* (Boston, 1999).
Barry H. Leeds, *The Enduring Vision of Norman Mailer* (Bainbridge Island, WA, 2002).
J. Michael Lennon, ed., *Conversations with Norman Mailer* (Jackson, MS, 1988).
Tony Tanner, "On the Parapet," in *City of Words: American Fiction, 1950–1970* (New York, 1971), pp. 344–371.

James Baldwin (1924–1987)

James Arthur Jones was born in Harlem, New York City, and became James Baldwin three years later when his mother married a Baptist preacher. David Baldwin denounced whites, and he brought up his stepson to share his hatred. Yet James Baldwin's fiction displays again and again the destructive qualities of such intolerance. As an author he early began to forge an independent voice, an independence that would later set him against early supporter Richard Wright, against black critics and publishers who wanted him to write a certain kind of fiction, and against black leaders who wanted his name for their particular brand of activism.

The Harlem Renaissance poet Countee Cullen was an important early mentor, encouraging Baldwin to apply to the well-known DeWitt Clinton High School in the Bronx, which Cullen himself had attended. As part of his work on the school magazine, *The Magpie*, Baldwin interviewed Cullen, the interview appearing in the Winter 1942 issue. In the same year that his stepfather died, 1943, Baldwin moved to Greenwich Village, where he worked as a waiter and continued with his writing. A friend introduced him to Richard Wright, whose influence helped Baldwin obtain a Saxon Memorial Trust Award to give him time to work on his first novel.

Baldwin began regularly writing reviews for *The Nation* and *The New Leader*, but early versions of his novel were rejected by both Harper and Doubleday. In 1948 he moved to Paris. Richard Wright had also moved to the city, but the relationship was strained the following year with Baldwin's criticism of the older writer in his essay "Everybody's Protest Novel," reprinted in *Notes of a Native Son* (1955). In arguing the limitations of the protest novel, particularly Stowe's *Uncle Tom's Cabin*, Baldwin claims of Wright's *Native Son* that "below the surface of this novel there lies, as it seems to me, a continuation, a complement of that monstrous legend it was written to destroy." Relations were completely broken when Baldwin's essay "Many Thousands Gone," also reprinted in the collection, directly criticized Wright's novel at greater length for its limited portrayal of black culture and tradition. "What the novel reflects – and at no point interprets," Baldwin argues, "is the isolation of the Negro within his own group and the resulting fury of impatient scorn."

The criticisms of Wright point to Baldwin's intentions in his own fiction, particularly his attempt to analyze the historical and cultural context for the racial and gender issues in his narratives. In other essays reprinted in *Notes of a Native Son* Baldwin contrasts the different histories of Africans in France and American Negroes, and explores the implications for identity and self-understanding of Americans' inability to face or understand the racial history of their own culture. Such themes are at the center of some of his best-known later stories, such as "Sonny's Blues" (1957) and "Going to Meet the Man" (1965).

Before the essays in *Notes of a Native Son* were collected, Baldwin found a publisher for his first novel, *Go Tell It on the Mountain* (1952). The autobiographical narrative is in three parts, set during a Saturday night church service. Fourteen-year-old John Grimes is converted, although with his conversion comes recognition of his homosexuality and a determination to defy the novel's David Baldwin figure, his father Gabriel. Baldwin's later comments on the novel suggested that it was not so much about religion as about finding the courage to love.

Baldwin returned to New York in 1954, having been awarded a Guggenheim Fellowship. He worked on a play, *The Amen Corner*, which was staged at Howard University in 1955. (This play was later produced on Broadway in the 1960s, as was his better-known *Blues for Mr. Charlie*.)

Baldwin's second novel, *Giovanni's Room*, appeared in 1956, having been rejected by several publishers. Baldwin was determined not to limit his fiction to the expectations of what a black writer's subject matter ought to be. The novel contains no African American characters, and the social alienation that is a central theme of the book is treated through the issue of homosexuality, not race. The white American narrator, David, is a character very conflicted about his homosexuality, and his lack of complete honesty to himself and to those closest to him finally leaves him isolated and wracked with guilt.

While working on his next novel, *Another Country* (1962), Baldwin published various essays, stories, and articles on a number of civil rights issues, including school integration, and the conditions in Harlem's public housing projects. He also responded to Norman Mailer's essay "The White Negro," and wrote on the last years of Richard Wright. *Nobody Knows My*

Name: More Notes of a Native Son (1961) collects these and a number of Baldwin's other essays from 1954 to 1961.

The narrative of *Another Country* explores relationships that involve interracial love, homosexuality, racial stereotypes, and professional jealousy. As in Baldwin's earlier fiction, the degree to which a character accepts and understands the motives and values determining identity and behavior governs success in love and – in this novel and in the novels to follow – artistic expression. The book was a bestseller despite some mixed reviews. A number of Black Nationalist writers, most famously Eldridge Cleaver in *Soul on Ice* (1967), used the novel to accuse Baldwin of catering to white audiences in his fiction, and of ignoring the more urgent political and civil rights abuses facing black Americans.

In these years Baldwin traveled a good deal within the United States and Europe. In 1961 he began spending time in Istanbul, a city he would revisit many times in the coming years. He spent much of 1963 in the United States, however, lobbying for the cause of Civil Rights. In this same year he collected two of his recent essays on race in the volume *The Fire Next Time*. The first essay examines the history of race relations in the United States, and the second the relationship between race and religion. The book was almost universally praised, recognized as an important contribution to the current dialogue on racial issues, and brought Baldwin a great deal of attention in the media. The following year, 1964, Baldwin was elected to the National Institute of Arts and Letters.

The role that had descended on Baldwin as an important spokesperson on racial issues began making major demands on his time. These commitments, coupled with his continued traveling between continents, disrupted the preparation of his next novel, *Tell Me How Long the Train's Been Gone* (1968). The central character is again an artist, here actor Leo Proudhammer, and again the narrative centers upon interracial love and bisexuality, emphasizing the power of forgiveness, generosity, and self-understanding. The novel has its admirers but was not treated particularly kindly by reviewers. Mario Puzo, for example, writing in the *New York Times*, thought the book narrowly polemical, and voiced what was a growing sense among some commentators that Baldwin's talents lay more in his powerful and influential essays than in his fiction.

Over the next few years Baldwin worked in Hollywood on an aborted screenplay on Malcolm X, continued to travel extensively, and participated in various dialogues and events, most famously a conversation with anthropologist Margaret Mead published in 1971 as *A Rap on Race*. In 1972 he published a book of essays, *No Name in the Street*, which included an account of the Civil Rights March on Washington in 1963, in which he had participated. His next novel, *If Beale Street Could Talk*, appeared in 1974. Like the central characters of Baldwin's two previous novels, protagonist Fonny is an artist, in this case a sculptor. His story is narrated by his wife Tish, and the events are based on the experience of Baldwin's former assistant Tony Maynard. Maynard was falsely accused of murder in Germany (an account appears in *No Name in the Street*) and Baldwin worked for his release for some years. As many critics have observed, the novel is Baldwin's most sustained examination of heterosexual love. His final novel, *Just Above My Head* (1979), covers 30 years in the lives of the Montana and Miller families. The focus is on the life and career of deceased gospel singer Arthur Montana, who achieves his greatest success in singing when he begins his openly homosexual relationship with Jimmy Miller, a relationship that is accepted by both families. The relationship between Arthur and Jimmy may be Baldwin's frankest treatment of homosexuality; certainly it is not deflected in Arthur's case by any suggestions of a complicating bisexuality.

In the last decade of his life Baldwin taught for part of the year at a number of colleges: Bowling Green College, Berkeley, and the University of Massachusetts, Amherst. He was also in frequent demand as a speaker. He published a selection of his poems, *Jimmy's Blues* (UK 1983, USA 1985), and collected his non-fiction from 1948 to 1985 as *The Price of the Ticket* (1985). In 1987 Baldwin was diagnosed with cancer of the esophagus, and died in December of that year. Among the speakers at his funeral acknowledging his achievement and importance were Toni Morrison, Maya Angelou, and Amiri Baraka.

Bibliography

The Library of America's *Early Novels and Stories* includes Baldwin's first three novels and a selection of stories, while his non-fiction is in a companion *Collected Essays* volume (both 1998). Baldwin's novels and essay collections are also generally available in paperback format.

Lawrie Balfour, *The Evidence of Things Not Said: James Baldwin and the Promise of American Democracy* (Ithaca, 2001).

Clarence E. Hardy III, *James Baldwin's God: Sex, Hope, and Crisis in Black Holiness Culture* (Knoxville, TN, 2003).

David Leeming, *James Baldwin: A Biography* (New York, 1994).

D. Quentin Miller, ed., *Re-Viewing James Baldwin: Things Not Seen* (Philadelphia, 2000).

John Barth (b.1930)

John Barth's novels have been accused of exhibiting such faults as pedantry, chauvinism, self-indulgence, unreadability, and a general disinterest in the world beyond the four walls of his study. Nevertheless he is recognized as one of the most important writers of post-modern fiction in American literature. In addition, his non-fiction essays, published in *The Friday Book* (1984) and *Further Fridays* (1995), have made valuable contributions both to the study of his own work and to discussion of post-modern fiction generally.

Barth was born in Cambridge, Maryland. After high school, and following a summer studying at the Julliard School of Music in New York City, Barth attended Johns Hopkins University, where he graduated in 1951 with a degree in creative writing. He moved on to the graduate program at Johns Hopkins, but having married in 1950 and soon with two children and a third on the way, he left to take a position as instructor in Pennsylvania State University's English Department.

His first major writing project at Penn State was the "Dorchester Tales," intended to be a cycle of 100 stories incorporating the history and tradition of Maryland's Eastern Shore. The story cycle is a recurring feature of Barth's subsequent fiction, an interest evidently first sparked by his student job at Johns Hopkins in the university's classics library. There he read many of the collection's oriental tale cycles. Barth abandoned the "Dorchester Tales" project when he had written about half of the planned tales, and turned to what would become his first two published novels, *The Floating Opera* and *The End of the Road*. The novels were completed by the end of 1955. Barth has commented that the two books are companion pieces: a "nihilistic comedy" and a "nihilistic tragedy."

The Twentieth-Century American Fiction Handbook   By Christopher MacGowan
© 2011 Christopher MacGowan

The Floating Opera (1956) was accepted by publisher Appleton, Century Crofts, but only on condition that Barth change his proposed ending. Narrator Todd Andrews is a lawyer writing in 1954 about a day in 1937 when he had decided to commit suicide – as his father had in 1930. Todd is trying to find a pattern or significance within the apparent randomness of existence, some clue that might help him understand his father's action. Like all of Barth's fiction, the narrative calls attention to its telling. In this case it is akin to a performance on the showboat that features centrally in the novel. Todd's plan is to blow up the steamboat during a performance, killing himself and hundreds of others in the audience, but this was the ending that the publisher objected to, insisting that the plan be just an individual act of suicide. When Barth republished the novel in 1967 he restored the original ending.

The Floating Opera received some respectful reviews but sold little. Publisher Appleton felt little incentive to publish a second novel that they felt was too similar to the first, thus *The End of the Road* did not appear until 1958, when picked up by Doubleday. In this second novel narrator Jake Horner gets into a philosophical debate with history student Joe Morgan: Jake's nihilism challenges Joe's relativism. Complicating the debate is the battle for the sexual favors of Joe's wife Rennie. This novel performed only slightly better in terms of sales and attention than its predecessor.

Even though both Todd Andrews and Jake Horner draw attention at times to the fictionality of their narratives, Barth came to feel that he had written two novels of realistic fiction, and took a more radical direction with his third novel, *The Sot-Weed Factor* (1960). The title is an eighteenth-century term for a tobacco merchant, and the novel takes as its starting point an actual poem of that title, a Juvenalian satire, published in 1708 by Maryland poet Ebenezer Cooke (*c*.1670–*c*.1732). Thus the novel announces that it is a text based upon a text, and within the novel Barth imitates, and sometimes parodies, a number of literary genres. Masquerades and word play abound, with the novel's artifice suggesting the arbitrariness of all patterning. Chapter headings mimic the long detailed summaries favored by eighteenth-century novelists to signpost the narrative to come. One example reads: "The Laureate is Exposed to Two Assassinations of Character, a Piracy, a Near-Deflowering, a Near-Mutiny, a Murder, and an Appalling Colloquy Between Captains of the Sea, All Within the Space of a Few Pages." Clearly the novel has affinities to an eighteenth-century text much better known than Ebenezer Cooke's, Laurence Sterne's *Tristram Shandy*.

In 1965, while completing his next book, *Giles Goat-Boy*, Barth accepted a teaching position at the State University of New York, Buffalo. The novel, published the next year, was far more successful in terms of sales than his previous three. Even more than in the earlier novels, *Giles Goat-Boy* emphasizes its own constructedness, and the various processes that the narrative goes through in transmission. These processes include the multiple frame devices surrounding the memoirs that George Giles dictates into the West Campus Automatic Computer (in this novel the world is one giant university). The computer edits the memoirs and turns them into printout tapes. George's son also edits the tapes before passing them on to writer-academic "J.B.," a figure whose career is similar to Barth's. J.B. also makes some changes prior to passing the narrative to the publishers. The publishers undertake further editing, and add an ambiguous "Publisher's Disclaimer." The novel has been read as a theological and political allegory, but then such a reading may itself be part of the satire. The commercial success of *Giles Goat-Boy* allowed the republication in 1967 of Barth's first three novels. As well as restoring the original ending to *The Floating Opera*, Barth cut 50 pages from *The Sot-Weed Factor*'s original 806.

Also in 1967 Barth published his influential essay "The Literature of Exhaustion." He asserts in this essay that possibilities within the traditional forms of narrative have largely been exhausted, but praises Jorge Luis Borges for confronting the issue and finding new possibilities and combinations. Barth revisited his argument in "The Literature of Replenishment" 13 years later to clarify that what he was looking for was a kind of post-modernism that would move on from modernism, but that would incorporate the past and history as well as the relativistic world of the post-modern.

Barth's fifth book, *Lost in the Funhouse* (1968), is a series of 14 fictions, most of which he had previously published. He designates particular media for each story – print, tape, or "live voice." To the paperback reprint the following year he added "Seven Additional Author's Notes" in response to some critical reactions to the book. The title of one of the stories is "The Title," while the book's "Frame-Tale" suggests that the structure of the book is a closed loop, the figure eight of a Moebius strip. Upon following the instructions in the story for folding and cutting the pages, the reader creates a text reading endlessly: "ONCE UPON A TIME THERE WAS A STORY THAT BEGAN ONCE UPON A TIME ..."

Barth won a National Book Award for his sixth book, *Chimera* (1972), made up of three novellas. "Dunyazadiad" is named for the sister of the *One Thousand and One Nights* narrator Scheherazade; "Bellerophoniad" is told by Bellerophon, killer of the Chimera in Greek mythology; and "Perseid," is narrated by Perseus, slayer of Medusa. All three principal narrators are joined by additional narrators, and the tales continue Barth's examination of the issues of contemporary storytelling while also acknowledging the traditions of the past.

Barth's first marriage had ended in divorce in 1969, and he remarried in 1970. In 1973 he returned to Johns Hopkins as Professor of English and Creative Writing, remaining at Hopkins until his retirement in 1990. His next novel, *LETTERS*, appeared in 1979, his first for 12 years. Six of the correspondents are taken from Barth's first six books, some of them later descendents of the original characters. The seventh is a new character, Germaine Pitt, Lady Amherst. The epistolary form recalls the beginnings of the English novel in such eighteenth-century works as Samuel Richardson's *Pamela* and *Clarissa*, but in Barth's novel the author exchanges letters with the characters and they with him. At times the characters are aware of their fictional status. Some decoding of various textual clues reveals the book's subtitle: "An old time epistolary novel by seven fictitious drolls & dreamers each of which imagines himself factual."

Barth returns to a more realistic mode in *Sabbatical: A Romance* (1982), although this story of former CIA officer Fenwick Turner and his wife Susan Seckler sailing the Chesapeake Bay still plays with point of view and degrees of certainty and uncertainty. *The Tidewater Tales* (1987) is in many ways a companion novel to *Sabbatical*. A number of the events in the earlier novel recur, and Fenwick and Susan turn up under what are apparently their "real" names, meeting the couple who are at the center of the new book, minimalist writer Peter Sagamore and his pregnant wife Katherine. The novel is more than twice as long as *Sabbatical*, and includes tales about Odysseus, Scheherazade, Don Quixote, and Huckleberry Finn. For all of the book's pleasures, and its loving evocation of the Maryland waters, some critics felt that the book was rather self-indulgent, and that some of its jokes wore thin, or were rather too obvious.

The frame story of *The Last Voyage of Somebody the Sailor* (1991) is set in a modern hospital room, but its multiple stories are told in both twentieth-century Maryland and in the world of *One Thousand and One Nights*, at the house of Sinbad. Sinbad tells his tales, as does his twentieth-century visitor Simon Behler, but the Arabian audience take Behler's modern details, such as cars and watches, to be fantasy. Locality, narrative, and identity are as fluid as ever in a novel that, at 573 pages, some reviewers nevertheless found rather overblown.

Self-referentiality, issues of identity, sailing, and a fictional narrator named "John Barth" are elements of Barth's 1994 *Once Upon a Time: A Floating Opera*. Here the fictional Barth, like his counterpart author, reached 60 in 1990, and considers that this work will be his last novel. The book teases with its possibilities of being autobiography, and a "Program Note" claims somewhat cryptically that the narrative "is not the story of my life, but it is most certainly a story thereof."

On With the Story (1996) marked Barth's first collection of short fiction since *Lost in the Funhouse*. The stories are interrelated in ways that emphasize again puzzles, patterns, and a self-consciousness about storytelling. The first story is titled "The End: An Introduction," while the story "Ever After," which might suggest a traditional ending, is not the last story. In *Coming Soon!!!* (2001) Barth again suggests that he is writing his last novel. Here he meets up with a version of the showboat from *The Floating Opera*, and with a young novelist who is a Barth-aspirant. Each agrees to write a novel about the other writing a novel, and the tales take off from there. While the book was received with some enthusiasm, the general critical reaction was that the novel was mainly of interest to diehard fans and academics. Repetition and trying a reader's patience had always been elements of Barth's repertoire; nevertheless few would disagree that, as the *New York Times* reviewer of this book noted, Barth's "marquee value" had dimmed somewhat since the days of *Giles Goat-Boy*.

Barth has continued to publish regularly into the twenty-first century. *The Book of Ten Nights and a Night* (2004) collects some previously published stories and adds the kind of frame that is a Barth hallmark. Some commentators noticed a darker tone within the playfulness of this book. *Where Three Roads Meet* (2005) is made up of three novellas: "Tell Me," "I've Been Told: A Story's Story," and "As I was Saying . . ." The third of the stories concerns the recollections of three elderly sisters who once inspired a now mysteriously vanished novelist. The linked stories of *The Development* (2008) are set in a rest home for the elderly in Tidewater, Maryland. But with *Where Three Roads Meet* and *The Development* the real John Barth makes clear that he has neither vanished nor retired.

Bibliography

Almost all of John Barth's novels are available in paperback format.

Zack Bowen, *A Reader's Guide to John Barth* (Westport, CT, 1994).
Stan Fogel and Gordon Slethaug, *Understanding John Barth* (Columbia, SC, 1990).
Patricia Tobin, *John Barth and the Anxiety of Continuance* (Philadelphia, 1992).

Toni Morrison (b.1931)

Toni Morrison published her first novel at the age of 39, and in 1993, the year after she published her sixth, she became the first African American writer to win the Nobel Prize for Literature. In addition to her importance as one of the nation's foremost contemporary novelists, Toni Morrison has been a major figure both as a creative writing teacher, and – during the 18 years in which she worked as a senior editor at Random House – as a mentor to many new and established authors.

Morrison was born Chloe Anthony Wofford in Lorain, Ohio. She changed her name to Toni while an undergraduate at Howard University, from which she graduated in 1953. She took the surname of her husband, Harold Morrison, a Jamaican architect, when the two married in 1958. Upon completing her undergraduate degree she received an MA from Cornell in 1955, and taught at Texas Southern University from 1955 to 1957, before returning to Howard to teach from 1957 to 1964. Her marriage to Harold Morrison ended in 1964, and the following year Morrison joined Random House, at first with subsidiary L. W. Singer in Syracuse, New York, and then in the New York City offices in 1968. At the same time Morrison taught courses at a number of universities, including Bard, Yale, and the State University of New York at Albany.

Morrison began writing her first novel, *The Bluest Eye*, while working in Syracuse, and published it in 1970. Set in 1941, the novel's primary narrator, Claudia MacTeer, tells the story of her friend Pecola Breedlove's obsession with conventional ideas of beauty. Pecola views beauty in terms of the blue-eyed, blonde-haired, white world of the Dick and Jane primer, excerpts from which open the novel and return at various times throughout the book. Another of Pecola's models is the child screen icon Shirley Temple. This

The Twentieth-Century American Fiction Handbook   By Christopher MacGowan
© 2011 Christopher MacGowan

desperate need to be loved for something she isn't consumes her, while Pecola's parents, like their daughter, also see greater value and beauty in whiteness. The reality is that their constant fighting is in stark contrast to the idyllic marriage of Dick and Jane's parents, and that at the age of 11 Pecola is pregnant with a baby resulting from being raped by her father. The novel is a commentary not only on the nature of desire, but also upon the institutionalized racism that produces such texts as the Dick and Jane series, and, as Morrison puts it in an "Afterword" published with the novel in 1993, the kind of "racial self-loathing" that makes Pecola feel "that it was better to be a freak than what she was."

Sula (1973) is almost as much about the African American neighborhood of Bottom in the town of Medallion, Ohio, as it is about the novel's title character. Like *The Bluest Eye*, the novel explores concepts of identity, and the values and assumptions by which we judge others. Nel Wright is challenged to come to an understanding of her one-time best friend Sula in a way that goes beyond conventional moral criteria. And the community of Bottom comes to some conclusions about Sula that turn out to be more self-serving than accurate.

In contrast to Morrison's first two novels, *Song of Solomon* (1977) focuses upon a male protagonist. The novel brings folklore and cultural heritage to the fore in the story of Milkman Dead discovering his Virginia ancestry and his vital role in passing on the individual and communal significance of what he discovers. Pilate and Circe are two of Milkman's most important teachers and both practice folk magic. True to their teaching, the narrative mixes realism and folklore in its telling. Pilate has no navel, and Circe is a figure everyone in town assumes is dead. And a myth central to the novel, and to Milkman's final understanding of what he has discovered, is the myth told by slaves of Africans who flew back to Africa rather than be enslaved.

Tar Baby (1982), Morrison's fourth novel, is her first to be set outside of Ohio. The narrative revolves around three couples, but most centrally around Son and Jadine, each of whom is associated with a different version of blackness – a difference that eventually dooms their relationship. Son's identity is tied to nature and to the all-black town of Eloe. Eloe's present differs little from its past. But Jadine's identity is contemporary, and she eventually leaves Son to return to her modeling career in Paris. The magic in this novel invites comparison to events in Shakespeare's *The Tempest*, with the wealthy white landowner Valerian serving as a Prospero figure, at one time controlling all on his island paradise, and Son suggesting a version of Caliban. The novel's title reference to the trickster story from Joel Chandler Harris's Uncle Remus tales has been applied both to Jadine, who at one point actually falls into tar, and to Son who, like Brer Rabbit, manages his own kind of escape from his fascination with her.

Beloved (1987) won Morrison the Pulitzer Prize, and the decision not to grant the novel the National Book Award too was a controversial one. Morrison took as the starting point for her complex narrative of slavery and the traumatic impact upon the lives of those who suffered under it the real-life story of Margaret Garner. Morrison came across the story while editing an African American folk history, *The Black Book*, while at Random House. Garner killed her daughter to save her from being returned to slavery, and was subsequently charged not with murder but with theft of her master's property. In the novel, most of the central characters lived as slaves at one point on the ironically named plantation Sweet Home, although the present of the novel occurs in the post-slavery years just after the Civil War. The novel explores the role of memory in the way that the disruption and violence of the slave past is either lived with or repressed. The narrative is built up separately through the stories of a number of characters, gradually moving toward the key events at Sweet Home, and the confrontation that caused Sethe Suggs to kill her child. From the first page that child is present in Sethe's home as a ghost, and she becomes even more of a presence later as she comes to dominate Sethe's life. Again the role of community is crucial, especially the individual acts of kindness and understanding that can shape and change a community's entrenched judgments.

In 1988 Morrison was elected to the American Academy and Institute of Arts and Letters. The following year she joined the Creative Writing Program at Princeton University where she taught until retiring in 2006. The year before being awarded the Nobel Prize Morrison published *Jazz* (1992). This novel, set in the 1920s, tells the story of the love triangle between Violet, her husband Joe, and Joe's young mistress Dorcas. The marriage is shattered by the affair, and by Joe's murder of Dorcas when he finds her involved with a younger man. The process of recovery for both Joe and Violet involves returning to the stories of their respective parents and grandparents in order to more fully understand the role of racism, violence, and passion in the culture that has shaped the lives of all three generations. Important to Violet's healing is her friendship with Dorcas's aunt, Alice Manfred, who helps her to understand Dorcas, and important to both Joe and Violet is their friendship with the aptly named Felice, Dorcas's friend. A controversial aspect of this novel is Morrison's use of an unnamed and sometimes unreliable narrator who intrudes at times with commentary. Arguably the device allows Morrison to engage her readers more fully in trying to comprehend the complexities of the characters' lives, but some readers find it a disruptive and at times limiting device.

Before publishing her next novel Morrison edited two books of essays on important media-influenced events of the 1990s. *Race-ing Justice, Engendering Power: Essays on Anita Hill, Clarence Thomas, and the Construction of Social Reality* (1992) takes up the issues surrounding the nomination of Clarence Thomas to the Supreme Court in 1991. In 1997 Morrison co-edited with Claudia Brodsky Lacour a book of essays, *Birth of a Nation'hood: Gaze, Script, and Spectacle in the O.J. Simpson Case*. Morrison's own contribution looks at what she sees as the hidden racism in the media's treatment of the murders and subsequent trial.

Morrison's next two novels were seen by some as charting familiar territory but in an overly schematic way. *Paradise* (1998) describes the clash of two communities, one the patriarchal town of Ruby and the other a group of five women living in the large house outside town known as the Convent. Nine men from the town descend on the women and murder them, yet the disappearance of their bodies, and suggestions of their reappearance elsewhere in various places, imply that both as individuals and in the communal spirit that they represent they live on in ways that the violence of the men from Ruby cannot extinguish. In *Love* (2003) the spiritual and financial legacy of long-dead hotel owner Bill Cosey is fought over by his child-bride Heed and his granddaughter Christine, who live together in the shuttered hotel. However, *A Mercy* (2008), set in the lawless, slave-holding Virginia of the 1690s, is generally seen as a more successful blending of history and mystery. In this novel Morrison goes further back in time than in any of her previous works to look at the foundations of what would become the world she has explored in her earlier novels.

Bibliography

Toni Morrison's fiction is readily available in paperback format.

Elizabeth Ann Beaulieu, ed., *The Toni Morrison Encyclopedia* (Westport, CT, 2003).
J. Brooks Bouson, *Quiet as It's Kept: Shame, Trauma, and Race in the Novels of Toni Morrison* (Albany, NY, 2000).
Lucille P. Fultz, *Toni Morrison: Playing with Difference* (Urbana, 2003).
Andrea O'Reilly, *Toni Morrison and Motherhood: A Politics of the Heart* (Albany, NY, 2004).

John Updike (1932–2009)

John Updike published more than 20 novels, many short stories, and hundreds of essays, reviews and poems, many of them in *The New Yorker*, the magazine with which he was associated for much of his career. His wide-ranging literary interests led him to write on many contemporary writers, American and foreign, as well as on some of the canonical American writers of the nineteenth and early twentieth centuries. He was always willing to be fair and appreciative of authors who did not write or think as he did. His interest was finally in the quality of the writing and in the wide range of possibilities available to the art of fiction. But if his critical interests were wide ranging, the characters, settings, and issues in his fiction were usually more narrowly focused. His novels and stories usually concerned middle-class Americans in small towns or the suburbs whose lives revolved around religious doubt, love, boredom, marriage, adultery, children, and facing the inevitable passage of time. But these subjects were treated with a wit and variety that, along with his lyrical prose, led Updike to be viewed from early in his career as a writer of the highest rank.

Updike was born in Shillington, Pennsylvania, the "Olinger" of a number of short stories and the setting for his novel *The Centaur*. His father was a poorly paid mathematics teacher at the local high school and his mother worked in a department store and wrote short stories. When Updike was 13 the family moved to a sandstone farmhouse owned by his mother's family 11 miles from Shillington, and there, Updike later claimed, his literary ambitions grew "out of sheer boredom." He wrote extensively in high school, and continued writing, and drawing cartoons, once he began attending Harvard University on a tuition scholarship. He married a Radcliffe student, Mary Pennington, in 1953, and the following year graduated with a Knox

Fellowship, which allowed him to attend the Ruskin School of Drawing and Fine Art in Oxford, England from 1954 to 1955. He then moved to New York City, sold some stories and poems to *The New Yorker*, and took a job as a staff writer on the magazine. In 1957 he resigned his position and moved with his family to Ipswich, Massachusetts, to concentrate on freelance writing. Updike and Mary Pennington separated in 1974, divorcing in 1976, and he married Martha Bernhard in 1977. As critics have noticed, there are many parallels between the gradual break-up of the first marriage and Updike's series of short stories concerning Joan and Richard Maple. These were collected as *Too Far to Go: The Maples Stories* (1979).

Updike's first book was a book of poetry, *The Carpentered Hen and Other Tame Creatures* (1958), but he published his first novel, *The Poorhouse Fair*, the following year.

Set in 1978, 20 years into the future from the date of the novel's writing, in a Home for the Aged, the book centers upon a moral debate between efficient administrative "prefect" Stephen Conner and ex-teacher John Hook, who is in his nineties. Hook is based on Updike's grandfather John F. Hoyer, who had died in 1953. The heartlessness of efficiency set against a rebellious imagination is one of the major themes of Updike's subsequent fiction, and is related to his interest in the difficulty of maintaining faith in a scientific age. When the book was reissued in 1977 Updike made a few corrections to the chronology and offered his own assessment of the novel in his introduction.

Updike's next book, *Rabbit, Run* (1960), is probably his best-known work. The novel is the first of four that follow the story of Harry "Rabbit" Angstrom, the following three appearing at roughly 10-year intervals. In this first of the series, Rabbit – there are many allusions to the Peter Rabbit stories – is dissatisfied with his sales job and a marriage resulting from an unplanned pregnancy, seeing them as a poor result of the aspirations he held when a high school basketball star. Rabbit is faced with a number of choices, torn between accepting his responsibilities and his sense that he could still achieve something of his earlier aspirations. Like the later Rabbit novels, the book is written in the present tense and there is little direct evaluation by the author of Rabbit's actions and decisions. There are, however, various judgments offered by the other characters. Rabbit runs from his pregnant wife, starts an adulterous affair with Ruth Beyer, is partly responsible for the death of his newly born daughter, and is faced with Ruth's threat that if he doesn't divorce his wife she will abort their child. The advice of two ministers is of little help to Rabbit in his anxiety about whether to return to his wife or stay with his mistress, and running from both is not necessarily any solution either. His difficult choice is, as the novel puts it, between "the right way and the good way."

Rabbit Redux (1971) finds the protagonist aged 36 and back with wife Janice. Updike picks up the narrative in the year of writing the novel, not where the story left off in the first book. He continues this practice with the next two books; thus Rabbit ages with his creator, and the books remain contemporary with the time of their composition. In this second of the series, which has been variously judged as both the least and the most interesting, Janice leaves Rabbit, and he takes into the house a black Vietnam veteran and a hippie runaway. Also on the scene is Rabbit's now teenaged son Nelson. The novel illustrates Rabbit's conservative politics and unthinking acceptance of received opinions, although during the course of events he has to examine some of these views. Rabbit's home is burnt by local citizens objecting to the interracial relationship of his house guests, and Rabbit finds himself indirectly responsible for another death. By the time of *Rabbit Is Rich* (1981) the golf-playing Rabbit is wealthy from his share of his now deceased father-in-law's car business. But material success brings him no closer to happiness or to his elusive sense of greater possibilities. Sex, both within and outside his marriage, provides him with some pleasure, and granddaughter Judy is some compensation for his own lost daughter; however, there is also a possibility that he actually has a daughter, that mistress Ruth Beyer did not abort their child. *Rabbit at Rest* (1990) sees Rabbit through retirement and death. A number of incidents and images in this final novel of the series parallel features of the first, including Rabbit's return to the basketball court. Rabbit remains a character who is not particularly sympathetic, who is even cruel at times to others, including his wife and the various women he sleeps with. Son Nelson causes him trouble, as does his car business; he commits adultery with his daughter-in-law, and near the end is still running. Updike published the four books together in 1995 as *Rabbit Angstrom: A Tetralogy*, adding an introduction and revising some factual and chronological details to unify the series, the last two novels of which were both awarded the Pulitzer Prize for fiction.

The Rabbit series is not the only group of related novels that Updike published, although it is his best known. Successful and much-traveled philandering Jewish writer Henry Bech is the subject of three collections of comic short stories: *Bech: A Book* (1970), *Bech Is Back* (1982), and *Bech at Bay* (1998). The first of the stories, "The Bulgarian Poetess," resulted from Updike's visit to the Soviet Union and Eastern Europe in 1964 as part of a State Department Cultural Exchange Program. Bech sometimes writes to and interviews Updike himself, and is in some ways Updike's ironic homage to what he recognized as the important contributions to post-war American fiction of such writers as Saul Bellow, Norman Mailer, and Philip Roth. The trilogy *A Month of Sundays* (1975), *Roger's Version* (1986), and *S* (1988) echo characters and incidents from Hawthorne's *The Scarlet Letter*. Like Hawthorne's novel, the trilogy explores the relationships of sex, religion, guilt, and sin. In the first novel the Reverend Thomas Marshfield, the Dimmesdale figure, seduces motel manager Ms. Prynne. In the second, a novel containing more scientific lore than any of Updike's other fictions, the narrator is theology professor Roger Lambert and, married to Esther, is the Roger Chillingworth figure. In the third of the series, the "S" of the title is Sarah Worth, descended from the Prynne family and with a daughter named Pearl. This epistolary novel is in Sarah's voice, her series of letters and audio tapes telling of the determined search for independence that makes her the target of a spiritual leader more lecherous than spiritual, although she finally sees through the fraud. Like Hawthorne's Hester Prynne, she exposes the hypocrisy of her community while herself being fraught with contradictions. Something of a companion novel is *The Witches of Eastwick* (1984), which explores evil and the occult in a contemporary suburban setting through a narrative filled with comic and parodic invention. Updike's last novel, *The Widows of Eastwick* (2008), published the year before his death, picks up the story of the three central characters 30 years after their escapades in the earlier book.

A number of other novels deserve particular mention in Updike's extensive *oeuvre*. *The Centaur* (1963), Updike's third novel, won him the National Book Award. Peter Caldwell tells the story of his science teacher father retrospectively from middle age, learning to appreciate his father more fully as he recounts the narrative. The quietly heroic sacrifices of George Caldwell, who is based on Updike's father Wesley, are paralleled in the book by the story of Chiron, the centaur who resisted Zeus to champion man, and who gave up his immortality to help Prometheus. The novel is arguably the author's most experimental fiction. Updike's biggest commercial success was *Couples* (1968), in which stories of multiple suburban adulteries illustrate a lifestyle where private pleasures far outweigh social commitment, and sex for many is a substitute for lost religious faith. For Updike, as elsewhere in his fiction, spiritual values beyond the merely physical might be found, but not through separation of the physical and the secular. George Caldwell's mythic dimension in *The Centaur* illustrates the importance of the unity, while in the central relationship of *Couples*, Piet Hanema must leave the angelic Angela for the earthy Foxy Whitman. Updike leaves suburbia and small towns behind in *The Coup* (1978), a novel set in the fictional country of Kush, a state that resembles Ethiopia. America is still very much a presence in this novel despite the foreign setting. Updike has suggested that the novel is an allegory of Watergate, and Marxist President Felix Ellelloù has a strong distrust of American interests in his country, although he learned his Marxism while an exchange student in the United States.

When Updike died of cancer in January 2009, he had published around 60 books, the result of a disciplined six-days-a-week writing regime. The closest that he came to overt autobiography is his *Self-Consciousness: Memoirs* (1989), in which he writes, among other things, of his home town, the psoriasis and stuttering that sometimes made him very self-conscious, his conservative position on the Vietnam War, and his thoughts on the possibility of an afterlife.

Bibliography

Most of John Updike's novels are available in paperback format or in hardcover from Alfred A. Knopf.

Jack De Bellis, ed., *The John Updike Encyclopedia* (Westport, CT, 2000).
Stacey Olster, ed., *The Cambridge Companion to John Updike* (Cambridge, 2006).
William H. Pritchard, *Updike: America's Man of Letters* (South Royalton, VT, 2000).
James A. Schiff, *John Updike Revisited* (New York, 1998).

Philip Roth (b.1933)

The relationship between autobiography and fiction is often a central issue in Philip Roth's books, particularly in his middle and late novels. Public details of Roth's life and career are woven provocatively and comically into narratives that are otherwise clearly fiction. Sometimes readers are teasingly invited to see parallels between the author and a protagonist, and at other times the tendency to such identification is mocked. In *Operation Shylock* (1993), for example, a character named Philip Roth, a writer, finds that a man in Israel is posing as Philip Roth. And the supposedly autobiographical *The Facts: A Novelist's Autobiography* (1988) begins with a letter from Roth to fictional Nathan Zuckerman asking advice, which Zuckerman answers in an epilogue by suggesting that Roth stick to fiction.

Roth was born in Newark, New Jersey, into a lower-middle-class Jewish family. After attending public high school he enrolled in the Newark College branch of Rutgers University, before transferring to Bucknell. At Bucknell, where he received a BA in 1954, he founded, edited, and wrote for the university's literary magazine. He began graduate work at the University of Chicago the same year, studying in a city associated with Saul Bellow, one of the writers whose career is often seen as an important and lasting influence on Roth's own. After receiving an MA in 1955, he joined the US Army anticipating being drafted, but was injured in basic training and discharged the following year. While in the army, and during his one semester of graduate study after his discharge, he began writing and publishing the stories and the novella that would appear in his first book, meanwhile supporting himself by teaching freshman composition at the university and writing reviews for *The New Republic*. Roth resigned his teaching position in 1958 and moved to New York City. In 1959 he married Margaret Williams. The two separated in

The Twentieth-Century American Fiction Handbook   By Christopher MacGowan
© 2011 Christopher MacGowan

1962 and in 1968 she died in an automobile accident. The troubled marriage is fictionalized in Roth's 1974 novel *My Life as a Man*.

In the year of his marriage, 1959, Roth published his first book, *Goodbye Columbus and Five Short Stories*, which went on to win the National Book Award. The title story contrasts the family of Newark-born narrator Neil Klugman with the upwardly mobile family of his girlfriend, Radcliffe-educated Brenda Patimkin. The Patimkins are striving for acceptance in the upper-class Protestant world of country clubs and material success, and to that end try to put their Jewish heritage behind them. Neil himself, while he understands Yiddish, does not follow religious law, but finds himself wary of what is lost in the Patimkins' social climbing. The stories in the book that had earlier received serial publication had already been denounced by some influential rabbis as the work of a "self-hating Jew." The charge was renewed with the appearance of the book, and marked the beginning of many accusations, particularly in response to books published in the early part of Roth's career, that he was anti-Semitic in his portrayal of Jewish characters and culture.

Following two novels that, like his first book, were in a realist mode, *Letting Go* (1962) and *When She Was Good* (1967), the latter a book set outside Jewish culture, Roth published the book with which he is probably still most associated, *Portnoy's Complaint* (1969). In the parody and caricature behind Alex Portnoy's confessions to his psychiatrist, Roth breaks many taboos of good taste. Alex's complaints are about his overbearing mother, ineffectual father, and generally the repressive culture of his Jewish background. His acts of rebellion include excessive masturbation and the desire for gentile girls, the "shiksas" that his mother is always warning him to avoid. Inevitably the novel brought further condemnation from the synagogues, although arguably its targets extend beyond those of Jewish American culture.

In addition to publishing his novels, Roth taught writing courses at a number of institutions through the 1960s, teaching at Iowa, Princeton, the State University of New York at Stony Brook, and the University of Pennsylvania. At the last named he taught for a semester annually into the mid-1970s, and he would later teach at New York's Hunter College from 1988 to 1991. Roth became the youngest member of the National Institute of Arts and Letters when he was elected in 1970. Two years later he was elected to the American Academy of Arts and Sciences.

In 1975 Roth began a relationship with English actress Claire Bloom; they married in 1990, separated in 1993, and divorced the following year. One result of the relationship was that Roth began to live half of the year in London into the late 1980s, and another was the unflattering portrait of

Roth in Bloom's *Leaving a Doll's House: A Memoir* (1996). Bloom's memoir reinforced the charge by some critics that Roth's fiction is deeply misogynistic.

Following *Portnoy's Complaint*, Roth's next novel, *Our Gang (Starring Tricky and His Friends)* (1971), is a political satire on Richard Nixon and his administration, particularly targeting what Roth saw as their abuse of language. *The Breast* (1972) is the fable of a professor who turns into a six-foot female breast, a narrative clearly influenced by Kafka, one of the writers most important to Roth. The protagonist of this novel, David Kepesh, is also at the center of two further novels, *The Professor of Desire* (1977) and *The Dying Animal* (2001).

Between the first two novels featuring David Kepesh, Roth published *The Great American Novel* (1973) and *My Life as a Man* (1974). In *The Great American Novel* narrator Word Smith parodies the writing styles of figures such as Melville, Hawthorne, and Hemingway, and tells the tale of the now defunct Patriot Baseball League. The novel satirizes consumerism, poor taste, and the debasement of language in sporting, political, and religious rhetoric. *My Life as a Man* begins Roth's fuller exploration of the relationships between fiction and biography. In this work he introduced novelist Nathan Zuckerman, who appears in nine further novels over the next three decades. Roth has described Zuckerman as a figure "whose existence was comparable to my own and yet registered a more powerful valence, a life more highly charged and entertaining than my own." Zuckerman's first appearance in this 1974 novel is as the creation of the fictional writer Peter Tarnopol. Two stories supposedly by Tarnopol tell of Zuckerman's child-hood, his rebellion against his Jewish background, his failed marriage, and his wife's death in an automobile accident.

Zuckerman reappears as the central character in a trilogy in which he is mostly interested in writing about himself: *The Ghost Writer* (1979), *Zucker-man Unbound* (1981), *The Anatomy Lesson* (1983), and an epilogue, *The Prague Orgy*, first published when the trilogy was collected in 1985 as *Zuckerman Bound*. *The Ghost Writer* was hailed as a return to form by those commentators who felt that Roth's fiction following *Portnoy's Com-plaint* had been largely unsuccessful. Zuckerman is the narrator in this novel, and he describes visiting writer E. I. Lonoff, a character usually read as an amalgam of Bernard Malamud and Henry Roth. Zuckerman reveres the older, reclusive Jewish writer, who serves as something of a surrogate father for Zuckerman. The situation is complicated by the unhappiness of Lonoff's wife, and by the presence of Amy Bellette, a dark-haired researcher whom Zuckerman imagines is diarist Anne Frank – not dead, but a concentration camp survivor. References to the fiction of Henry James, and to Nathan's disagreement with his father over autobiographical incidents that his father feels will shame the family if published, contribute to the novel's play between fiction and reality.

Zuckerman is a famous author by the time of *Zuckerman Unbound* thanks to his *Portnoy*-like novel *Carnovsky*. Set in 1969, one theme of this second novel in the trilogy is the price of fame. Strangers assume that Zuckerman is one with his protagonist in the famous novel, and address him as Carnovsky. And Zuckerman finds himself being harassed by fellow Newark native Alvin Pepler, a figure who once had fleeting quiz show fame. Zuckerman receives letters accusing him of anti-Semitism, and is forced to recognize how much the publication and success of his novel has hurt his family. His marriage is broken, and when he returns in his chauffeur-driven limousine to view his childhood neighborhood in Newark he finds it an urban ruin. The novel was generally well received, although at least one reviewer wished that "Roth would stop apologizing for *Portnoy's Complaint*."

Zuckerman continues his series of losses in *The Anatomy Lesson*. His parents are dead and he feels distant from the Jewish identity that was so much a part of the subject matter of his fiction. Four women obligingly offer their support and favors, but they help him no more than the alcohol and drugs that he turns to. He begins the novel with back and neck pain, probably psychosomatic, loses the support of important critic Milton Appel, previously an admirer of his writing (as Roth had lost the support of Irving Howe in Howe's 1972 essay "Philip Roth Reconsidered"), suffers writer's block, decides to give up writing for a medical career, and finally suffers a fall which leads to his mouth being wired shut. If the book is Roth's comment on the available subjects of fiction, then the only subject might be the lack of a subject, although the problem is arguably Zuckerman's, not Roth's. At any rate, in *The Prague Orgy*, visiting the birthplace of Kafka to obtain a lost Yiddish manuscript by a writer probably murdered by the Nazis, Zuckerman finds evidence of such repression in 1970s Soviet-dominated Czechoslovakia that he begins to reconsider his own values and writing. The dead end of *The Anatomy Lesson* may now be behind him.

Nathan Zuckerman and his brother Henry are the protagonists of Roth's next novel, *The Counterlife* (1987). The novel's chapters offer alternative versions of their lives, sometimes repeating similar details. Henry dies during an operation in one part of the novel, for example, and survives the operation in another to become a militant Zionist. He takes up Nathan's manuscript when Nathan becomes the one who dies. Nathan's English wife demands to be freed from the text, and she urges Nathan to defy author Philip Roth and to take charge of his own life. The novel is both a commentary upon fiction, the variety of its possible narratives, and the various alternative lives anyone might lead – the title's counter-lives. Roth commented in an interview in the year of the book's publication: "Normally there is a contract between the author and the reader that only gets torn up at the end of the book. In this book the contract gets torn up at the end of each chapter . . . We are all writing fictitious versions of our lives all the time, contradictory but mutually entangling stories that, however subtly or grossly falsified, constitute our hold on reality and are the closest thing we have to the truth."

Definitions of Jewishness and degrees of anti-Semitism are a central issue of *The Counterlife*, as they continue to be in Roth's next two self-reflexive novels, *Deception* (1990) and *Operation Shylock: A Confession* (1993). Between these two novels Roth published a well-received biography of his father, *Patrimony* (1991). In *Deception* a character named Philip has written Philip Roth's novels, including some that involve a character named Zuckerman. The central issue of fact and fiction here revolves around a diary that Philip's English lover discovers and that Philip insists is actually a writing exercise. *Operation Shylock* is more centrally focused on Israeli issues. Character Philip Roth travels to Israel to confront an imposter with many of his characteristics whose plan is to repatriate Israelis of European and American descent to their countries of origin. The purpose of the plan is to avoid what he sees as the inevitably violent consequences of Zionism. While, like many other post-modern narratives, the novel highlights the fragility of assumptions about narrative and character continuity, it is more unusual in its concern with broader issues of contemporary politics.

Sabbath's Theater (1995) leaves the self-reflexive mode behind somewhat, although the protagonist, elderly and suicidal Mickey Sabbath, is usually read as a Portnoy-like character now turned elderly. Although the novel received mixed reviews, it won Roth a National Book Award. And his next novel, *American Pastoral* (1997), won a Pulitzer Prize. In *American Pastoral* Nathan Zuckerman returns, this time to recall his Newark childhood, and to relate, mostly through his imagination, the story of a figure whom the young Nathan greatly admired in high school, Seymour "Swede" Levov. Although Jewish, Levov is not the angst-ridden figure of much of Roth's fiction. He is an athletic hero, serves in the marines, marries an Irish American beauty, joins the family business, and prospers financially. But his success and popularity blind him to the alternative kinds of America that he has to confront when in the late 1960s his pampered daughter rejects her privileged background and joins a group of violent urban terrorists. She is raped, becomes destitute, and takes up a religion of extreme non-violence that, since it extends to plant life, makes eating difficult for her. Unlike the focus of his earlier novels, Roth's interest here is more with the parents and their confused pain over the direction of their children's lives.

Nathan Zuckerman also narrates Roth's next two novels, although, as with *American Pastoral*, he is not the central subject. *I Married a Communist* (1998) does give an account of Nathan's early search for mentors, but the main story is of Marxist Ira Ringold, partly as told to Zuckerman by Ira's brother, Murray. Set in the McCarthy-era 1950s, the novel recounts Ira finding fame as a soap opera actor on radio, marrying cast member Eve Frame, quarreling with her about her daughter from a previous marriage, and, with the marriage over, becoming blacklisted when Eve writes a memoir that exposes him as a communist. The book was generally considered less successful in its attempt to integrate its characters with the wider world of the 1950s than *American Pastoral* had achieved for the 1960s. Many commentators noted the parallels to Roth's relationship with Claire Bloom, and *I Married a Communist* is often seen as Roth's response to Bloom's *Leaving a Doll's House: A Memoir*. The last novel of this trilogy narrated by Zuckerman is *The Human Stain* (2000), in which he tells and imagines the story of lightly colored, non-Jewish Coleman Silk, who passes himself as white and Jewish. In this novel Nathan Zuckerman has reached a passive old age – a perfect position, in some ways, for his unobtrusive and sympathetic portrait of his neighbor and friend.

After the return of David Kepesh in *The Dying Animal*, Nathan Zuckerman reappeared, in what Roth has said is Nathan's final appearance, in *Exit Ghost* (2007). Between these two novels Roth published two others. *The Plot Against America* (2004) is a political fable that imagines a fascist President Charles Lindbergh elected in 1940 on a peace platform sympathetic to the Nazis. Part of the success of the book is the way Roth weaves actual historical events into his fictional history. The book also suggests some implicit parallels with the presidency of George W. Bush. *Everyman* (2006) rehearsed more familiar themes of childhood memories, sexual pleasures, and the onset of old age. *Exit Ghost* brings back, as well as Zuckerman, the legacy of the deceased E. I. Lonoff, as well as the now aged Amy Bellette.

The protagonist of *Indignation* (2008) is young Marcus Messner, who suffers the consequences of trying to think for himself, firstly within his family, and then with the authoritarian Dean at Winesburg College – attendance at which spares Marcus from the Korean War draft. As in *American Pastoral*, the confused and despairing parent – here Marcus's father back in the Jewish neighborhood of Newark – is treated sympathetically in the novel. Marcus's rebellion is far more innocent and typically adolescent than that of Swede's daughter, but the nature of the rebellion and the kind of penalty exacted is one measure of the differences between the 1950s and the 1960s as seen in the two novels.

The prolific Roth, in his late seventies as the new century's first decade ended, showed no sign of slowing down. *The Humbling* appeared in 2009 to mixed reviews, and in October 2010 he published *Nemesis*, a story of failure and guilt set in mid-century New Jersey.

Bibliography

Roth's fiction from 1959 to 1991 has been published in five volumes by The Library of America (2005–2008), and his more recent novels are generally available in paperback format.

Ross Posnock, *Philip Roth's Rude Truths: The Art of Immaturity* (Princeton, 2006).
Elaine B. Safer, *Mocking the Age: The Later Novels of Philip Roth* (Albany, NY, 2006).
Mark Shechner, *Up Society's Ass, Copper: Rereading Philip Roth* (Madison, WI, 2003).
Debra B. Shostak, *Philip Roth – Countertexts, Counterlives* (Columbia, SC, 2004).

Don DeLillo (b.1936)

Don Delillo had been publishing for some time before establishing his reputation with *White Noise* (1985) and confirming it with *Libra* (1988) and *Underworld* (1997). The universe of his novels is one where language, media, and consumerism so package and transmit the real that for many of his characters this secondary version replaces authentic experience. In addition, the novels posit a complex system of connections between corporations and government agencies that produce forces aimed at defining and exploiting the individual. But for all the bleakness of this vision, many commentators find a suggestion of transcendent possibilities in DeLillo's work. The author himself has suggested in interviews that the novel is the form in which the presence of the forces that package and replace the real can best be exposed, and – at least to some extent – might be foiled.

DeLillo was born in an Italian American neighborhood in New York City and received a BA in Communication Arts from Fordham University in 1958. After college he worked as an advertising copywriter for five years, publishing a few short stories, before committing himself to a career as a freelance writer. He began writing his first novel, *Americana*, five years before it was eventually published in 1971. The novel is narrated by former network television executive David Bell, who has realized that while at the network he identified himself entirely in terms of media images. He recalls that his father, a television advertising executive, used his children as an audience to test commercials. In an attempt to break away from this media imprisonment Bell travels west, working with a group making a documentary. But he fails to find any part of America that is not the product of media culture and its images, so he retreats to a desert island, from where he narrates his story. An important part of Bell's search is his retracing President Kennedy's route through Dallas on the day of his assassination. The assassination is central to DeLillo's thinking, particularly in his earlier novels, about the impact of media upon contemporary culture; for DeLillo the Kennedy assassination is the first major media event of the television age.

End Zone (1972), as indicated by the title of the institution that its football-playing narrator attends – Logos College – is concerned with the ordering structures of language. These structures shape themselves in this novel into racial, religious, and cultural stereotypes, and also suggest relationships between sport, violence, and nuclear war. As in *Americana*, the narrator can only avoid these structuring forces by a self-imposed isolation. In the novel that appeared the following year, *Great Jones Street* (1973), set in the world of rock stardom, Bucky Wunderlick tries to withdraw from the media management of his life, only to find that even his withdrawal is exploited for commercial gain. Whether Bucky's attempts to withdraw are eventually successful or not remains an open issue in the novel.

DeLillo ventures into science fiction territory with *Ratner's Star* (1976). A message from a distant galaxy, vastly complex mathematical problems, and an attempt to develop a universal language based on mathematical principles – together with a massive corporation planning to use such knowledge for its own ends – are all part of a narrative that posits the final uncertainty of the cosmos despite any of the systems that try to define it. The overly abstract titles of the book's two sections suggest the structures that try to contain, explain, and thus distort, reality: "Adventures: Field Experiment Number One" and "Reflections: Logicon Project Minus One."

Players (1977) is DeLillo's first novel to incorporate terrorism as one of its main elements, and has contributed to his reputation as a novelist who appears to foresee what will later become major cultural concerns. Pammy and Lyle Wynant are in a bored marriage and both work within systems of control: Lyle on the New York Stock Exchange, and Pammy for an organization called the Grief Management Council. Adultery, and adventures generated from seeing too many spy movies, form part of the couple's unsuccessful attempts to overcome their boredom. Much of the same ground is covered in *Running Dog* (1978), this time involving a US senator, the market in erotica, and the commercial value of a supposedly erotic movie made in Hitler's Berlin bunker in the last days of World War II. DeLillo brought a greater degree of realism into his work in *The Names* (1982), as he would in the novels that followed. The novel is set chiefly in Greece and India, and concerns a murderous, international cult that tries to counter chaos through its ordered, systematic actions.

Within the Gladney family of *White Noise* (1985), the parents' lives are ruled by paranoia, and the children, who are the offspring of this and various earlier marriages, live in a world in which the weather forecast on television is truer than the actual weather. In the threatening, electronic, and poisonous surroundings that make up the world of this novel, language shades into euphemism, drugs promise to eliminate the fear of dying, images replace reality, consumerism rules, and the horrific legacy of National Socialism is translated into the abstract academics of Hitler Studies.

White Noise established Delillo as a major novelist, and *Libra* (1988) reaffirmed his position. Involving three years of research, this historical fiction takes up DeLillo's long-held interest in the Kennedy assassination, illustrating his view that a conclusive, linear account of causes and events is impossible and that chaos, randomness, and chance had as much if not more to do with the events in Dallas than any amount of planning. One of the central narratives traces the biography of Lee Harvey Oswald: his manipulation by various groups interested in action against the President, his writing in what he calls his Historic Diary, and his obsession with seeing himself as an actor about to become, through his role as gunman, a star. Another narrative strand explores the schemes of a group of ex-CIA agents who see themselves as victims of the Bay of Pigs fiasco and plan an attempted assassination that will implicate the Castro government they want overthrown. And trying desperately to find an order within the ever-increasing detail that he uncovers about these events is Nicholas Branch, a former CIA man who has been charged by the agency with the task of writing a secret history of the assassination. But the multifaceted construction of DeLillo's novel, moving back and forth between history and the interior dialogues of its characters, offers the only kind of qualified order that the author feels might be discoverable or imaginable.

DeLillo's next novel, *Mao II* (1991), is concerned with the problem of artistic integrity and independence in a consumer culture, and one where, additionally, terrorists exercise more and more control over events. The book was written against the background of Salman Rushdie being condemned to death by the Ayatollah Khomeini for his novel *The Satanic Verses*. In *Mao II* novelist Bill Gray takes a stand against terrorist threats, and against the ideologies of such leaders as the Reverend Moon and Mao Tse-tung, ideologies that would subsume within mass movements the voice and identity of the individual. The novel opens, for example, with a mass wedding ceremony conducted by the Reverend Moon. The book has been seen by many as DeLillo's most personal, although for some commentators he is sometimes so close to his material – DeLillo publicly supported Rushdie's position – that he falls into passages of authorial pontification.

History and fiction continue to mix in *Underworld* (1997), an 827-page novel covering the 1950s to the 1990s which was nominated for a National

Book Award and a Pulitzer Prize, and came second (to Toni Morrison's *Beloved*) in a 2006 *New York Times* poll of distinguished writers, critics, and editors, who were asked: "What Is the Best Work of American Fiction of the Last 25 Years?" Protagonist Nick Shay's story shares space with such figures as J. Edgar Hoover and Lenny Bruce, and such events as the Cuban Missile Crisis, the Soviet Union's atomic weapons program, and a famous baseball game in 1951 (the last two events form the headlines on the *New York Times*'s front page of October 4, 1951, which DeLillo has said inspired the book). DeLillo followed this expansive novel with the much shorter *The Body Artist* (2001), a kind of domestic ghost story that traces the widowed Lauren Hartke as she tries to understand and live with her husband's suicide. Identity becomes mysterious in this novel, both in Lauren's own transformations as a performance artist and in the ambivalent figure she discovers haunting her house – or her mind – a Mr. Tuttle, who seems to know a great deal about her husband and her marriage.

Cosmopolis (2003) received a mixed reception, lacking many of the more realistic elements that usually accompany the fantastic elements in the author's later fiction. The novel tracks billionaire money-manager Eric Packer's day-long ride through a congested and action-filled mid-town Manhattan in his gadget-filled stretch limo on his way to get a haircut. His adventures on the journey include sexual trysts, coming across his wife several times, losing vast sums of money, and encountering an assassin, a riot, and a movie crew.

Some of the mixed reception accorded *Cosmopolis* appears to have come from expectations that this writer who had seemed to prophesy the rise of terrorism would be just the one to put the September 11, 2001 attacks on the World Trade Center at the center of a powerful novel. However, the events of September 11 were the subject of an essay by DeLillo in the December 2001 issue of *Harper's Magazine*, and eventually they were the setting for his 2007 novel *Falling Man*. The novel does not aim at the kind of panoramic view of events undertaken in some of his earlier novels, but focuses on the troubled marriage of a middle-class Manhattan couple and the people who surround them. While the novel's title describes the narrative in a number of ways (and possibly invites comparison to Saul Bellow's 1944 *Dangling Man*), one particular reference is to a performance artist who appears from time to time in the city dangling from a wire and safety harness, his action a reminder of a famous photograph depicting one of the doomed victims from the upper floors of the North Tower falling to his death. The performance artist provokes and disturbs the city with his sudden appearances. The complex reaction of the audience suggests something of the difficulty of making a recent major traumatic event the subject of art, as well as suggesting that

DeLillo himself sees the role of the contemporary novelist as not to shirk such a challenge, whatever the difficulties.

Cosmopolis was followed by *Point Omega* (2010), which has the Iraq war as its background, and centers upon Richard Elster, his daughter Jessie, and a documentary filmmaker named Finley who is interested in filming Elster. Contemporary events and the role of the media, particularly their impact upon human relationships and values, continue to be one of DeLillo's central concerns.

Bibliography

All of Don DeLillo's novels are readily available in paperback format.

Peter Boxall, *Don DeLillo: The Possibility of Fiction* (London, 2006).
Thomas DePietro, ed., *Conversations with Don DeLillo* (Jackson, MS, 2005).
Joseph Dewey, *Beyond Grief and Nothing: A Reading of Don DeLillo* (Columbia, SC, 2006).
John N. Duvall, ed., *The Cambridge Companion to Don DeLillo* (Cambridge, 2008).

Thomas Pynchon (b.1937)

On the whole, Thomas Pynchon has preferred not to involve himself directly with the publicity and marketing of his books, and his desire for privacy has meant that details of his personal life, even basic biographical details, are few and sometimes speculative. There are few photographs of the author in the public domain. Nevertheless some biographical details are matters of public record, and Pynchon himself sometimes provides hints in the essays, reviews, and introductions that he publishes from time to time.

Pynchon was born in Glen Cove, on Long Island, New York, and grew up in nearby Oyster Bay, where he attended high school. He entered Cornell University in 1953 to study engineering physics, took two years off to serve in the US Navy, and completed his degree, having switched to English, in 1959. Possibly, while at Cornell, he attended some of the classes taught by Vladimir Nabokov, whose work is in some ways a forerunner to Pynchon's own.

Pynchon began to publish stories in some leading literary reviews in the years just before and just after graduation. He republished five of them in *Slow Learner* (1984) and added an extraordinary introduction in which he apologizes to the reader for what he now sees as the faults of most of the stories. There are, he warns the reader, "some mighty tiresome passages." He excuses their publication on the grounds that they might at least show beginning writers what faults to avoid. Of the best known and most frequently anthologized of these stories, "Entropy," Pynchon claims that when writing the story he knew very little about entropy, and that he still does not fully understand it. Yet discussion of Pynchon's work often uses the role of entropy in his fiction as a starting point. Of particular interest in this volume is the story "Under the Rose," which Pynchon revised for chapter three of *V*, and, despite Pynchon's caveats, "Entropy." The latter story describes the events in two apartments, one on the second floor and one on the third floor of the same building. In one apartment a temporary order is imposed on increasing disorder, while in the other order threatens to wind down to a halt. The relationship of order to chaos is a central one in Pynchon's fiction, along with questions about who is imposing the order, whether it is imagined or imposed by some authoritarian force, and the degrees of isolation or community that might be the result of such order.

In the early 1960s Pynchon worked for the Boeing Company in Seattle as a technical writer, an experience which probably contributed to the presence of the Yoyodyne Corporation in his first two novels. The first of them, *V*, was published in 1963. Two separate stories come together at the end of the novel – coming together, as many have observed, in the V of the title. In the first, the somewhat passive Benny Profane moves around, from Norfolk, Virginia, to New York City, accompanied by a barmaid from Malta named Paola Maijstral, and a group who call themselves the Whole Sick Crew. Meanwhile Herbert Stencil, whose diplomat father left a journal containing a reference to the enigmatic "V," tries to track down the identity of the female figure designated by the letter. Stencil's narrative covers many of the major political events of the first half of the twentieth century, events in which the enigmatic V may or may not have made an appearance. As happens often in Pynchon's work, the reader's task takes on some of the quest characteristics of the central character, in this case evaluating possible clues to the identity of the elusive V, and looking for connections between the two story threads. The act of reading and interpretation is a major issue in *V* and in all of Pynchon's subsequent fiction, as are the elusive relation-ships between fact and fiction, and the assumptions behind the kind of historical and fictional genres that conventionally record them.

In the dismissive remarks about his writing in the introduction to *Slow Learner* Pynchon does not spare his much-praised second novel, *The Crying of Lot 49* (1966). In this book Pynchon explores further the issues of interpretation, coincidence, ambiguity, genre, communication systems, and manipulation. Because the novel has a single narrative point of view and is told chronologically, it is usually the work suggested as the best introduction for readers new to Pynchon's work. Oedipa Maas, whose days as a housewife find their greatest excitement from the hostess of a Tupperware party having perhaps put too much kirsch in the fondue, sets off on a quest to interpret the legacy of Pierce Inverarity. She may be the victim of her own desperate need to believe in a world beyond the mundane; she may be the victim of the malicious plotting of an aggrieved ex-lover; or she may have been introduced to, or stumbled upon, an alternative, underground form of communication practiced by isolated groups, and groups within groups. The alternative system that she may or may not have discovered is in defiance of the monopolistic and monolithic institutions of government, and is an alternative to the cultural, commercial, and political forces that push people toward conformity – toward the mass that echoes Oedipa's name. It is no surprise that in 2003 Pynchon contributed an introduction to a reissue of George Orwell's novel of totalitarian nightmare, *1984*.

The 760-page *Gravity's Rainbow* (1973) secured Pynchon's reputation, although it was not to the taste of the editorial board of the Pulitzer Prize committee. The fiction jury unanimously recommended the novel for the prize, but in rejecting the recommendation various members of the full board reportedly found the book "unreadable," "turgid," "overwritten," and in parts "obscene." The novel did win the National Book Award (shared with Isaac B. Singer's *A Crown of Feathers*). Like Pynchon's previous novels, the book challenges conventional ideas of the literary, leaving ambivalent the status of many key episodes, and through a series of false leads raising questions about the importance or irrelevance of many of its over 400 characters. The book has multiple narrators, multiple intersecting plots and subplots, multiple digressions, and is encyclopedic in the range of subjects that it covers. The main narrative is set in the closing months of World War II and the months that follow, where the gradually deteriorating US Army Lieutenant Tyrone Slothrop (his name an anagram of sloth and entropy) searches for a rocket numbered 00000 with a special component called the S-Gerät, and is in turn being followed by various others with various motives. The book's range of knowledge, comic invention, and ambition have been almost universally praised, guidebooks have appeared to help with the dense and multiple allusions, and the book has inevitably been the subject of many and varied interpretations.

Apart from publishing the early stories of *Slow Learner* in 1984, Pynchon did not produce another book for 17 years, although a few essays and reviews appeared from time to time. When *Vineland* (1990) was published it was generally met with reviews more mixed than those of Pynchon's previous novels. Set in northern California in the 1980s, when a group returns to the scenes of their 1960s hippie community, the novel sets the world of Ronald Reagan's America against the hippie group's spontaneity and independence. The novel has more references to popular culture than Pynchon's earlier books, and less esoteric scholarly allusions. The world of *Vineland* is slightly less dark, less a world inviting paranoia in its characters, than the previous three novels.

In 1990 Pynchon married his literary agent, Melanie Jackson, and dedicated his next book, *Mason & Dixon* (1997), to her and to their son Jackson. This novel, which returns to the length of *Gravity's Rainbow*, is written in the language and style of eighteenth-century histories. But as always in Pynchon's work, the narrative calls into question the reliability of any one version of the past, or any one idea of order. Set just before the Revolutionary War, the central characters are the title's Charles Mason and Jeremiah Dixon, melancholy astronomer and more boisterous surveyor, who drew the famous line separating North and South. For many readers, the two characters are the most fully drawn in all of Pynchon's fiction. The story is narrated by the Reverend Wikes Cherrycoke in his sister's Philadelphia parlor, and told to a shifting audience of relatives young and old. Arguably his narrative shifts in emphasis depending on his audience at any particular time. Along with details from historical record, the tale incorporates myth, fantasy, anecdote, digressions, and a parade of such historical figures as Benjamin Franklin, George Washington, Thomas Jefferson, and Samuel Johnson. While the story is set in the Age of Reason, science and reason cannot explain clocks that can talk to each other, an amorous automated duck, a man who metamorphoses into a beaver, and a Learned Dog – all of which turn up in this novel.

Against the Day (2006) at 1085 pages is even longer than *Gravity's Rainbow* and *Mason & Dixon*. The novel is set in the two decades leading up to World War I and features the multiple array of characters, plots, subplots, histories, and puzzles now familiar to Pynchon's readers. The book is told in the style of a number of genres, the framing device being the adventures of the Chums of Chance, a *Boy's Own* set of characters sailing the skies in their hydrogen airship. The two main narratives, more often left behind than followed, involve the Traverse family seeking revenge for the murder of their father, and a complex set of intrigues taking place across Europe that are leading inexorably to the Great War. The novel divided critics, although the general assessment was that for all the brilliant set pieces and the comic inventiveness the multiple threads of the novel finally did not quite cohere, and that none of the characters have the substance that the previous novel brought to its portraits of Mason and Dixon. *Inherent Vice* (2009) keeps to the framework of the mystery mode; here the ethos of Raymond Chandler and Dashiell Hammett is set in 1970, at the end of hippie dreams of lethargic freedom. The world of Orwell's *1984* is on the horizon.

There is no general agreement on which is Pynchon's most important novel. *Gravity's Rainbow* is most often cited, but *Mason & Dixon* has its supporters, and some would argue for *Against the Day*. *The Crying of Lot 49* is generally considered too short to be in the running, yet it draws few of the complaints that are made even by the most enthusiastic readers of the other novels – that sections could be cut, that the comedy sometimes falls flat, that there is dazzle where there might be depth. What is almost universally agreed is that since his first novel in 1963, the provocative, entertaining, and reclusive Pynchon has been one America's major novelists.

Bibliography

All of Pynchon's novels are available in paperback format.

Ian D. Copestake, ed., *American Postmodernity: Essays on the Recent Fiction of Thomas Pynchon* (Oxford and New York, 2003).

Stefan Mattessich, *Lines of Flight: Discursive Time and Countercultural Desire in the Works of Thomas Pynchon* (Durham, NC, 2002).

Tony Tanner, *"The Rubbish-Tip for Subjunctive Hopes: Thomas Pynchon's Mason & Dixon,"* in *The American Mystery* (Cambridge, 2000), pp. 222–238.

Weisenburger Steven, *A Gravity's Rainbow Companion: Sources and Contexts for Pynchon's Novel* (Athens, GA, 2006).

Joyce Carol Oates (b.1938)

Joyce Carol Oates is such a prolific writer that sometimes the sheer range and number of her publications become themselves the subject of discussion. In interviews she has described her disciplined routine of writing up to 10 hours a day, of writing first drafts in longhand, and putting finished manuscripts aside for a period in order to review them later from a less immediate perspective. She has published at least one book a year since her first in 1963, and by 2004 was close to having published 100. In addition to her novels she has published short stories, poetry, essays, reviews, plays, young adult fiction, children's books, and – under pseudonyms – mysteries and thrillers. She is often compared to Flannery O'Connor in that much of her fiction is concerned with themes of violence, obsession, and sexuality, sometimes accompanied by elements of gothic horror. Her fiction regularly explores the relationship of inherited traits and experience as they make up a character's motivation, identity, and fate, often depicting the complex relationships within families, sometimes across generations. Sudden acts of evil or violence in her fiction can shatter individual lives or whole families. At times real events are behind the deaths, violence, or tragedy in her fictions; for example *Black Water* (1992) contains incidents similar to the Chappaquiddick incident involving Senator Edward Kennedy, and *Blonde* (2000) is a fictional account of the life of Marilyn Monroe, narrated posthumously by the actress herself. Both of these books were finalists for the Pulitzer Prize. The novel *My Sister, My Love: The Intimate Story of Skyler Rampike* (2008) echoes the case of the murdered six-year-old JonBenet Ramsey, and the title story of *Dear Husband* (2009) recalls the drowning by Andrea Yates of her own children.

The Twentieth-Century American Fiction Handbook   By Christopher MacGowan
© 2011 Christopher MacGowan

Oates was born into a working-class family in Lockport, New York State. Both her father and grandfather were steel mill workers. Many of her novels are set in the western part of the state and reflect the rural community of her childhood. She graduated from Syracuse University in 1960 with a degree in English, and received an MA from the University of Wisconsin, Madison, in 1961, where she met and married fellow graduate student Raymond Smith. She started work on a doctoral degree at Rice University the following year but it was never completed. In 1962 she began the teaching career which would take her to the University of Detroit, the University of Windsor in Ontario, and finally to Princeton University. (Detroit and its suburbs is another setting that appears in a number of Oates's novels.) Oates and her husband founded *The Ontario Review* while at Windsor, and the journal published its last issue in 2008 when Smith died. In 2009 Oates married Charles Gross, a psychology professor at Princeton.

Oates's talent began to be recognized early. While still an undergraduate at Syracuse she won the *Mademoiselle* college fiction prize. Her first book was *By the North Gate* (1963), a collection of stories, followed by her first novel, *With Shuddering Fall*, the following year. The first of her books to gain significant attention was *A Garden of Earthly Delights* (1967), which was nominated for a National Book Award, as were three novels that followed: *Expensive People* (1968), *them* (1969), and *Wonderland* (1971). Of the four, *them* went on to win the award.

A Garden of Earthly Delights tells the story of Clara Walpole, born in a migrant labor camp, and the male figures most important to her attempts to rise out of poverty: her abusive father, manipulative lover, wealthy farmer husband, and dysfunctional illegitimate son. The novel is the first of what Oates originally intended as a trilogy covering different classes in American society, but when she published *Wonderland* the trilogy became a quartet. The four books were reissued under the collective title "The Wonderland Quartet" 40 years later. For the reissue Oates substantially rewrote *A Garden of Earthly Delights* ("to present its original characters more clearly," she explained, "unoccluded by an eager young writer's prose"). *Expensive People* is the first-person confession of Richard Everett, child of a privileged but careless upbringing, whose father is caught up in his corporate successes, and whose mother moves between affluent country club living and mysterious trips away from her family to mix in more bohemian circles. The setting for *them* is urban Detroit. The novel follows three generations of the working-class Wendall family, beginning in the Depression and leading up to the Detroit riots of 1967. The "them" of the title, as Oates explained in her 1999 essay, "*Them* Revisited," are the "poor whites" separate from "us" the readers, "in our democratic nation, a category of *them* at whom we can gaze with pity, awe, revulsion, moral superiority, as if across an abyss." The fourth novel, *Wonderland*, is at bottom an examination of the nature of personality, its shifting shapes and forms suggesting the changing shapes of Alice in the Lewis Carroll novel that gives Oates's book its title. Jesse, whose father shoots himself and the rest of the family, struggles to discover an identity that is his own rather than one that is merely a response to the succession of sometimes violent and grotesque events of his life. Oates rewrote the ending of this novel for the 1972 paperback printing, giving the novel slightly less of a downbeat conclusion.

With *Bellefleur* (1980) Oates produced the first of a number of ambitious gothic novels, moving away for this series from the realism of her earlier work. The 1980 novel was followed by *A Bloodsmoor Romance* (1982) and *Mysteries of Winterthurn* (1984). *Bellefleur* tells the story of various members of the rich and influential Bellefleur family over several generations. The family home is an enormous mansion in familiar Oates territory in New York State. The narrative's temporal contradictions and shape-shifting events are described in realistic terms, only obeying, as Oates pointed out in an "Author's Note," the logic of the imagination: "the implausible is granted an authority and honored with a complexity usually reserved for realistic fiction." "*Bellefleur* is a region," she insists, "a state of the soul, and it does exist; and there, sacrosanct, its laws are utterly logical."

Because It Is Bitter, and Because It Is My Heart (1990) was Oates's fifth novel to be nominated for a National Book Award. Set in the late 1950s and early 1960s, the book describes how the prevailing racial attitudes of the time prevent the two central characters, Iris and Jinx, who are white and black, from fulfilling the attraction that they feel for each other. *We Were the Mulvaneys* (1996) examines the disintegration of the prosperous Mulvaney family, as told in retrospect by the youngest child, Judd; a disintegration which begins with the rape of Judd's 17-year-old sister Marianne by a high school senior. The aftermath of the assault deeply affects the lives of both parents and all of the children. Marianne's brother Patrick, for example, becomes obsessed with avenging his sister, while the father, Michael, becomes an alcoholic, his business goes to pieces, and his marriage is ruined. Only many years later, with the father gone and lives mended to some extent by time, is healing possible. This novel became Oates's first major bestseller when it was chosen in 2001 for the popular book club run by Oprah Winfrey.

In the first decade of the new century three of Oates's novels that have received particular attention are *Blonde* (2000), a finalist for both the Pulitzer Prize and the National Book Award; *The Falls* (2004), which uses Niagara Falls to reflect the powerful forces that impact upon the lives of the novel's characters; and *The Gravedigger's Daughter* (2007). *The Gravedigger's*

Daughter, Oates's thirty-sixth novel, is based upon the biography of her grandmother. This is a story, Oates has said, that she felt she could tell only after both of her parents had passed away.

Of the many volumes of well-received, often prize-winning, short stories that Oates has collected, a later volume of particular interest is *Wild Nights!* (2008), in which she imagines the last days of Edgar Allen Poe, Emily Dickinson, Henry James, Mark Twain, and Ernest Hemingway. As well as the fascination of a talented writer writing on other writers, and on the subject of writing itself, Oates also speculates interestingly on how those writers might have viewed their contemporary and future readers.

Oates has demonstrated her own sense of some of the century's most important American writers in her selection for *The Best American Essays of the Century* (2000), co-edited with Robert Atwan. The selection mirrors the range of American voices across the century, and includes Mark Twain, T. S. Eliot, Zora Neale Hurston, James Baldwin, Vladimir Nabokov, E. B. White, Eudora Welty, and Joan Didion. A useful complementary volume is her edition of *The Best New American Voices 2003* (2002). These 15 stories, taken from work produced in writing programs from across the country, give some indication of the kind of contemporary writing that Oates most admires.

Bibliography

Joyce Carol Oates's most important novels and story collections are available in paperback format.

Gavin Cologne-Brookes, *Dark Eyes on America: The Novels of Joyce Carol Oates* (Baton Rouge, 2005).
Brenda O. Daly, *Lavish Self-Divisions: The Novels of Joyce Carol Oates* (Jackson, MS, 1996).
Greg Johnson, *Invisible Writer: A Biography of Joyce Carol Oates* (New York, 1998).
Monica Loeb, *Literary Marriages: A Study of Intertextuality in a Series of Short Stories by Joyce Carol Oates* (Bern, 2002).

Raymond Carver (1938–1988)

Raymond Carver made his reputation writing short stories, a form imposed on him to a large extent by economic necessity. His stories are often about blue-collar families living lives of quiet despair or feeling emotions they can barely articulate or comprehend – feelings heightened, not deadened, by alcohol. In interviews he often named Hemingway and Chekhov as two of the writers he most admired, and one of his last stories, "The Errand," centers upon the early death of the Russian writer. Carver admired Chekhov's view that stories did not need to be about extraordinary people accomplishing extraordinary and memorable deeds. This ordinariness was matched, particularly in Carver's earlier stories, by a minimalist style that arguably went even further than Hemingway's in its paring down of detail.

Carver was born in Clatskanie, Oregon. His father worked as a laborer and his mother at such transient jobs as sales clerk or waitress. The family moved around a lot during his childhood, as his father found work at lumber mills first in Washington State and then in California. Carver married early, soon after finishing high school in 1956, and over the next two years he and Maryann Burk had two children. Both parents struggled to provide for the family while holding various low-paying jobs, but were also determined to further their educations beyond high school. Carver had already developed the desire to write before entering college, and when he enrolled in 1958 at Chico State College, he was fortunate to have as a writing teacher John Gardner, not yet published but later to become a nationally known novelist. As Carver recalled in his essay "John Gardner: The Writer as Teacher," Gardner helped him to focus his reading, and generously gave him the key to his faculty office to use at weekends, knowing that Carver needed a quiet place to write. There, Carver goes on to say, surrounded by Gardner's boxes of

The Twentieth-Century American Fiction Handbook   By Christopher MacGowan
© 2011 Christopher MacGowan

unpublished manuscripts, "I undertook my first serious attempts at writing." With Gardner's encouragement Carver founded, and edited, the first issue of a short-lived literary magazine, *Selection*. Included among its pages in the first issue was a poem sent in by William Carlos Williams, who would become a major influence on Carver's poetry, and in the second issue appeared Carver's first published story, "The Furious Seasons" (reprinted in a revised version in *Call If You Need Me* [2001]). After a stint at a sawmill in 1960, Carver transferred to Humboldt State College, where he co-founded another magazine, *Toyon*, which published more of his early stories.

When Carver graduated from Humboldt in 1963 he enrolled at the Iowa Writers' Workshop on a small scholarship, but, needing to support his family, he returned to California after a few months and found work as a janitor at a hospital. He wrote in whatever spare time he could manage to set aside, sending out his stories. In 1966 he joined a poetry workshop at Sacramento State College, where the English Club in 1968 published a collection of his poems. But two important events occurred in 1967 that began to change his writing career. The first was that he obtained his first professional job, working as an editor for Science Research Associates in Palo Alto. As a result of this position he had more time to write, and he met writer and editor Gordon Lish, who worked nearby and would have an impact upon Carver's career for some years to come. The other major event was that a story he had published in a Chicago magazine in December 1966 was selected by Martha Foley for the prominent annual, *The Best American Stories 1967*. The story, "Will You Please Be Quiet, Please," became the title story of Carver's first major collection in 1976.

The skill of "Will You Please Be Quiet, Please?" lies in the way that Carver illustrates the gradual escalation of an exchange between husband and wife, from an apparently casual question that has a private meaning for her, into a revelation insisted upon, despite himself, by the husband. The story then follows the husband out into the seedy bars and dance parlors where he tries both to understand and to forget the revelation. But he really has nowhere else to go, and his return to an ambiguous sexual healing might be the saving of his marriage, or the beginning of a long period of torment for husband, wife, and children.

Carver stayed with Science Research Associates until 1970, although he took a year's leave while working there to be with his wife when she won a scholarship to Tel Aviv University. As Carver admitted in later interviews, alcoholism became a serious problem for him around this time. Nevertheless, with severance pay from Science Research Associates and a National Endowment for the Arts Award, he had the free time to write a number of the stories that would later be part of his first major collection. Meanwhile, a second volume of poems, *Winter Insomnia*, appeared in 1970.

As a result of Carver's increasing prominence he obtained a number of one-year visiting positions in writing programs. Three of these were at University of California campuses – Santa Cruz, Berkeley, and Santa Barbara – and another at the University of Iowa. The Capra Press in Santa Barbara published limited editions of his prose and poetry, but his work received national circulation when he placed both poems and stories with *Esquire*, where Gordon Lish was now fiction editor. For three successive years, 1973 through 1975, Carver's stories were included in the annual volume *Prize Stories: The O. Henry Awards*. His stories began to appear regularly in various publications, although many of them were magazines read chiefly by academics and other writers. However, alongside this increasing success Carver's alcoholism grew worse, and because of it he was unable to complete his year at Santa Barbara. Finally, after a number of hospitalizations, on June 2, 1977, he was able to stop drinking.

In 1976 Gordon Lish placed 22 of Carver's stories with McGraw-Hill, and they formed his first major collection, *Will You Please Be Quiet, Please?* The volume went on to be nominated for a National Book Award. The stories were written between 1962 and 1975 and because of this time span the book is less cohesive than Carver's later collections. The three stories from the O. *Henry Awards* volumes are included: "What Is It?," "Put Yourself in My Shoes," and "Are You a Doctor?" Many of the stories in the collection cover the lives of working people with low-paying jobs, dissatisfied with and trapped in their lives. In "Put Yourself in My Shoes," a writer trying to write without much success encounters a bitter couple who tell him stories they insist are excellent material for fiction. In the course of telling their stories they provide their reluctant listener with an important lesson about human sympathy. Whether the lesson destroys his future as a writer, or is the beginning of his ability to write more successfully, is left an open question – although Carver in an interview suggested the more positive reading. This story is probably as close as Carver gets to meta-fiction, and is often read as his own comment on storytelling.

Will You Please Be Quiet, Please? was dedicated to Maryann Carver, but around the time of its publication the couple began to live apart, and they divorced in 1982. Maryann Carver has written her own affectionate if sometimes grim record of her years with the writer, *What It Used To Be Like: A Portrait of My Marriage to Raymond Carver* (2006). At the end of 1977 Carver met poet Tess Gallagher. In 1979 they began living together, and they were married in 1988 in the last weeks of Carver's life. Gallagher has written her own account of the impact of Carver on her life in *Soul Barnacles: Ten More Years With Ray* (2000).

Following the success of *Will You Please Be Quiet, Please?*, in 1978 Carver won a Guggenheim Fellowship, and in 1978–1979 he was writer-in-residence at the University of Texas, El Paso. In 1980 Carver and Gallagher accepted permanent positions on the creative writing faculty at Syracuse University, and in 1981 Knopf published his second major collection, *What We Talk About When We Talk About Love*. Squalor, bleakness, loss, mere attempts to survive – these are common themes in the stories, which were both praised and criticized for their minimalist narrative style and their lack of introspection. In the title story, two couples talk and drink themselves into a mood that matches the darkness that slowly engulfs them. The story is almost all dialogue, and Carver conveys through minimal extra detail the tension and quiet desperation between the four at the table. Language seems just a cover for the fears, desires, anger, and despair behind the talk of love, talk that finally falls silent, leaving only darkness and "human noise."

In recent years there has been some discussion of the role Gordon Lish played in editing these stories. Lish had now become an editor at Knopf and the archives recording his work with Carver (now at Indiana University's Lilly Library), suggest that, particularly in *What We Talk About When We Talk About Love*, some of Lish's revisions were quite extensive – usually cutting, occasionally rewriting. The archived correspondence between writer and editor suggests that Carver became increasingly resistant to Lish's changes after this second collection. In *Where I'm Calling From* (1988), a volume of new and selected stories, Carver returned in a number of cases to his original versions edited by Lish. An example of a well-known story that changes in this way is the 1981 volume's bleak "The Bath," which becomes, with its cuts restored, a story of reconciliation in the 1988 volume's printing, where it is titled "A Small, Good Thing." This restored, longer version, when published separately in 1983, won Carver the O. Henry Award for best story of the year.

In 1981 Carver sold his first story to *The New Yorker*, "Chef's House," and subsequently became a frequent contributor to the magazine. At the same time he left behind the pared-down mode of *What We Talk About When We Talk About Love*, and turned to the more expansive style that characterizes his last stories. This change is noticeable in the story "Cathedral," which provided the title of his next collection, *Cathedral* (1983). The misanthropic narrator, a man with no friends – as his wife reminds him – begins his account of a blind man's visit in a cynical, mocking, jealous tone. The blind man is an acquaintance of his wife. At first the evening follows what is apparently a familiar course, eating and drinking to excess. But before exhaustion and drink can bring the narrator sleep (a sleep, he confesses, often broken by nightmares), he realizes a surprising empathy with the blind visitor. Similar moments occur in other stories in the volume, which went on to be nominated for a Pulitzer Prize. Whether this expansiveness and greater concern with human sympathy was because of Carver's happier personal circumstances, or because Gordon Lish was no longer wielding an editorial pencil, has been a matter of debate.

Carver was able to give up his teaching position at Syracuse when in 1983 he was awarded one of the Mildred and Harold Strauss Livings, $35 000 a year for five years. His main creative efforts for the next two years went into poetry. He published two volumes of verse, *Where Water Comes Together with Other Water* (1985) and *Ultramarine* (1986), he contributed to *Poetry*, and in 1985 was awarded the magazine's prestigious Levinson Prize. Carver's national stature was recognized by his induction in 1988 into the American Academy and Institute of Arts and Letters. But in the previous year he had been diagnosed with lung cancer, and the cancer returned as a brain tumor in 1988. Before he died in August of that year he published a book of new and selected stories, *Where I'm Calling From* (1988), and completed a book of poems that was published posthumously the following year as *A New Path to the Waterfall*. Uncollected and unpublished writings have continued to appear from time to time since his death, including some of his reviews of other writers, the most notable collection being *Call If You Need Me* (2001). Robert Altman's award-winning film *Short Cuts* (1993) was based on nine of Carver's stories and his poem "Lemonade." The stories and poem were reissued in that year under the title *Short Cuts*, with a short but perceptive introduction by the director recording his own response to reading, and then filming, Carver's work.

Bibliography

The Library of America has published Carver's *Collected Stories* (2009), which includes the manuscript and published versions of *What We Talk About When We Talk About Love*. Carver's individual collections are also available in paperback format from Random House/Vintage.

Arthur F. Bethea, *Technique and Sensibility in the Fiction and Poetry of Raymond Carver* (New York, 2001).

Sam Halpert, *Raymond Carver: An Oral Biography* (Iowa City, 1995).

Sandra Lee Kleppe, *New Paths to Raymond Carver: Critical Essays on His Life, Fiction, and Poetry* (Columbia, SC, 2008).

Kirk Nesset, *The Stories of Raymond Carver: A Critical Study* (Athens, OH, 1995).

Carol Sklenicka, *Raymond Carver:A Writer's Life* (New York, 2009).

Louise Erdrich (b.1954)

Karen Louise Erdrich was born in Little Falls, Minnesota, of mixed Native American (Chippewa/Ojibwa) and German American ancestry. Erdrich's characters are themselves often of mixed race and live within a culture impacted both by the traditions of reservation life and by the outside forces of nearby towns and cities that encroach upon those traditions. The lives of her characters are also impacted by the actions of the federal government, historically in the land allotment schemes that tried to turn Native Americans into individual farmers, and the government schools that sought to integrate the children into white culture by minimizing their heritage – and also through such more recent actions as federally funded employment projects and the granting of tribal casino licenses. The novels are often told through multiple narrators, crossing different time periods and moving back and forth between generations. Many of the novels are set within the Ojibwa reservation in North Dakota, an actual reservation for which Erdrich has invented fictional – but often partly autobiographical – characters, as well as the nearby fictional town of Argus. The technique has often been compared to William Faulkner's novels of interconnected generations set in the fictional Yoknapatawpha County, Mississippi, although Erdrich has pointed out that the form also has roots in traditional Chippewa storytelling.

Erdrich grew up in Wahpeton, North Dakota, where her parents both taught at the local Bureau of Indian Affairs School. An important family figure who reappears in various guises in her fiction was her maternal grandfather, Pat Gourneau, who was tribal chair of the Turtle Mountain Band of Chippewa. Erdrich attended local Catholic schools before entering Dartmouth College in 1972 as a member of its first co-educational class. The

The Twentieth-Century American Fiction Handbook   By Christopher MacGowan
© 2011 Christopher MacGowan

fusion, and sometimes conflict, of Catholic and traditional tribal religious beliefs is another recurring theme of her fiction.

While an undergraduate at Dartmouth, Erdrich met Michael Dorris, a newly arrived professor of anthropology, who would become her husband and writing partner some years later. Erdrich's poetry and fiction won her some prizes at the college, and upon graduation she started work for the North Dakota Arts Council's Poetry in the Schools Program. Both before and during her college years Erdrich worked at a number of the jobs that reappear in her novels, such as weighing dump trucks and hoeing sugar beet. In 1979 she graduated with a Master's degree from Johns Hopkins University, where her main creative work continued to be in poetry, and she moved from there to Massachusetts to edit the Boston Indian Council newspaper, *The Circle*. She was supported by writing fellowships from the MacDowell and Yaddo Colonies, and for a time worked as a textbook writer for the Charles E. Merrill Company, where she published a textbook for young readers and writers.

Erdrich met Michael Dorris again when returning to Dartmouth to give a reading. Since arriving at the college Dorris had founded and was directing Dartmouth's Native American Studies program. The two began to comment on each other's writing through correspondence, and in 1981, when Erdrich served as Dartmouth's writer-in-residence, the two married. Erdrich legally adopted the three Sioux children that Dorris had already adopted as a single father.

In interviews and other accounts of their writing practices Erdrich and Dorris made clear how close their writing collaboration became. Drafts would go back and forth and both writers had to be in agreement on every word for a book to be submitted for publication. The writer of the first draft would be the author of record, and the couple only published two books under joint authorship, both in 1991: *Route Two*, the story of a family trip through Minnesota, North Dakota, and Montana, and the novel *The Crown of Columbus*. Erdrich also wrote an introduction to Dorris's best-known book, *The Broken Cord* (1989), an account of Reynold Abel, one of the children Dorris had adopted, and who suffered from fetal alcohol syndrome, at that time a condition little recognized. Dorris had a productive literary career in his own right. In addition to his scholarly work in Native American Studies and *The Broken Cord* (which won a National Book Critics Circle Award), he published a number of well-received novels. In the first years of the 1990s, however, various strains began to tell on the marriage. Dorris, as Erdrich revealed in later comments, suffered from severe depression. In 1991 Reynold Abel died of his injuries after being struck by an automobile while crossing the street. Dorris became the subject of abuse allegations by some of the couple's children, and in1995 the two separated. In 1997 Dorris took his own life.

In the early 1980s Erdrich worked on some short stories in collaboration with her sister Heidi (as "Heidi Louise") and on potboiler romance fiction with her new husband (as "Milou North"). But her literary career began in earnest when she won the $5000 Nelson Algren Award in 1982 for the short story "The World's Greatest Fishermen." The following year she won a National Magazine Fiction Award for "Scales," a story which used her dump truck weighing experience, and which went on to be included in the *Best American Short Stories of 1983* volume, where she was in the company of John Updike and Raymond Carver. Also in 1983 one of her poems, "Indian Boarding School," won a Pushcart Prize. These successes led to two book publications the following year – a volume of poems, *Jacklight*, and the novel that would win her a National Book Critics Circle Award and become a national bestseller, *Love Medicine*.

Love Medicine (1984) introduces the themes, setting, and many of the characters of Erdrich's subsequent North Dakota novels. She commented in a 2001 interview with Paul Gray for *Time*: "A few years ago, I finally decided that I was working on one long novel ... I stopped being concerned about whether the same characters show up or not ... If they show up, they have to show up."

A revised version of "The World's Greatest Fishermen" serves as the novel's opening chapter, "Scales" forms another chapter, and other parts of the book had appeared as separate short stories too – a practice that Erdlich continued with subsequent novels. "The World's Greatest Fishermen" begins with the death of June Morrissey, an event that affects various members of her family in different ways in this novel and in the books to come. The novel begins in 1981 and ends in 1985, but during the course of the narrative there are chapters that go back to 1934, and chapters that cover a number of the decades in between. Of the five families at the center of the novel whose stories interweave across generations – the Nanapushes, the Kashpaws, the Pillagers, the Lazarres, and the Morrisseys – some are Native American and some mixed-blood. June Morrissey's background illustrates how these families are interrelated. She is the daughter of a Lazarre and a Morrissey, is adopted by Eli Kashpaw and marries Gordie Kashpaw. She has an affair with Gerry Nanapush, whose father is a Pillager, and their child, Lipsha Morrissey, is adopted by Gordie's parents, a Kashpaw who married a Lazarre. These relationships, when they are formalized, are sometimes traditional Chippewa marriages and sometimes Catholic marriages. The characters are to different degrees associated with such aspects of traditional heritage as healing, living close to nature, and respecting communal ties, or with the pull of the towns and cities outside the reservation, even though the racism of whites and feelings of displacement and alienation limit and sometimes destroy the lives of those who travel beyond the tribal community. Alcoholism is rampant on the reservation, particularly but not only among the men, and the nuns and priests nearby add as much to the general sense of displacement and fractured heritage as they provide any kind of spiritual comfort. But there are survivors: in this novel the trickster figure Gerry Nanapush, whom no state prison can hold, and two strong older women, Lulu and Marie, formerly lovers of the same man, who use the forum afforded by tribal politics to limit where possible the outside exploitation of tribal labor and land.

Erdrich's next novel, *The Beet Queen* (1986), tells the story of the Adare family, particularly Dot Adare, a white woman with some Native American background who is a relatively minor character in *Love Medicine*. Nearby Argus rather than the Indian reservation itself is the setting for many of the events in this novel. The family history is a tangled one of abandoned children and multiple sexual relationships, the consequences of distrust, despair, and love. The narrative is more focused than in *Love Medicine*, although it still covers 40 years and is again told through multiple narrators.

Some aspects of *The Beet Queen*'s plot appeared contrived to a few commentators, a criticism that has accompanied a number of Erdrich's novels. The combination in this and the earlier novel of modernist and post-modernist techniques with the kind of storytelling usually associated with myth and magical realism is unusual in Native American writing, and provoked criticism from Leslie Marmon Silko, who argued that the language and structure of Erdrich's novels called attention to themselves in a way that minimized the political, social, and cultural realities of contemporary Native American life.

Whatever the merits of Silko's criticism (made in a 1986 review of *The Beet Queen* titled "Here's an Odd Artifact for the Fairy-Tale Shelf"), for most readers Erdrich's next novel, *Tracks* (1988), is her most overtly political. The events in *Tracks* take place between 1912 and 1924, before those of the previous two novels. In these years much of the reservation land is being lost to lumber companies. There are two narrators, one more unreliable than the other: the pureblood, Nanapush, is the grandfather of Lulu from *Love Medicine*, and the other narrator is Pauline, who becomes a nun and is the mother of Marie Lazarre from the first novel. Both narrators focus on Fleur Pillager, Lulu's mother – who is also the subject of a short story that Erdrich published separately and which won first place in *Prize Stories: The O. Henry Awards*. The narration in the novel never enters Fleur's mind directly, but she emerges as one of Erdrich's fullest, most complex characters through the perspectives offered by the two narrators.

In 1989 Erdrich published a second book of poems, *Baptism of Desire*, and 1991 saw the two books to which both Erdrich and Dorris put their names.

The Crown of Columbus has its admirers, but its tale of two Dartmouth professors on an adventure in the Bahamas has received less critical attention than most of Erdrich's other novels. In 1993 Erdrich co-edited that year's *Best American Short Stories*, and in the same year published an expanded edition of *Love Medicine*. The four-and-a-half additional chapters correct some of the inconsistencies that had cropped up from details in the later novels, provide some additional background information, and relate more of Lyman Lamartine's entrepreneurial adventures in preparation for his role in *The Bingo Palace*, published the following year. The narrative of *The Bingo Palace* is set within the year following the most recent events in the expanded *Love Medicine*. At the center of the novel is the desire of Lipsha Morrissey and his uncle Lyman for a new character, the unmarried mother Shawnee Ray Toose.

The non-fiction *The Blue Jay's Dance* (1995) describes Erdrich's experiences as mother, wife, and writer within a family that had grown to include the three daughters born following her marriage. She has commented that the one birth year that the book describes – from pregnancy, through birth and a return to writing – is a composite of her experiences with all three. Erdrich's next novel, *Tales of Burning Love* (1996) brings back the engineer, Jack Mauser, who was with June Morrissey on the night that she died, as told in the first chapter of *Love Medicine*. The much-married, mixed-blood Chippewa Mauser – his current wife is Dot Adare – is the subject of tales recounted to each other by his four surviving wives when they find themselves snowbound together after attending a funeral for his faked death. The tale telling brings the women together and the multiple perspectives reveal a more complex Jake Mauser than had first appeared.

The Antelope Wife (1998) is the first novel that Erdrich published after the suicide of her estranged husband. In a prefatory note she records that the novel was written before his death, but the novel's suicide and its account of two failing marriages have inevitably suggested possible autobiographical elements. The book introduces a new set of characters, members of the Ojibwa now living in Minneapolis. The Nanapushes, Kashpaws, and other families from the North Dakota novels are back in *The Last Report on the Miracles at Little No Horse* (2001), which returns to the harsh early years of the reservation, tells the story of the priest Father Damien whose identity and role is assumed by a woman, and provides more details on the life and manipulations of Sister Leopolda from *Love Medicine*. The novel was a finalist for the National Book Award for Fiction.

The German side of Erdrich's mixed ancestry is behind *The Master Butcher's Singing Club* (2003), set between the two world wars and telling the story of German immigrant Fidelis Waldvogel, who settles in Argus.

The novel has been dramatized by Marsha Norman and premiered at the Guthrie Theater, Minneapolis, in fall 2010. *Four Souls* (2004) picks up the story of Fleur from *Tracks* as she hunts down the man who built his Minneapolis mansion of trees felled on the reservation land he had purchased. The elderly Nanapush who adopted Fleur is again a narrator, as he was in *Tracks*, and the other narrators are the sister-in-law of the timber baron and Nanapush's common-law wife Margaret. The serious revenge story involving Fleur is offset by a more comical revenge plot concerning Nanapush and one of Margaret's admirers. For some critics the various stories in *The Painted Drum* (2005), while individually powerful, do not come together as well as those elsewhere in Erdrich's fiction. The drum turns up in New Hampshire, part of the estate of a family descended from an Indian agent who had worked on the Ojibwa reservation.

The multiple narrators of Erdrich's fiction, the family histories entwined across generations, the mix of small town and reservation life, and the language that describes events that can be harshly realistic, mythic, or almost magic, are all put in the service of a murder mystery in the Pulitzer Prize-nominated *The Plague of Doves* (2008). The powerful revelations in this book stem as much from the way in which the family histories trace back to the murder and the racist act that is its aftermath as they do to the solution of the murder itself decades later. There is also in this book a more assured weaving of symbols than in some of the novels – particularly in the doves of the title, with their spiritual associations of peace and death, and their place in nature as the multiple flocks of passenger pigeons, threatening the crops in their thousands but themselves doomed to extinction, like the town of Pluto in which much of the story is set.

In a departure from the sweeping scope of *The Plague of Doves* and Erdrich's other novels, *Shadow Tag* (2010) remains focused on the corrosive marriage of Irene and Gil, a Minnesota couple, both of Native American heritage, whose creative collaboration and domestic problems inevitably recall some of the details of Erdrich's own marriage. Irene keeps a diary that she knows her husband will read, and another in which she records her true feelings and which she makes sure is kept from his eyes.

In addition to her novels, short stories (collected, with some previously unpublished, in *The Red Convertible* [2009]), poetry, and non-fiction, Erdrich has also published children's books. One of them, *The Birchbark House*, illustrated by the author, was a finalist for the National Book Award for Young People in 1999. In that same year Erdrich moved with her youngest children to Minnesota, where in 2000, along with her sister Heidi, she opened the bookstore Birchbark Books. The store has been successful and has an active website, although Erdrich noted in June 2010, reflecting upon the store's tenth anniversary and the difficulties of its first months – "thank god I kept my day job."

Bibliography

Louise Erdrich's fiction is published by HarperCollins, and is generally available in paperback format.

Peter J. Beidler and Gay Barton, *A Reader's Guide to the Novels of Louise Erdrich*, revised and expanded edition (Columbia, MO, 2006).

Allan Chavkin and Nancy Feyl Chavkin, eds., *Conversations with Louise Erdrich and Michael Dorris* (Jackson, MS, 1994).

Allan Richard Chavkin, ed., *The Chippewa Landscape of Louise Erdrich* (Tuscaloosa, 1999).

Brajesh Sawhney, ed., *Studies in the Literary Achievement of Louise Erdrich: Native American Writer* (Lewiston, NY, 2009).

Lorena Laura Stookey, *Louis Erdrich: A Critical Companion* (Westport, CT, 1999).

Sherman Alexie (b.1966)

Sherman Alexie writes in a number of genres, sometimes within the same volume. His work includes poetry – in both free and formal verse – short stories, novels, essays, songs, and screenplays. He has won poetry slam competitions, has performed as a stand-up comedian, and has directed one of his screenplays. Alexie is of Spokane and Coeur d'Alene descent, and his work reflects this Native American background (Alexie prefers the word "Indian" in his writing). His themes include isolation, alcoholism, domestic violence, and the oppression, stereotyping, and general mistreatment of Native Americans and their heritage by the dominant culture – particularly in popular films, television series, songs, and sports. Contemporary consumer culture infiltrates the world of his characters, although they usually have little money. The setting of the earlier fiction is usually the Spokane Reservation, in Washington State, while the later narratives are more often set in Seattle.

Alexie was born on the Spokane Reservation and was educated there until he began attending the white high school in nearby Reardan. He attended Gonzaga University from 1985 to 1987, and Washington State University in Pullman from 1988 to 1991. Alcoholism seriously impaired his college work, and although he managed to conquer his drinking problem in 1992, he did not receive his degree until 1995. Such was his early success that he was awarded an Alumni Achievement Award along with his BA. In this same year, 1995, Alexie married his wife, Diane.

At Washington State Alexie took a creative writing class with Chinese American author Alex Kuo, who became an important mentor. Shortly after finishing college he received two Fellowships: a Washington State Arts Commission Poetry Fellowship in 1991 and a National Endowment for the Arts Poetry Fellowship in 1992. He then made a remarkable debut, publishing four books in two years. One of them, *The Business of Fancydancing*, was singled out as a *New York Times* "Notable Book of the Year," and another, *The Lone Ranger and Tonto Fistfight in Heaven*, is frequently taught in contemporary literature courses.

When *The Business of Fancydancing* (1992) was published by Brooklyn's Hanging Loose Press, a number of its poems and stories had already appeared in various journals and magazines. Alex Kuo's introduction to the collection characterizes Alexie's work as having "escaped the pervasive influence of writing workshops, academic institutions and their subsidized intellect." In what is generally considered Alexie's bleakest book, there is little possibility of escape from the world of alcoholism, subsidized housing, poor nutrition, racist tribal police, and "Crazy Horse Dreams" – escapist fantasies that offer a form of release for a short while. In the title poem, fancydancing is a money-raising "business" performed to win prize money for drink. The book's longest story, "Special Delivery," illustrates the role of imagination and humor in the attempts to survive the violence, drunkenness, and dead-end boredom of reservation life. Thomas Builds-the-Fire, the central figure in this story – a storyteller who can find no audience – is one of the recurring characters in Alexie's work.

Old Shirts & New Skins (1993) and *First Indian on the Moon* (1993) also mix poetry and prose genres, and continue the depiction of a native culture reduced, isolated, rootless, and crudely co-opted by Hollywood and television. In "My Heroes Have Never Been Cowboys," for example, the cowboys' six-shooters never need reloading, God looks like John Wayne, and in Westerns the Indians are always extras.

All four of these early books illustrate what continue to be major characteristics of Alexie's writing: humor, directness, and surprising turns and juxtapositions of language and incident. Of the four, *The Lone Ranger and Tonto Fistfight in Heaven* (1993), Alexie's first publication by a major commercial press, did most to establish his reputation. The book won the PEN-Hemingway Award for best first book of fiction. In his introduction to the 2005 reissue, which adds two new stories, Alexie describes the impact of the prominent positive review given *The Business of Fancydancing* in the *New York Times*. He was beset by agents and producers looking to turn him into a more commercial writer and seeking to cash in on his moment of fame. In the introduction he acknowledges that the stories are bleaker than those in his later work – "reservation realism" is his term for their approach – and he concedes the autobiographical elements that he had earlier minimized. This introduction is written with the same kind of dry, sometimes bitter, humor that enters the stories, humor that helps the characters to fight off boredom, and to live with violence, loss, and alcoholism. The narratives' unexpected turns often take the form of stories within stories, memories that form a bridge with the main narrative and add to the story's culminating action, or inaction. The title story's various narrative levels, for example, include a 3 a.m. visit to a convenience store, a troubled relationship with a now lost girlfriend, bored joblessness, and a basketball game.

One of the stories in *The Lone Ranger and Tonto Fistfight in Heaven*, "This Is What It Means to Say Phoenix, Arizona" – in which storyteller Thomas drives with Victor to collect the ashes of Victor's father – became the basis of the film *Smoke Signals* (1998), for which Alexie wrote the screenplay. The film was made with an all-Native American cast and crew, and won numerous awards, including two from the Sundance Film Festival. Alexie's other film work includes writing and directing the 2002 film *The Business of Fancydancing*, and writing the short film *49?* (2003), which documents an Indian chant style.

Victor Joseph and Thomas Builds-the-Fire are among a number of characters who reappear from Alexie's earlier books in his first novel, *Reservation Blues* (1995). The story concerns the Indian rock band Coyote Springs and their difficulties getting a recording contract in the white music industry. Reaction to the novel has tended to recognize the power of its individual stories, while suggesting that they don't fully sustain the larger narrative structure of the book or fully integrate the mythic and historical material into the contemporary story. Alexie's second novel, *Indian Killer* (1996), a murder mystery, also met with some qualified reviews. The novel is set in Seattle and follows three Indians living in the city (including Alexie's most fully developed female character, Marie Polatkin) at a time when a serial killer is loose. The murders are of white men, and the police suspect that the killer is an Indian. The novel contains some sharp satire on those whites who write, edit, or teach Indian materials while having little knowledge of Indian life beyond popular stereotypes or secondhand knowledge.

Following these two novels, Alexie published a number of books of poems, and two further books of stories – *The Toughest Indian in the World* (2000) and *Ten Little Indians* (2003). In reviewing the former, Joyce Carol Oates drew attention to Alexie's position outside of more mainstream Native American writing: Alexie is "the bad boy," she writes, "mocking, self-mocking, unpredictable, unassimilable." The first of these collections continues Alexie's exploration of compromised heritage and identity. The stories are contemporary but the problems go back generations, exacerbated by dead-end work, violence, and stereotyping. The only release, as in the title story, is a tentative communal suffering, and a return to the reservation is both a comfort and a defeat. In *Ten Little Indians* the central characters are more likely to be successful professionals, trying to make their way outside the reservation, but always in the midst of a white world in which an Indian might be told on the street by a stranger, with no sense of the irony, to go on back to his own country.

Flight (2007), Alexie's first novel for more than 10 years, is an ambitious and fast-paced story of 15-year-old half-Indian Zits – his name coming from the pimples on his face – whose anger and frustration lead him to plan an act of mass murder. But in the midst of the shooting he is transported back in time to some key moments in American history, including the Battle of Little Big Horn just before Custer's arrival, and into the body of a flight trainer unknowingly preparing one of the 9/11 terrorists. His time travel shows him perspectives beyond the merely violent, perspectives that invite tolerance rather than rage, and that involve a broader sense of community.

Some reviewers categorized *Flight* as young adult fiction, while recognizing its adult themes, but Alexie's *The Absolutely True Diary of a Part-Time Indian* (2007), published the same year, with cartoons by Ellen Forney, is his first novel explicitly for that age group, and won its author the National Book Award for Young People's Literature. "I think the world is a series of broken dams and floods," writes narrator Arnold Spirit Jr., "and my cartoons are tiny little lifeboats." Frankly autobiographical, the story of Arnold's demoralizing experience in the reservation school, his transfer to the nearby white school (where he is the only Indian apart from the mascot) and the problems and opportunities it brings him, is told with an economy and humor that for some readers makes it Alexie's best work to date in an *oeuvre* that, with its author barely 40, already includes more than 17 books.

Bibliography

Sherman Alexie's novels and story collections are available in paperback format.

James Cox, "Muting White Noise: The Subversion of Popular Culture Narratives in Sherman Alexie's Fiction," in *Studies in American Indian Literature* 9.4 (1997), 52–70.
Daniel Grassian, *Understanding Sherman Alexie* (Columbia, SC, 2005).
Arnold Krupat, "The 'Rage Stage': Contextualizing Sherman Alexie's *Indian Killer*," in *Red Matters: Native American Studies* (Philadephia, 2002), pp. 98–121.
David L. Moore, "Sherman Alexie: Irony, Intimacy, and Agency," in *Cambridge Companion to Native American Literature*, ed. Joy Porter and Kenneth M. Roemer (Cambridge, 2005), pp. 297–310.

Part 3

Key Texts

Part 3

Act Tens

Theodore Dreiser, *Sister Carrie*, New York: Doubleday, Page & Co., 1900

Before publishing *Sister Carrie*, his first novel, Dreiser had worked as a reporter in Chicago, St. Louis, and Pittsburgh, and as an editor in New York. He had written a few short stories but most of his writing experience had come from journalism or from publishing articles in magazines. This tale of seduction, theft, adultery, and bigamy set in Chicago and New York came out of the world he had reported on in his journalism, coupled with some incidents from the sexual misadventures of one of his sisters.

Dreiser had the good fortune to have as a reader at publishers Doubleday, Page, the novelist Frank Norris, author of *McTeague* and *The Octopus*, but the misfortune to run up against the conventional morality of senior partner Frank Doubleday when he finally read the book in manuscript. Dreiser had produced a narrative in which the sexual misdeeds of a young woman are rewarded, not punished; where Carrie's first seducer is better off at the end of the novel than at its beginning; and where even the thief, adulterer, and bigamist Hurstwood meets his fate more from the ruthlessness of a financial partner, the impersonality of the city, and his no longer being a young man, than as a direct result of his elopement and seduction of Carrie. The Doubleday firm were obliged under contract to publish the book, which they did reluctantly, but they printed only about 1000 copies and did not publicize or market the novel. Consequently the book received little attention in the United States when it first appeared, although it sold well with an English publisher in Britain who published a truncated version. It was not until 1907,

The Twentieth-Century American Fiction Handbook   By Christopher MacGowan
© 2011 Christopher MacGowan

when the novel was reissued in the United States, Dreiser having purchased the plates himself from the Doubleday firm, that the book began to receive attention and recognition.

From its first pages *Sister Carrie* is an urban story. The train where Carrie first meets Drouet is traveling to Chicago, and Chicago and New York are the main settings for the novel. Toward the end of the century both cities are growing fast, bringing opportunities for wealth and success, but also creating a class of the working poor at the mercy of any economic downturn. In dramatizing the increasing social stratification, the novel includes the desperate struggle for survival among the homeless, unemployed, and penniless men haunting the Bowery, the grinding routines of the working girls at a shoe factory in Chicago – reduced for 10 hours a day to becoming adjuncts to their machines – the labor struggles of the Brooklyn transit strike, and the world of the rich and materially comfortable, together with the growing number of establishments that cater to their expensive pleasures.

The novel illustrates the widening gap through the fates of its central characters, and in the function of its settings. The saloon that Hurstwood manages for Fitzgerald and Moy is a meeting place for the financial, social, and sporting elite, but is also a place where Hurstwood can meet and be on social terms with Drouet. Hurstwood himself can bridge both worlds, manner and dress counting as much as personal wealth in his success. By contrast, Carrie's success in New York bars Hurstwood from meeting her; he is literally thrown out of the theater in his last attempt to ask her for help. As Hurstwood discovers, social stratification is ruthlessly enforced, and the city's most wretched can be easily ignored. As part of the novel's account of its social machinery it provides a careful account of the dollars and cents cost of eating, rent, car fare, and clothes, and measures them against the inadequate wages and predatory employment practices suffered by the working poor. The narrator stops giving Carrie's salary once she achieves the fame that brings her starring roles, for it is finally irrelevant to satisfying her material needs, while Hurstwood's decline is measured out in terms of his slowly decreasing savings.

Frank Norris, reading the manuscript for Doubleday, Page, found a novel reflecting, as did his own work, the views of Thomas Huxley and Herbert Spencer, whose social theories took a mechanistic view of evolution, and saw society as driven by the same evolutionary principles as biological organisms – particularly the need for survival and the search for pleasure. Dreiser's novel suggests in a number of ways the inevitability of the events that unfold. The first two chapter headings incorporate the language of scientific process: "The Magnet Attracting: A Waif Amid Forces" and "What Poverty Threatened: Of Granite and Brass." Later chapter titles include

"The Machine and the Maiden" and "The Lure of the Material." Important events that shape a character's fate are as inevitable as they are matters of chance – the safe locking before Hurstwood can return his employers' money to the drawer, Hurstwood being spotted with Carrie out driving, or the maid in Drouet and Carrie's apartment house revealing details of callers to Drouet.

The terminology of the chapter headings is matched by the detached tone of the narrative voice, further suggesting a scientific account of forces at play. The novel's frequent analogies to animal instincts and behaviors reinforce the biological determinism behind the characters' motives and responses. Many chapters begin with generalized observations on human behavior (often very gender specific) or the human condition, observations illustrated by the scenes that follow. Chapter 8, for example, begins with the observation: "Among the forces which sweep and play throughout the universe, untutored man is but a wisp in the wind" (70). Civilization, the narrator goes on to assert in the next sentence, is in a "middle stage," wholly guided by neither instinct nor reason.

Rich or poor, comfortable or desperate, all are driven by desire in this novel: sexual desire, the attraction of material goods and the glamour of showy wealth, or just an obscure hope that saving from meager earnings will provide a better future, or that tomorrow will bring work, or that the next passer-by will give the needy beggar the price of a bed or a meal. Many desires in the novel remain unrealized, or, if achieved, prove empty or transient. But there are some characters who are motivated by sympathy and even selflessness. The "Captain," penniless himself, nightly begs passers-by on Broadway for money to provide beds for every one of the more than a hundred homeless men who line up to wait for him to collect enough for the cheap lodgings that are an alternative to the streets; a baker distributes bread at midnight, a loaf to any hungry unfortunate who might need it to survive a little longer; and the manager who takes pity on the desperate Hurstwood at the hotel and employs him even though there is no immediate need for extra help.

The degree to which a character can avoid allowing biological appetite, an insatiable materialism, or illusion to completely drive his or her life is illustrated by Ames, whose views stem from a degree of reflection rare in the characters of this novel, and whose values parallel some of the author's. But Ames needs the space afforded by material comforts in order to maintain his critical distance from the values of his comfortably-off relatives the Vances. Thanks to Ames, Carrie – a star in the world of escapist entertainment that Dreiser's novel sets itself against – is reading the realist author Balzac at the height of her musical-comedy fame. Cynical about sex and romance, she sees behind, if with more feeling than understanding, the purpose of the industry she serves; an industry, and public, that knows her by the last of the three false names that she adopts. The title of the novel, however, insists upon her biological identity of "sister."

Dreiser's examination of the role of the media in this novel, the theater in which Carrie finds success, and the newspapers that allow Hurstwood to forget his troubles foreshadows what becomes a major theme of twentieth-century American literature: the role of the media in feeding dreams, providing escape from the grinding repetition of a mundane existence, and perpetuating the uncritical faith in America as the place in which impossible things can happen. Many novels follow *Sister Carrie* in ruthlessly exposing the mechanism of such illusions. And yet, as this novel also acknowledges, without some kind of hope an individual could be reduced to asking Hurstwood's final exhausted question to himself just before his suicide – "What's the use?" (453).

The novel was early criticized for what some saw as its amorality. It then became a famous example of a writer's need to face down publishers and critics who would limit freedom of expression. In more recent criticism commentators have explored the complexities of Dreiser's naturalism, the ways in which his narrative complicates what might otherwise have been a mechanistic set of events designed to illustrate a theory. And the novel's carefully detailed accounts of such settings as Hurstwood's bar, the shoe factory, and the new department stores in the growing cities have made *Sister Carrie* an important text for critics interested in the social and cultural background out of which this and other turn-of-the-century American novels arose.

Bibliography

The text of the 1900 edition is published by The Library of America, *Theodore Dreiser: Sister Carrie, Jennie Gerhardt, Twelve Men* (New York, 1987) and is also available in paperback printings from many publishers. The University of Pennsylvania Dreiser Edition's *Sister Carrie*, edited by Thomas P. Riggio (rev. edn., Philadelphia, 1998) restores material that Dreiser cut from the first edition.

Donald Pizer, ed., *New Essays on Sister Carrie* (Cambridge, 1991).
David E. E. Sloane, *Sister Carrie, Theodore Dreiser's Sociological Tragedy* (New York, 1992).
Priscilla Wald, "Dreiser's Sociological Vision," in *The Cambridge Companion to Theodore Dreiser*, ed. Leonard Cassuto and Clare Virginia Eby (Cambridge, 2004), pp. 177–195.
James W. West III, *A Sister Carrie Portfolio* (Charlottesville, VA, 1985).

Henry James, *The Wings of the Dove*, New York: Charles Scribner's Sons, 1902

The Wings of the Dove is the first of Henry James's three late novels in which he returned to the international theme of his earlier work, the relationship of America and Europe. But these later novels are written in a much denser, more nuanced style than such early works as *The American* (1877) and *The Portrait of a Lady* (1881). The term often applied is "indirection," where both the Jamesian narrator and the central characters themselves speak in terms oblique and guarded, even where, as in the case of this novel, the central issue might be expressed in quite brutal terms – a secretly engaged couple try to deceive a terminally ill young American heiress into leaving a bequest that, unknown to her, would give the engaged couple the fortune to marry on their own terms.

James's notebooks reveal that he conceived of the basic situation as early as 1894, during the period when he was trying, unsuccessfully, to write for the stage. In his notes he considers two different endings, one for the novel and one for the play, although neither is as powerful or ambiguous in its understatement as the scene between Morton Densher and Kate Croy that closes the 1902 novel.

In James's Preface, written for the New York edition of his works in 1909, he notes that he was unable to interest any magazine publishers in serializing the novel, but that this failure brought the advantage of his being able to arrange the novel without having to give thought to the commercial needs of serialization. He recognized, he notes, that he had two stories to tell, that of

The Twentieth-Century American Fiction Handbook   By Christopher MacGowan
© 2011 Christopher MacGowan

Densher and Kate Croy, and that of the doomed Milly Theale. Thus he felt free to delay the introduction of Milly until the third of the novel's 10 books while he set up the circumstances that restrict the relationship of the English couple. In these early pages, Kate, whose motives are arguably immoral and quite ruthless in her plan to deceive Milly, is shown as something of a victim. Her father is guilty of behavior so appalling that neither Kate nor the author want to describe it, and he remains even to the end of the novel a hovering presence blighting her life and that of her close relatives. Kate's Aunt Maud rescues her from this trap, but in opening up opportunities for her only encloses her in another – the requirement that she marry well as a condition of her continuing patronage. Densher is not, of course, Aunt Maud's idea of a suitor; therefore the couple's engagement must be a secret one. James's Preface describes the rich opportunity these opening books gave him to set up the situation into which the innocent Milly Theale walks, but – often his severest critic – he feels that in retrospect the result was inadequate, the details often too sketchy.

The opulent Lancaster Gate house to which Aunt Maud brings Kate is just one of the central places that figure importantly in the narrative. It serves as a contrast to the gloomy surroundings of Kate's sister, Mrs. Condrip. But Kate and Densher can meet in neither place freely, and their courtship takes place in the parks and public gardens of London. Important too is the grand house called Matcham, where the most important "match" is one that the company agree Milly has with a painting in the Matcham collection by Bronzino of a finely dressed, beautiful but enigmatic young woman. Yet the association with the figure from the past only reminds Milly of her own mortality and begins her consultations with the eminent physician Sir Luke Strett, who sees her into her final days in Venice. The beautiful but dying Italian city is another important place in the narrative. It has its own important contrast between the magnificent Palazzo Leporelli, which Milly rents in what can only be a temporary splendor, and where Densher courts her as part of Kate's scheme, and Densher's own dingy rooms where Kate becomes his mistress as his condition of following through on her plan. By contrast with these confining but expressive places, Milly and her companion Mrs. Stringham enter the novel with a view of the Alps, the world seeming at the feet of the young Boston heiress, only to inexorably close down for her in the months to come.

Much of James's interest, as often in his later fiction, is in the moral questions that his characters face. Kate's deception may seem heartless, but her scheme is her attempt to forge her own future instead of that laid out for her by Aunt Maud, and even by her sister and father, both of whom imagine benefits to themselves from Kate's association with Maud. Kate herself at one point warns Milly about the dangers for her American friend of their growing friendship, and Kate appears to genuinely love Densher. Her instincts in love are borne out by the behavior of the suitor whom Aunt Maud has in mind for Kate. Lord Mark proposes at different times to both Kate and Milly, trading the status of his title for the money that he needs, an exchange when it comes to Kate that meets with Aunt Maud's full approval. He is quick to tell Milly of Densher and Kate's secret engagement when Milly rebuffs his proposal (the source of his knowledge remains unclear to Densher, and possibly to Kate too). The act is certainly a vindictive one, but on the other hand he is enlightening Milly where Kate and Densher are deceiving her.

Thus Kate's ruthlessness could be argued as a response to restrictions upon her freedom of choice that the narrative itself to some extent condemns, and Lord Mark's actions are capable of being looked at in more than one way. But much more ambiguous are the final actions and motives of Morton Densher and Milly Theale – Densher's refusal of the bequest and Milly's act of making it. The novel gives no direct account of Densher's last meeting with Milly, or of her motives in asking to see him again in spite of what Lord Mark has told her. As a result, different interpretations are possible of the novel's ending. For some critics, Milly's action is a generous attempt to allow the man she has fallen in love with the happiness that she is doomed to forgo. Such a reading sees Millie's act as selfless, her own sacrificial act in full recognition of the evil represented by Kate and Densher's deception. But Milly may also be putting Densher in a position where it is materially possible but morally impossible for him to marry Kate. Importantly, for a reading that sees the bequest in terms of possible redemption – for Milly, Densher, or both – the news is timed to reach Densher on Christmas Eve.

The difference here is the degree of awareness imparted to Milly's action. She may be a character whose morality lies on a different plane than that of Kate and Densher – she is, as a number of allusions make clear, the "dove" of the title. She may be testing Densher, or again she may be testing the fidelity of the love between the engaged couple. But then again Milly may not want to believe Lord Mark's claims, for reasons and needs of her own, or she may love Densher despite recognizing the truth of Lord Mark's revelation. Within these various possibilities her bequest might be made entirely as a gesture for Densher alone, or it might be made to Densher for one or another reason, in terms of his relationship with Kate.

As for Densher, Kate suspects that he fell in love with the dying Milly on their last meeting in Venice, and Densher gives no direct response to the suggestion. But while he is still willing to marry Kate immediately, he wants no part of the money that was the goal of their deception, either because of his love for Milly, his rejection of that part of Kate that schemed for it, or his recognition that taking it would be an immoral act that would blight their future together. But whatever the motives behind the bequest and its refusal, and whether redemption or loss is the final outcome of events, the relationship between Kate and Densher can never be the same, as Kate tells him in the last words of the novel – that may also be the last words ever between the couple.

Bibliography

Henry James, *The Wings of the Dove*, ed. J. Donald Crowley and Richard A. Hocks (2nd edn., New York, 2003). Reprints the 1909 New York Edition text, with corrections, and includes some useful critical essays as well as James's Preface and a selection from his Notebooks.

Anna Kventsel, *Decadence in the Late Novels of Henry James* (New York, 2007), pp. 57–134.

David McWhirter, *Desire and Love in Henry James: A Study of the Late Novels* (Cambridge, 1989), pp. 83–141.

William Stowe, "James's Elusive *Wings*," in *The Cambridge Companion to Henry James* (Cambridge, 1998), pp. 187–203.

Yasuko Tanimoto, *A New Reading of the Wings of the Dove* (Dallas, 2004).

Edith Wharton, *The House of Mirth*, New York: Charles Scribner's Sons, 1905

Edith Wharton first began thinking about the novel that became *The House of Mirth* in 1900. Two alternative titles that she considered for the narrative of the last 17 months of Lily's Bart's life were "A Moment's Ornament" and "The Year of the Rose." But the title that she chose comes from Ecclesiastes: "The heart of fools is in the house of mirth." All three titles suggest the fragility of Lily Bart's position as she graces, and is then expelled from, wealthy New York Society. Wharton started writing the novel in 1903 and completed it in March 1905. Two months earlier it had begun an 11-month serial run in *Scribner's Magazine*, where Wharton had been publishing travel articles and short stories for more than 15 years. She had been a prolific writer, authoring nine books in the previous eight years, but this novel required her most sustained period of writing. When *The House of Mirth* was published at the end of 1905 it became a bestseller. More than 140 000 copies were printed by year's end, and for the first two months of 1906 it was the best-selling novel in the country, bringing its author national and international fame.

The House of Mirth is arguably the first accurate portrait of wealthy New York society in American fiction. This is a world in which houses and gardens, furniture and social events, are judged by the prevailing standards of grace and tasteful opulence; where hostesses vie for the most distinguished guests and the most entertaining parties, the entertainments following the social season between New York City and Newport, Rhode Island – with occasional visits to Europe. Wharton's narrative also describes what lies behind the glitter: the social rivalries, the sexual intrigue and exploitation, and the initiations that those who wish to break into the social elite must undergo. Also part of the novel are the various imitative social groups further down the scale of wealth, as well as the world of the working girls who sew the finery displayed at the opulent parties, and finally the world of those living barely above poverty.

This social spectrum is traversed by Lily Bart, who, like her mother before her, has the taste and connections to be part of a social world that is financially beyond her means. For fortunes earned can also be lost, as happened to Lily's father. The newly rich are ready to replace those who falter, as is the case with Mr. Rosedale, who at various times in the novel offers Lily the financial means that would keep her within the social elite.

Lily is able to use her beauty and training to be as manipulative as any member of the group, whether to obtain invitations to the season's events, or to create safe if loveless marriage possibilities for herself. But her constrained financial situation makes her a vulnerable figure both to men seeking to take advantage of her lack of means, and to the women who purchase her company for their own covert ends. But for all of her undeniable selfishness and lack of self-reflection, she is finally not ruthless enough to survive and prosper in the world she covets. She is an easy victim for a hostess seeking to cover up adultery to save her marriage to a husband she neither loves nor respects – but whose wealth supports her social position, and whose foolishness blinds him to her sexual adventures.

Lily, at 29, is under the pressure of time to find herself a wealthy husband. But her inconsistencies leave her socially compromised despite her fundamental innocence. The social crime is appearing to be guilty, not the actual question of innocence or guilt. Rosedale believes her quite innocent of the behaviors that ostracize her, but he needs her social rehabilitation before he can marry her.

The key relationship in *The House of Mirth*, the one that frames the beginning and end of the narrative, is between Lily and Lawrence Selden. The moral questions of the novel, including the distinctions between surface impressions and truth, are central in the scenes where these two meet, and are behind their inability to find the happiness that a full understanding of each other would bring. On three occasions they become aware of the love that could bring them together, and on each occasion Lily provides Selden with a glimpse of that self beyond the social ornament that angles for a wealthy husband, and that he assumes motivates her central values and actions. On the first of these the two spend an afternoon in the countryside away from the Trenor house party at which they are both guests, unaware of time until other guests intrude upon their world. To be with Selden Lily neglects the doting

Percy Gryce, insipid heir to a fortune, marriage to whom would seal her place in the wealthy social milieu. Gryce remains a distraction that stops both Lily and Selden recognizing the significance of their rare afternoon. On the second occasion, Lily appears at an entertainment put on by the Brys. For her role in a series of arranged tableaux she selects a figure from a Reynolds painting. When she is able to "embody the person represented without ceasing to be herself," Selden realizes his love for her (141–142). But on the following evening he glimpses Lily in the act of escaping late at night from the town house of would-be adulterer Gus Trenor. Selden automatically assumes the validity of appearances – Lily leaving the house of a married man late in the evening when his wife is absent, a man to whom social gossip claims Lily is under heavy financial obligations. On the third occasion, by destroying the letters that she could use as blackmail, an exhausted and demoralized Lily chooses the morality associated with her love for Selden over the action that could win her Rosedale and restore her social position. In this final meeting with Selden, "the external aspect of the situation had vanished for him as completely as for her." At the time Selden "felt it only as one of those rare moments which lift the veil from their faces as they pass," but he is at her door the next morning having realized the significance of what they have missed for each other (326).

That Selden is the male correspondent to the married Bertha Dorset in the letters that Lily destroys further complicates her moral choices when she considers using the letters. In her pursuit of suitors, Lily always sees Selden as not wealthy enough to be one of the candidates, and he assumes the same, enjoying what he calls at one point the "wonderful spectacle" of watching her (68). But in arriving at Lily's boarding house too late, Selden is forced to recognize that if she were to forgo the social role for which she had been brought up, and to which she had devoted so much ingenuity, that self beneath "the veil" would needed more recognition and support than he had ever been able to offer her.

Selden needs to be a sympathetic character in order for the final scene to resonate with lost opportunity. He is an independent, critical observer of the social scene, tries to help Lily with advice at some crucial moments, and recognizes the qualities of Gertie Farish. But recent analyses of the gender roles of the novel are more critical of Selden, seeing him centrally implicated in the patriarchal moral framework that allows one code of behavior for men while imposing on women the strict conditions of virginity before marriage, and domestic subservience and fidelity afterward. The letters, after all, could have destroyed Bertha Dorset's marriage if Lily had used them, but they would have done little long-term damage to Selden's reputation. Sympathetically read, Bertha, like many of the other women in the novel, is obliged for her social position to marry a dull man, and must resort to duplicity in order to retain any sexual vitality. From this perspective Selden is almost as much a sexual predator as Trenor.

A contrast, life affirming in a quite literal way, is Nellie Struther's baby, part of a family which, in its near poverty, gives Lily her first sense, just before her own death, of "the continuity of life" (337). And unlike the actions of those who judge Lily by appearances only, and who estimate her value in social rather than human terms, Nellie's husband George knows of Nellie's past and accepts her. Nellie was able to resist the fate that poverty, ignorance, and the broken promises of a traveling salesman had prepared for her thanks to George's love. As a consequence Nellie, unlike Lily, can say: "I did n't see why I should n't begin over again – and I did" (332).

Bibliography

The Library of America edition, *Edith Wharton: Novels* (New York, 1985), prints the 1905 text, which is also available from many publishers in paperback format.

Deborah Esch, ed., *New Essays on The House of Mirth* (Cambridge, 2001).
Judith P. Saunders, "*The House of Mirth*: An Unsuccessful Mate Search," in *Reading Edith Wharton Through a Darwinian Lens: Evolutionary Biological Issues in Her Fiction* (Jefferson, NC, 2009), pp. 7–34.
Carol J. Singley, ed., *Edith Wharton's The House of Mirth: A Casebook* (Oxford, 2003).
Linda Wagner-Martin, *The House of Mirth: A Novel of Admonition* (Boston, 1990).

Willa Cather, *My Ántonia*, Boston: Houghton Mifflin, 1918

Like her earlier novels *O Pioneers!* and *The Song of the Lark*, *My Ántonia* drew upon Cather's childhood years in Nebraska, where she grew up surrounded by newly arrived families from Norway, Sweden, and Czecho-slovakia (the "Bohemians" of the novel). Ántonia is based upon Cather's childhood friend Annie Sadilek, whose father, like Ántonia's, committed suicide. The book is dedicated to Carrie and Irene Miner, whose family become the Harlings in the novel. Ántonia's story is told following an introduction in which an unnamed "I" and the novel's narrator Jim Burden, who both grew up in the same Nebraska town, recall "a Bohemian girl whom we had known long ago and whom both of us admired." They both feel that "more than any other person we remembered, this girl seemed to mean to us the country, the conditions, the whole adventure of our childhood."

In the 1918 printing the narrator of the Introduction suggests that they both write their recollections of Ántonia, but in a revision for the 1926 printing that shortens this Introduction, Jim has already been writing down what he remembers of Ántonia. The narrative that Jim writes is as much his story as Ántonia's, and in fact she disappears for stretches of the novel, only to be heard about second hand. Jim Burden's story, like Cather's, takes him away from Nebraska, and helps to give the novel the wider context that makes *My Ántonia* both a powerful regional novel, and a narrative that puts the stories of its pioneers into the larger context of a changing, growing conti-nent. As in all of Cather's novels, those changes involve considerable loss, and Jim's return to the places and persons of his childhood involves a recognition of that loss, one further marked by his own unsuccessful marriage, and his sense of the unrealized, probably impossible, direction that his feelings for Ántonia might have taken. The book's epigram is Virgil's "Optima dies ... prima fugit," recalled by Jim Burden as "the best days are the first to flee" (876). But as always in Cather's contrasts of past and present, there is the question of whether failures in the present produce a misleadingly sentimental and nostalgic sense of the past – as a form of escape, and of dealing with present disappointments. Jim's marriage in New York is loveless, and his constant traveling as a railroad lawyer leaves him no stable home, unlike his childhood years. Thus, as Joseph Urgo has argued, it could well be that Jim's life of movement requires his mythologizing of Ántonia's rootedness. Frances Harling calls him "romantic" for his glamorizing "the country girls."

But whatever romantic nostalgia there may be in Jim's recollection of Ántonia herself, his descriptions of pioneer life incorporate many examples of its difficulties and tragedy. His narrative describes the near-starvation of Ántonia's family during their first winter on the plain, the primitive housing of the immigrant families, and the relentless, backbreaking task of making the land fit for farming. He also recalls the story of the herd of wolves attacking the wedding party back in Russia and the actions that turn Peter and Pavel into pariahs; the tramp who throws himself into the threshing machine and is cut to pieces; the attempted rape of Ántonia by Wick Cutter, and his later murder and suicide; the story of the Negro pianist Blind d'Arnault; and, most centrally, the quiet, despairing suicide of Mr Shimerda, unable to give up his identification with the country he left behind, but pleading with Jim to teach Ántonia the language that she will need in order to have a future in the new land.

Jim shares his childhood with Ántonia and the other "hired girls," Lina Lingard and Tiny Soderball, in the town of Black Hawk (the novel's version of Red Cloud, where Cather herself grew up). The connection of their childhood and community to the land is captured in the novel's famous image of a plough against the sunset, momentarily "heroic in size, a picture writing on the sun" (866). But this important moment occurs at a picnic Jim has with the girls in what will be his last summer in Black Hawk, and also the last summer of his childhood. Jim, Lena, and Tiny all go on to lead lives that take them far away, where they can become part of the growing continent in the new century. But whereas they can each make choices about opportunities – Jim to move east with his college tutor, Lena to market her dressmaking skills, and Tiny to be part of the tough world of prospecting – Ántonia's only chance of moving away is marred by the trusting nature that leaves her unmarried, pregnant, and abandoned. Her feelings about her life when Jim sees her again in middle age are complicated in the novel by being filtered through his own needs.

Jim becomes part of the transmission of stories that binds the next generation to the pioneers, as he tells his stories to Ántonia's children, and is himself a figure in the stories that Ántonia's children have heard from their mother long before Jim returns to see her. But Jim's place in this transmission is not the same as Ántonia's, and not only because his future visits will be timed around his work for the railroad, and his escape from his loveless marriage in New York (about which there is much more detail in the 1918 version of the Introduction). Jim's father and mother died in Virginia, and on his journey out to live with his grandparents he has the sense that he has left his dead mother and father behind. Ántonia, on the other hand, traveling the same road on the same night, travels with her father, and although he does not survive that first winter she grows up and works the fields beside his grave. He thus supplies a physical continuity to her life, a continuity continued through the many children of her marriage. Mr. Shimerda's violin, which he never played in his new country, is now played, albeit imperfectly, by the grandchildren he did not live to see. Jim shares with the father the phrase "My Ántonia" that titles Jim's manuscript and thus the novel, and his title – and the degree of awareness he brings to so titling it is judged differently by different readers – incorporates the side of Ántonia that is part of this physical continuity, as well as the part of Ántonia that is described by the boyhood friend who brings the larger context of a complex, urban, industrial America to the perspective that his account offers.

Jim Burden's title "My Ántonia," a phrase also spoken by Mr. Shimerda, suggests to some readers an approach to the novel in terms of its gender issues. From this perspective, the novel's title suggests Jim's desire to define Ántonia, a male definition resisted by the more independent and arguably more successful Lena and Tiny. Both of Ántonia's parents, one could argue, are victims of gender (as well as class) discrimination. Mr. Shimerda's family ostracizes him after his marriage to a servant girl, thus immigration for Mrs. Shimerda represents an opportunity for her family to make a future away from such prejudice. Yet while Mr. Shimerda, who came to the New World reluctantly, becomes an icon of continuity for both Ántonia and Jim, Mrs. Shimerda is viewed, when Jim is a child, as grasping and crafty, and holds nothing like the place that her father does in Ántonia's memory in later years. Ántonia, in such a reading, is passed on as if a commodity from father to Jim, with the result that the definition of "My Ántonia" is one shared by both males. Ántonia also functions, one could argue, as in some sense a substitute to Jim for his wife back in New York, who leads her own life separate from him. Ántonia's brother, Ambrosch, is another oppressive figure in her life, obliging her to work in the fields and thus lose the opportunity for an education in the new Black Hawk school, an opportunity that is given to Jim. In Black Hawk, Mr Harling is an oppressive, joyless figure in the Harling household who wants to restrict Ántonia's leisure time. Her escape to employment with Wick Cutter only results in Cutter's attempts to rape her. Her trusting nature is abused by Larry Donovan. And even in her marriage she is in effect a domestic slave, producing children for husband Cuzak, finding ways to feed and clothe them to bring her husband something of the mobility enjoyed by Jim. And Jim titles his final section "Cuzak's boys," as if Ántonia's identity has been obliterated by her husband's, and her daughters are no important part of the story alongside the boys. "I like to be like a man," Ántonia tells Jim in the first summer she knows him, when she is proud of her work in the fields, but the restrictions and demands made upon her are those demanded by men of a woman (801). In such a reading, the play *Camille*, about the doomed Marguerite Gautier, that Lena and Jim watch has particular significance, as does Peter and Pavel's story of the attack of the wolves. In this latter case their desperate plan is to lighten the load and escape the wolves by throwing out the bride, not the groom – here marriage for the bride turns into literal annihilation.

How far to take such a reading depends upon the degree to which a reader judges Jim Burden sympathetically, or takes a more critical perspective. Certainly in a number of her other novels Cather dramatizes the limitations that male attitudes seek to impose upon women, while her own life and career speak to the value that she gave to independence. But it could equally be argued that in amending his manuscript title "Ántonia" to "My Ántonia," as the narrator of the Introduction recounts, Jim is acknowledging the personal and inevitably limited nature of his version of her story – recognizing that Ántonia herself is larger and more complex than any one account of her can convey.

Bibliography

The Library of America, *Willa Cather: Early Novels and Stories* (New York, 1987), prints the first edition text, and includes the 1926 Introduction in the notes. The current Houghton Mifflin printings use the 1926 text. For a scholarly edition see *My Ántonia: The Willa Cather Scholarly Edition*, ed. Charles Mignon (Lincoln, NE, 2003)

John J. Murphy, *My Ántonia: The Road Home* (Boston, 1989).
Sharon O'Brien, *New Essays on My Ántonia* (Cambridge, 1999).
Susan J. Rosowski, ed., *Approaches to Teaching Cather's My Ántonia* (New York, 1989).
Joseph Urgo, "Introduction," in *My Ántonia* (Toronto, 2003), pp. 9–32.

Sherwood Anderson, *Winesburg, Ohio*, New York: B. W. Huebsch, 1919

Sherwood Anderson was an important influence on the early work of Ernest Hemingway, William Faulkner, and a number of other writers from the 1920s and 1930s, and *Winesburg, Ohio* was the book that made his reputation. The *Winesburg* stories are set in the Ohio of the 1890s, when the full impact of the industrial revolution, and the growth of such major cities as Chicago, was starting to change the isolated community life of the small rural town. Anderson was always most successful in the short story form, and with these loosely linked stories he found the ideal framework for linking his stories to the broader narrative and thematic range usually associated with the novel. The stories of Chekhov and James Joyce have often been cited as probable influences, and Anderson was aware too of the sexual frankness in the work of D. H. Lawrence. The *Winesburg* "tales," to use Anderson's term, reject the standard form of the commercial magazine story structured around a linear plot, one that often provided a twist or surprise at the end. Instead the tales in *Winesburg* center around a key epiphanic moment, usually but not always associated with the book's sometimes absent central protagonist, George Willard. Details that might fill a string of chapters in a novel from another writer are summarized in an opening paragraph, as in this opening to "Paper Pills":

> He was an old man with a white beard and huge nose and hands. Long before the time during which we will know him, he was a doctor and drove a jaded white horse from house to house through the streets of Winesburg. Later he married a girl who had money. She had been left a large fertile farm when her father died.

The girl was quiet, tall, and dark, and to many people she seemed very beautiful. Everyone in Winesburg wondered why she married the doctor. Within a year after the marriage she died. (35)

Such details are merely surface details for Anderson. For the same reason physical description is also minimal in *Winesburg, Ohio*. In the story "Death" the narrator comments of Dr. Reefy and Elizabeth Willard:

the man and the woman sat looking at each other and they were a good deal alike. Their bodies were different, as were also the color of their eyes, the length of their noses, and the circumstances of their existence, but something inside them meant the same thing, wanted the same release, would have left the same impression on the memory of an onlooker. (221)

The physical details and "circumstances of their existence" might have interested a turn-of-the-century realist reacting against the symbolist writing of an earlier generation, or the writer of a plot-driven story, but Anderson structures his tale around the "something inside them" that "wanted the same release." Even language is superficial for Anderson if it makes claims to delineate exactly what this "something" is. The book's characters often make such a claim as part of their confusion, but the stories do not. The important communication between characters, when it occurs, is not signaled through dialogue. The story "Mother" ends with an exchange between George and his mother Elizabeth in language that is almost identical to an earlier exchange between them before the key event of the story: George's instinctive acceptance of his mother's values over his father's, and Elizabeth's isolated joy at the discovery. In the anticlimactic and perfunctory exchange that closes the story neither character conveys anything of this to the other: "'I think you had better go out among the boys. You are too much indoors,' she said. 'I thought I would go for a little walk,' replied the son stepping awkwardly out of the room and closing the door" (48).

On the broadest level, the book describes the impact of the industrial revolution upon small-town life. Communities break up, to be replaced by the anonymity of cities, while the idealistic optimism of American possibilities has been reduced to outworn and misleading rhetoric. The book insists that part of maturity, for the nation and for central figure George Willard, is the acceptance of limitation as a way to continue to grow, to avoid becoming a prisoner of the past. The importance of this acceptance of limitation is mirrored in the book's narration, its language, and the framework within which the "tales" are set.

Most of the stories concern characters who allow the "truth" of a key moment in their past to dominate their lives, remaining trapped in that past moment and becoming what the book terms "grotesques." Wash Williams hates all women because of the actions of his ex-wife and his mother-in-law, and Wing Biddlebaum gives up being a teacher and is ashamed of his expressive hands because of a misunderstanding by one boy. Sex, for a number of characters, is dangerously confusing because it seems to offer an escape from isolation beyond the moment of shared passion. Alice Hindman grows into a lonely middle age waiting for the return of a lover from the city because, years before, she and Ned Currie had declared in the moments after their lovemaking, "Now we will have to stick to each other, whatever happens we will have to do that" (114). Alice and her lover try to extend the significance of the event beyond the moment, and Alice becomes trapped by language. In the world of *Winesburg* marriage is the social codification of such a trap. A number of characters, mostly women, feel trapped in their marriages. Yet in "The Untold Lie" Ray Pearson realizes that his years of marriage, for all their oppression, have brought him most of the happy moments of his life. Recalling those moments, he cannot give a definitive answer to his fellow farmhand Hal Winters, who seeks advice on whether or not to marry his pregnant lover.

The book's narrative framework reinforces its refusal to claim definitive statement. In the opening story, set apart from the stories that follow, the oral narrator describes his encounter with an "old writer." The old man has a "dream that was not a dream," in which he recalls a procession of "grotesques." In writing his manuscript "The Book of the Grotesque" the old writer avoids becoming a grotesque himself by not publishing the book; the manuscript retains its status as a production of the moment, not a definitive statement of his experience. The old writer also keeps alive what the narrator calls the "young thing" inside himself. This quality, associated most fully with women in the book, is the ability to grow and to absorb new experience – "to dream," in the book's terms, an ability that the book argues is usually lost after adolescence (22–24). This loss is reinforced by dreams and imagination being seen as unimportant, or as feminine, in a male-dominated cultural hierarchy which values the skills associated with commerce – efficiency, competitiveness, and economic success.

The oral narrator recounts that he saw "The Book of the Grotesque" just once, and that it "made an indelible impression on my mind" (23). This "impression" is the basis of the stories that the narrator goes on to tell and that make up *Winesburg, Ohio.* Thus the old writer's text is an indirect source, another version of the tales, as are, insists the oral narrator, his own versions – their spontaneity emphasized by calling the narration "talk." He directly addresses the reader at times as if the reader were part of an audience gathered around a speaker, and he will return to a description or idea if dissatisfied with his first attempt to express it. Further complicating the source of the tales, as several critics have noted, a number of them suggest contemporary versions of classical myths, myths which themselves often have several versions.

The limitations of language are part of the book's central theme – that in order to live in the modern world it is necessary to recognize that truths are relative, time-bound, and always subject to change. Thus the narrator's language remains purposely vague at key points of the tales. When George Willard and Helen White share a silent evening together, and without the confusion of sexuality each recognizes a new sophistication in the other, the narrator only says, "they had for a moment taken hold of the thing that makes the mature life of men and women in the modern world possible" (243). Earlier in the book Kate Swift tells George that if he wishes to be a writer he must "stop fooling with words" for "the thing to learn is to know what people are thinking about, not what they say" (163). The oral narrator is the kind of storyteller that Kate Swift describes, and Kate's view reflects Anderson's larger point in this book that the responsibility of writers is to show an alternative to the America that has suppressed the potential contribution of women, and has become a place where machines replace imagination, social institutions become oppressive, and the routines of city life substitute anonymity for community.

George Willard leaves the town with the potential still to grow and learn, to avoid becoming a grotesque. He remembers "little things" as he departs Winesburg, having inherited his mother's imagination, and having accepted limitation – the time-bound place of the key moments of his life. With such an acceptance, the past, Anderson argues, can be a foundation for "the dreams of his manhood," and not a trap (247). George's evening with Helen suggests her potential too, and others in the book – the young child, Tandy, and the coach of the town's baseball team, Joe Welling – may also be figures who avoid becoming grotesques, the one because of her youth and the other because of his passionate excitement about new ideas.

The book's refusal to analyze, or even clarify explicitly, its central themes led to the accusation by some critics in mid-century that the book was sentimental, its emotional scenes neither explained nor earned. Another complaint, argued most prominently by Lionel Trilling, was that although Anderson thought he was opening up new subject matter for fiction, particularly through his frank treatment of sexual themes, actually he severely limited the range of his own work by confining himself to describing adolescents and adolescent emotions. As more recent discussions have recognized, such views do little justice to the complex unity of form, language, character, and theme in a book that, while claiming to be artless, argues passionately for the importance of art and the artist.

Bibliography

Sherwood Anderson, *Winesburg, Ohio: Penguin Classics* (New York, 1992). *Winesburg, Ohio*, ed. Ray Lewis White (Athens, OH, 1997), is a scholarly edition. Many paperback printings are also available from various publishers.

John E. Bassett, *Sherwood Anderson: An American Career* (Selingsgrove, PA, 2006).

John W. Crowley, ed., *New Essays on Winesburg, Ohio* (Cambridge, 1990).

Walter B. Rideout, *Sherwood Anderson: A Writer in America*, 2 vols. (Madison, WI, 2006, 2007).

Ray Lewis White, *Winesburg, Ohio: An Exploration* (Boston, 1990).

Sinclair Lewis, *Babbitt*, New York: Harcourt, Brace, 1922

Babbitt was the second of the series of successful and influential novels that Sinclair Lewis published in the 1920s that brought him by 1930 the Nobel Prize in Literature, the first American writer to win the award. *Main Street* (1920) had satirized the values of the American small town, and became the best-selling American novel of the first quarter of the century. With *Babbitt* Lewis turned his attention to the mid-sized city.

The Zenith of the novel is set in the Midwest and bears some resemblances to Cincinnati, where Lewis undertook some of his extensive research for the novel – research into business practices, language, and organizations. In the first paragraphs of the book Zenith is described as "a city built – it seemed – for giants." But the central character, the man who gives the novel its title, is "nothing of the giant" (489–490). Babbitt is married with two children, a member of the correct middle-class political and business groups in the city, and an excellent salesman. He runs his real estate business in a way that ignores the occasional ethical ambiguities of some of his transactions, transactions that do not cheat individuals so much as the city's taxpayers, while making all participants in the chain of the transactions a handsome profit. Babbitt slowly recognizes the emptiness of his materialism and his worship of technological progress, values that he has allowed to govern his business and domestic life. He realizes that his values and relationships are as mechanical as the machines he so admires. His largely impotent rebellion against the city, and the individuals and groups who represent its power, ends when he returns with relief but resentment to the protection, and rewards, of conformity.

The Twentieth-Century American Fiction Handbook   By Christopher MacGowan
© 2011 Christopher MacGowan

While composing the novel Lewis debated whether to keep the city in the foreground, together with the people and events that surround Babbitt, or whether to focus more fully on the central character himself. In opting for the latter he faced the problem of how to go more deeply into the mind of a man whose main interest was his ordinariness – his representative nature – and still keep him interesting. In his manuscript revisions Lewis cut many passages that give more complexity to Babbitt than he has in the final version. But the novel is the more successful for Babbitt's lack of self-knowledge, his not fully thinking through the reasons for his dissatisfaction and thus not bringing a deeply held purpose and direction to his rebellion. He becomes all the more easily a prey to the various forces that surround him.

At times, however, the point of view shifts briefly to a broader perspective, to events that only indirectly affect Babbitt, but which point up the power of the city as an autonomous force in itself. In the scene in which various cities compete for the publicity and status of hosting the annual State Association of Real Estate Boards Convention, the cities almost take on an identity of their own as characters, eclipsing the largely interchangeable individuals and groups representing them.

In Zenith consumer and business ethics govern attitudes toward education, art, religion, and even language, the culture of the city reinforcing the dehumanizing and mechanical power of its buildings and suburbs. Babbitt's son, Ted, at one point wants to drop out of high school and skip college in order to take a correspondence course with the "Shortcut Educational Pub. Co." on "Power and Prosperity in Public Speaking." The "inspiring educational symbol" at the top of the advertisement is a row of dollar signs (556–558). Babbitt objects to his son's plans without recognizing that his own values differ little from those driving the promise of the circular. Graduating from college, Babbitt argues, has more marketable status. Babbitt himself at one point in the novel has the status of a renowned orator, although the ideas and language of his speeches are a collection of clichés that tell his business audiences only what they want to hear. He delivers the required content with style. Babbitt's business letters are vague, full of slang, and often ignore grammar. They are quietly polished and corrected by his stenographer Miss McGoun, although he is irritated by her changes. The letters as Babbitt dictates them to her are another version of the exchanges that he has with his business colleagues at the Zenith Athletic Club (neither athletic nor a club) and similar places.

In making the Annual Address at the dinner of the Zenith Real Estate Board, Babbitt characterizes New York, Chicago, and San Francisco as "cursed with unnumbered foreigners," before dismissing the "moth-eaten, mildewed, out of date, old, European dumps ... that aren't producing anything but boot-blacks and scenery and booze," in order to finish by praising Zenith's plumbing and knowledge of loose-leaf ledgers (652–653). Nevertheless, some of the city's major buildings are a pastiche of foreign styles. The Athletic Club itself is a mixture of Gothic, Roman Imperial, Spanish Mission, Chinese Chippendale, and Tudor, with "a somewhat musicianless musicians'-gallery, and tapestries believed to illustrate the granting of Magna Charta" (540). Chum Frink, the local poet who also applies his talents successfully to advertising copy, is greeted with applause at a Boosters meeting when he makes a plea for the city to "whoop it up for Culture and a World-Beating Symphony Orchestra" in order to increase tourism and Zenith's status. But Zenith's advocate of culture also notes that of course he prefers jazz to "some piece by Beethoven that hasn't any more tune to it than a bunch of fighting cats," and while the symphony conductor must be "one of the highest-paid conductors on the market," he can't be "a Hun" (721–722).

To help his Presbyterian pastor, Dr. John Jennison Drew, increase attendance at the failing Sunday school Babbitt applies business and military methods to the problem, soliciting the help of a press agent who then moves on to a personal publicity campaign for Dr. Drew. Not surprisingly, when late in the novel the troubled Babbitt consults the pastor with questions about salvation, he finds the cleric's concerns driven more by earthly matters than spiritual ones, his schedule organized to the minute much like any busy business executive.

As Babbitt comes to feel dissatisfaction with the routine of his business and family life, he gropes for ways to discover an identity that isn't the anonymous one thrust upon him as the price of business success. He tries fantasy, dreaming of a sexualized version of his earlier "fairy child" dream, and later imagines a life lived among the unspoiled woods and rivers of Maine (490, 579, 689). But when reality displaces fantasy, he acts out his rebellion in terms of dissipation and a dulling sensuality.

Unlike his even more desperate friend Paul, Babbitt never takes his rebellion beyond the point where the business community of Zenith might offer him the chance of redemption. Myra Babbitt's illness and Babbitt's fear of business ruin and social isolation end his rebellion once he is given an opportunity to join the Good Citizen's League. The social forces that isolate the rebel are strong ones, and only a character with the kind of strong convictions held by the liberal Seneca Doane can live with the consequences of ideas that threaten the interests of his own class. Lewis comments overtly toward the end of the novel that while the ruling class of all countries want to perpetuate the class structure that keeps them on top, "American Democracy," while not implying "any equality of wealth ... did demand a wholesome sameness of thought, dress, painting, morals, and vocabulary" – and is more vigorous than any in seeking to impose it (835). The power of money is one way this is done – for example, businesses withholding advertising from a troublesome newspaper, just as Babbitt begins to lose staff, clients, and business opportunities when he does not conform.

Babbitt's marriage had been as empty as Paul's; husband and wife did not listen to each other, and Babbitt, like Paul, has an adulterous relationship. The male bonding of the business community excludes wives, and Babbitt is quite prepared to cover up Paul's adultery and later to perjure himself at Paul's trial to help his friend. Only late in the novel does Babbitt realize his wife's dissatisfaction with her own dull routine, although he is not sympathetic to her particular escape fantasy when she makes him sit through a lecture by Optimist and Metaphysical Seer Mrs. Opal Emerson Mudge. But the prospect of her dying from acute appendicitis brings much appreciated help from the professional men who had been isolating Babbitt for his views and behavior, and allows Babbitt to see that his marriage and family are the closest things to a human relationship that the mechanical world of the city and his job allow him. His isolation would be all but complete without Myra; "she was not merely A Woman, to be contrasted with other women, but his own self . . . in muttered incoherencies they found each other" (828, 830). Babbitt returns to conformity, and is welcomed and rewarded for his return. But from such self-knowledge as he gains from his failed rebellion he realizes what would be the human cost to his son of imposing the same oppressive conditions upon him.

With the success of *Babbitt* the words "Babbitt" and "Babbittry" passed into the American language. Upton Sinclair, H. L. Mencken, and Virginia Woolf were among those who reviewed the novel with praise, but from the first there were critical voices. Edith Wharton, to whom the book is dedicated, thought Babbitt too much purely a product of his environment, and looked for more development of his character. Other commentators have objected that the novel is more a series of set pieces, always a danger for a satirist, than a developed narrative. There have been complaints that Babbitt's motives in rebelling need more careful explanation, or that the novel offers no remedies for what it portrays. For some others, Lewis has difficulty balancing the Babbitt with whom we are to have sympathy with the Babbitt who is the object of the satire. Whether such objections are serious flaws, or whether, like Twain before him, the humorist and satirist could be allowed some inconsistencies as necessary to hit his targets, is a judgment for individual readers. Certainly the novel's lively treatment of identity, technology, gender roles, and business and religious ethics keep it fresh and relevant more than 75 years after its first appearance.

Bibliography

An authoritative text is printed in The Library of America's *Sinclair Lewis: Main Street & Babbitt* (New York, 1992), and the novel is also available in paperback printings from a number of publishers.

Michael Augspurger, "Sinclair Lewis' Primers for the Professional Managerial Class: *Babbitt, Arrowsmith,* and *Dodsworth*," *Journal of the Midwest Modern Language Association*, 34, 2 (Spring 2001), 73–97.

Simone Weil Davis, "The Pep Paradigm: Masculinity, Influence, and Shame in *Babbitt* and *The Man Nobody Knows*," in *Living Up to the Ads: Gender Fictions of the 1920s* (Durham, NC, 2000), pp. 46–79.

James M. Hutchisson, *The Rise of Sinclair Lewis: 1920–1930* (University Park, PA, 1996).

Glen A. Love, *Babbitt: An American Life* (New York, 1993).

F. Scott Fitzgerald, *The Great Gatsby*, New York: Charles Scribner's Sons, 1925

F. Scott Fitzgerald's first two novels, *This Side of Paradise* (1920) and *The Beautiful and Damned* (1922), caught the new carefree, morally relaxed atmosphere of the affluent in the early 1920s, and both had been bestsellers. The power of wealth and the allure, to an outsider, of its apparently limitless possibilities is a theme in much of Fitzgerald's fiction, but his third novel is where for the first time he explores it most fully. The novel was not the financial success he had hoped for, although there were critics who early recognized the nature of his achievement. Fitzgerald struggled with the composition of his much delayed fourth novel, *Tender is the Night* (1934), and was trying to return to something of the shorter, disciplined form of *The Great Gatsby* in *The Last Tycoon*, unfinished at his death in 1940.

The Great Gatsby explores what money can and cannot buy, and broadens the theme to include the history of the continent itself. A place of enchantment to the Europeans who first viewed it, in the present the dreams it evoked are crushed by a wealthy elite ruthless enough to know how to use the power of money. Jay Gatsby's single-minded dream to "repeat the past" with Daisy Buchanan is doomed to fail, for all his newly acquired riches, given the corruption and carelessness that in this novel the continent's history has produced. The omnipotent figure watching over Gatsby's fate is not the providential God imagined by the Puritans and other early religious pioneers, but a commercial advertisement, itself abandoned and in disrepair, looking over the valley of ashes that separates Long Island's East and West Egg from New York City: "The eyes of Dr. T. J. Eckleburg ... blue and gigantic – their retinas ... one yard high" (23).

The Twentieth-Century American Fiction Handbook   By Christopher MacGowan
© 2011 Christopher MacGowan

Gatsby's story is told by narrator Nick Carraway, who is distantly related to Daisy as well as being a college acquaintance of her husband Tom. As events unfold, Nick gradually comes to learn the true story and identity of his extravagant neighbor: how James Gatz reinvented himself as Jay Gatsby, and of his early history with Daisy. The source of Gatsby's wealth is never explicitly spelled out, but is clearly illegal, vast, and profitable.

What wealth allows Gatsby is the ability to purchase the showy house from whose grounds he can look across Long Island Sound at Daisy's dock, and in which he can throw enormous parties, virtually open to all-comers, in hopes that she will attend one of them. But what having money brings Tom Buchanan is an apartment in New York City for meetings with Myrtle, his mistress, the power to distract Myrtle's husband by dangling the possibility of a car sale that would help the garage owner's financial plight, and the resources to keep Myrtle's sister quiet if necessary at the inquest into Myrtle's death. But most importantly, money brings Tom the ability to marry and keep Daisy. Her insecurities finally drive her loyalties, rather than her marital unhappiness or her love for Gatsby. As Tom's malicious re-counting of the sources of Gatsby's income makes clear to her, the wealthy background that she and Tom have known since birth means that they share what in the world of this novel is something much more powerful, stable, and practical than her shared past with Gatsby. Tom is ruthless, racist, violent, and unfaithful, but an unhappy Daisy stays with him – for in this novel "practicality" defeats dreams, and part of that practicality is recognizing what money can and cannot buy.

Nick Carraway's own story mirrors the central narrative in important ways. Like Gatsby, he moves from the Midwest to the East, but while Gatsby's fortune is made illegally, Nick's place in the world of money, banking, and bonds is legitimate. Like Gatsby, Nick has left a girl behind, but in his case this is an engagement that he wanted to break. His initial reactions to learning more about Gatsby are annoyance, curiosity, and a rather patronizing incredulity. As an attendee at Gatsby's parties Nick is fascinated by the splendor and sheer extravagance of the setting and the behavior; for a while the world of Gatsby's parties is one with the attraction of New York and of the financial success that he could achieve there. Added to this is his attraction to Jordan Baker, professional sportswoman, friend of Daisy's, whose morally suspect values Nick can initially set aside.

Gatsby reawakens in Nick a capacity to dream that returns him to memories of his midwestern childhood, and that brings him a profound respect for the grandeur and audacity of Gatsby's impossible hopes. His story is in part the story of this reawakening. After meeting Gatsby and attending one of his parties, Nick can say of the city:

I began to like New York, the racy adventurous feel of it at night, and the satisfaction that the constant flicker of men and women and machines gives to the restless eye. I liked to walk up Fifth Avenue and pick out romantic women from the crowd and imagine that in a few minutes I was going to enter into their lives, and no one would ever know or disapprove. Sometimes, in my mind, I followed them to their apartments on the corners of hidden streets, and they turned and smiled back at me before they faded through a door into warm darkness. (56)

Elsewhere Nick describes crossing the Queensboro Bridge to come upon a view of New York that seems to offer a "wild promise of all the mystery and the beauty in the world," a city where "Anything can happen now that we've slid over this bridge ... anything at all ..." (68–69).

Some of Gatsby's party guests are also inspired to wild, imaginative flights, particularly in their speculations on the identity of their mysterious host. But such an imagination is dangerous when it fixes upon a woman more pragmatic than romantic. Daisy, for a short time, is also caught up in Gatsby's dream, escaping from the resigned cynicism that had become her way of coping with marriage to Tom. But Gatsby loses her in a raw scene at New York's Plaza Hotel, when Tom, accompanied by the sounds of Mendelssohn's Wedding March drifting in from a wedding party in a nearby room, exposes the criminal source of Gatsby's money and Gatsby demands, impossibly, that Daisy deny having ever loved her husband. In the ensuing events the three outsiders, Gatsby, Myrtle, and Wilson are killed, while Tom and Daisy disappear, taking their "baggage with them" (164). As Nick puts it: "They were careless people, Tom and Daisy – they smashed up things and creatures and then retreated back into their money or their vast carelessness, or whatever it was that kept them together, and let other people clean up the mess they had made ..." (179).

Only one of Gatsby's hundreds of summer party guests – and none of his business acquaintances – comes to the funeral. The one guest, "the man with owl-eyed glasses," is more an embodiment of the eyes of Dr. T. J. Eckleburg that watch impassively over the ash heaps than a mourner of Gatsby (174). His association with the ash heaps links him to Wilson, who appears an "ashen, fantastic figure" in the moments before he kills Gatsby; both killer and mourner are figures of death come to claim another dream and dreamer for the ash heaps (161).

Bibliography

F. Scott Fitzgerald, *The Great Gatsby* (New York, 1992). *The Great Gatsby*, ed. Matthew Bruccoli (Cambridge, 1991), is a scholarly edition, and an early version of the novel, *Trimalchio*, ed. James L. West III (Cambridge, 2000), is available in the same Cambridge Fitzgerald Edition series. The Bruccoli text is now used in the Scribner's paperback edition cited above.

Ronald Berman, *The Great Gatsby and Modern Times* (Urbana, 1994).
Claudia Johnson, *Class Conflict in F. Scott Fitzgerald's The Great Gatsby* (Detroit, 2008).
Roger Lathbury, *The Great Gatsby* (Farmington Hills, MI, 2000).
Richard Lehan, *The Great Gatsby: The Limits of Wonder* (Boston, 1990).

Ernest Hemingway, *In Our Time*, New York: Boni & Liveright, 1925

The 1925 version of *In Our Time* was Hemingway's third book, but his first with a commercial publisher. The first two books had appeared in limited printings with expatriate publishers based in France and contained some of the material that would eventually appear in the 1925 book. *Three Stories and Ten Poems* (1923) contained two stories, "Out of Season" and "My Old Man," that were included in *In Our Time*. Hemingway had planned to include the third story, "Up in Michigan," too, as the first story in the volume, but publisher Liveright objected to it on account of its sexual content (it was first published in the United States in 1938 in *The Fifth Column and the First Forty-nine Stories*). A volume titled *in our time* appeared in a printing of 170 copies the year after *Three Stories and Ten Poems*, and this book consisted of 18 short vignettes, 15 of which frame the longer stories in the 1925 publication, two of which in the 1925 book became distinct stories ("A Very Short Story" and "The Revolutionist"), and one of which became the concluding "L'Envoi." Further complicating the bibliographical history of *In Our Time*, in the 1930 reissue by Scribner's Hemingway added another story before the first vignette – titled "Introduction by the Author" in this edition and "On the Quai at Smyrna" in later editions of the collection.

Critical discussion of *In Our Time* as a book with its own structural and thematic patterns, as opposed to the discussion of individual stories, is relatively recent. The book was somewhat overshadowed by the success of the two novels *The Sun Also Rises* (1926) and *A Farewell to Arms* (1929) and two other collections of stories. When Scribner's published *The Fifth Column and the First Forty-nine Stories*, all three short story volumes tended to be viewed as the same kind of miscellaneous collection. *In Our Time* was not reissued again as a separate volume until 1962.

Discussion of influence is particularly pertinent in the case of this book because the individual stories illustrate the remarkable developments in Hemingway's work over a period of just two or three years, as he responded to and adapted his early models.

This development is clearly illustrated in three of the volume's stories concerning the relationship between father and son. "My Old Man," the earliest story in *In Our Time*, reveals the influence of such Sherwood Anderson tales as "I Want to Know Why" and "The Egg." In "My Old Man," the quiet desperation of the youthful narrator's love for his father is accompanied by an account of the world of fraud and corruption surrounding his father that the narrator does not fully comprehend. In "The Doctor and the Doctor's Wife," by contrast, Nick Adams is more aware of the father's weakness, but despite his emotional allegiance to the father over the mother, the story reveals some of the demons within the father of which the young boy is hardly aware. But in "Indian Camp" the tension, affection, and isolation of father and son are described in an economical, objective manner that is a good deal closer to Hemingway's mature style.

Two literary models often cited for the structure of *In Our Time* are Anderson's *Winesburg, Ohio* (1919) and T. S. Eliot's *The Waste Land* (1922), while the book has also been discussed as a Cubist text. Hemingway admired Anderson's book of loosely related stories, and had met the older writer in Chicago. Eliot's poem, winner of the prestigious *Dial* Prize in 1922, made dramatic use of juxtaposition to complicate thematic complexity, and presented short, apparently disconnected incidents to set scene and mood. Other influences often cited include James Joyce's collection of stories, *Dubliners* (1914), and the prose of Gertrude Stein. Hemingway adapted what he learned from such models to what he already knew from his work as a journalist about writing clear, concrete, economical prose.

Stein's practice of repetition in order to eschew abstraction is put to effective use in the stories. For example, when Nick Adams has made his camp in the first part of "Big Two-Hearted River," he stops to enjoy the results of his work, and a series of short, repetitive sentences slow down and break up the narrative into the series of discrete moments that record Nick's experience:

> Nick was happy as he crawled inside the tent. He had not been unhappy all day. This was different though. Now things were done. There had been this to do. Now it was done. It had been a hard trip. He was very tired. That was done. He had made his camp. He was settled. Nothing could touch him. It was a good

place to camp. He was there, in the good place. He was in his home where he had made it. Now he was hungry. (139)

This is the language of sensation, and part of Nick's comfortable pleasure comes from the exertions of a day that has dulled his mind's ability to pull him away from these immediately pleasurable sensations.

Nick's disciplined camping and fishing routine, his living with and using nature, serves as a healing process in the two-part story that closes the book. The story does not spell out what Nick's wound is, although the account begins with Nick stepping off a train to find the town that formerly stood there burned to the ground almost without trace. The earlier stories and vignettes suggest an association of the burned town and Nick's isolation with the impact of World War I, not just upon Nick Adams, but upon everybody – whether soldiers or civilians – whose lives have been caught up in it.

The world that Nick tries to recover from on his fishing trip, as suggested in the book's earlier stories and linking passages, is one where nature can be both beautiful and cruel, where love brings as much confusion and pain as it does pleasure, where friendship may end at any moment, and where violence, fear, and death are ever present. Both sides in the war have devalued language, using such abstractions as patriotism, valor, glory, and heroism to promote and justify wholesale slaughter. The accounts in the vignettes of actions played out under extreme pressure suggest similar forces at work behind the more understated events of the stories. There are no heroic gestures in the penultimate vignette, the hanging of Sam Cardinella, and in "L'Envoi," which closes the book, the Greek king acknowledges the need for ruthlessness in order to survive in a dangerous, violent world.

Although from the 1930 edition on the book carried the warning "there are no real people in this volume; both the characters and their names are fictitious," the characters are sometimes thinly disguised portraits of members of the expatriate community living in France. The stories also reflect the author's mid-west childhood and adolescence, his wartime service in the Red Cross ambulance corps, his subsequent injury and convalescence, and the tensions in his marriage to first wife Hadley Richardson (to whom the book is dedicated). Nick's cruelty toward Marjorie in "The End of Something" is echoed by the behavior of Luz in "A Very Short Story." The marriages in "The Doctor and the Doctor's Wife," "Mr. and Mrs. Elliot," "Cat in the Rain," and "Out of Season" are all troubled in various ways. George and Nick know in "Cross-Country Snow" that because of Nick's impending fatherhood they may not ski together again. The pleasure of skiing together must not be dissipated by putting it into words; it is "too swell to talk about," and "There isn't any good in promising" (109, 112).

In the years since Hemingway's death some important critical discussions have centered more fully on the autobiographical aspects of the book, taking account of newly available manuscript evidence, in particular earlier versions of some of the stories. Some of the posthumously published texts, and new biographical details, suggest a more insecure sexuality in the author than his aggressively masculine public persona ever conceded. Such material has drawn attention to the gender issues in the book, complicating discussions of the impact in the stories that heterosexual attraction can bring to the simpler, if inevitably barren, joys of male companionship. Also receiving fresh attention are the book's themes of fatherhood, abortion, incest, marriage, androgyny, sexual repression, and impotence, and their impact upon writing, the war, and the necessarily limited expectations of what might be possible in the future.

Nick can begin the healing process in the final story because nature offers him a degree of renewal and continuity. He can guide himself by the river, and after walking a few miles he finds that the grasshoppers there are not blackened by the fire that has destroyed the town. In Nick's largely silent two days by the Big Two-Hearted River he remembers Hopkins giving his friends objects "to remember him always by," rather than going through the rhetorical formulas of parting. Even so, the group throws around plans for a future meeting that never happens and that are scarcely believed at the time. The understated pain and loss in the three sentences that summarize Nick's recollection of Hopkins are the essence of the narrative style that Hemingway found for this book: "They said goodbye and all felt bad. It broke up the trip. They never saw Hopkins again" (141). This is a narrative style that in its sparse detail mirrors the starkness of the world it describes, and in its clipped tone reflects the stoicism necessary to face that world. These repressed feelings of regret and longing will, Nick realizes, one day have to be faced – just as he will have to face the swamp further upriver. That awareness is part of living "in our time," and Hemingway's prose finds a way to record it.

Bibliography

In Our Time (New York, 2008). The book is often reprinted by Scribner's in paperback editions.

Milton A. Cohen, *Hemingway's Laboratory: The Paris in our time* (Tuscaloosa, 2005).

Nancy R. Comley and Robert Scholes, *Hemingway's Genders: Rereading the Hemingway Text* (New Haven, 1994).

Michael S. Reynolds, *Hemingway: The Paris Years* (New York, 1989).

Matthew Stewart, *Modernism and Tradition in Ernest Hemingway's In Our Time* (Rochester, NY, 2001).

William Faulkner, *The Sound and the Fury*, New York: Jonathan Cape and Harrison Smith, 1929

The Sound and the Fury, Faulkner's fourth novel, is his second to take place in the fictional Yoknapatawpha County that he set in his native Mississippi. The first, *Sartoris*, was published in January 1929 and *The Sound and the Fury* appeared nine months later in October. The much more complex and challenging later novel was turned down by Harcourt, Brace, who had published *Sartoris* only after insisting upon cutting down the manuscript, and thus was published by Cape and Smith, Smith having been the editor at Harcourt, Brace who had supported publication of *Sartoris*. Like most of Faulkner's novels, the book was out of print by the 1940s, but sections of the novel were reprinted in *The Portable Faulkner* in 1946, and the full text became available later that year in a one-volume edition that also included *As I Lay Dying*. *The Sound and the Fury* has since been recognized as one of Faulkner's major works, and one of the major works of American fiction.

Yoknapatawpha County and its residents would appear in many of Faulkner's novels and stories for the next 30 years. Quentin Compson, narrator of the second section of the novel, reappears along with his Harvard roommate, Shreve McCannon, in *Absalom, Absalom!*, published seven years after *The Sound and the Fury* – although concerned with events much earlier. As another example, the Snopes family, who have a relatively minor role in *As I Lay Dying* (the next Yoknapatawpha novel to be published following *The Sound and the Fury*), become the subject of a late trilogy: *The Hamlet* (1940), *The Town* (1957), and *The Mansion* (1959).

The Twentieth-Century American Fiction Handbook   By Christopher MacGowan
© 2011 Christopher MacGowan

Each of the first three sections of *The Sound and the Fury* covers a day narrated by one of the three Compson brothers. The novel's present is Easter weekend April 6, 7, and 8, 1928, although Quentin's section is set 18 years earlier, on the day of his suicide. The assumptions, arrogance, and suffering revealed by the narration are part of the novel's picture of a defeated South haunted by the corruption of slavery and the moral blindness that sought to justify it. The fourth and last section of the novel is recounted by an objective narrator, although the focus of the narration for much of the section is the old and ailing black servant Dilsey, whose presence across the years, and whose qualities of faith, sympathy, and patient suffering, are in marked contrast to the torment and fragmentation of the Compson family. The four sections circle around many of the same events, each section a part of how the history of the Compson family shapes the events of the Easter weekend.

Caddy, the brothers' only sister, is a central presence in the narratives despite her absence, rejected both by her family and her morally suspect husband. Her lack of a narrative section is consistent with the suppression of the female voice in the chivalric codes of the pre-Civil War South that had given the Compsons their aristocratic status. Caddy appears almost entirely as a projection of her father and brothers' different emotional needs and obsessions.

The mentally retarded Benjie narrates the first section, making little distinction between past and present. The detail of his narration fuses multiple past events with what he sees, hears, and feels, moment by moment, on April 7, 1928. Faulkner provides some clues to time shifts by italicizing certain passages, and a further chronological clue comes from which particular young boy from Dilsey's family is assigned the care of Benjie. The particular experience that sends Benjie's narration into his own subjective experience of time might be a single word spoken by another, his own sensory response – perhaps to cold or fire – or an overpowering emotion. But Benjie's narration is not a chaotic set of arbitrary impressions. Even if his sensory or emotional recall of an event from the past experienced as the present is briefly interrupted by an event in the actual present, Benjie always returns to complete what was interrupted. And what initially appears to be Benjie's confusing application of male and female pronouns to the name Quentin is an accurate distinction between the novel's two characters with that name, his eldest brother and Caddy's daughter.

Benjie is also accurate in his narration of dialogue, and often from that dialogue events outside of his sense experience and awareness can be inferred. To take a small example, early in the section Benjie is with Luster and some other boys, and Luster is looking for a coin that he has lost in the branch of a nearby river. Benjie's description of Luster looking for the lost quarter is followed by an account of an apparently related action:

> then they splashed and fought in the branch. Luster got it and they squatted in the water, looking up the hill through the bushes.
>
> "Where is they." Luster said.
> "Aint in sight yet."
> Luster put it in his pocket. They came down the hill.
> "Did a ball come down here." (16)

Benjie does not see the ball come from the adjacent golf course into the water, and so he does not describe the event, only the result – the boys splashing in the water. He does not infer from the golfer's question that the boys are looking for a ball and adjust his account, he only describes the exchange and the response. The reader's understanding of the antecedent of "it" shifts from the quarter to the golf ball in light of Benjie's fidelity to the world of his senses, but there are no antecedents in Benjie's world any more than there is a past separate from the present. (One consequence of the proximity of the golf course is that the players' recurring call of "caddy" is a torment to him, since he imagines that the absent sister whose sympathy and affection always brought him such comfort is close by, Benjie having no sense of the events that brought about her exile.) Overall, the structure of his narration suggestively mirrors the first physical description of him, a description supplied by the objective narrator in the fourth section: "a big man who appeared to have been shaped of some substance whose particles would not or did not cohere to one another or to the frame which supported it" (274).

If Benjie's experience is a continual present, his eldest brother Quentin, sent to study at Harvard by his father, is trapped by the desperate wish to return to a past and a place that once could have offered him an identity, a code of values, and a role. He is constantly reminded during his day wandering in the countryside outside Cambridge of the increasing distance between that past and his present, by the ticking and chiming of clocks, the movement of the sun and shadows, and the flow of the Charles River. Benjie's narration makes no distinction between his present and his past, but Quentin, in contrast, is painfully aware of the difference. His identity is so caught up in the past that his narrative continually shifts to past events, events recalled with increasing desperation as his day progresses. Quentin's narration replays furious discussions with his father, whose response to Caddy's promiscuity – and the fragmentation of the family along with the broader culture that sustained his authority – is to replace the chivalric values passed on to his eldest son with an alcohol-driven cynicism and sexual disgust. In response Quentin constructs a personal theology within which he and Caddy are damned, he for his suicide and she for the promiscuity that he wants to insist is incest. This damnation, as he imagines it a number of times in his narrative, would keep them together apart from others, in *"a hell beyond that: the clean flame the two of us more than dead. Then you will have only me then only me then the two of us amid the pointing and the horror beyond the clean flame"* (116).

The devastation wrought upon Quentin by his father's cynicism is all the greater because his mother offers no alternative. Mrs. Compson is herself a product of the passivity assigned to women under the chivalric code. She sees the transmission of that code to the eldest son as an entirely masculine affair. She both resents her assigned role and uses it to avoid taking any responsibility for the events that engulf her children. This absence leaves Quentin open to the impossible chivalric ideals instilled by his father, and leaves Caddy victim to the confusion of emotional need and the powerful sexual energies awakening in her body.

Jason Compson's cynically exploitative attitudes toward women, including his mother, sister, and niece, are in stark contrast to the chivalric obsessions that bring his brother such despair. His bitter and cruel humor deflates the lost values that so torture Quentin. As a younger son he considers himself unfairly disinherited, but tells himself that he has no illusions about the consequences – one of which, he thinks, is that he is a clear-eyed modern, independent man freed from the legacy of Compson history. In fact his narrative makes clear that he is as driven by the past as his two brothers. In his fast-paced account he is continually late arriving at his destination, whether just missing the girl Quentin, or too late to catch the changes that would reward his market speculations. He views all relationships in financial terms: Caddy's pregnancy robbed him of a good job at a bank, Quentin's suicide after the sale of family land had paid for Harvard selfishly robbed him of an inheritance, the black servants are lazy and exploitative. Appropriately, his girlfriend Lorraine is a prostitute. Jason's furious pace finally stops in section four, when, exhausted and sick from chasing Quentin and the money that she escaped with, he has to pay a Negro to drive him back to Jefferson. Isolated rather than independent, he cannot even find comfort in the thought of being with Lorraine, since those thoughts quickly shift to dollars and cents, and then to renewed fury at being outwitted by a woman.

Section four, set on Easter Sunday, places Dilsey within the cycle of seasonal change. She is the first central character to experience time and landscape as something beyond personal projections. The novel is all the more powerful for not sentimentalizing the woman who tries to meet as best she can the needs of her own family as well as those of her Compson employers.

She treats Benjie with more kindness than he is shown by any of his own family now that Caddy has gone, and takes him to the Easter service that quiets his misery. Her faith brings her belief in a future that transcends the time-bound history which so torments the Compsons, and allows her a sense of unbroken connection to the past of her suffering race. By contrast, Mrs. Compson's empty gestures toward faith bring her no comfort. Her unopened Bible lies at the end of her bed in a darkened room; her son Jason, fruitlessly chasing money and the girl Quentin, is too rushed to even recognize the religious festival; and Quentin rationalizes his suicide by a purely private theology constructed out of his own desperation.

With the girl Quentin having escaped, and Caddy disowned by the family, the Compson line is represented at the end of the novel by the corrupt and violent Jason, the mentally retarded Benjie, and the largely supine Mrs. Compson. In an Appendix that Faulkner prepared in 1945 for *The Portable Faulkner*, he set out at some length the past history of the Compson family as well as its future. That future is already implicit in the narrative of this strongly determinist novel. But although not part of the novel itself, the Appendix is an interesting record of the author's sense of the larger familial and historical background to the generation whose suffering and decline forms the narrative of *The Sound and the Fury*.

Bibliography

William Faulkner, *The Sound and the Fury* (New York 1990). This Vintage edition prints the "corrected text" as established in 1984.

John T. Matthews, *The Sound and the Fury: Faulkner and the Lost Cause* (Boston, 1991).
Charles A. Peek and Robert W. Hamblin, *A Companion to Faulkner Studies* (Westport, CT, 2004).
Noel Polk, ed., *New Essays on The Sound and the Fury* (Cambridge, 1993).
Stephen M. Ross and Noel Polk, *Reading Faulkner: The Sound and the Fury* (Jackson, MS, 1996).

Zora Neale Hurston, *Their Eyes Were Watching God,* Philadelphia: J. B. Lippincott, 1937

Hurston's second novel came in for a good deal of criticism from black male writers upon its publication, most famously from Richard Wright, who argued that the novel's use of myth, dialect, and tradition exploited the "quaint" aspects of Negro life that particularly appealed to white audiences. He also felt that the novel presented the life of blacks in the South as too carefree, and that its romantic, lyrical prose was a step backward from the social realism and protest writing that had followed the achievements of the 1920s Harlem Renaissance.

Some of the central features of Hurston's novel certainly run counter to Wright's sense of the issues that black fiction should engage. The two central male figures in the novel, Joe Starks and Tea Cake, are active, energetic, and charismatic, but the novel focuses on its central female character, Janie, who at times is very passive within the narrative, and whose voice is supplanted third-person narration. The novel is sometimes critical of its black characters and black communities. Individuals and groups can be cruel to others and to animals; the men are generally sexist and have few qualms about beating their wives. Some of the black characters, Joe Starks and Mrs. Turner in particular, make racist distinctions between blacks. The crowd that comes to Florida's Everglades for seasonal work on "the muck," are people "ugly from ignorance and broken from being poor" (282). They gamble and get drunk when they get paid, and assume that Janie is guilty of murder before learning any details of Tea Cake's death. A series of predatory black suitors try to win Janie

The Twentieth-Century American Fiction Handbook   By Christopher MacGowan
© 2011 Christopher MacGowan

after Joe leaves her a wealthy widow, and even Tea Cake – who has little interest in her money – beats her when another man is interested in her, even though on his part he creeps into the cover of the fields with the sexually willing Nunkie.

None of the central black characters fight against the subservient position imposed by whites, and some of them benefit from the whites' patronizing protection and charity. To most of the characters, white power and racism are an immutable fact – always a presence and potentially dangerous – a fact that has to be accepted and somehow lived with. Janie's grandmother has to accept the sexual victimization by the owner of the plantation where she is a slave, and Janie, two generations later, does not speak up in the white court that puts her on trial, just passively trusting in their mercy and understanding. Her relationship with Tea Cake and journey to "the muck" lead her deeper into her own black heritage, but the end result produces in her no fuller understanding of gender, violence, poverty, or race, although what she retains for herself from the experience (but does not communicate to Phoebe) is a wholeness that is the major triumph of her narrative. Part of that triumph is to turn against, even to hate, her grandmother – the victim of slavery who brought her up in the absence of the child's mother. And although money could not purchase this triumph, Janie is hardly a representative figure when she returns to Eatonville, since she is significantly wealthier than any other member of the black community.

Thus the novel, so against the grain of the largely male-dominated African American writing of its time, was out of print and hard to find by the early 1970s, when it was rediscovered along with Hurston's other work – largely by writers, scholars, and teachers of the new Black Studies programs forming nationwide. The more contemporary assessment of the novel sees the author's study of African American myth and folklore (at Barnard College and Columbia University and with the support of two Guggenheim Fellowships) not as producing a picturesque background of local color, but as recording within a powerfully imagined narrative an authentic account of the dialect and traditions that bind together a culture. This culture is a shared heritage born out of slavery, suffering, and poverty that is a support, a comfort, and even a delight to the community it brings together. This is the heritage and communal experience that for 20 years Joe Starks keeps Janie isolated from, and that subsequently her time with Tea Cake allows her to discover and share.

Although the novel begins with Janie's return to Eatonville, where she starts to tell her tale to friend Phoebe, the narration shifts to, and largely remains, in a third-person voice – and her tale broadens to become the story of her whole life. One of the critical issues in discussion of the novel is this shift in voice. Janie also requests that Phoebe tell the story to the town, and earlier she is silent for whole stretches of the narrative, most strikingly for some readers in the courtroom scene when she is on trial. One reading suggests that Janie's voice becomes a collective one for her race and gender, as she recognizes in asking Phoebe to speak for her. As for her silence when on trial, 20 years of marriage to Joe Stark teaches her that she should keep quiet when powerless, and this is possibly the position that experience has taught her to take in the courtroom.

Janie's grandmother tells her that love is an impractical and even dangerous hope as the young girl is married off to a local black farmer to protect her from the kind of sexual exploitation that the grandmother herself suffered. But Janie, whose romantic imagination is expressed from the first in terms of nature and natural processes, yearns for something more than the servitude and humiliation she suffers at the hands of Logan Killicks.

Janie's grandmother was both victimized and protected by whites, although she manages to achieve a small degree of independence. Whites remain largely on the margins of Janie's story, but their actions constantly impact upon her life and that of the black communities, actions sometimes benevolent, sometimes exploitative, but most often merely thoughtless of the consequences to a race so separate from their own concerns. Captain Eaton and Mr. Laurence give 50 acres to the black community, but Joe Starks recognizes the limitations of the gift if the town is to have any chance at self-sufficiency. The white lawyers, the judge, and the police in Palm Springs make sure that Janie is tried and acquitted within hours after Tea Cake's death, their sensitivity a marked contrast to Tea Cake's friends, who would condemn her. But the protection is double-edged in that the black community is simply denied a voice in the proceedings. Earlier, in the floods that follow the hurricane, whites had claimed all the protective high ground on the bridge at Six Mile Bend, forcing the exhausted Tea Cake and Janie onto the route that results in his death. Later, in Palm Springs, while the groups pressed into service recovering bodies are multiracial, the bodies themselves, their race obliterated by the force of the catastrophe, must be searched and the race identified. The graveyards are segregated, and only white bodies receive burial in coffins, while black victims are thrown into a ditch.

However, the impact of white presence upon black lives past and present is most telling in the hours before the hurricane strikes, in the scene that gives the novel its title. Tea Cake is a gambler, and is willing to chance fate when the hurricane threatens. But he wants the advantages on his side, and rationalizes that the "white folks" haven't left, although they surely would if the storm were going to be really dangerous (301). In giving this power and prescience to whites he ignores the actions of the fleeing Native Americans. This passive and misplaced trust takes in generations of cultural history, and a servitude once physical but now a way of thinking born of limited opportunities, continuing racial division, and the whites' continued and uncompromising hold on power.

But when Tea Cake's group is confronted with the undeniable and increasing power of the storm, their sense of where to look for protection moves beyond race to "Old Massa," a God-like figure personified in terms of slave heritage, but with a power beyond the merely human. "They seemed to be staring at the dark," the narrator reports, "but their eyes were watching God" (305). The crucial difference between "staring" and "watching" is the difference between passivity and Tea Cake's decision that they must flee, and also the difference between following a spiritual rather than a racial guide. Hurston's black characters are not angry rebels, they confront forces – racial, natural, and spiritual – against which their own powers are limited, and their understanding of that confrontation is often expressed in mythic rather than social or political terms. As Hurston's title makes clear, and as Janie's story illustrates, this confrontation is hardly the story of passive acquiescence against a background of local color, which is how the novel was characterized by some of Hurston's contemporary critics.

Janie leaves her husband to follow Joe Starks on a journey that promises to take her toward the horizon that figures in her dreams as offering love and a future free of restriction. Joe's energy, inventiveness, and self-confidence build the community of Eatonville, but his hierarchical and sexist views keep Janie from participating in the communal life of the town. The distance that he insists she keep reinforces his own status, although he fully shares in the humor, tall tales, and gossip that he keeps her from. He insults her publicly, a humiliation that culminates in a public beating. She can only speak frankly without punishment when he is on his deathbed. The result is her isolation in marriage and within the community, her horizons as far away as they ever were but still yearned for by the imaginative self kept separate from her life with Joe.

Janie's choices for a partner among her suitors after Joe Stark's death come down to an undertaker, trading in finalities, and the creative, penniless gambler Tea Cake who promises a new future. Tea Cake, like Joe, is a leader, but his leadership is inclusive not hierarchical, and their life together is shared not compartmentalized. Two telling incidents in their relationship are Tea Cake enjoying and claiming part ownership of Janie's hair – a particular feature of her beauty that Joe made her keep hidden in a head rag, and a key motif through the novel. The other is Janie's casual dress at Tea Cake's funeral. She is "too busy feeling grief to dress like grief," in contrast to the formal mourning clothes she wears at Joe's funeral and behind which she hides her true emotions (330). Janie pulls "in her horizon like a great fish-net" when she returns alone to Eatonville and it becomes part of the dress with which she clothes both body and soul (333). With Tea Cake she had journeyed to that horizon, and in the resulting peace she can now make her own choices.

Bibliography

The Library of America printing, included in *Zora Neale Hurston: Novels and Stories* (New York, 1995), is based on the first and only edition published in Hurston's lifetime, as is the frequently reissued Harper trade paperback.

Michael Awkward, ed., *New Essays on Their Eyes Were Watching God* (New York, 1990).

Henry Louis Gates, Jr. and K. A. Appiah, eds., *Zora Neale Hurston: Critical Perspectives Past and Present* (New York, 1993).

Neal A. Lester, *Understanding Zora Neale Hurston's Their Eyes Were Watching God: A Student Casebook to Issues, Sources, and Historical Documents* (Westport, CT, 1999).

Cheryl Wall, ed., *Their Eyes Were Watching God: A Casebook* (New York, 2000).

Djuna Barnes, *Nightwood*, London: Faber and Faber, 1936; New York: Harcourt, Brace, 1937

Although *Nightwood* was published in the second half of the 1930s, its story is set in the 1920s Paris and Berlin of the American expatriates, and Barnes had begun the novel much closer to that decade. In 1921 Barnes had become the Paris correspondent for *McCall's* magazine. In that year she met and for some years lived with Thelma Wood, the model for Robin Vote in the novel. *Nightwood*'s complexly told narrative of a lesbian love triangle had been rejected by almost every publisher in the United States (Clifton Fadiman at Simon and Schuster had told her that no standard publishing house would take it) before T. S. Eliot, after some initial hesitation, saw it into print at Faber and Faber, making some editorial changes to material that he feared could be judged obscene. Eliot went on to write an introduction which traces his response to the manuscript over a number of readings, recording that "it took me, with this book, some time to come to an appreciation of its meaning as a whole" (xvii). Eliot was particularly struck by Doctor O'Connor's furious and despairing monologues, although he initially felt that they rather overbalanced the book. Eliot's comments also introduced the 1937 American edition, and the New Directions edition when James Laughlin brought the novel back into print in 1946. The novel was well received on its first appearance, and its admirers included Dylan Thomas and William S. Burroughs. But its complex and difficult narrative made it a book often more respected than read, until the revival of interest in Barnes's work in the 1970s that firmly established *Nightwood* among the most important American novels of the century.

The Twentieth-Century American Fiction Handbook   By Christopher MacGowan
© 2011 Christopher MacGowan

A younger version of Doctor O'Connor appears in Barnes's 1928 novel *Ryder*, although in *Nightwood* he is capable of much deeper feeling and suffering. His title, like that of his friend the Baron, is fake. He is not a licensed doctor, he lives on the brink of being discovered by the law, and he has very little money – stealing, and trying with as much dignity as he can muster to get others to pay on social occasions. Although male, he dresses for sexual encounters as a female. His language, like his drinking, is as much an attempt to fend off despair as to communicate, and by the end of the novel, in a drunken, exhausted monologue, he has completely given in to his dark mood. But he recognizes, more fully than the triangle of lovers, the character of the "night" as part dream, part real, part fantasy, and part "legend." He more fully understands Robin's connection with the night than any of her three lovers (surreptitiously applying some of her makeup on himself when he is called to revive her) although this knowledge, and the demands made on him because of that knowledge, finally undermine his attempts to be an uninvolved observer. He is in fact at the center of the triangle. He exclaims to Nora, "why, sweet God, my girl, I helped to bring you into the world!" (21); he introduces the Baron to Robin and suggests the later marriage; and, mistakenly, thinks that he introduced Robin to Jenny, bringing about the break between Nora and Robin that causes Nora such torment.

"I have a narrative, but you will be put to it to find it," the doctor tells the unhappy Nora at one point, and equally the key narratives in this novel are to be found elsewhere than in the book's external events (104). The chronological signposts are there but are few, since each character in the novel is, through a combination of love, obsession, despair, or desperation, caught up in his or her own time, each linked in some way to the mysterious and compelling figure of Robin Vote. The broader structure of the novel does lay out the story chronologically: from the birth of Baron Volkbein in 1880, to the scene early in the 1930s when Nora and her dog discover Robin in the decaying chapel on Nora's estate. Yet juxtaposed against this forward narrative movement, chapters three, four and five all end with an account of the same evening – the evening of the carriage ride, and Nora seeing Robin with Jenny in the garden.

Robin's room is decorated like a jungle, suggesting her place between the bestial and the human in her appetites and wanderings. Her bed is "surrounded by a confusion of potted plants, exotic palms and cut flowers, faintly over-sung by the notes of unseen birds" (37). Her "flesh was the texture of plant life, and beneath it one sensed a frame, broad, porous and sleep-worn." She is like a sleepwalker, part child and part "desperado," and these qualities govern her activities when she leaves each of her lovers to go out into the night (38). Robin represents for her three lovers, Nora, Jenny, and the Baron, something daring, imaginative, and creative, vulnerable yet threatening, and attractive in its careless hedonism. These qualities are missing in their own more limited, more structured lives. Part of the appeal to Robin of each of the three lovers is that each of them appears to have a sympathy for the transformations of identity and performance that might match her own, although they finally turn out to be too rigid: the Baron's concern with history, Nora's limited imagination, and Jenny's mere appropriation of others' emotions, "teeming with second-hand dealings with life" (72).

As the doctor knows, and tries to explain to Nora, Robin's magnetic appeal is connected to "the night," in particular, says the doctor, "French nights." "Every day is thought upon and calculated," he tells Nora, "but the night is not premeditated. The Bible lies the one way, but the night-gown the other." Americans, the doctor explains, try to separate day and night: "we tear up the one for the sake of the other; not so the French." Nora tells the doctor, "I never thought of the night as a life at all – I've never lived it," but at three in the morning she learns things about him that are new to her: learning how poor he is, and of his cross-dressing. "I used to think," Nora confesses, "that people just went to sleep, or if they did not go to sleep that they were themselves, but now … now I see that the night does something to a person's identity, even when asleep" (87–89).

The doctor's account of the night indicates what the Americans find unfulfilling about the country that they leave behind in order to live in Paris. For many of the characters, part of getting away from the calculated morality associated with "the Bible" is the attraction of Catholicism. Catholicism's iconography and theatrical rituals, akin to the opera and circus that the expatriate characters also enjoy, involve a full recognition of sin as part of the promise of absolution. The doctor seeks answers to his ambivalent sexuality in a Catholic church, and in his final, drunken moments in the novel is being taken home by an ex-priest. The Baron, born of a Christian mother and a Jewish father, embraces a fake Christian heritage, and his son even as a child wishes to "enter the church" (115). Jenny Petherbridge treats religion as she does opera, as a source of artifacts from which to appropriate emotions, while Nora, "an early Christian; she believed the word," learns about night, sin, and the fluidity of gender through her nocturnal wanderings in search of Robin (56).

The emotions of loss in this novel are associated with degrees of obsession about the past. Robin is able to forget, but the others cannot. Nora's dream of inviting Robin into her grandmother's house is matched in the Baron's case by the family portraits of his grandparents, portraits that are actually of performers. One of Jenny's "second hand dealings" is her interest in purchasing one of these portraits from the Baron, in order to be closer in some way to Robin. Whether through the rituals of Catholicism or the artifice of the circus and the opera, each character's response to loss and despair is itself a performance – one played out amidst the artifice of false titles, aristocratic and medical, and fluid gender identities. And all such artifice is compounded by the transformations of night, that "dark door," as the doctor calls it, through which Robin escapes (87).

Bibliography

The New Directions edition (New York, 2006) carries Eliot's introduction and a preface by Jeanette Winterson. *Nightwood: The Original Version and Related Drafts*, ed. Cheryl J. Plumb (Normal, IL, 1995), presents Barnes's text before the pre-publication revisions.

Phillip Herring, *Djuna: The Life and Work of Djuna Barnes* (New York, 1995).

Jane Marcus, "Laughing at Leviticus: *Nightwood* as Woman's Circus Epic," in *Silence and Power: A Reevaluation of Djuna Barnes*, ed. Mary Lyn Broe (Carbondale, IL, 1991), pp. 221–250.

Deborah Parsons, "Djuna Barnes: Melancholic Modernism," in *Cambridge Companion to the Modernist Novel*, ed. Morag Shiach (Cambridge, 2007), pp. 165–77.

Diane Warren, *Djuna Barnes' Consuming Fictions* (Aldershot, UK, 2008).

John Steinbeck, *The Grapes of Wrath*, New York: Viking, 1939

Prior to writing his Pulitzer Prize and National Book Award-winning novel *The Grapes of Wrath*, in the mid-1930s Steinbeck wrote a series of articles for the *San Francisco News* on the plight of the tens of thousands of migrants flocking into California from the dust bowl conditions of the Midwest. These families had been evicted from farms that had sometimes been in the family for two or three generations. In the course of writing the articles Steinbeck met and traveled with Tom Collins, administrator of the Arvin Sanitary Camp, one of a number set up by the Federal Farm Security Administration to provide some basic amenities to the migrants. Collins provided Steinbeck with much important background information, and the Arvin Camp served as the model for the Weedpatch Camp in the novel. Collins shared the dedication of the book with the novelist's first wife, Carol Henning.

The *Grapes of Wrath* was Steinbeck's third novel on the plight of migrant workers in California, following *In Dubious Battle* (1936) and *Of Mice and Men* (1937). The title comes from the second line of "The Battle Hymn of the Republic," which Steinbeck had printed on the endpapers of the original edition. While the narrative follows the journey and sufferings of the Joad family, their story alternates with interchapters that describe from a broader perspective the impact of the drought, the trials of a 2000-mile migration, and the hostility and exploitation that the migrants encountered in California upon their arrival. The interchapters make clear that the Joads' experience is both representative and inevitable.

The migrants are victims of nature and of economic change. Already vulnerable because of drought and the Depression's impact upon farm prices, they are forced to borrow from the banks that, in conjunction with large landholding associations, take over and consolidate the small farms. Tractors replace mules and ploughs, knocking down the homes of the evicted farmers as they plough up the newly acquired fields. The farmers are exploited by those who buy the possessions they are forced to sell in order to pay for the journey, and again by those who sell them the ancient trucks and cars upon which they hope to cross the mountains and desert to reach California. Thirteen people and a dog begin the journey in the Joads' overloaded 1925 Hudson.

Such federal government protections as a minimum wage, regulation of working hours, child labor laws, unemployment and welfare benefits, and safe working conditions only came later in the 1930s. In *The Grapes of Wrath* the government camp at Weedpatch is safer than the impromptu Hooverville camps that can at any time and on any pretext be terrorized and even set on fire by local law officials. But the government camps can do little to alleviate starvation, and the only work that they can provide is in lieu of the dollar-a-week rent. The Joads, grateful for the humane treatment and sanitary conditions that the government camp brings them, are forced by hunger and lack of work to leave after a month. Some existing laws work to contribute to the family's suffering. Tom Joad violates the parole that requires him to stay within the borders of a state in which he is homeless and unemployed. When Grandpa dies the family cannot afford to obey the law that requires them to report his death, and they bury him in an unmarked grave in a cornfield.

Grandpa's death, on the first night of the journey and still within the state borders, begins the migration's pressure upon the authority structure of the family. The subsequent changes are part of the novel's exploration of the responsibility of individuals to the family and to the larger community, the possibilities of collective action, and the transformation of religious faith into a more secular, political, but still mystical, sense of hope.

The choreography of the family gathering at which the Joad family makes its decision when to move west reflects the gendered authority that subsequent events will realign, but not completely disrupt. The family meets near the truck, the new center of their lives that replaces the lost house and the surrounding fields. Pa and Uncle John squat at the center, and Grandpa, whose position is now only "honorary and a matter of custom," faces them (317). The younger men – Connie, Noah, Tom, and for the first time Al – join the other men, and the women and children take their places behind the squatting males.

But events upon the journey and in California require a strength and courage that Ma Joad shows more than any other member of the family. Pa Joad recognizes his inability to lead, and concedes authority without fully accepting or understanding the shifting positions within the family. As Ma Joad puts it: "Man, he lives in jerks ... Woman, it's all one flow, like a stream, little eddies, little waterfalls, but the river, it goes right on. Woman looks at it like that" (660). Ma insists that the family try to stay together, refusing to accept the plan agreed to by the men that the family split up when it appears that a necessary car repair will cost a two- or three-day delay. In that instance she enforces her will with the threat of violence, and later in California she advances upon an armed deputy with her iron skillet and forces him back. In the novel's climactic scene, through sheer force of will she gets Pa, John, and the children to a barn and out of the immediate threat of the flood. The barn may provide only a temporary respite from the starvation and death to come, but for the moment Ma's wordless request to Rose of Sharon to breastfeed the starving man they find inside with his young son, and Rose of Sharon's willingness to comply, are final reminders in the novel of actions that only women can undertake. Nevertheless the novel's interchapters open and close with the suggestion that the women still look to the men for reassurance and for whatever hope is possible. At the novel's opening "the women" look to see the response of "their men" to the drought and dust bowl conditions. They feel relieved, and "safe," to see that the faces of the men are "hard and angry and resistant" (213). As long as this anger is not replaced by hopelessness and despair, they feel, there will be no defeat. And in the final interchapter the women still look for this anger in the men. As the narrator summarizes, echoing the novel's title, "the break would never come as long as fear could turn to wrath" (671).

Just as the interchapters lay out a broader context for the narrative of the Joads, the mythic dimensions of their journey provides a larger backdrop to the story of Casy, the former preacher, whose values and mission Tom Joad vows to continue. The migrant journey has biblical dimensions: out of the land of famine, across the wilderness of the desert, and into the fruitful and fertile valley – although in this case the promised land is advertised in handbills printed in their thousands to mislead the migrants and bring to California a labor pool in such numbers that desperate families will work even for starvation wages. There is a suggestion that the flood at the end of the novel might bring the fundamental change that various characters, especially Ma, predict but cannot articulate. What the spring following the rains certainly brings is the renewal of the land: the "tiny points of grass" and "the hills ... pale green with the beginning year," along with new crops and the possibility of employment after three starving winter months of no work (671).

Casy is the first person that Tom meets on the road to the abandoned Joad farm, and their stories intertwine in important ways. Casy no longer has the faith to fulfill his communal role of preacher, and to him prayer seems to offer no solution to the deprivation he sees around him. But the older members of the Joad family still seek the solace of prayer and he responds with language that reflects his own confusion but still meets their needs. Casy's final response to his crisis of faith is more thoughtful than the older generation's wish for tradition, more social than John's self-torment, and more tolerant than the fundamentalist Christians at the government camp. The path he takes is an important one for the novel's view of collective identity and responsibility, a view that is mystical, but also, in its call to action, humanist and political. Casy sacrifices himself for Tom at the Hooverville Camp, and in jail finds some of the answers that he has been searching for. He uses the rhetorical skills of his days as a preacher for the service of workers seeking a fairer wage, and while the deputy who kills him answers only with violence, Tom Joad has listened. His final speech to his mother upon their separation is one, as he tells her explicitly, that echoes Casy's: "maybe like Casy says, a fella ain't got a soul of his own, but on'y a piece of a big one" (656). The movement for justice transcends the death of any one individual.

The vision of community action that is shared by Casy and Tom mirrors the sharing behind the family's journey from the beginning. The Joads take Casy along with them, and would have taken Muley too, had he wanted to leave. The sharing continues when they meet and travel with the Wilsons, and later with the Wainwrights – a union that the future marriage of Al and Aggie will make permanent – and finally with the selfless action of Rose of Sharon in the barn. On a broader level mutual support appears in the Hooverville Camp, as the makeshift community shares prospects of work, or rumors of possible group resistance. In the largely self-governed Weedpatch Camp, united action defeats the outside attempts to cause serious trouble that would bring in the deputies.

But the novel offers no comfortable solutions in its final pages. The operators of the Hooper Farms get their way in breaking the strike, and there are starving families enough to work for a wage that will not even purchase a family meal at the overpriced company store. The Joad family continues to fracture, with Tom on the run and Al looking to start his own life, and any possibility of work remains a season away for the exhausted men, women, and children taking shelter in the barn. While the future could be read through Tom's speech on following Casy's lead, or the interchapter's description of the first signs of spring, it could equally be seen in Rose of Sharon's shattered marriage, and the stillborn child that Uncle John sends down the floodstream toward the town as a concrete example of what has been visited upon the migrant families. The government camp offers dignity and relative safety, but no solution to the desperate need for work. And there are many more Hoovervilles than Weedpatches. Understandably, the unemployed workers in California see the influx of migrants as unneeded competition in their own search for scarce work. With so much unemployment there remains a surplus of fruit that would bring prices below subsistence level for the farmers – thus the destruction of the surplus, even in front of the starving families who cannot afford to pay for it.

The Grapes of Wrath has come in for criticism on a number of counts. The novel's focus on the plight of the migrant workers has led some to see it as less an imaginative work than a social document of its time. The authorial commentary in the interchapters has been seen as heavy-handed and artless. John Gardner, in *The Art of Fiction*, argued that while Steinbeck knew a great deal about the migrant workers, he knew very little about California farming, and that as a result the book is unbalanced by its overly reductive presentation of the treatment accorded to the migrants. And the final scene of Rose of Sharon breastfeeding the dying farmer is sometimes condemned as unmotivated and sentimental. But such comments are in the minority, and *The Grapes of Wrath* is firmly established as one of the major American novels of the century.

Bibliography

The Library of America printing, *The Grapes of Wrath and Other Writings: 1936–1941* (New York, 1996), edited by Robert DeMott and Elaine Steinbeck, corrects some editorial errors in the first edition. This first edition is the basis of the Penguin Classics printing (New York, 2006).

Barbara A. Heavilin, *John Steinbeck's The Grapes of Wrath: A Reference Guide* (Westport, CT, 2002).
John Steinbeck, *Working Days: The Journals of The Grapes of Wrath 1938–1941*, ed. Robert DeMott (New York, 1989).
Rick Wartzman, *Obscene in the Extreme: The Burning and Banning of John Steinbeck's The Grapes of Wrath* (New York, 2008).
David Wyatt, ed., *New Essays on The Grapes of Wrath* (New York, 1990).

Richard Wright, *Native Son,* New York: Harper and Brothers, 1940

Richard Wright's *Native Son* was the first book by an African American to be picked up by the Book of the Month Club. The resulting visibility helped the book sell almost a quarter of a million copies in three weeks, and made Wright the foremost, and wealthiest, African American writer of his generation. However, the adoption came at the price of requiring the author to rewrite some parts of the novel, and this revised text was the only version available for many years. But in 1991 the Library of America brought out an edition based upon the bound page proofs originally sent to the Book of the Month Club, and this text is now the basis of Harper's trade edition.

In 1938 Wright had published a book of stories, *Uncle Tom's Children,* which dealt with the suffering inflicted by racism, but he came to feel that the book's impact was blunted by the emotional content of its narratives. In *Native Son* he set out to write a much starker novel where the issues of responsibility were more complex. The implications of its two murders go beyond the arguments raised in the trial of Bigger Thomas, or the biased reporting of the media, or the fury of the crowds outside the courtroom demanding what they consider justice. Bigger seeks some control over his actions and possibilities within a white-dominated culture that is organized around limiting that control. His attempts to break out of the limitations are sometimes petty, sometimes furiously angry, and finally murderous. The novel exposes the fallacies of a liberalism that fails to recognize the radical reforms necessary to reverse racial injustice, and points to the limitations of a generally well-intentioned Communist Party. For Wright in this book, the

The Twentieth-Century American Fiction Handbook   By Christopher MacGowan
© 2011 Christopher MacGowan

white-controlled media, market economy, and political system together work to perpetuate the economic inequalities, racial divisions, and mutual misunderstandings that result in the grief brought upon the families, black and white, who are affected by the murders. The two victims themselves fail to understand the social dynamics in which they are caught. Mary Dalton is naïve in her attempt to overcome an entrenched system of racial injustice through well-meant gestures of inclusion, and Bessie doesn't recognize the extent to which sex and alcohol contribute to her passivity and vulnerability.

In a talk that Wright gave at Columbia University shortly after the novel was published, "How 'Bigger' Was Born" (subsequently added to printings of the novel), he observed that most of his preliminary thinking about the book involved "learning about Bigger, what had made him, what he meant." He continued, "When the time came for writing, *what had made him and what he meant* constituted my plot" [Wright's emphasis] (454). In a number of ways in the novel Wright makes clear that "what had made" Bigger makes inevitable the direction of his life. The titles of the novel's three chapters, "Fear," "Flight," and "Fate," give one indication of this inevitability. Bigger's mother tells him in the opening scene that "the gallows is at the end of the road you traveling, boy," and shortly after this prediction the novel's narrator observes that "the moment he allowed what his life meant to enter fully into his consciousness, he would either kill himself or someone else" (9–10). Bigger also senses this inevitability: "I feel like something awful's going to happen to me," he tells his friend Gus, and, a little later, "It's like I was going to do something I can't help" (20, 22). To his lawyer, Max, just before facing trial, Bigger reflects, "Now I come to think of it, it seems like something like this just had to be" (358).

Bigger's sense of his fate is tied to the largely inarticulate and impotent anger he feels at being excluded by virtue of his color from the world of plenty open to whites, a world glimpsed in the newspapers and cinema – a world epitomized by the life of Mary Dalton. Max emphasizes at the trial the impact of racism and economic inequality on Bigger's actions, and asks the judge to weigh the additional guilt of all who tolerate or contribute to such conditions. Max has sympathy for but does not spare Mary's bereaved parents: Mr. Dalton, whose company owns the rat-infested building in which the Thomas family lives, and who profits from the racial segregation of the city's real estate, and Mrs. Dalton, whose well-intentioned attempts at social work are paralleled by a blindness both symbolic and actual.

The Daltons' well-intentioned but naïve charity brings Bigger into the margins of their privileged world, where he crosses a racial divide at which every other experience of his life had forced him to halt. Thoughtlessly, Mary Dalton puts Bigger in the position of having to deceive his new employer, while later, with Jan, the two treat him as an equal, displaying their social conscience rather than recognizing the confusion and embarrassment that they are causing him. When Bigger has to get the intoxicated girl home alone, he has no choice but to help her to her bedroom. And when Mrs. Dalton enters the room, the cultural forces that Max tries to explain in the courtroom result in a death that is both accidental and inevitable. Nevertheless, the judge, the state's attorney, the media, and the mob crowding the court and the streets outside view the case to varying degrees as a matter of individual not social responsibility. The case also reinforces their stereotype of a black man's predatory and opportunistic attitude toward white women.

While much of the broader social commentary of the novel is given to Max's courtroom speech, Max has limitations in his understanding of Bigger, as does Jan, although both are treated in the novel with the sympathy that Wright held for the Communist Party despite his differences with it (differences usually connected to the Party's attempts to influence his writing). One of Bigger's important discoveries is that not all whites are part of a conspiracy to limit his opportunities, and central to this discovery is that the Communist Party, and Max and Jan in particular, do not judge him solely on the basis of his race.

Wright's narrative problem, as he recognized, is that a character largely driven by emotion, and shown as reacting to forces in his or her environment, will usually not be able to articulate the broader perspective upon events that the novelist may require. As a result *Native Son*, like many other naturalist fictions, relies upon narrative commentary to articulate that perspective, and – in the case of this novel – Max's courtroom argument. Bigger does not begin to reflect with any real degree of self-consciousness on the circumstances of his life until he responds to Max's questioning in prison. Generally, Bigger's experiences move him in the direction of the kind of collective unity advocated by the Party. He had felt that he had little in common with others of his race. He had rejected the religion that comforts his mother and sister – quite explicitly when the preacher sent by his mother visits him in his cell. He also finds no sense of community in the folklore or history of his race. But through his conversations with Max, for the first time he gains a sense of a possible "union, identity . . . a supporting oneness, a wholeness which had been denied him all his life" (362). But in a foreshadowing of Wright's later interest in existentialism, Bigger's recognition of a communal identity exists alongside his sense of having for the first time struck out against a world that previously he had faced with only an impotent, furious fear. As he tries to explain to the horrified Max shortly before his execution, "I didn't know I was really alive in this world until I felt things hard enough to kill for 'em ... I feel all right when I look at it that way" (429).

Wright points out in "How 'Bigger' Was Born" that he is prepared to sacrifice verisimilitude for thematic purposes. The example he uses in his essay is the unlikely gathering in Bigger's cell, all at the same time, of the major figures in his personal life along with characters associated with the Mary Dalton murder and the upcoming trial. "I wanted those people in that cell to elicit a certain important emotional response from Bigger," Wright records. "And so the scene stood. I felt that what I wanted that scene to say to the reader was *more important than its surface reality or plausibility*" (458). Similarly, the coincidence of Bigger and Gus seeing a newsreel of Mary Dalton on a Florida beach only hours before Bigger meets her serves Wright's theme of the media's role – teasing with a world forbidden to the two black men, and thus contributing to the inevitable confusion, and danger, when Bigger actually meets her in person.

The symbolism of the novel is integrated into its verisimilitude to various degrees, but as with the cell and cinema scenes, thematic issues are paramount for Wright. The furnace in the Dalton basement burns red as it consumes the remains of Mary Dalton during Bigger's interrogation by the family, Britten, and the newspaper reporters. Its heat and color make the basement a kind of personal, isolating hell for Bigger. But the central color symbol in the novel is the whiteness that surrounds, limits, threatens, and finally engulfs him. A massive snowfall closes all routes out of Chicago after Mary's death, and his attempt at flight is made against the background of the snow blanketing the streets. Bigger sees Mrs. Dalton in Mary's bedroom as "an awesome white blur" (86). Other examples are the Daltons' white cat acting accusingly toward him; the water tower, "huge and round and white looming up in the dark" upon which he is finally trapped (265); the white wall of his cell; and the "white looming mountain of hate" that he senses in the courtroom and the mob outside (361).

Following the novel's enormous success, Orson Welles (having just finished *Citizen Kane*) staged a version of the novel on Broadway in 1941. In the early 1950s, Ralph Ellison's *Invisible Man* pushed *Native Son* into the background somewhat, and James Baldwin in an influential essay complained that the book reinforced stereotypes. But Max's warnings in his courtroom speech of "looming ... violence" if nothing changed (warnings shortened at the insistence of the Book of the Month Club, and virtually eliminated by the American censor from the 1950 film version of the novel) made the book appear prophetic in the turbulent racial climate of the 1960s (402). Although in recent years the book's importance has been more fully realized, it has received some criticism for its focus being almost exclusively on the plight of black men. In addition, Wright himself has been faulted for being less than welcoming to black writers whose work took a less confrontational approach to race than his own. In particular he has been attacked for his hostility toward the work of Zora Neale Hurston, a writer whose characters, unlike Bigger Thomas, can often find comfort in the religion and folklore of their race. Wright himself appears to have recognized the need to explore the plight of black women as well as men. In "How 'Bigger' Was Born" he notes that "With what I've learned in the writing of this book ... I am launching out upon another novel, this time about the status of women in modern American society" (461). But this planned novel was never finished.

Bibliography

Richard Wright, *Native Son* (New York, 2005), with an introduction by Arnold Rampersad.

James Baldwin, "Everybody's Protest Novel," in *Notes of a Native Son* (Boston, 1984), pp. 13–23.
Ana Maria Fraile, ed., *Richard Wright's Native Son* (Amsterdam and New York, 2007).
Keneth Kinnamon, ed., *New Essays on Native Son* (Cambridge, 1990).
Andrew Warnes, *Richard Wright's Native Son* (New York, 2007).

J. D. Salinger, *The Catcher in the Rye*, Boston: Little, Brown, 1951

The Catcher in the Rye is one of the most widely read American novels of the second half of the twentieth century, and also one of the most frequently banned in high schools. Before the appearance of the only novel published in his lifetime, J. D. Salinger had published short stories in such magazines as *Colliers*, *Esquire*, *Harper's*, and *The New Yorker*, including two stories, "I'm Crazy" in 1945, and "Slight Rebellion Off Madison" in 1946, that are earlier versions of parts of the novel. His subsequent published fiction was sparse, consisting of stories centering around the Glass family, the last of which appeared in 1965. In the last 40 years of his life the author become almost as famous for his reclusiveness as for his writing.

The events of the novel occur over 48 hours in Christmas week 1949. Narrator Holden Caulfield, 16 then and 17 now, describes his hours in Manhattan between leaving, a few days early, the latest preparatory school he has been expelled from, and sitting in Central Park watching his sister Phoebe riding the park's carousel. A short epilogue finds Holden in a psychiatric hospital, where he is as much concerned with what he is not going to say as anything else.

Like a famous predecessor, Huckleberry Finn, Holden is a confused but independent adolescent feeling oppressed by the social and cultural pressures coming to bear upon him – and disgusted by the hypocrisy of the adults he encounters. Holden, like Huck, plans to escape "somewhere out west," but while Huck might actually make his escape, Holden concludes by the end of

The Twentieth-Century American Fiction Handbook   By Christopher MacGowan
© 2011 Christopher MacGowan

his narrative that whether out west, or in a tomb reconstructed in New York's Metropolitan Museum, "You can't never find a place that's nice and peaceful, because there isn't any" (257, 264).

Much commentary on the novel has centered upon the character of its narrator. A central issue has been whether he is responsible to some degree for his own fate, or whether he is a victim of the mid-century culture that he abhors but cannot escape. He despises "the movies," and yet spends part of the only full day covered by his narrative watching a film at Radio City. Sometimes he fantasizes or acts out scenes from movie conventions. He is quick to distance himself from others by calling them "phonies" or "morons," but admits that some of his own actions are "phony." The very quality for which Salinger has often been praised, capturing the language and attitudes of disaffected adolescence, illustrates how much Holden is a product of the culture that surrounds him.

Holden's relationship to his siblings is associated with the wish he some-times expresses to stop time, a symptom of his crisis about growing older. He is closest to his dead younger brother, Allie, whose baseball mitt covered with poems he has in his suitcase at school. And Allie is the protector he turns to at a moment of deepest crisis when he thinks that he might "disappear" (257). Holden's close relationship to his brother D.B. also belongs in the past since D.B. has, Holden feels, sold his writing talent "to the movies" in moving to Hollywood. Phoebe is a comfort to him at the end of the novel although he rejects her plea to join his planned escape west. His pleasure and comfort at watching Phoebe go round and round on the carousel comes in part from the very circularity of its journey. And earlier he comments, "That's one nice thing about carrousels, they always play the same songs" (272).

Although the desire to stop time or return to the past becomes particularly acute toward the end of Holden's narrative, time and consciousness of his age are issues always close to the surface. He looks older than he is, and can sometimes purchase alcohol even though underage. His age is also an issue in his casual encounters with older women, including the prostitute sent to his room by the elevator operator. Sex and drinking put pressure on him to act with a knowledge and sophistication that he has not yet had the time to acquire. "The best thing" for Holden about the displays in the American Museum of Natural History "was that everything always stayed right where it was. Nobody'd move" (157). He is very disturbed by the vulgarity that defaces the Egyptian tomb display at the Metropolitan Museum of Art, another potentially timeless place, and by the same desecration in Phoebe's school, the school he went to "myself when I was a kid" (259). The school for Holden is no longer the refuge for Phoebe that it had been for him. Holden also uses humor and exaggeration to try to deny the value of time as any kind of exact measure. The examples are many, for instance he calls the secretary in the Principal's office at Phoebe's school "some old lady around a hundred years old" (261). And he applies the same treatment to himself. He tells the reader that the carousel in the park "played that same song about fifty years ago when *I* was a little kid" (272).

Holden's attitude toward telling his story is an important part of his characterization. He both resents his need for an audience and wants to limit his obligations to it, but recognizes that it is necessary for the expression of his voice – in a literary sense for his very existence. In his first sentence he declares that as far as personal and family background is concerned he is not going to go into "that David Copperfield kind of crap . . . my parents would have about two hemorrhages apiece if I told anything pretty personal about them. They're quite touchy about anything like that, especially my father" (3). The final pages of the novel reflect his ambivalence toward readers (and in the light of his creator's subsequent career, perhaps J. D. Salinger's ambivalence too). Describing his happiness watching Phoebe on the carousel, he confides, "God, I wish you could've been there." But in the short epilogue that follows, he declares of "all this stuff I just finished telling you about" that "I'm sorry I told so many people about it" (275–277).

Holden tells his story in a way that reflects his tastes in literature and drama. His favorite author, after brother D.B. (before he went to Hollywood), is Ring Lardner, and Holden's narrative is told in the colloquial, self-revealing style of many of Lardner's first-person stories. He admires the reckless dreamer Jay Gatsby of F. Scott Fitzgerald's novel, but has little regard for the stoic, disciplined Frederick Henry of Hemingway's *A Farewell to Arms* and calls the novel itself "a phony book" (182). A number of times Holden makes clear that he approves of digression, for example when he tells his former teacher Mr. Antolini the story of a student who was yelled at in Oral Expression class for the supposed fault. Against Antolini's more academic claims for simplicity and unity, he counters, "Some things you just can't do that to" (240). Elsewhere Holden declares that he hates "those dumb stories in a magazine . . . with a lot of phony, lean-jawed guys named David . . . and a lot of phony girls named Linda or Marcia" (70). In keeping with Holden's liking for spontaneity he criticizes what he sees as the self-conscious mannerisms of Sir Laurence Olivier, the showing off of Greenwich Village piano player Ernie, and the performances of Alfred Lunt and Lynn Fontanne, who "didn't act like people . . . They acted more like they knew they were celebrities and all" (164).

After sister Phoebe, the two most important girls in Holden's narrative are Jane Gallagher and Sally Hayes. Holden feels close enough to Jane that he once showed her Allie's baseball glove, and is anxious on the evening that he leaves Pencey that roommate Stradlater might have "given her the time" on a date (99). Holden himself is a virgin, and the concern for Jane reflects both his sense of platonic friendship with her, and his own sense of inadequacy alongside a roommate who is a senior. His own relationship with this daughter of a neighbor is clearly very special to him, and his thoughts return to her and her evening with Stradlater a number of times. Holden actually arranges to meet Sally Hayes, who, unlike Jane, is very good-looking, but for whose intelligence Holden has little respect. As further evidence of his emotional confusion, he can convince himself that he is for the moment in love with Sally, although he is acutely aware of her self-conscious mannerisms. When he tries to share his mood and desire to escape with her, and even invites her to join him, she is full of commonsense objections. In the wild swing of emotions that characterize Holden's moods, the two end up hating each other, and Holden confesses, "I don't even know why I started all that stuff with her . . . about going away somewhere" – and "probably wouldn't've taken her even if she'd wanted to go with me" (174). The confused emotions aroused by Sally contrast with the comfort he finds in thinking about his time with Jane, a comfort all the more easily disturbed by the thought of her evening with Stradlater.

While sexuality and the pressures of time confuse Holden, he receives little help from the conversations that he has with teachers at the beginning and end of his narrative. Mr. Spencer, the history teacher from Pencey, is elderly, smells of the medicine he is taking for a bad cold, tells Holden that he should think about his future, and reiterates the Principal's dictum that "Life *is* a game that one plays according to the rules" (12). Such clichés have little impact upon the disaffected Holden, who nevertheless is honest about his failure to study for Mr. Spencer's history examination. Mr. Antolini's advice is less formulaic, and he tries to comfort Holden by reminding him that there have been others "just as troubled morally and spiritually as you are right now," some of whom have "kept records of their troubles" (246). Antolini is sometimes read as speaking for Salinger, although he has consumed a large number of highballs and is rather insensitive to Holden's obvious exhaustion. Nevertheless, his comment might be one of the motivations behind Holden writing his narrative. But the sanctuary and potential guidance that Antolini provides is ruined for Holden by the intrusion, once again, of sexuality, or – if Holden's interpretation is just the product of his own sexual insecurities – at any rate, by the teacher's inappropriate and insensitive behavior.

Holden decides to call Mr. Antolini after telling Phoebe of his dream to be a "catcher in the rye." For Holden, to be "the catcher in the rye" is to be part of a game different from that in Mr. Spencer's clichéd advice, and also to have a purpose. As Phoebe reminds him, the allusion is to Robert Burns's poem

"Comin' thro' the rye," the song of an isolated girl surrounded by paired couples. Holden hears a six-year-old singing the song near Broadway. The boy's pleasure lifts Holden from his depression for the moment, but the boy's mistake "If a body catch a body" (instead of "If a body meet a body") is how Holden remembers the line when he tells Phoebe of picturing himself as the only "big" kid among "all these little kids playing some game in this big field of rye … Thousands of little kids." His job is to save any child who in the excitement goes too close to the nearby cliff. He tells Phoebe "that's the only thing I'd really like to be" (224–225).

Holden appears to abandon his role of savior when he accompanies Phoebe to Central Park. Watching his sister on the carousel, he is concerned that in reaching for the gold ring she might fall from her horse; however, "I didn't say anything or do anything. The thing with kids is, if they want to grab for the gold ring, you have to let them do it, and not say anything. If they fall off, they fall off, but it's bad if you say anything to them" (273–274).

The contradiction might be one example among many of the contradictions that arise from Holden's tendency to universalize his feelings, even if they apply only to one particular moment. For some commentators, his disturbing experience with Mr. Antolini contributes to the changed attitude, while others see his visit to the Egyptian tomb as a symbolic death that makes his mood more fatalistic. The gold ring might also suggest, more broadly, adult ambition and its material focus – a material focus instilled in children even in their amusements. And there are inevitable punishments, Holden might be recognizing, for those who criticize this materialist system; such punishments as the hospital where he is taken to be cured, and where, with regrets, he tells his story.

Bibliography

J. D. Salinger, *The Catcher in the Rye* (Boston, 2001).

Joel Salzberg, ed., *Critical Essays on Salinger's The Catcher in the Rye* (Boston, 1990).
Jack Salzman, *New Essays on The Catcher in the Rye* (Cambridge, 1991).
J. P. Steed, *The Catcher in the Rye: New Essays* (New York, 2002).
Pamela Hunt Steinle, *In Cold Fear: The Catcher in the Rye, Censorship Controversies and Postwar American Character* (Columbus, OH, 2000).

Flannery O'Connor, *Wise Blood*, New York: Harcourt, Brace, 1952

Flannery O'Connor began writing the first of her only two novels in 1946 while living and studying in Iowa City for her MFA degree, going on to publish four of its 14 chapters separately between 1948 and 1952. Like all of O'Connor's fiction, the novel is infused with the author's religious faith, a Catholicism severe enough in the way its implications are played out to puzzle some readers as to exactly where the story directs their sympathies.

The book received relatively little attention when it first appeared and eventually went out of print, but O'Connor's rising reputation in the ensuing 10 years led her later publishers Farrar, Straus and Giroux to reissue the book in 1962. In a short "Author's Note" accompanying this second edition, O'Connor called the book "a comic novel." The term "comic" may seem curious for a novel in which the central character blinds himself with quicklime, in which there are two, possibly three, violent murders, where a young girl is morally lost and sent to a "detention home" (220), where a young boy is friendless and confused, where the police are callous thugs, three of the preachers are fraudulent, and Mrs. Flood the landlady is a ruthless materialist out to get whatever money she can from her blind tenant. But the comedy, for O'Connor, lies in the contorted and sometimes desperate ways in which the characters avoid considering the future state of their souls by turning to the short-lived satisfaction of physical appetites and material needs.

As with many of O'Connor's central characters, the ferocity of Hazel Motes' attempts to deny original sin, and thus his need for salvation, only reflect the greater power of the spiritual truth that he refuses to acknowledge.

The Twentieth-Century American Fiction Handbook   By Christopher MacGowan
© 2011 Christopher MacGowan

On first arriving in the city he visits a prostitute, and later has sex with an underage girl. He has "a strong confidence in his power to resist evil" and convinces himself that his soul is "not there" (17, 18). Hazel aggressively challenges strangers on the state of his or of their redemption. "I AM clean," he tells the waitress at the Frosty Bottle. "If Jesus existed, I wouldn't be clean" (87). He tells Sabbath Hawks, "Nobody with a good car needs to be justified," and at a gas station he tells the attendant that it is "not right to believe anything you couldn't see or hold in your hands or test with your teeth" (109, 208). Standing on top of his car, he preaches "the Church Without Christ."

Hazel looks like his grandfather, a "circuit preacher" who had predicted of the boy that "Jesus would have him in the end!" (14, 16). The likeness is just one of a number of doubles in the novel: Hazel blinds himself as Asa Hawks had failed to do, Hoover Shoats employs Solace Layfield to double for Hazel, and the "ape" in the city park matches the actor dressed in the Gonga suit who is himself replaced by Enoch Emory. The names of the characters also suggest doubles alongside their biblical counterparts. As Margaret Earley Whitt has pointed out (in *Understand Flannery O'Connor*, 1997), Hazel suggests Hazael King of Syria (2 Kings 8–13) who oppressed the Israelites, Enoch's worship of false idols contrasts with the biblical Enoch who "walked with God" (Genesis 5:24), and Asa Hawks's running from Christ at the moment of intending to blind himself aligns him with Asa, a king of Judah who was chastised for putting his trust in the king of Syria, not in God (2 Chronicles 16).

Although Hazel tries to deny his need for salvation, the force of what he is trying to deny attracts a number of other characters in the novel to him, although their reasons, and their awareness of what they are attracted to, differ in important ways. Hazel's journey toward accepting his need for salvation includes rejecting the alternatives offered by these figures.

The friendless Enoch Emory seeks a transcendent meaning in various material objects and self-invented rituals, discarding each one when it fails to fulfill his need, and he ends the novel translated from human to animal – the condition, for O'Connor, of one who does not heed the condition of the soul. The "long red foyer" and dark tunnels of the cinema where he spends one afternoon prefigure the hell that movie star Gonga tells him to go to (138). Emory thinks Hazel's denial of Christ a source of potential friendship between the two, not seeing beyond the superficial parallels to what, for O'Connor, are their similar more urgent spiritual needs.

Mrs. Flood is similarly attracted to Hazel for reasons beyond those that she recognizes; she covets the money to be gouged from his government allowance, and enjoys the companionship of someone who is dependent upon her.

She has a fierce need to control the world around her, but half-realizes the limitations of her materialism when at the end of the novel she stares into Hazel's dead eyes and sees him "moving farther and farther away, farther and farther into the darkness" (236).

The material values of two other women in the novel are associated more with sexual temptation. While Mrs. Flood has plans to marry Hazel, her motives stem from needing official sanction of her rights to his property rather than from sexual designs. Hazel's sexual initiation comes with Mrs. Watts, an act that is part of his attempted nihilism. His sexual initiation is likened to the Fall, for he finds her address in a toilet stall decorated with "something that looked like a snake" on its door (26). His later plans to seduce Hawks's underage daughter Sabbath Lily are part of his intention to provoke her father, although Sabbath turns out to be the sexual aggressor. Sabbath is initially attracted by what she thinks are Hazel's carnal, sacrilegious values. Taking over the mummified figure stolen, then abandoned, by Enoch, she enacts a parody of motherhood. When Hazel violently rejects her claim to be "Momma," throwing his own mother's glasses away at the same time, Sabbath speaks a truth that he is not yet ready to fully acknowledge: "I seen you wouldn't never have no fun or let anybody else because you didn't want nothing but Jesus." In the world of Sabbath's inverted values, such a desire is "mean and evil" (188). Her remark echoes an earlier comment of Enoch's, who tells Hazel scornfully, "I knew when I first seen you you didn't have nobody nor nothing but Jesus" (54).

Sabbath's father, Asa Hawks, recognizes Hazel's spiritual conviction as a passion similar to that which had also driven him when he announced publicly that he would blind himself – only to flee just before committing the act. Hazel, impressed in turn with Hawks's apparent spiritual conviction, wants to challenge it by defying Hawks to convert him. Hazel's Church Without Christ is intended to both provoke and impress the older man. When Hazel later blinds himself, his action is both to align himself with one who ran from Jesus, but also to follow through on the conviction that he realizes Hawks lacked. Hazel's act is a private act, just as for O'Connor the final condition of one's soul is an individual decision, but Hazel avoids the melodrama produced by Hawks's public announcement.

One-time radio preacher Hoover Shoats sees Hazel's Church Without Christ as a potentially lucrative business, a way to make money by offering a "new jesus." Hazel's own preaching has a desperate integrity because of the power of what he is trying to deny, even though his words are finally little different from those of Hoover or of Solace Layfield, the man Shoats hires to double for the uncooperative Hazel. Solace dies acknowledging his need for salvation, although Hazel, at this point, is focused only on the urgency of murdering a double whose duplicity of actions, motives, and performance too closely mirror his own contradictions.

The last important distraction that Hazel must separate himself from is the "rat-colored car" with which he murders Solace Layfield. It must join the other material objects that he discards, a list that includes a potato peeler, a hat, unspent money, and the physical pleasures offered by the bodies of Sabbath Hawks and Mrs. Watts. The car, Hazel tells the salesman when he buys it, is "mostly to be a house for me," because "I ain't got any place to be," and it also serves as the platform from which he preaches (69). Hazel's rude and aggressive responses to the officer who asks for his driver's license suggest that Hazel wants to provoke the patrolman to run the car over an embankment. With the car destroyed, he can begin seeking God's house, the "place" where, for all his denials, he needs "to be."

Mrs. Flood's failed attempt, with her own eyes closed, to follow "the pin point of light" in Hazel's dead eyes is the culmination of a central motif of vision in the novel (236). Mrs. Wally Bee Hitchcock, facing Hazel on the train into Taulkinham, is drawn to his eyes, which seem to her "almost like passages leading somewhere" (4). Sabbath Hawks recognizes that Hazel's eyes "don't look like they see what he's looking at but they keep on looking," although in keeping with her appetites she merely finds the quality physically attractive (105). The movie houses outside which Hazel, and later Hoover, preach offer through the projector lens escapist images from a mechanical eye. The first of the trio of films that Enoch watches is about a scientist named "The Eye." And finally, Hazel Motes' name directly refers to this important motif. The "mote" in his eye stops him from seeing clearly what he needs to see, producing the "Haze" that O'Connor often shortens his name to in the narration, and linking both character and reader to Christ's question in the Sermon on the Mount: "And why seest thou the mote that is in thy brother's eye; and seest not the beam that is in thy own eye?" (Matthew 7:3.).

Characters in O'Connor's fiction who are too lazy and trapped in habit to think for themselves often speak in clichés when making moral judgments, not realizing that the cliché could also point them to a much deeper understanding of good and evil, and thus to the necessity of salvation. Such clichés sometimes supply O'Connor with a title, and examples from her short stories are "A Good Man Is Hard to Find," "The Life You Save May Be Your Own," and "Good Country People." In *Wise Blood* nobody offers more clichés in such a short space of time than does Mrs. Hitchcock on the train into Taulkinham, but Enoch Emory supplies the novel with its title. He accuses an indifferent Hazel of thinking "you got wiser blood than anybody else," and trusts the instincts of his "wise blood" as he invents, only to discard, his empty rituals (55). For O'Connor, however, the true "wise blood" runs in the veins of a body that recognizes its need to accept the blood shed by Christ, blood made manifest in the mystery of the Catholic mass. The dying Hazel finally acknowledges this need when the two young policemen find him lying in a drainage ditch. "I want to go on where I'm going," he tells them, and in thoughtlessly murdering him as they take him back to Mrs. Flood, they unknowingly allow him this all-important wish (234).

Bibliography

Flannery O'Connor, *Wise Blood* (New York, 2007).

Connie Ann Kirk, *Critical Companion to Flannery O'Connor* (New York, 2008).
Michael Kreyling, ed., *New Essays on Wise Blood* (New York, 1995).
Douglas Robillard Jr., ed., *The Critical Response to Flannery O'Connor* (Westport, CT, 2004).
R. Neil Scott, *Flannery O'Connor: An Annotated Reference Guide to Criticism* (Milledgeville, GA, 2002).

Ralph Ellison, *Invisible Man,* New York: Random House, 1952

Ralph Ellison recalls in his introduction to the thirtieth anniversary edition of *Invisible Man* that he started writing the novel in a Vermont garage in 1945. Since the late 1930s he had been publishing reviews, essays, and short stories, mainly for left-oriented journals. Ellison's novel won the National Book Award in 1953 and almost universal acclaim, but it would be the only novel that he published in his lifetime. A version of the unfinished *Juneteenth* appeared five years after his death, in 1999.

Invisible Man is an ambitious integration of several different literary techniques, as well as African American folklore, blues, and jazz. In his own comments on the book, Ellison noted that he used three different styles to reflect the stages of his narrator's journey: naturalism for his high school and college life in the South, expressionism for his experiences in New York City, and surrealism for the final stage of his narrative when his various public identities are stripped away. Such variety, along with the improvisatory musical forms, matches the unnamed narrator's realization that when he finally emerges from his subterranean "border area" he must adopt a fluid relationship to the world, one that will help him resist attempts by others to impose a fixed identity upon him that would restrict future roles and possibilities (5). Similarly, Ellison countered claims by critics who took issue with his departing from the protest literature of his early mentor, Richard Wright, asserting that the complex history and contemporary role of the Negro in the United States was more complex than could or should be contained in any one style or genre.

The Twentieth-Century American Fiction Handbook   By Christopher MacGowan
© 2011 Christopher MacGowan

The invisible man's narrative involves the taking on and shedding of various restrictive identities imposed on him by institutions and organizations for their own benefit. These institutions and organizations are associated in the novel with machines, either actual machines – as in the hospital where he is treated after the accident at Liberty Paints – or the machine-like operation of the Brotherhood, where history is claimed to be a science and individuals must subsume their identities to the movement as a whole. At the black college that he attends and is expelled from, the students have "uniforms pressed, shoes shined, minds laced up, eyes blind like those of robots" (36). These machine-like forces are further associated in the novel with the power of electricity, a force by which others can control him. One example is the grotesque entertainment for the white businessmen that he is forced to participate in as a schoolboy, and another is the powerful spotlight that blinds him before his first speech for the Brotherhood – of whose purposes he remains for some time in the dark. Eventually he finds a way potentially to regain control, tapping electricity illegally from Monopolated Light & Power for the 1369 lights that illuminate his subterranean refuge.

The narrator wins his scholarship to the black college (based upon the Booker T. Washington-founded Tuskegee University that Ellison attended from 1933 to 1936) as reward for his speech accepting the position of humility and gratitude that his white patrons want to hear. The speech is the first of many that he makes in the novel, some spontaneous and some programmed. These speeches are made with differing motives – many, like the first one, for rewards from whites.

Before President Bledsoe removes him from the college for showing white trustee Norton a side of Negro life that Norton's condescending paternalism had never imagined, the narrator receives a lesson in the complexities of leadership, language, performance, motive, and influence from Bledsoe's frank admission that "This is a power set-up," and also from the rhetoric of the blind Reverend Barbee (142). Barbee's account of the life and death of the Founder – which incorporates the principles of compromise and cultural assimilation advocated by Washington, although he is not mentioned by name – invokes biblical parallels to endow a messianic quality to the Founder. Similar myth-making rhetoric then endows many of the same qualities on "his living agent, his physical presence," disciple Bledsoe (134).

Barbee's blindness is matched with the sightless eye of Brother Jack. Sight, surface appearance, light, and darkness are all major motifs in the novel, connected to the invisibility that the narrator discovers is both his misfortune and his potential power. Sight, like language, serves to organize the world outside the self but also, as the narrator discovers, serves others in their imposition of an identity upon him. When he tries to hide behind dark glasses on the streets of Harlem, he is mistakenly identified on almost every corner as Rinehart, whose multiple identities include "the runner . . . the gambler . . . the briber . . . the lover and . . . the Reverend" (498). Similarly, what the viewer brings to seeing the college's bronze statue of the Founder "lifting a veil that flutters in hard, metallic folds above the face of a kneeling slave" determines interpretation. The narrator puzzles whether the veil is "really being lifted, or lowered more firmly in place; whether I am witnessing a revelation or a more efficient blinding" (36). The description matches the famous Booker T. Washington Memorial at Tuskegee University, and the narrator's comments reflect the concern of some black leaders, particularly W. E. B. Du Bois, about Washington's views.

At Liberty Paints the narrator's task of mixing a few drops of black into cans of milky brown paint to produce the company's "Optic White" is another example of the relationship of sight to surface appearance. Even when the mixture does not completely absorb the black, as when adding the wrong liquid results in a white tinged with gray, the paint still looks white to foreman Kimbro. The government buildings for which the paint is intended reinforce through this whiteness the power structure of which "slave driver" Kimbro is part, even though the white is an optical illusion and merely a surface coating (199). In fact, as the narrator discovers, the quality of the paint is actually dependent upon the knowledge and experience of a black man. Brockway, working in the basement that is another of the novel's subterranean environments, mirrors President Bledsoe in his use of this power. He insists upon working alone, and is prepared to sacrifice the narrator or anybody else to retain the control that gets him the attention and what he imagines is the respect of "the Old Man," the company's white owner.

As the narrator subsequently discovers, the Brotherhood, just as much as Brockway and Bledsoe, is concerned finally only with furthering its own power and control. The narrator's emergence from the machines of the hospital after the explosion at Liberty Paints suggests both a robotic identity and – since he is rescued and comforted by the maternal Mary – a parody of the virgin birth. Appropriately, two background incidents, a funeral and a woman beginning labor, accompany the narrator's first meeting with Brother Jack. Jack has red hair, the organization's parties are held at the Chthonian, and the alcoholic wife of one of the key backers is named Sybil. The Brotherhood's scientific analysis of history denies the importance of race or the role of racial difference in the history that its methods purport to explain. The blindness of this analysis is revealed not only in Brother Jack's false eye, but in the past of Brother Tarp and the fate of Tod Clifton – both Brotherhood members who disappear. The wounded Tarp, seen for a moment by the narrator as his own grandfather, is the victim of an injustice that mirrors slavery in all but name. Tod Clifton, recognizing that he has acted the role of a puppet, in effect commits suicide by resisting arrest, shot, even though unarmed, by a white patrolman.

Some of the key moments of potential understanding for the narrator occur through chance meetings. Two of these occur before he is forced to leave the college, with Trueblood and with the doctor/veteran at the Golden Day. Having none of the manipulative rhetoric of Reverend Barbee, the two speak honestly – bitterly, in the case of the veteran – about their experiences.

Two casual meetings on the streets of Harlem are also significant. At a point when the narrator is still fooled by the letters that Bledsoe had told him to deliver to a number of trustees, supposedly for possible employment, he meets a man disposing of unused blueprints. The narrator is unable to fully engage in the old man's repartee, only dimly recalling the songs and slang from his childhood. The white-directed oratory that won him a place in the college has replaced the language of his upbringing. Although the narrator's initial response is irritation, he does eventually acknowledge their common heritage. But the limitations resulting from the boundaries that the narrator sets up between his past and present are revealed in a key exchange with the old man about the blueprints. "Folks is always making plans and changing 'em," the old man remarks of the discarded rolls of paper. "That's a mistake," returns the narrator, "You have to stick to the plan." The old man, "suddenly grave," replies, "You kinda young, daddy-o" (175).

The old man himself has multiple identities, "a piano player and a rounder, a whiskey drinker and a pavement pounder." He advises the narrator that he will need to learn such "good bad habits" – a lesson in fluid identities that the invisible man will learn only later when repeatedly mistaken for Rinehart (176).

The second meeting is with a yam seller, following his experience at Liberty Paints. In contrast to the language that he can only dimly recall with the blueprint carrier, the odor of the yams brings back vivid memories of home and school. Initially he is cautious, wanting only one, and although he returns for two more yams, enjoying the freedom of eating on the street and indulging his appetite unrestrained, the lesson that the incident might teach him about the relationship of his identity to his remembered past is lost in a lack of balance, and in petty anger. Inevitably, one of the yams turns out to be "frost-bitten" and his exuberant and unbalanced sense of freedom quickly passes (265).

The main rival to the Brotherhood on the streets of Harlem, Black Nationalist Ras the Exhorter, offers no solutions for the narrator with his anti-white rhetoric. Ras sidesteps what the narrator terms "the beautiful absurdity of ... American identity" through his identification with Africa, and particularly Ethiopia (559). To claim such an identity is to confront the legacy of slavery by an impossible return to the past. The self-defeating nature of Ras's rhetoric is revealed through his transformation into Ras the Destroyer, and his incongruous appearance on the night of the race riot, a spear-carrying figure "upon a great black horse ... dressed in the costume of an Abyssinian chieftain" complete with fur cap and shield (556).

From the cellar hideout where the narrator begins and ends the novel, he wrestles with the need to integrate his own past with that of his race and his country, and at the same time to find an "American identity" that can be his own without necessitating isolation – that can be social without bringing excessive restriction. In the subterranean "border area" he can slip between potentially restrictive identities, in contrast to white trustee Norton, encountered in the subway vainly seeking directions to "Centre Street" (578).

Important to the narrator's task in the cellar is his continued puzzling over the dying advice of his grandfather: "I want you to overcome 'em with yeses, undermine 'em with grins, agree 'em to death and destruction, let 'em swoller you till they vomit or bust wide open" (16). At various points in the novel the narrator misunderstands or dismisses the advice, but he comes back "again and again" to the words. He comes to no final conclusions, but recognizes that they must concern division only in the sense that division recognizes diversity. The old man, he realizes, must have been affirming a principle greater than the violence, selfishness, and condescension that produced slavery – and that characterize many of the narrator's own experiences – a principle of "American identity" that could allow individual difference while still offering a share in the community for all. The painful history of the black race in America, the narrator reflects, makes all the more crucial that "we, most of all ... affirm the principle, the plan in whose name we had been brutalized and sacrificed" (574). But as the narrator begins to consider re-emerging from underground, he tells his readers directly that the need to continue affirming the principle belongs just as much to "all the others" (574). Despite the past, and all the division behind the activities of the college, its trustees, the paint factory, the Brotherhood, and Ras the Exhorter, the consequences of the principle's destruction would, the narrator reminds his readers, be a loss for all.

Bibliography

Ralph Ellison, *Invisible Man* (New York, 1995).
John F. Callahan, ed., *Ralph Ellison's Invisible Man: A Casebook* (New York, 2004).
Michael D. Hill and Lena M. Hill, *Ralph Ellison's Invisible Man: A Reference Guide* (Westport, CT, 2008).
Ross Posnock, ed., *The Cambridge Companion to Ralph Ellison* (Cambridge, 2005).
Eric Sundquist, *Cultural Contexts for Invisible Man* (Boston, 1995).

Jack Kerouac, *On the Road*, New York: Viking, 1957

The freewheeling travels that form the basis of *On the Road* occurred between 1947 and 1950, and Jack Kerouac began trying to write a novel about them as early as 1948. After a number of false starts, in April 1951 he taped together some sheets of teletype paper and began the version which, after several revisions, was finally published in 1957. The April 1951 version was finished in about six weeks, contains no paragraphs or chapter divisions, and, unlike the version finally published, uses the real names of such traveling companions as Allen Ginsberg and Neal Cassady – the latter a figure who would subsequently appear in works by Tom Wolfe and Ken Kesey. This earlier version was published in 2007, on the fiftieth anniversary of the novel, as *On the Road: The Original Scroll*, and includes a number of articles on the novel, its textual history, and its social and political context.

In the published version, not only are names changed (Ginsberg becomes Carlo Marx, Cassady becomes Dean Moriarty), but some other identifying details are changed too. The journey begins in Paterson not, as it actually did, in Ozone Park, Queens, and Kerouac's mother becomes his aunt. Experiences are intensified, sometimes telescoped. Some details are omitted – the sexual adventures described in the novel, for example, give little to no account of the homosexual experiences of Cassady, Ginsberg, or Kerouac himself.

Kerouac's first novel, *The Town and the City*, was published in 1950, an event recorded in *On the Road*, but after some early attention the book faded from view. In the years that followed he unsuccessfully shopped *On the Road* to publisher after publisher and worked on the numerous unpublished manuscripts listed by Ginsberg in the 1956 dedication to *Howl*, a dedication that Kerouac shared with Cassady, William S. Burroughs, and Lucien Carr.

The Twentieth-Century American Fiction Handbook　By Christopher MacGowan
© 2011 Christopher MacGowan

Kerouac's novel had to wait for other expressions of the rebellious post-war youth movement to appear before he found a publisher – such as the success of "Howl," the apotheosis of James Dean, and the advent of Elvis Presley.

Kerouac used notebooks and letters from the trips to supply details for his novel, and made the frantic physical and verbal energy of Dean Moriarty, the Cassady character, its center. Kerouac brings immediacy to the narration by having a first-person narrator, Sal Paradise, record the events in which he sometimes participates and is sometimes a bystander, and has Sal passing little or no judgment on the actions of others, their values, or the condition of their lives – and only rarely evaluating his own. Sal's spontaneous wonder at the beauty and sweep of the American landscape seen from hitchhiked rides, buses, or travel bureau cars is conveyed in the same tone as scenes of drunken debauchery and states of drug-fueled ecstasy or confusion.

Much of the power of the novel, in addition to that brought by its remarkable central figure, comes from Kerouac's economical yet vivid descriptions of the various characters met by chance on the road or encountered in weekend-long binges, characters caught up for the moment in the maelstrom around Dean Moriarty. Sal and Dean, sometimes together, sometimes alone, and sometimes with others, hurtle between the east and west coasts, using Denver as a kind of stopping-off point. The traveling, drinking, drug-taking, and sexual conquests are mostly spontaneous events, chance often dictating who is currently in the city, where a night of drinking ends up, or, if traveling, who the fellow travelers are. The trips are made with little money. Destinations are never final, commitments to lovers – despite a side of both Dean and Sal that wants to settle down – are broken. The breathless activity is only halted by Sal's occasional visionary introspection, and the sense he sometimes has of his isolation and of the purposelessness of the traveling and indulgence.

Sal begins the novel a naïve traveler, unlike the experienced Dean. His first day hitchhiking west leaves him stranded on Bear Mountain and forced to return to the city where, disheartened, he takes a bus to Chicago. Most of the time Sal lets Dean initiate events. Dean does most of the talking, and most of the driving. Sal is fascinated by Dean's frantic energy, even to the extent of overlooking Dean's selfishness and insensitivity – for example, Dean abandons Sal on two important occasions, in San Francisco and in Mexico City.

A key moment in the relationship occurs during their third trip when Sal, now with money from his publisher, does not immediately follow Dean as usual, but invites Dean to follow him to New York, and on to Italy:

> Now his eyes were blank and looking through me. It was probably the pivotal point of our friendship when he realized I had actually spent some hours

thinking about him and his troubles, and he was trying to place that in his tremendously involved and tormented mental categories. Something clicked in both of us. In me it was suddenly concern for a man who was years younger than I, five years, and whose fate was wound with mine across the passage of the recent years. (189–190)

Like all plans involving Dean Moriarty, these plans are supplanted by chance meetings and sudden changes of direction. And while this moment brings Sal closer to Dean, shortly afterwards Dean is criticized ruthlessly to his face by Galatea and others in the room. The other perspectives upon Dean, here and elsewhere, contribute to the rich characterization of the central character and complicate Sal's perspective on him – itself at times ambivalent, although always sympathetic. The passage quoted above also illustrates the crafted spontaneity of Kerouac's prose. Although a moment set in the past, the suggestion of words flowing from mind to page is reinforced by the narrator stopping for the moment to qualify "years younger" with the exact number, "five years," as if only recalling it a few words later.

Kerouac's father, Leo, had died in the spring of 1946 and his death is much more a feature of the "scroll" version of the novel than in the published version. The focus in the published version is on the unsuccessful search for Dean Moriarty's missing alcoholic father, "Old Dean Moriarty," who becomes a character in the novel even in his absence, and is in Sal's thoughts at the end of the novel along with thoughts of Dean himself. Various rumors suggest that he is working in one place, or in jail in another. He comes to represent both a lost continuity and a lost inheritance, not only biologically but also as a representative of the displaced migrants and hobos from the 1930s who never recovered from the Depression, never themselves settled down, and whose children are living a wilder, more self-destructive version of their fathers' wanderings. A similarly ghostly figure in the novel is the "shrouded stranger" met in Sal's dreams and perhaps on the road, a reminder of aging and death, but also of a fellow traveler pointing the way to roads beyond the physical and time-bound.

Music and sex are two unifying features of the various trips. Sal listens to bop in Chicago, and "I thought of all my friends from one end of the country to the other." Bop allows for individual, introspective expression by a performer, and extended solos, in contrast to the more programmed, group dynamics of big bands. The spirit of bop matches the freewheeling individualism of Sal and his group. Sex, like jazz, bop, drugs, alcohol, and speed, can bring ecstatic states of consciousness akin to the mysticism that is the closest the novel's characters come to conventional religion. But for all of Dean's adventures in casual sex, he always returns to the two women he had married,

Marylou and Camille, sometimes seeing both of them at different times in the day, rushing from one end of the city to the other. On the same night that Dean marries for the third time, he leaves his new wife, Inez, jumps on a bus, and crosses the continent to rejoin Camille.

Sal's few idyllic weeks with the Mexican girl Terry on his first trip foreshadow the drive to Mexico City in part four, and Sal's view there of a culture and people that he sees as rooted in living traditions and crafts. With Terry and her young son Sal finds a degree of peace, even love, and lives for a while the hard life of a transient cotton picker. But his own clumsy attempts at picking the crop, and his experience of the bare level of subsistence that the little pay allows, undercut his attempts to romanticize the life of the other migrants, or wax too lyrical on the joys of working with "the brown moist earth" (96). He must remain an outsider when Terry visits her family, dropped off a quarter-mile away to watch the family scene "across the sad vineyards of October in the valley," while "huddled in the cold, rainy wind" (98).

Sal is as just as distant from the Indian people that he and Dean pass just outside Gregoria on the road to Mexico City. The term that Sal uses, "Fellahin," is borrowed from Oswald Spengler's *The Decline of the West*, where for Spengler they are the "residue" of a civilization's decline. Kerouac adapted the term to mean "primitive" peoples across the earth, threatened by Western culture but uncorrupted by it:

> I was alone in my eternity at the wheel ... like driving across the world and into the places where we would finally learn ourselves among the Fellahin Indians of the world, the essential strain of the basic primitive, wailing humanity that stretches in a belt around the equatorial belly of the world ... They were great, grave Indians and they were the source of mankind and the fathers of it. (280)

But this moment of "eternity" for Sal remains an alternative finally unavailable to him, as unavailable as Old Dean Moriarty is for Dean, or Leo Kerouac is for Jack. During his stay Sal enjoys aspects of Mexico – the tolerant police, the easy availability of girls and drugs – but the people remain distant and the interaction transient and commercial.

In the novel's coda both men are still traveling, but Sal's journey is much more circumscribed, almost a parody of his earlier freedom. He is sitting in a Cadillac with a concert ticket for Duke Ellington at the Metropolitan Opera, with companions who refuse to allow Dean Moriarty to come in from the cold to share the ride uptown. Sal is sorry to be going to the concert and sorry to be refusing Dean, but he is accompanied by Laura, "to whom I'd told everything about Dean" (307). Dean turns the corner and goes out of sight, starting yet another journey west, but Sal's telling of Dean's story, as he sits next to "the girl... that I had always searched for and for so long," comes to its close in this novel, although as "Cody Pomeray" the irrepressible Cassady would appear in a number of Kerouac's subsequent works (304).

Bibliography

Jack Kerouac, *On the Road* (New York, 2003), with an introduction by Ann Charters. A Fiftieth Anniversary Edition of *On The Road* appeared in 2007 as a hardcover (New York, 2007).

Hillary Holladay and Robert Holton, eds., *What's Your Road, Man?: Critical Essays on Jack Kerouac's On the Road* (Carbondale, IL, 2008).

Robert Holton, *On the Road: Kerouac's Ragged American Journey* (New York, 1999).

Jack Kerouac, *On the Road: The Original Scroll*, ed. Howard Cunnell (New York, 2007).

Paul Maher, Jr., *Jack Kerouac's American Journey: The Real-Life Odyssey of On the Road* (New York, 2007).

Vladimir Nabokov, *Lolita,* Paris: Olympia Press, 1955; New York: Putnam, 1958

In his short essay "On a Book Entitled *Lolita*," written to accompany the excerpts from the novel published in the *Anchor Review* in 1957, Vladimir Nabokov tells of his efforts to find a publisher for the book in the United States. Four publishers, he records (actually five, according to biographer Brian Boyd), turned him down, either on the grounds that the novel was pornography, or because in their view both author and publisher risked jail if it were printed. The novel found a publisher in Paris in 1955 with Olympia Press, although Olympia had a history – evidently unknown to the author – of publishing titles which could only reinforce the perception that the novel actually was pornographic. The French government did ban the book, along with a number of other Olympia titles, for more than a year. The novel received little attention until novelist Graham Greene listed *Lolita* in a review as one of the three most important books of 1955, and sparked a spirited debate in the English press. The *Anchor Review* excerpt marked the first tentative United States publication of pages from the novel. American publishers continued to hesitate, fearing a costly court battle. However, when Putnam published the book the following year they encountered no legal trouble. The novel was banned by a number of libraries, but immediately became a bestseller, its sales fueled as much by its notoriety as by interest in its literary qualities. Nabokov later observed that a whole generation of American mothers stopped considering the name Lolita for their newly born girls. The town of Lolita in Texas considered changing its name to Jackson. The success of *Lolita* gave impetus to the translation and reissue of Nabokov's

The Twentieth-Century American Fiction Handbook   By Christopher MacGowan
© 2011 Christopher MacGowan

earlier novels and stories written in his native Russian, including in 1986 the publication of a previously unpublished manuscript from 1939, translated as *The Enchanter*, that is an early treatment of the themes that would appear in the later novel.

Nabokov's note for the *Anchor Review* was published in the Putnam edition, and has been included in all subsequent editions of the novel. As such it offers a counter to the claims made by the author's invented editor John Ray, Jr. in his "Foreword." John Ray purports to introduce the narrator and the text, although he is himself – J.R. Jr – one of the first of the many doubles in the novel, a list that includes the narrator's lawyer, Clarence Clark, and, most centrally, narrator Humbert Humbert.

John Ray claims that his qualifications as editor include being the winner of "the Poling Prize," although he doesn't go on to note that the manuscript that he is introducing contains more references to Poe than to any other author, or that the all-important predecessor of Lolita, Annabel Lee, derives her name from one of Poe's best-known poems (3). Appropriately, the tragic Annabel's name is at the center of Lo-lee-ta's own. Although two of the central characters are thus arguably literary constructions, John Ray offers supposed details for "old-fashioned readers" about "the destinies of the 'real' people beyond the 'true' story." Hidden in this playful paragraph, disguised within the anagram "Vivian Darkbloom," is the inventor of all of the novel's characters. Of little help to "old fashioned readers" is John Ray's information that a "Mrs. Richard F. Schiller" died in childbirth, since Lolita's marriage is not reported by Humbert until more than 300 pages into his narrative. John Ray's defense of the novel is that despite the "moral leprosy" of author Humbert, the book will no doubt interest "psychiatric circles," and, most importantly, will have an "ethical impact" and provide a "lesson" for "the wayward child, the egotistical mother" (4–6). Nabokov's closing essay, however, makes quite clear that he does not consider himself in any sense a writer of moral fiction.

Humbert confesses late in his narrative, "I suppose I am especially susceptible to the magic of games," and John Ray's "Foreword" is the first of the many "games" that Humbert's creator plays in this novel (233). Important events occur during games of tennis and chess, Humbert plays games with language, and Quilty plays games in the hotel register entries that record his trailing of Humbert and Lolita on their second long trip – teasing Humbert with a medley of puns, anagrams, and pseudonyms worthy of, perhaps even imagined by, the narrator himself. But the central game is played with the reader – directly addressed more than 20 times by Humbert – any reader who, following John Ray, looks for the book to obey either the conventions of realistic fiction or of "reality"; and perhaps for it to be a thinly disguised version of real events, with the narrator's voice a projection of the author's, and a narrative culminating in the strictures, however artfully integrated, of a moral lesson.

The coincidences in the narrative tease with suggested significance, but finally reflect the patterning of its artifice and the game of words. For example: the street number of the Haze house in Ramsdale and the traveling couple's room number in *The Enchanted Hunters* are the same, 342, which is also the number of "hotels, motels, and tourist homes" that Humbert registers at in trying to track down Quilty and Lolita (248). Camp Q shares an initial with Quilty, whose nickname is "Cue." The death of Humbert's mother, Lolita's fears, and one of Quilty's plays are all related to lightening. The extent to which such coincidences permeate Humbert's narrative has been annotated in Alfred Appel's edition of the novel. Appel notes, for example, that Humbert and Lolita spend 52 weeks on the road on their first trip; there are 52 lines in the poem that Humbert addresses to her after she has left him; Quilty is "the author of fifty-two successful scenarios" (298); and all three major characters die in 1952. Further, Humbert and Quilty both appear to recognize in advance the significance of 52 in Humbert's (at that point unwritten) narrative by focusing on the license plate numbers "Q32888" and "CU88322" recorded among the 342 hotel registers (251). As well as referring to Quilty's nickname and being almost mirror images of each other, the numbers add up to 52, the number, appropriately, of playing cards in a deck.

Humbert cites a number of texts as external evidence of his narrative's veracity, but they all reinforce the fictional status of the novel itself. In *Who's Who in the Limelight*, for example, Vivian Darkbloom again makes an appearance, and the entries for Roland Pym, Clare Quilty, and Dolores Quine all have echoes of Poe, of sexual appetites that rival Humbert's, and relate to Lolita's drama interests. Other texts have an even more problematic status. The list of Lolita's classmates at her Ramsdale school adds to the novel's many doubles by containing four sets of twins, and is part of a series of journal entries by Humbert from a diary "destroyed five years ago" but brought into the narrative "courtesy of a photographic memory" that at other points in the narrative is far less reliable (40). Entries that Humbert cites from the Ramsdale *Journal* and later the *Briceland Gazette* are equally problematic. Charlotte's letter confessing her love for Humbert is destroyed, an important snapshot of Annabel is lost, and John Ray's suggestion that references to Humbert's "crime" can be found in "the daily papers for September–October 1952" is merely vague (4).

The doubles in *Lolita* suggest, along with the many Poe references, and Humbert's reference to himself at one point as "Mr Hyde," that the story might be in the doppelgänger genre (206). One suggestive thread of the novel's wordplay implies that Quilty is a manifestation of Humbert's guilty conscience: Guilty – Quilty – Clare Quilty, clearly guilty – guilty of crimes in a quilt-covered bed – a character created by the pen, the quill. At one point Quilty exists as a French phrase in a letter from one of Lolita's girl friends – "qu'il t'y" (223). Sometimes Humbert believes that he must be inventing the series of different colored convertibles that he suspects of tracking the couple, and that he might be fusing into one identity the multiple admirers whom Lolita attracts during stops on their second journey. Toward the end of the novel Humbert and Quilty start to form a common identity. When Humbert wants to practice his aim before shooting Quilty he shoots a hole in his own sweater. When he finally confronts Quilty, Humbert is dressed in black, as if a shadow of his prey, while Quilty is dressed in a "purple bathrobe, very like one I had" (294). And when they grapple on the floor singular pronouns become plural: "We rolled all over the floor . . . he rolled over me. I rolled over him. We rolled over me. They rolled over him. We rolled over us" (299).

But the double genre, like the romance and detective story genres, which Humbert's tale also visits, is parodied – all three would impose restrictions upon the world of fiction that Nabokov rejects. Poe and Stevenson's double stories present clearly demarcated good and evil characters, but Humbert and Quilty are a much more ambiguous pairing. Romance may dictate the plot of Quilty's play *The Enchanted Hunters*, with its "profound message . . . that mirage and reality merge in love," but *Lolita* offers no such romantic closure (201). The 17-year-old Lolita, no longer a nymphet, rejects Humbert's offer to return to him. And as a detective story the narrative is full of ambiguous and unresolved clues, while the criminal's confession is written by the detective himself (and is a parody of T. S. Eliot's "Ash Wednesday").

"On a Book Entitled *Lolita*" makes clear the kind of reader that Nabokov seeks for his novel: one who enjoys the pleasures of imagination and the sophisticated play of language. However, in the years since the novel's publication, public attention – and the attention of lawmakers – has increased awareness and concern about the sexual exploitation of children. A reasonable question that some readers may ask is – is the sexual exploitation of a middle-school child a suitable subject for humor, even humor and skill at the highly sophisticated level of this novel? Nabokov is clearly a writer driven by the desire to expand the possibilities of his craft, and to explore the possibilities of language, and he does not endorse any of the attitudes or behavior of the novel's characters. But a contemporary reader of *Lolita* does not have to be one of John Ray's "old-fashioned readers" to find the question coming to mind – even if that contemporary reader's sympathies are finally with the author's insistence that the act of writing and reading fiction takes place firmly in its own world of "aesthetic bliss" (314).

Bibliography

Vladimir Nabokov, *Lolita* (New York, 1997); *The Enchanter*, trans. Dmitri Nabokov (New York, 1991); *The Annotated Lolita*, ed. Alfred Appel Jr. (New York, 1991).

Leland De La Durantaye, *Style Is Matter: The Moral Art of Vladimir Nabokov* (Ithaca, 2007).

Zoran Kuzmanovich and Galya Diment, *Approaches to Teaching Nabokov's Lolita* (New York, 2008).

Lance Olson, *Lolita: A Janus Text* (New York, 1995).

Ellen Pifer, ed., *Vladimir Nabokov's Lolita: A Casebook* (New York, 2003).

Joseph Heller, *Catch-22*, New York: Simon and Schuster, 1961

As Joseph Heller points out in his 1994 preface to *Catch-22*, the novel "won no prizes and was not on any bestseller list" in the United States when it first appeared (2). But when the novel was reissued in paperback in 1962, it captured the growing anti-war sentiments of many readers, and went through 15 mass-market reprintings in the next two years. Such was its popularity that the book provided a new term for the language: "Catch-22" is defined by *Webster's Dictionary* as "a frustrating situation in which one is trapped by contradictory regulations or conditions."

The novel's examples of Catch-22 are many. Central to the narrative is the predicament of Yossarian, bombardier in the air force in Italy in World War II. Catch-22 dictates that a flier driven to insanity because of the dangerous bombing missions must have his requests to be grounded or sent home denied because his response to the near-suicidal missions is in fact a sane one. Catch-22 allows for the enforcement of its rules because its enforcers – the police, superior officers, and general bureaucracy – "have a right to do anything we can't stop them from doing" (407). Even more importantly, as Yossarian comes to realize, although Catch-22 does not exist, "everyone thought it existed" (409). The assumption is reinforced by the repetition, efficiency, hierarchy, and discipline demanded by a military organization such as the air force of this novel. The demands of the larger organization – the squadron, and more broadly the whole war effort against the enemy – provide cover for the private motives of officers who punish non-conformists. Yossarian has no alternative, as far as the system is concerned, but to fly missions until he is killed or until the war is over, even though the former is much more likely in the immediate future, and even though replacement fliers are trained and available. Individuality is dangerous and is punished in various ways. Dunbar is marked to "disappear," and "the soldier in white" is reduced to a mass of bandages, a small black hole, and two jars that recycle liquids through him. Since in his condition all individual characteristics beyond apparent weight and size are obliterated, he can be replaced later with another "soldier in white." Snowden's death, his insides spilling out from his flak suit in front of Yossarian, is a reminder, to which the narrative returns many times, of the vulnerable human flesh beneath the blank surface and bureaucratic abstraction.

Within a system sanctioned by Catch-22, the hospital's psychiatrist can tell Yossarian: "You've got a bad persecution complex. You think people are trying to harm you . . . You have no respect for excessive authority or obsolete traditions" (299). The Chaplain can be asked whether he is "guilty or innocent" of "crimes and infractions" that his accusers "don't even know about yet" (386). An official form can state that a man is dead even if the man himself is present to confirm that he is living, as happens with Doc Daneeka – or that a man is alive even though everyone in the camp knows that he was killed before officially reporting for duty, as happens to Mudd. Official forms confirm the validity of statements made on other official forms – the system's confirmation process taking on an autonomous authority of its own that is impossible to deny with mere facts. Mirroring this version of the trap, Major Major finds that all forms that he signs circle back to him for another signature, attached this time to dozens more forms that have themselves been circulating for signatures.

Catch-22 allows figures in authority to use those below them ruthlessly for their own advancement, since regulations demand that men obey the orders of their superiors in rank even if those orders run counter to the squadron's other regulations. Although the demand for obedience is sup-posedly for the good of the group, it actually serves the purposes of manipulative individuals. "You're either *for* us or against your country. It's as simple as that," Colonel Korn tells the unhappy Yossarian (423). This tactic is taken to an extreme by Captain Black's "Glorious Loyalty Oath Crusade," actually a campaign against his rival, Major Major. Elsewhere, rivals General Peckham and General Dreedle issue orders driven by their own personal tastes, ambitions, and jealousies. On one mission, General Peckham is more concerned with the aesthetics of a bomb pattern than with the military purpose of the bombing, which itself is so abstractly conceived as to ignore the deaths of the supportive civilians that the bombing will bring about. Meanwhile Colonel Cathcart is always confused as to which General he should impress to gain his own promotion. To draw attention to himself he continues to increase the number of missions that the men in his group must fly well beyond the number required by the squadron. He does this at no physical risk to himself (beyond a plot to murder him that never gets underway). The desire for publicity leads him to base some of his decisions on the editorial needs of the *Saturday Evening Post*. Two officers who do succeed in being promoted are both associated with the machine-like processes of the system. The foolish Lieutenant Scheisskopf is obsessed with the discipline and patterning of parades, while the reluctant Major Major is promoted by an IBM computer.

The military organization in the novel allows Heller to satirize through exaggeration some basic tenets of American culture. The monetary rewards associated with initiative are what drive Milo and win him wide approval – even when he contracts with the Germans to bomb his own side. His energetic pursuit of profits is complemented by his assurance that free enterprise benefits all, that everybody gains as a member of "the syndicate." Milo's enterprises flourish because of the unthinking acceptance of such principles without regard to how they are being used. Force of habit, he explains to Yossarian, allows him to make a profit by buying eggs from Malta for seven cents apiece and selling them to the mess halls in Pianosa for five cents through a complex scheme that includes buying from and selling to himself. The values that empower Milo and allow his schemes are as inhuman as the larger system within which he operates. His activities contribute to Snowden's suffering when his "borrowing" of supplies from the plane's medicine kit results in Yossarian finding no morphine with which to ease the pain of Snowden's fatal wound.

Major Major finds a way to "disappear" himself by only taking appointments for times when he is absent. The more desperate and isolated Yossarian needs to stay alive long enough to find a way out of the traps endorsed by Catch-22. The hospital provides a temporary haven, a place where, unlike the war zone, death is not arbitrary and usually not sudden. But here too there are dangers.

When Yossarian is on official rest leave in Rome he indulges in sex, drink, and food and can almost forget the missions that he must return to. But he sees a different Rome when he walks the streets without official leave. He cannot blot out the scenes of suffering and violence that he witnesses despite his attempts to walk away, to close his eyes, or put his hands over his ears. This human suffering is, however, ignored by the military machine, where deaths are largely numerical abstractions. When Yossarian is arrested for being in Rome without leave papers, the police focus on the flier and show no interest in the body of a murdered woman, or the murderer who is right in front of them.

As Yossarian's desperation grows he becomes increasingly isolated, losing his friends one by one. His emotional needs lead him to fall in love with every prostitute he meets, and he becomes so blunted to genuine affection that he doesn't recognize it when it is offered. The escape that he seeks is finally supplied by Orr, whose name aptly suggests an alternative. Orr uses routine against the enforcers of routine by becoming the flier who is *expected* to go down on a mission, and thus is able to rehearse his escape quite within the restrictions imposed by Catch-22. Yossarian's selfless pledge to look for and rescue the 12-year-old sister of "Nately's whore" and take her with him has been criticized as sentimental, but his motives indicate the human, caring qualities that have both threatened his existence within the system and allowed him the chance to survive – qualities learned from the horror of Snowden's death, and his night walking in the streets of Rome without leave papers.

The novel offers no guarantee that Yossarian will find the "kid sister" or survive his journey. But Heller's sequel to *Catch-22*, titled *Closing Time*, published 33 years later, finds the now aged Yossarian in New York, with billionaire Milo and the Chaplain. "Should I ever write another sequel," Heller writes in his 1994 Preface, Yossarian "would still be around at the end" (5).

While *Catch-22*'s influence has always been recognized, the novel has been criticized for what some see as its excessive length, lack of structure, and the uneven quality of its humor. For more sympathetic readers, the novel's startling narrative and time shifts, its play with the contradictions and multiple meanings of language, its double negatives and black humor all serve as a mirror to Yossarian's, and the author's, dodging and weaving – refusing to be tied down to overly oppressive convention. Ex-P.F.C. Wintergreen's subversive manipulations on duty at the center of the communications network is one way to protest the machinery of oppression, and the novel's endorsement of Yossarian's escape is another. Language may be a trap in this novel, but literature is subversive. After all, this is a set-up in which introducing the names of T. S. Eliot and Washington Irving into the system produces official bewilderment, and not a little chaos.

Bibliography

Joseph Heller, *Catch-22*, with an updated preface by the author (New York, 2004).

Frederick Kiley and Walter McDonald, eds., *A Catch-22 Casebook* (New York, 1973).

James Nagel, *Critical Essays on Catch-22* (Encini, CA, 1974).

Stephen W. Potts, *Catch-22: Antiheroic Antinovel* (Boston, 1989).

Jon Woodson, *A Study of Joseph Heller's Catch-22: Going Around Twice* (New York, 2001).

William S. Burroughs, *Naked Lunch*, Paris: Olympia Press, 1959; New York: Grove, 1962

William S. Burroughs writes in the *"Atrophied Preface"* section near the end of *Naked Lunch* that "You can cut into *Naked Lunch* at any intersection point," noting just before this invitation that "sooner or later" most of the characters who populate the book "are subject to say the same thing in the same words, to occupy, at that intersection point, the same position in space-time" (186). As such comments indicate, *Naked Lunch* does not have a conventionally arranged plot or clearly distinct and developed characters. The book has no consistent narrative viewpoint, and characters are introduced only to suddenly disappear. There are satirical episodes alongside detailed descriptions of narcotic addition, and scenes of drug withdrawal agonies and violent individual and group sexual activities alongside parodies of such genres as romance and crime novels. The tone veers between slapstick and scientific analysis. Sometimes a scene (or to use Burroughs's term, a "routine") will extend for two or three pages, and sometimes it will be a fragment or a sentence; on occasion a scene is set out as if the book were a play script. A few lines or verses of a song might accompany a scene, while the section headings might locate the narrative for the moment in a place or with a person, but might instead repeat a particular phrase within the section. "Notes" in parentheses sometimes explain specialized vocabulary; one scene is accompanied by an "alternative," while another, the writer advises, was written in a state of drugged "intoxication" (124, 91).

The circumstances of the book's publishing history had a direct impact upon its arrangement. The narcotics addiction that plagued Burroughs from the mid-1940s and would continue, with occasional periods of non-use, for the rest of his life hindered his organization of the typescripts. In the mid-1950s his friends Jack Kerouac and Allen Ginsberg visited Burroughs in Tangier, where he had lived since 1953, and helped with the typing and organization of the various drafts – a visit that Kerouac describes in his 1965 book *Desolation Angels*.

Lawrence Ferlinghetti, who had published Ginsberg's *Howl* in 1956, rejected Burroughs's manuscript when Ginsberg offered it in 1958. But the publication of sections of the book in a Chicago journal produced a Post Office ban on the grounds of obscenity, and reignited the interest of Paris publisher Maurice Girodias. Girodias and his Olympia Press were always on the look-out for English-language books, whether pornographic or literary, that had run afoul of the censor or had scared off American publishers. (Olympia Press was the first publisher of Vladimir Nabokov's *Lolita*.) Sensing some timely publicity from the Post Office ban, Girodias gave Burroughs two weeks to get a manuscript ready for the printer. Burroughs and his friends sent off the various sections of the book as they were retyped, and Burroughs intended to put the sections into a final order when he received the galleys. But author and publisher agreed when the galleys arrived that the arrangements as they now stood worked best. As it happened, Burroughs had recently met and become interested in the work of visual collage artist Brion Gysin, and had begun to develop what he called the "cut up method" that he would use in some of his later writing. Thus Burroughs's preparation of the typescripts to meet Girodias's deadline allowed the book to reflect the techniques that the author had recently been discussing with Gysin.

When Grove Press began to prepare their edition in 1960, with Burroughs's concurrence the Grove edition included some material that was in the version rejected by Ferlinghetti but not included in the Olympia Press printing. In addition, Burroughs agreed that the Grove edition include in an appendix his "Letter from a Master Addict to Dangerous Drugs," a first-person account of his struggle with addiction first published in January 1957. He also agreed that the edition include his article "Deposition: Testimony Concerning a Sickness," which describes treatment of his addiction with apomorphine. The appendix gained another addition in the 1966 printing, following the prosecution of a bookseller in Massachusetts for offering the novel, and the eventual ruling by the Massachusetts Supreme Court on July 7, 1966, that the book was not obscene. (This would be the last major obscenity trial of a literary text in the United States.) The book's defenders in court included

Norman Mailer and Ginsberg, and the 1966 addition reproduced some of the trial testimony. The story of the various editions and additions is told by editors James Grauerholz and Barry Miles in their 2001 "restored text," which removes a number of apparently unintended repetitions, corrects the spelling of many proper names, and adds in a further appendix some earlier and alternative versions of various "routines." This edition quotes as testament to the novel's ongoing reputation and influence such writers as Terry Southern, Marshall McLuhan, Mary McCarthy, Anthony Burgess, and Joan Didion.

The prevailing theme in the book is entrapment by external forces that threaten to take over the individual's identity and liberty. "I can feel the heat closing in," the book begins (3). The threatened individual is often named "William Lee," Burroughs's authorial pseudonym for his first book, *Junkie*, published in 1953 by Ace in a cheap pulp edition (complete with sensational cover and with the subtitle "Confessions of an Unredeemed Drug Addict"). Sometimes the narration is in William Lee's voice, and at other times it is third person.

The forces that threaten to take over are multiple. They include drugs and drug dealers; the agents tracking down drug users – sometimes to use the drug themselves; sadistic doctors and technocrats working for various hospitals and state organizations; and the instruments of government and media demanding uniformity and obedience to their dictates, however oppressive or degrading. The freedom that is being threatened is sometimes freedom of thought, and sometimes physical – the threat of imprisonment or death, or the freedom to practice homosexual or heterosexual sex without restriction. Resistance to the threats results in the sadistic punishments, bizarre experiments, and excessive violence that the book describes in sometimes vivid detail. Individuality, for Burroughs, can also become lost within an organizational role, or be subsumed by the biological drives of the body.

Dr. Benway appears a number of times as an agent of various departments. Along with "Fingers" Schafer and Dr. Berger, he is one of the nightmarish authority figures whose claims to heal actually threaten annihilation, both physical or mental; they are figures who might rip a patient's body apart on the operating table. At one point Benway is working for the "Ministry of Mental Hygiene and Prophylaxis" (155). Before becoming an "advisor to the Freeland Republic" he worked for the equally repressive Annexia, "where his assignment had been T.D. – Total Demoralization" (19). Benway's methods are insidious rather than dramatic and sudden, and aim at total control. With dispassionate approval he tells Dr. Schafer "about the man who taught his asshole to talk," only to have it take over his body and reduce him to "one all-purpose blob" (110).

The city of Interzone, where Benway and his fellow doctors operate, suggests a nightmarish vision of Tangier. The Moroccan city had the status of an International Zone until 1956 and a reputation as a center of espionage. But Burroughs's city exists as much in mental as physical space, a fluid, unstable landscape in which change could happen at any moment. The Interzone sections of the novel contain some relatively conventional satire – on bureaucracy, consumer culture, and the effects of colonial occupation – alongside heightened scenes of excess, many of them sexual and violent. Interzone is also the home of the mysterious Islam Inc., the organization that employs the narrator.

The origins of tycoon A.J., owner of Islam Inc., are also obscure, as are the company's goals. A.J.'s entrepreneurial activities are global, his affiliations a mystery, and his many interests linked by an exuberant homosexual exhibitionism. His nationality follows the rise and fall of world powers, "His English accent waned with the British Empire, and after World War II he became an American by Act of Congress" (122).

A.J. is an "agent like me," the narrator records, but nobody knows "for whom or for what" (122–123). A.J. claims to be "independent," but "there are no independents any more" in Interzone (130). Lee himself belongs to the Factualists, who oppose the annihilation techniques of the Liquefaction party and their plan to merge "everyone into One Man" (123). The Factualists also oppose the Divisionists, whose program advocates division and the growing of exact replicas of themselves. Rather than the goal of One Man, the Divisionist program would lead to complete loss of individual difference, "one person in the world with millions of separate bodies" (137). The fourth party in Interzone is more directly concerned with controlling the mind rather than the body. The Senders are ignorant of what they are sending, have a "rabid fear of any *fact*," and their interest in sending to others takes over any interest in receiving (136). Against these forces threatening mind and body the Factualists cling to their own world, their desires, and their physical independence. Burroughs makes such a claim for writing in the *Atrophied Preface*: "There is only one thing a writer can write about: *what is in front of his senses at the moment of writing*" (184).

Against the programmers, killers, and oppressors, Burroughs sets the sudden juxtapositions and transitions of his narrative, peopled with characters who may, like Benway and The Sailor, reappear; who may, like "Jane," die within two pages of being introduced; or who may be fluid and double, as with Lee and the first-person narrator. "Lee the Agent" does manage to run, at least for the moment, from some of the forces that are threatening him. In a daring escape he outsmarts and kills City Narcotic Squad veterans Hauser and O'Brien, although the Department, in a reassertion of control, subsequently denies their existence. In the last pages the escapee is driving with Bill Gains in the Republic of Panama, "back to sex and pain and time and *yagé*," a journey that parallels Burroughs's own travels in South America from January to July 1953, when he exchanged a famous series of letters with Ginsberg about his search for the plant (183).

Bibliography

William S. Burroughs, *Naked Lunch: The Restored Text*, ed. James Grauerholz and Barry Miles (New York, 2001). A hardcover "Fiftieth Anniversary Edition" (New York 2009) adds an afterword by David Ulin.

Michael B. Goodman, *Contemporary Literary Censorship: The Case History of Burroughs' Naked Lunch* (Metuchen, NJ, 1981).

Oliver Harris, *William Burroughs and the Secret of Fascination* (Carbondale, IL, 2003).

Oliver Harris and Ian MacFadyen, eds., *Naked Lunch @ 50: Anniversary Essays* (Carbondale, IL, 2009).

Davis Schneiderman and Philip Walsh, eds., *Retaking the Universe: William S. Burroughs in the Age of Globalization* (London, 2004).

Saul Bellow, *Herzog*, New York: Viking, 1964

Although *The Adventures of Augie March* (1953) won Saul Bellow the first of his three National Book Awards, *Herzog*, for which he received the second award, and which was his first bestseller, established the international reputation that would eventually win him the Nobel Prize in 1976. Some critics and fellow writers have faulted his work for what they see as trying to take the novel back to nineteenth-century conventions rather than exploring the possibilities opened up by post-modern writing. But in his Nobel Prize speech Bellow argued that the more radical position was the attempt to restore the relevance of art and literature to central human concerns. The writers he most admired and found of interest, he remarked in a 1966 *Paris Review* interview, were Dreiser, Hemingway, Fitzgerald, Faulkner, Joyce, and D. H. Lawrence. The bestseller status of *Herzog*, he speculated in the same interview, seemed to have happened because it "described a common predicament" and "appealed to Jewish readers, to those who have been divorced, to those who talk to themselves, to college graduates, readers of paperbacks, autodidacts, to those who yet hope to live awhile, etc."

Bellow's earlier novels, as has often been observed, are either narratives of exuberant invention, or stories that focus upon a troubled, isolated character. In *Herzog* Bellow combines both. The narrative is driven by the brooding Moses E. Herzog's mostly unsent letters to friends, family, acquaintances and public figures alive and dead, and also by his memories – which range from the manipulations and betrayals of his second wife Madeline and his best friend Valentine, to recollections of his childhood in Canada, his mother's early death, his father's various careers, and his own first marriage. Herzog revisits

The Twentieth-Century American Fiction Handbook   By Christopher MacGowan
© 2011 Christopher MacGowan

these memories and composes his unsent letters while living alone in Ludeyville, a village in Western Massachusetts so small that it is "not on the Esso map." Herzog observes to his rich, urbanite brother, Will, that the location is "*The edge of nowhere. Out on the lid of Hell*" (358).

The letters, musings, and mental excursions into the past are part of Herzog's attempt to recompose a sense of self severely shaken by the manipulations of Madeline and Valentine. This attempt at recovery involves exploring his various identities as son, brother, scholar, father, husband, friend, and at least two national identities, as well as his Jewish heritage. This sense of self is particularly complex, he reflects, for modern man "deprived of the firm ideas of the seventeenth century, clear, hard, theorems" (117). "*There is someone inside me*," he acknowledges early in the book, "*When I speak of him I feel him in my head, pounding for order*" (14). But externally that order has fallen apart. Both of his children are living with their mothers. His academic career has derailed, he has squandered his father's legacy on the unsaleable Massachusetts property where he now finds himself, and his family is living in Chicago – a move, it turns out, resulting from his manipulation by Madeline and Valentine. Herzog recalls telling his friend Asphalter of the unsent letters, "I go after reality with language. Perhaps I'd like to change it all into language"; his purpose is to "conjure up a whole environment" to prevent the "escape" of Madeline and Valentine (296).

Clearly Herzog needs to put Madeline and Valentine's betrayal behind him, while trying to maintain his relationship with daughter June and her half-brother Marco, but this will not happen while he loses himself in the language constructions of his letters. Now in a relationship with Ramona, a figure as vivid and theatrical as he earlier found Madeline and Valentine, he needs to learn from the past, not repeat it. His scholarly career will not revive through unsent letters to other scholars and mental reviews of their works. But these are difficult issues for Herzog to confront, and his attempts leave him doubting his own sanity. He realizes that he needs to keep his suffering in proportion, and that this is a task made more complicated by recent Jewish history. For example, the one legacy of the Holocaust is a more brutal, impersonal "standard" that makes more difficult, even self-indulgent, definitions of self that are built upon personal troubles (162). Herzog gains further perspective on what he realizes is his privileged existence from listening to the routine arraignments of some petty criminals while he waits for a lawyer friend, and again in Chicago from his temporary cellmates – a sleeping drunk and a silent Negro boy – before he is bailed out by his brother.

Even more important to his recovery is the horrific story he hears in a New York courtroom of a neglected and murdered child. "I fail to understand," he tells himself after listening to the witnesses in the murder case, and begins his recognition that language can be an inadequate substitute for reality, how "people who spend their lives in humane studies" can "imagine once cruelty has been described in books it is ended" (258–259). His initial reaction is to fear a possible parallel between the child's doomed life and the babysitter's story of Valentine leaving daughter June outside in a car while the two lovers argued inside the house. Determined to see for himself, and approaching with his father's loaded gun, he has to watch, however painfully, Valentine's tender care of June, and hear her own reassuring version of the car story. The actual experiences reorder the "constructions" that his language had created, and also help him to understand the role of the gun in his relationship with his father (296). He can begin to recover from the past what is actual, and to recognize what in the more recent past is only part of his web of verbal order.

Herzog must also find a way to avoid allowing himself to be defined by others in what amounts to another kind of abdication of self. He imagines the interpretation that Madeline puts to others about his character and actions, and hears it for himself in the Chicago police station. He also sees first hand the example of the pathetic Hoberly still pursuing his lost relationship with Ramona, and the almost comical extent of Asphalter's grief for his lost partner, a monkey. On the other hand, Herzog's successful brother Will can only achieve this success through a life of "duty and routine" that allows him no "private or 'personal' side" (334). And Valentine's self is absorbed by his success in "mass communications," his being everything for everyone socially and professionally (234). This danger is particularly acute for Herzog because it makes him so vulnerable to manipulation by such bullying, intense, theatrical individuals as Madeline and Valentine, and even by the gentler, sexually theatrical Ramona. He wonders at one point whether "he really had inwardly decided years ago to set up a deal – a psychic offer – meekness in exchange for preferential treatment" (168).

Herzog knows that he has to come to terms with time, age, decay, and change, not just within the large cultural abstractions of the History of Ideas, but also within his own life and the lives of those close to him. He has to move from near obsession to more balance. The obsessive quality leads him to recollections of a crumbling New York and its throngs of dying old men and women, to seeing subway graffiti as "Minor works of Death," to recalling the slow decay of his stepmother moving through his dead father's house, and to remembering his mother's and father's deaths – following them in imagination even into the ground (193). His responses are those of an idealist who has discovered a more complex world. Characteristically, as high school class orator he had taken his text from Emerson. And staring at a photograph of himself "taken when he got his M.A.," he sees a man who "refused to know evil" although "he could not refuse to experience it. And therefore others were appointed to do it to him" (266–267).

Nature, as actually present around and even inside his ill-kept house in the Berkshires – as opposed to the Nature of Romantic Studies – helps him to restore some of the balance. Sleeping in a hammock in his overgrown garden, leaving a nest of owls alone in the light fixture so as not to disturb them, he is strong enough to turn down brother Will's suggestion that he check in to a hospital, and can keep Ramona at a distance while still allowing her into his life. This degree of restored order, however temporary and privileged, allows him some relief from the burden of memory, and allows the composition of the unsent letters to stop. "At this time," the novel concludes, as he achieves this temporary respite, "he had no messages for anyone. Nothing. Not a single word" (371).

Bibliography

Saul Bellow, *Herzog* (New York, 2003), with an Introduction by Philip Roth. The Library of America edition, *Novels 1956–1964* (New York, 2007), which also includes *Seize the Day* and *Henderson the Rain King*, contains some useful annotations to the novel.

Harold Bloom, ed., *Saul Bellow's Herzog* (New York, 1988).
Gloria L. Cronin and Ben Siegel, eds., *Conversations with Saul Bellow* (Jackson, MS, 1994).
Daniel Fuchs, *Saul Bellow: Vision and Revision* (Durham, NC, 1984), pp. 121–154.
Jonathan Wilson, *Herzog: The Limits of Ideas* (Boston, 1990).

Thomas Pynchon, *The Crying of Lot 49*, Philadelphia: Lippincott, 1966

Thomas Pynchon's second novel, *The Crying of Lot 49*, was preceded and followed by the encyclopedic *V* (1963) and *Gravity's Rainbow* (1973), the latter winning Pynchon the National Book Award. While there is some critical debate over which of these three novels and those that followed is the most successful, *The Crying of Lot 49* would certainly be on the short list for many critics. It is generally considered the most accessible of Pynchon's novels, and contains many of the characteristic themes of his fiction.

The search that Oedipa Maas undertakes as executrix of Pierce Inverarity's estate leads her to consider many of the questions that the novel itself raises about interpretation, language, the media, technology, isolation, history, and the role and value of fiction. Oedipa searches for an order or frame within which to understand the information unearthed, or imagined, as she explores the legacy. But her motives are in part, too, a wish to break away from a life, and more broadly a culture, too programmed; a life and culture that traps her in a world of Tupperware parties, where the main excitement is the hostess adding too much kirsch to the fondue. "And how had it ever happened here," she asks herself near the end of the novel, "with the chances once so good for diversity?" (176). From the beginning of her search she is open to the possibilities of an alternative. Driving into San Narciso, its name suggesting the narcissism that is a central issue in the novel, Oedipa looks down a slope at the "ordered swirl" of houses that are like a "printed circuit" and imagines that "a revelation . . . trembled just past the threshold of her understanding" (16).

Oedipa is faced with a failing marriage, a consumer culture that demands uniformity, and a world in which aberrations are either explained away through therapy, or escaped through drugs, alcohol, and sex. The possible alternative revealed by Inverarity's legacy, and linked in some way to the Trystero, is an alternative peopled with the disinherited and with outsiders who refuse to conform. But Oedipa is as disturbed by the possibility that the Trystero does exist as she is by the possibility that it doesn't. At times she follows up energetically on the increasing number of clues and coincidences, but at other times she holds back, and when she does hold back, possible witnesses die and clues disappear.

Her relationship with Inverarity is linked to a painting that she saw on a trip with him before her marriage, a painting that illustrates "the confinement" which, "Rapunzel-like," she felt in her own "tower." The painting, by the Spanish-Mexican surrealist Remedios Varo (1908–1963), depicts:

> a number of frail girls with heart-shaped faces, huge eyes, spun-gold hair, prisoners in the top room of a circular tower, embroidering a kind of tapestry which spilled out the slit windows and into a void, seeking hopelessly to fill the void: for all the other buildings and creatures, all the waves, ships and forests of the earth were contained in this tapestry, and the tapestry was the world. (12–13)

"*Shall I project a world*," Oedipa writes in her memo book early in her search, echoing the painting (76). And another of the many coincidences that confront and confuse her is when, upon checking into a hotel in Berkeley, she finds a reproduction of another Varo painting in her room.

Oedipa's names suggest her need for love. Her surname indicates the representative nature of her need in an America in which individuals are subsumed into a "mass," while her first name indicates that what is inherited can be emotionally confusing, even tragic. And what is inherited includes the marketing of love and sex by radio stations such as Mucho's KCUF, by musicians such as the Paranoids, and by the emblem of "Echo Courts" with its 30-foot sheet metal painting and "a concealed blower system that kept the nymph's gauze chiton in constant agitation, revealing enormous vermillion-tipped breasts and long pink thighs at each flap" (18). One of the groups possibly associated with the Trystero search are the Inamorati Anonymous, dedicated to helping others avoid the addiction of falling in love.

The Trystero offers Oedipa a possible rescue from her isolation and anonymity, although whether Inverarity or her own imagination serves as potential knight errant remains an open question. Inverarity may have recognized her need for an escape, and provided her with the means to one; he may have wished to undermine her marriage to Mucho; or he may – dead or still alive – have organized an elaborate hoax in order to make her think that she has found an escape that is, in fact, all of her own making.

Thus a central issue in Oedipa's search is the problem of interpretation and the related problem of meaning. Oedipa is unsure what status to give to what could be called the perceiver's share of this meaning – to fantasy, dreams, hallucinations, and to interpretation that might be colored by need and preconception. She spends a night wandering around San Francisco, but "later, possibly, she would have trouble sorting the night into real and dreamed" (112). Director and actor Randolph Driblette has his own views on the relationship of text and performance, telling her that words are merely "rote noises to hold line bashes with," and that reality lies in the head that responds and interprets (75).

Oedipa encounters problems not only with interpreting the meaning of words and signs, but also in determining the status of historical record. She encounters a series of convoluted narratives each a mixture of facts – verifiable inasmuch as the facts are corroborated in various external texts claiming to be true records – and details found in no histories except those embedded in the novel. For example, the history of the Thurn and Taxis postal system, which operated in Europe from the Middle Ages to the mid-nineteenth century, is well documented in many histories. But in order to trace its transformation into an organization which opposed state monopolies and systems of government control, Oedipa, and her sources, move into specu-lation. The status of recorded history is finally uncertain, its distinction from legend, rumor, and fiction not always clear. As a result, Oedipa is never sure whether the connections she is making are true, are part of the fiction created by herself, or are part of an elaborate hoax planted by Inverarity.

The wild narratives that appear to blend fiction and historical narrative follow a course similar to that of the can of hair spray that Oedipa drops in her hotel bathroom, its "high-speed caroming" such that "God or a digital machine, might have computed in advance the complex web of its travel" (29). The plots of such narratives as *Cashiered* and *The Courier's Tragedy*, the stories of the Peter Pinguid Society, the Inamorati Anonymous, the Scurvha-mites, the account of Dr. Diocletian Blobb's *Singular Peregrinations*, and the history of the Trystero itself are similarly unpredictable in their direction, but may have a logic to their paths unknown to Oedipa.

A question for reader and novelist that has its parallels in Oedipa's quest is: to what degree do the histories, fictions, absurd and suggestively symbolic names (Hilarious, Inverarity, Fallopian), and "caroming" narratives have any significant connection with the world outside of the novel, and do they need to? Vladimir Nabokov, one of Pynchon's teachers at Cornell University, celebrated the self-contained pleasures of reading and writing fiction. Nabokov is an appropriately teasing presence in *The Crying of Lot 49*; one of the Paranoids' songs refers to "Humbert Humbert," the infamous narrator of *Lolita*, and suggests a possible rivalry with the singer:

> What chance has a lonely surfer boy
> For the love of a surfer chick,
> With all those Humbert Humbert cats
> Coming on so big and sick?
> For me, my baby was a woman,
> For him she's just another nymphet; (141–142)

But Pynchon's novel is more ambivalent about the status and value of fiction than Nabokov's lyrical justification of the "aesthetic bliss" that fiction can provide. As Tony Tanner has observed in *City of Words* (1971), the acronyms associated with the Trystero, DEATH and WASTE, suggest that "Pynchon himself is ambivalent about his own fiction making," while the wild narratives confirm that "the anxiety about the status of *all* plots is so deeply a part of the subject of the book."

Further evidence of this anxiety comes from the novel's treatment of visual, aural, and printed media and their relationship to marketing. Not only are language, signs, history, narratives, and interpretation all of uncertain status in the novel, but the various media through which information is transmitted add their own distortion. When Oedipa's psychiatrist suffers a breakdown, the police ask her to try to delay his possible suicide because, "TV folks would like to get some footage through the window" (132). She is subsequently interviewed by husband Mucho, reporting the event for his radio station, who refers to her as "Edna Mosh" to allow for "distortion" in transmission, assuring her that "It'll come out the right way" (134–135). The text of *The Courier's Tragedy* is unstable, the play existing in different editions, one an unauthorized, unsigned, paperback reprint that is the source of a line crucial for Oedipa and, on at least one night, for director and actor Driblette. The television station showing the Baby Igor film *Cashiered* mixes up the reels, complicating an already unlikely plot. Lawyer Manny DiPresso, a lawyer turned actor, has played the part of lawyer Metzger in a TV pilot film, and "the casting had been typically Hollywood: they didn't look or act a bit alike" (49). The Paranoids, both involved in events and offering a chorus-like commentary at the same time, pretend to be English to match the current fashion among rock groups.

Of course, *The Crying of Lot 49* and its famous author are themselves necessarily caught up in this same process of media and marketing. A novel, too, might distort what it transmits; its publisher is looking for a return in the market; and its author usually presents himself or herself to the public in association with the book's publication. Thomas Pynchon, it would appear, recognizes the irony. The distortion is built into the narratives of the book, and the novelist himself is among the most reclusive and least photographed of authors, keeping biographical information on his covers to an absolute minimum, and playing virtually no role in the marketing of his books. In this case the author's legacy is the novel itself – there to be interpreted.

Bibliography

Thomas Pynchon, *The Crying of Lot 49* (New York, 2009).

J. Kerry Grant, *A Companion to The Crying of Lot 49* (Athens, GA, 1994).
Patrick O'Donnell, ed., *New Essays on The Crying of Lot 49* (New York, 1991).
Thomas H. Schaub, ed., *Approaches to Teaching Pynchon's The Crying of Lot 49 and Other Works* (New York, 2008).
Tony Tanner, *Thomas Pynchon* (London, 1982).

Philip Roth, *Portnoy's Complaint,* New York: Random House, 1969

In a long career that has produced a number of distinguished novels, Philip Roth is still best known by many readers as the author of *Portnoy's Complaint.* Some of the subsequent novels may receive more scholarly commentary, but the 1969 work remains Roth's best-selling book, and the burden of its fame is a theme that comes up at times in some of his later semi-autobiographical fiction.

Narrator Alexander Portnoy pleads at one point in the monologue to his psychoanalyst Dr. Spielvogel, a monologue that forms all but the final lines of the novel, that he is desperate to "be somehow sprung . . . from this hopeless, senseless loyalty to the long ago" (219). What he means by the "long ago" are the oppressive years of his childhood, and the continuing pressures and expectations of his disappointed parents. On a broader scale, the family and culture within the New Jersey neighborhood where Alex (and Roth himself) grew up are the foundation of a Jewish identity that Alex both clings to and fiercely resents.

To his analyst Alex delivers a sexually frank account of his various relationships and masturbatory obsessions. His moral rebellion against the expectations of Jewish identity, and the religious and social rituals that accompany it, leads him to undertake a series of sexual relationships with non-Jewish girls, "shikses," that, because of the accompanying guilt, shame, and ambivalence, never carry, on his side, any emotional commitment. Alex gives each of the girls a label, as if to deny the personal, human qualities that would make them something more than stages in his confused rebellion: thus he refers to "The Pumpkin," "The Pilgrim," "The Monkey" (a caricature, some argue, of Roth's first wife, Margaret Martinson), "The Lieutenant," and "The Jewish Pumpkin."

Alex's relationship in college with Kay Campbell, "The Pumpkin," sets the pattern of contradictions in the relationships to follow. Spending Thanksgiving with Kay and her family in Iowa in his freshman year is an important act of defiance for Alex, but at the same time he has to tell his parents that this college friend is male. He feels guilt and regret at being absent from the familiar family holiday routines that, at the same time, he feels trapped by. Even though years earlier Alex insisted in family arguments that he had rejected his parents' religion, his interest in Kay disappears when she makes clear that she has no intention of converting to Judaism. The legacy of this particular relationship years later is his assumption that she has made a perfect wife for someone somewhere, that she is a model of stability and support, in contrast to his own mass of confusions and contradictions.

For Alex, having sex with a girl like Sarah Abbott Maulsby, "The Pilgrim," is to "stick it up their backgrounds," those "generations of Maulsbys … buried in the graveyard at Newburyport, Massachusetts, and generations of Abbotts in Salem" (235–237). Sarah's solid and envied "place in American history," so unlike the immigrant history of his own family, means for Alex "not much room there for love" (240). She represents to him, he tells Dr. Spielvogel, a small gesture of revenge on the executives running the Boston & Northeastern insurance company that so exploited his father.

"The Monkey," Mary Jane Reed, while beautiful, and a sexual athlete who astonishes and excites Alex, represents another kind of "American history" with her working-class, West Virginia mining background. Just as Alex wanted Kay to convert, and urges Sarah to be less inhibited sexually, he tries to transform the poorly educated Mary with a reading list and lessons in social graces. He is anxious, ashamed, and guilty over what his relationship with her might reveal publicly, and condemns her for the circumstances of their meeting that he, not she, initiated. Mary is for him finally another sexual entertainment, as the triangle in Rome with Italian prostitute Lina makes clear. Earlier in their relationship he had recognized, and been very disturbed by, his realization "that she is also a human being – A *human being! Who can be loved!*" But immediately he distances himself from responsibility – "But by *me?*" (194).

Alex abandons Mary to fly to Israel, as if seeking affirmation of the identity and heritage that he so resents. However, the legacy of his treatment of Mary, and his identity as an American, foil his attempted sexual encounters with "The Lieutenant" and "The Jewish Pumpkin." His liaison with "The Lieutenant" ends abruptly with his fear of having been infected by the Italian prostitute.

The encounter with Naomi, "The Jewish Pumpkin," he calls "My final downfall and humiliation," and it sends him to the psychoanalyst's couch (258). Naomi's social and political egalitarianism is at one with her rhetoric and lifestyle, unlike Alex in his position as Assistant Human Opportunity Commissioner in New York City. Naomi attacks his acceptance of American economic and moral values, as well as exposing many of the motives and contradictions behind his attitudes. His response is the desire to dominate her sexually, and at the same time to convince himself that he is in love with her. Love in this case is both an attempt to justify his sexual aggression, and a link to the oppressive love behind his mother Sophie's demands, demands that produced and still produce in him guilt, shame, and humiliation.

Alex's father sees his son as a vicarious source of liberation, "from ignorance, from exploitation, from anonymity." Where his father "had been imprisoned, I would fly" (8–9). To this end Jack Portnoy adds to the pressure that his wife exerts on Alex to be the best and brightest at school, and wants Alex to hold on to his Jewish heritage, yet at the same time not to be held back by it. The pressure and contradictions lead Alex to ask, "Doctor, what should I rid myself of, tell me, the hatred . . . or the love?" (27). And in one confused memory, he is unsure whether he recalls his mother condemning his father for adultery with the cashier he has brought home, or chastising Alex himself for one of his many failures. In the recollection he at times takes the place of his father, projecting his own sexual guilt, as well as sharing with his father the role of victim in a household dominated by Sophie Portnoy.

Alex's narrative begins with his mother. She is "The Most Unforgettable Character I've Met," his first heading announces, and the narrative itself begins with the pronoun "She" that for Alex requires no antecedent (3). The demands that she makes of Alex about religion, family, hygiene, illness, school performance, and appearance are accompanied by threats of banishment that puzzle, frighten, and finally alienate the young boy. His acts of rebellion in the monologue include the comic exaggeration of her character, and the vulgar language that is his answer to her many euphemisms.

A number of events outside of the immediate family contribute to Alex's sense of exile. The ruthlessness of Uncle Hymie in breaking up cousin Heshie's engagement with the beautiful blonde Alice Dembosky heightens Alex's resentment at his extended family and influences the direction that this resentment takes in his adult relationships. Heshie's death on the Normandy beaches the year after Uncle Hymie's lies and bribery have done their work only heightens the impact of the episode on Alex. The suicide of 15-year-old Ronald Nimkin also makes a deep impression, particularly the detail of the suicide note in which the boy dutifully passes on a message for his mother – a final submergence of his own identity and voice to her needs and approval. Like a good son, Ronald had for years attended the piano lessons demanded by his mother to develop what she and the other women in the building had insisted was his musical genius. For Alex, Ronald is a fellow sufferer. Alex imagines his own suicide in a movie pastiche at the close of his narrative, refusing to surrender to the police despite their intention to come in "guns blazing" (274).

Two important memories associated with baseball reveal Alex's sense of what he, and other Jewish sons of his generation, have lost in leaving the closely knit Jewish communities of their past. The movement is both a physical one, moving away from the neighborhood to follow opportunity, and one forced by the inevitable shifts of time as the neighborhoods themselves change. Alex tells the psychoanalyst of the pleasure he used to find playing center field on the local softball team:

> you can't imagine how truly glorious it is out there, so alone in all that space . . . Because center field is like some observation post, a kind of control tower, where you are able to see everything and everyone, to understand what's happening the instant it happens . . . Oh, how unlike my home it is to be in center field, where no one will appropriate unto himself anything that I say is *mine!* (69)

As the recollection indicates, playing center field gave him an identity as an individual but also allowed him to be part of a group; it brought a sense of space that was not isolation, and a sense of possession that was not disputed. The isolated masturbatory acts in the locked bathroom serve as a kind of desperate attempt to recover such a quality at home, sexual fantasies involving a part of the body intimately and indisputably his own.

The second baseball memory is of being a spectator, sometimes with his father, watching other fathers, neighborhood men playing on Sunday mornings. He has this recollection as the plane descends into Israel, a land where he thinks he will find community but only feels more exiled. The memory of the Sunday mornings reinforces his sense that the boyhood pleasure of playing in center field, and everything that it represents, cannot be carried over into his adulthood. The fathers' Sunday morning game is part of an earlier, more closely knit generation. Understandably, its relaxed humor, the shared pleasures of a few hours away from women and family, has a strong appeal for the young Alex. "How I am going to love growing up to be a Jewish man!" he recalls feeling at such moments, "Living forever in the Weequahic section, and playing softball on Chancellor Avenue from nine to one on Sundays . . . I want to grow up to *be* one of those men" (244–245). But there is to be no such shared Sunday morning sanctuary for Alex. For him, routine becomes oppressive, finding personal space a constant and guilty battle, and the anxiety over what "is *mine!*" drives the physical and cultural obsessions that bring him to the couch of Dr. Spielvogel.

Bibliography

Phillip Roth, *Portnoy's Complaint* (New York, 1994), with a new afterword by the author. The Library of America printing, *Novels 1967–1972* (New York, 2005), which also includes *When She Was Good, Our Gang,* and *The Breast*, contains some useful annotations.

Harold Bloom, ed., *Philip Roth's Portnoy's Complaint* (Philadephia, PA, 2004).
David Brauner, "Masturbation and Its Discontents, or, Serious Relief: Freudian Comedy in *Portnoy's Complaint*," *Critical Review* 40 (2000), 75–90.
Ross Posnock, *Philip Roth's Rude Truth: The Art of Immaturity* (Princeton, 2008).
George J. Searles, ed., *Conversations with Philip Roth* (Jackson, MI, 1992).

Leslie Marmon Silko, *Ceremony,* New York: Viking, 1977

The novel that became *Ceremony* began, Leslie Silko recalls in a preface to a recent edition, as "a funny story about Harley" and his drinking, before evolving into a narrative of Native American lives ruined by liquor, and more broadly the account of a culture, already driven from its traditional lands, now in danger of losing its traditional stories and rituals (xvi). The novel insists upon the importance of these stories in part by incorporating them into its narrative methods. It also describes the forces that try to destroy them, beginning with the reservation schools, where they are ridiculed by the teachers who set white science against traditional healing. In the novel the stories and rituals are a vital part of the healing and purification ceremonies needed both for survival and for a restoration of balance.

Often considered the most important novel of the Native American Renaissance, *Ceremony* combines Western narrative methods and Native American mythology largely derived from Pueblo and Navajo sources. Events are told in both prose and poetry, with the poetry reserved for the Native American version of the story as related by Ts'its'tsi'nako, Thought-Woman, who foretells that "the only cure / I know / is a good ceremony" (3). Tayo, the half-white, half-Laguna World War II veteran at the center of the novel, is alienated from both white and Native American culture. He is haunted by his cousin Rocky's brutal death in the Philippines, where along with other Native Americans – only noticed by the government when needed for the war – they were fighting to defend a land already taken from them. Tayo is in danger of becoming another "crazy Indian," descending into the same alcohol-ridden fate as his mother, Harley, and Leroy before he is set on the path of being

The Twentieth-Century American Fiction Handbook   By Christopher MacGowan
© 2011 Christopher MacGowan

healed through the ceremony performed by Old Betonie and his helper Shush. Although Tayo's journey to Mount Taylor is vital to his own healing, it has larger cultural significance, the novel makes clear, as a journey foretold in prophecy.

What makes Old Betonie's healing work is his recognition of the need to change and adapt the old ceremonies. Tayo's earlier visit to a more traditional healer, the Laguna elder Old Ku'oosh, had failed, as had the modern medicine of the Los Angeles hospital. Betonie's ceremony changes with times and needs, as reflected in the calendars, telephone books, and other records piled in his hogan above the town of Gallup. He is himself a mix of Navajo and Mexican and tells Tayo the story of his grandfather, Descheeny, who took a young Mexican girl for his bride and who recognized along with her this need for the ceremonies to change in order to be effective. "It cannot be done alone," she had warned Descheeny. "We must have power from everywhere. Even the power we can get from the whites" (139).

The chronicle of loss that broadens Tayo's story further includes Harley, Leroy, and Emo, usually drunk, and often threatening to drag Tayo into the destructive and violent chaos of their own lives. The novel also tells the story of Helen Jean, a young woman who leaves the reservation and whose life, and inevitable death, follows a similar pattern to that of Tayo's mother. Important, too, are Tayo's Uncle Josiah and the Mexican woman Night Swan. She knows the source of the spotted cattle who later play such an important part in Tayo's journey, while her seduction of him serves as a modern parallel to the story of Descheeny and the Mexican girl that Betonie would later recount.

Betonie makes clear to Tayo upon finishing the rituals that the ceremony is not finished. He foretells the role of the stars, the cattle, and the mountain in the journey to come, as well as the role of a woman who will figure importantly in the task. He must undertake the journey with faith in the ceremony's power, although it will be a faith that falters at times. He must also reconnect to a land and landscape whose aridity is, within the larger tale, a reflection of his own condition. This landscape has a beauty and importance within the healing ceremonies despite its violation by the whites' uranium mining, and the larger destruction suggested by the atom bomb experiments at the nearby Trinity Site.

The novel's detailed, lyrical description of the landscape of Taylor Mountain, where Tayo searches for Josiah's spotted cattle, parallels the closer contact with the land and its animals that Tayo comes to experience. The drought at the beginning of the novel gives way to fertility and renewal. Tayo's careful respect for the mountain lion is repaid when its tracks distract the ranch hands who have captured him, while his knowledge of how animals shelter helps him to survive the blizzard. This respect for and knowledge of nature proves him worthy to meet the hunter, to see Ts'eh again, to recover the cattle, and to continue his healing.

Within the larger ceremony represented by Tayo's journey are the various ceremonies performed on the mountainside by Ts'eh. Tayo's participation in these rituals reinforces his love for her, and then continues his healing the following summer. When they finally part he is strong enough to resist the destructive threat represented by Harley and Leroy, although he still finds difficulty resisting the drunken forgetfulness offered by his fellow veterans. The label of "Crazy Indian" would be very easy to take on. He has to "call up the feeling the stories had, the feeling of Ts'eh and old Betonie," and put aside the doubts he has sometimes had about the ceremony's power. Ts'eh warns him to be wary of "Friendly voices," while Betonie had told him that "They will try to stop you from completing the ceremony" (215, 115). But Ts'eh had also assured him that he could change the way that the whites and those who assist them want to end the stories – in violence and defeat.

Tayo learns from Betonie that "His sickness was only part of something larger, and his cure would be found only in something great and inclusive of everything" (116). Toward the end of his journey Tayo realizes that "everything" includes the testing in July 1945 at the Trinity Site of the first atomic bomb. This event is witnessed by the seer figure Old Grandma, one of Ts'its'tsi'nako's listeners. The light from the explosion she understands as a "sun rise," and in that sense a threat to the "sun rise" that affirms the success of the ceremony for Tayo. For the bomb is a destructive force, albeit in different ways, to Tayo and to the Japanese whom Tayo and Rocky had been fighting – and potentially a destructive force for all humankind. Tayo finally recognizes why he saw his uncle Josiah's face on the face of a Japanese prisoner in the Philippines half a world away: he was granted a premonition of the common fate of the dispossessed Native Americans, of the bombed people of Hiroshima and Nagasaki, and possibly of the human race itself.

Bibliography

Leslie Marmon Silko, *Ceremony* (New York, 2006). This "Anniversary Edition" of the novel carries an introduction by Larry McMurtry and a preface by Silko.

Ellen L. Arnold, ed., *Conversations with Leslie Marmon Silko* (Jackson, MI, 2000).
Allan Chavkin, *Leslie Marmon Silko's Ceremony: A Casebook* (New York, 2002).
Lynn Domina, *Understanding Ceremony: A Student Casebook to Issues, Sources, and Historical Documents* (Westport, CT, 2004).
Robert M. Nelson, *Leslie Marmon Silko's Ceremony: The Recovery of Tradition* (New York, 2008).

Alice Walker, *The Color Purple,* New York: Harcourt Brace Jovanovitch, 1982

The Color Purple was a large critical and commercial success, winning both a Pulitzer Prize and the American Book Award in 1983, and it has also been the basis of well-received film and musical versions. With this novel Alice Walker became the first African American woman writer to win the Pulitzer Prize for fiction.

The epistolary form of the novel allows Walker to give full voice to two black sisters whose futures take very different directions once they are forced to separate as young women, but whose lives trace a similar emotional arc. Celie is the sister whose early life is shaped by a stepfather who is as abusive as Albert, the husband to whom her stepfather gives her away – along with a cow. Her children are taken from her, and she writes letters to God as the only outlet through which she can share her feelings and mitigate her isolation. Once she discovers that Nettie is still alive, she begins to address the letters to her distant sister, even though uncertain that they will reach their destination. In fact for years the letters are intercepted and hoarded by Albert. Her emotional isolation is also tempered by finding in Albert's mistress, Shug Avery, a lover and companion. Meanwhile Nettie's story takes her away from rural Georgia to Europe and then Africa as companion to a missionary couple, where eventually, like Celie, she finds love, marrying the widowed Samuel.

Despite the distance separating them, the two sisters share their love for each other over the many years of writing letters, the grammar, vocabulary,

The Twentieth-Century American Fiction Handbook   By Christopher MacGowan
© 2011 Christopher MacGowan

and spelling in the letters reflecting the different direction each sister's life has taken. Celie, the more emotional sister, suffers from her stepfather ending her education early, following the first of her two pregnancies by him. Nettie, the more successful student at school, is also forced to end her education early, but the articulate and sophisticated expression of her letters reflects her travels, her missionary work, and the close company of the relatively well-educated Samuel and Corrine.

As well as recording the lives of the two sisters, the letters also tell the stories of a number of other important characters. In Celie's case these include her stepchildren, the aggressive and independent Sophie, and the even more independent Shug Avery. Through Nettie's letters the novel tells the story of the two children taken away from Celie, recounts the missionary work of Samuel and Corrine, and describes the central figures in the Olinka village, a community faced with the destruction of its livelihood and culture by the encroachment of the rubber industry.

Within the different lives and circumstances of the two sisters the novel suggests important similarities between developments in America and Africa, and one central theme of the novel is the greater understanding that comes for some characters from the recognition of this kinship. Many of these connections are tied to the theme of race, particularly through the oppressive power exercised by whites, and to limitations placed upon women by the patriarchal structures of commerce, religion, marriage, and education.

Celie learns that her father was lynched by white men because his dry goods store took too much black business away from the white merchants. Shug Avery draws Celie's attention to a newspaper item where "they building a dam so they can flood out a Indian tribe that been there since time" (210). One of Shug's sons works on an Indian reservation, a mirror to the missionaries working with the Olinkas, but the Indians are so demoralized by their treatment that "nothing strangers say mean nothing" (268). The Native American culture, the novel makes clear, is being destroyed by forces similar to those destroying the homeland and culture of the Olinkas in Africa. One result of the destruction of the Olinka culture, however, is the breaking up of its patriarchal laws, along with the limitations that those laws imposed upon opportunities for women and girls. Under the new conditions the Olinka women can achieve a degree of financial independence through paid employment, and can insist upon their daughters being granted educational opportunities. Such changes allow Tashia to marry Adam, once she breaks free from the cultural barriers imposed on her earlier. At the same time Celie's letters tell their own version of such changes. She reports the financial success of Shug Avery's singing career, and the more provincial success of Squeak (Mary Agnes). Celie herself finds a source of independent income in her talent for making pants, and makes her home in the house that she inherits from her father. Even the abusive Albert becomes feminized, taking up sewing and genuinely regretting his earlier brutality.

This challenge to patriarchal oppression also extends to Celie's conception of God. In a "Preface" that Walker added to later printings of the book she notes that many commentators have not recognized the religious themes of the novel. The God conceived as a "patriarchal male supremacist," Walker argues, becomes in the novel a spirit within "trees, stars, wind, and everything else." Celie, in her awakening to what has been her own oppression by men, initially confuses dismissing the patriarchal concept of God with losing a sense of the divine altogether. She feels, she tells Shug, that "the God I been praying and writing to is a man. And act just like all the other mens I know," concluding that he is "deef" (192–193). But Shug convinces her that "You have to git man off your eyeball, before you can see anything a'tall," and that God is "inside you and inside everybody else" (197, 195). Shug concedes, recognizing the links of patriarchy, religion, and racism, "Ain't no way to read the bible and not think God white," but in a comment that highlights the novel's title she declares, "I think it pisses God off if you walk by the color purple in a field somewhere and don't notice it" (195–196). Nettie also discovers the links of racism and patriarchy in the attitude of the whites who run the Missionary Society of New York. Ideas of "duty" and of the superiority of white Europeans to Africans govern the Society's sense of its mission. But in her final letter, Celie's opening salutation aligns her conception of God with that in Walker's preface: "Dear God. Dear stars, dear trees, dear sky, dear peoples. Dear Everything. Dear God" – while the Olinka people's worship of the "roofleaf" is similarly broad and encompassing (285).

Despite the critical praise that the novel has received there have been some objections. Some commentators view the ending as overly sentimental. And Celie's many years passively accepting abuse have produced charges that Walker is reinforcing a racial stereotype, that rewarding the tolerance of such abuse is irresponsible, and that in addition Celie's passivity is so extreme as to be unrealistic – especially for the period in which the novel is set, the 1920s to the 1940s. More sympathetic responses to the novel see Celie as breaking the stereotype of the black woman who suffers abuse in silence – pointing to her relationship with Shug Avery, and her standing up, eventually, to Albert. Some black male critics, in particular, have suggested that there is an almost complete lack of sympathetic black male characters in the novel. Alternatively, some readers see the novel providing a voice to the story of abused black women, a story long silent, they feel, in many narratives shaped by black males.

Bibliography

Alice Walker, *The Color Purple* (Orlando, FL, 2003), with a preface by the author.

Harold Bloom, ed., *Alice Walker's The Color Purple* (Philadephia, 2000).
Kheven LaGrone, ed., *Alice Walker's The Color Purple* (New York, 2009).
Maria Lauret, "The Color Purple," in *Modern Novelists: Alice Walker* (New York, 2000), pp. 90–120.
Janet L. Montelaro, *Producing a Womanist Text: The Maternal as Signifier in Alice Walker's The Color Purple* (Victoria, BC, 1996)

Sandra Cisneros, *The House on Mango Street*, Houston: Arte Publico, 1984

Sandra Cisneros's novel of eighth-grader Esperanza Cordero growing up in a poor Mexican American neighborhood in Chicago was one of the first books by a Chicana writer to be adopted for mainstream literature courses across the country. It was first printed by a small press associated with the University of Houston, but in 1991 appeared under the Vintage imprint of Random House and gained a much larger distribution.

Through a series of short, lyrical vignettes Esperanza describes a year living on Mango Street in the first house that her parents have owned, after years of rentals and "moving a lot." The house is a poor substitute for the "real house" that the family had dreamed of buying. Esperanza describes in some detail its cramped interior and the bricks "crumbling in places," as well as the other houses on Mango Street and its surroundings (3–4). The neighborhoods around Mango Street are dividing along ethnic lines. One girl whom Esperanza meets offers to be her friend, but "only till next Tuesday," because on that day her family is moving a few streets further north. Aping the language learned from her parents, she tells Esperanza that "the neighborhood is getting bad" (13). Esperanza at this point in her narrative has a growing but still naïve understanding of the experiences that she begins to encounter, experiences that will bring her awareness of racism, sexuality, violence, death, and the trap of gender roles – particularly for women. But she finishes the year with a confident sense that her bilingual skills, her imagination, and her ability to write stories will free her from Mango Street – and just as

The Twentieth-Century American Fiction Handbook   By Christopher MacGowan
© 2011 Christopher MacGowan

importantly, that she will be able to revisit the past with affection and sympathy without being defined or trapped by it.

Esperanza is named after her great-grandmother, whose independence was lost with marriage, and "looked out the window her whole life" (11). Little has changed in succeeding generations for many of the women on Mango Street. Their lives are limited by traditional gender roles, and sometimes too by the violence of their husbands. Esperanza, determined not to inherit her great-grandmother's "place by the window," sees examples of restricted lives all around her (11). Her mother confides that she dropped out of school "because I didn't have nice clothes," and cautions Esperanza not to make a similar mistake (91). Her father came to the United States trapped by his limited English, eating only "hamandeggs" for three months because "that was the only word he knew" (77). Living nearby, Mamacita is isolated by the nostalgic memories of the Mexico she has left behind, and is all the more devastated when her baby boy begins picking up his first words of English, the language that will inevitably distance him from the heritage that she both mourns and fears she will not be able to share. Her own English is limited to eight words. Details that Esperanza does not know remain untold, but she records what she sees and hears of these and other women's lives on Mango Street, not with a full understanding of the causes behind their private sorrows, but with sympathy and a growing determination to avoid such a fate.

The stories of girls only a little older than herself bring Esperanza closer to understanding how the lives of women on Mango Street can become so restricted. Marin's dreams of independence are essentially passive, akin to Esperanza's parents hoping to win the lottery to buy their dream house. Marin "is waiting for ... someone to change her life," perhaps by marrying her secret boyfriend in Puerto Rico, or through meeting "someone in the subway who might marry you and take you to live in a big house far away." Closer to Marin's actual future is the plan that her guardians have "to send her back to her mother with a letter saying she's too much trouble" (26–27).

Sally's fate is sketched out more fully. She has a reputation among the boys at school, and is severely beaten by her father more than once as a result. Esperanza is sympathetic to her and fascinated by Sally's sexuality and her way of dressing. Some of Esperanza's account – such as imagining Sally wanting a room all to herself in "a house, a nice one," far from Mango Street – could be a projection of the younger girl's sympathy and identification. She trusts Sally, and does not realize Sally's active part in the sexual games with the boys. For Esperanza, "the stories the boys tell in the coatroom, they're not true" (82). But Esperanza's naïveté turns dangerous when she is assaulted at a carnival while waiting "such a long time" for Sally to return from meeting a boy. The crudity and violence of the assault remove all Esperanza's fantasies derived from "the storybooks and movies"; like Sally, they had "lied" (99). Sally's marriage in another state soon afterward leaves her another trapped woman, living with a violent husband who "doesn't like her friends," and trapped in her own house "because she is afraid to go outside without his permission" (102).

The fascination with Marin and Sally is part of the growing awareness of her own sexual power that Esperanza begins to feel, and fear, through the year of her narrative. The early vignette "Boys & Girls" records that "the boys and the girls live in separate worlds" (8). But a number of later episodes illustrate this childhood division giving way to the more complex, confusing, and dangerous world of young adulthood. When Esperanza and her friends are given a bag of shoes, shoes small in size but provocatively adult, they strut around on the street, enjoying their ability to attract the distant stares of the men who watch them. But they are frightened when a drunk approaches Rachel and invites her to come closer. The playful sexuality that enters the girls' jump rope songs begins to separate Esperanza from younger sister Nenny. Esperanza's naïveté is taken advantage of by an "older Oriental man" at the job she takes to help pay for Catholic school (54). Later she is frightened but fascinated by the power she seems to have over Sire, and she records a confused, defiant, and lyrical recognition of the forces awakening in her:

Everything is holding its breath inside me. Everything is waiting to explode like Christmas. I want to be all new and shiny. I want to sit out bad at night, a boy around my neck and the wind under my skirt. Not this way, every evening talking to the trees, leaning out my window, imagining what I can't see. (73)

But following the assault at the carnival Esperanza is ready to respond to voices who urge her to recognize other possibilities within herself, voices that reinforce her mother's admonition to "study hard" (91). She is helped by the example of Alicia, who undertakes the domestic duties that her widowed father considers "a woman's place" but then "studies all night" for her university courses "because she doesn't want to spend her whole life in a factory or behind a rolling pin" (32). Through Alicia, Esperanza understands that Mango Street will always be a part of her life even though she needs to move away. And Esperanza also recalls the dying Aunt Lupe, who had told her, "You just remember to keep writing, Esperanza. You must keep writing. It will keep you free" (61). However, Minerva's desperate condition is a reminder that the act of writing is no simple panacea. Minerva, "only a little bit older" than Esperanza, writes poems, and the two read their poems to each other, but Minerva is already the mother of two children and is trapped in a cycle of violence with a husband who is always leaving, and then always returning with empty promises to reform (84).

At the end of her year of writing Esperanza recognizes the potential power of an imagination that talks to the trees, that made a mysterious place of the monkey garden, and that filled with wonder at the music box in Gil's Furniture Store. This power, she realizes, can bring her independence. Her Mexican American heritage can expand this gift rather than limiting it. This independence includes, importantly, retaining control of her sexual power and sexual choices, a theme explored more fully and explicitly in other works by Cisneros.

Bibliography

Sandra Cisneros, *The House on Mango Street: 25th Anniversary Edition* (New York, 2009), with an introduction by the author.

Harold Bloom, ed., *Sandra Cisneros's The House on Mango Street* (New York, 2009).
"Sandra Cisneros: Two Interviews," in *Conversations with Contemporary Chicana and Chicano Writers*, ed. Hector A. Torres (Albuquerque, 2007), pp. 191–243.
Catriona Rueda Esquibel, *With Her Machete in Her Hand: Reading Chicana Lesbians* (Austin, 2006), pp. 95–103.
Claudia Johnson, *Patriarchy in Sandra Cisneros's The House on Mango Street* (Detroit, 2010).

William Gibson, *Neuromancer,* New York: Ace Science Fiction Special, 1984

William Gibson's first novel, *Neuromancer,* beginning a trilogy that is followed by *Count Zero* (1986) and *Mona Lisa Overdrive* (1988), is generally credited with popularizing the term "cyberpunk." *Neuromancer* remains the most famous example of the subgenre. Unlike most science fiction texts it has found its way onto a large number of college mainstream fiction courses, and is the continuing subject of academic talks and articles. The novel's account of "the matrix" and "cyberspace," the setting for much of its narrative, has been seen as anticipating the widespread development of the internet.

The near-future world of *Neuromancer* is not the utopia of much 1940s and 1950s science fiction, and its heroes are not the brave captains or brilliant scientists of such earlier narratives. The novel does, however, contain many elements from earlier popular fiction, and commentators have noted that in some respects cyberpunk writing is not as radical as it may seem. Gibson himself has cited William S. Burroughs, Jack Kerouac, and Allen Ginsberg as important early influences, while the narrative voice of the novel has affinities with 1940s detective fiction, particularly the work of Raymond Chandler, as well as with 1940s film noir. The name of the central character, Case, suggests such detective fiction, as well as the technology-saturated world in which *Neuromancer* is set. Like many private eyes in such detective fiction, Case is an anti-establishment outsider, a loner, at the mercy, in this novel, of the pervasive multinational corporations who have taken over from nations and states, and of the violent anarchy of the urban underworld that has grown up on the fringes of this corporate power. "Night City," one such area in the urban underworld, "was like a deranged experiment in social Darwinism" (7). As with much detective fiction, the novel's sympathies are not with the morally suspect police. In *Neuromancer* these are the "Turing Registry agents," who have international jurisdiction to ensure that artificial intelligence constructs never take actions independent of their human masters. Characteristically, the central female characters, Linda Lee and Molly Millions, are femme fatales, seductive and dangerous – a threat to Case's life, bound to desert him in one way or another, and thus an inevitable source of emotional wounds if he allows himself to feel or expect too much. The world that surrounds the narrative action is a night world, dark and artificially lit; even the light, clouds, and sunshine of the space colony Freeside are an artificial projection. Such staples of the 1940s detective genre as the seedy bars, world-weary bartenders, mysteries of Chinatown, and violent henchmen all have their counterparts in the world of *Neuromancer*.

The novel's dystopia is set in the aftermath of a destructive, but limited, World War III. A ruthless capitalism centered upon catering to pleasure and advancing new technologies governs almost every aspect of the social order. Technology allows all manner of modifications to the human body, from life-extending implants and transplants for those who can pay for them, to physical enhancements that can make parts of the body a deadly weapon. Poisons are more sophisticated and lethal. Mind-control and pain-killing drugs have a new and powerful potency. But the new drugs are also more destructively addictive. Case and Linda Lee are both addicts as the novel begins, and Case's drug habits are only curbed by an operation (performed without his consent) that changes his biochemistry.

In common with many post-modern fictions there are forces at play that lie beyond the protagonist's power to fully comprehend, forces attempting to control and even threaten the protagonist's life. Often, as in *Neuromancer*, if there is a single personality directing events, that person is obscured behind various masks and surrogates.

Matters are further complicated in *Neuromancer* in that the boundaries between what is human and what is machine are blurred in a number of ways. Not only can internal organs and body parts be replaced, and human-like clones created, but an individual can be reassembled into another identity, as happens when Wintermute reassembles Corto to become the recruiter Armitage. In addition, personality can be preserved beyond death in what the novel calls a "construct." Case is reliant in his mission to infiltrate the cyberdefenses of the Tessier-Ashpool Corporation upon the skills of the dead McCoy Pauley, preserved, not happily, as such a "ROM personality matrix." Wintermute, directing the whole mission, is itself an Artificial Intelligence complex programmed by the deceased Marie-France Tessier to reach beyond its Turing-policed limitations in order to merge with the "AI" called Neuromancer. The goal of the merger is to unite Wintermute's "hive mind" with Neuromancer's "personality," a union intended by Marie-France to make immortal the family's control of the super-corporation. The power of super-corporations is sufficiently abstract and mechanical that when Case asks Wintermute, once the merger is complete, what has changed, the reply is, "Things aren't different. Things are things" (259). Nevertheless, the direction of human events recedes further from human control when Wintermute subsequently answers the transmission of an AI in the Alpha Centauri star system.

Clearly the novel can be read as symptomatic of many of the cultural issues of the early 1980s, including American anxiety about the increasing dominance of Japanese technology; the dehumanizing potential of increasingly sophisticated medicine and surgeries; the blurring of reality and imagination by the vicarious experience offered by video and computer games, and by what came to be called virtual reality; the power of multinational corporations; the appeal and dangers of drug use; uncontrollable urban sprawl and decay; and the increasing lack of privacy in a world filled with more and more sophisticated tracking devices. In *Neuromancer* such issues are blended into the genre conventions of science fiction, a genre where projections of the future often reflect concerns with the direction of the present. In fact, one suggestive reading of the novel argues that *Neuromancer* was so enthusiastically embraced by the science fiction community (the first book to win the genre's three major literary awards) in part because it dramatizes developments in the marketing of science fiction itself, in particular the consolidation of bookstores and the takeover of niche publishers by media conglomerates interested in publishing only famous names. Terry Carr, editor of the Ace Specials series in which *Neuromancer* first appeared, saw the series as an attempt to restore something of the genre's distinctive outlaw quality while borrowing some of the mass marketing strategies of the conglomerates to promote the novels selected. In *Neuromancer* machines battle with corporations for power, but the novel's hero has his health restored, finds work, and keeps a degree of independence. The victor, Wintermute, is interested in power, but not only to make money. Appropriately, the winner reaches out to the stars.

Bibliography

William Gibson, *Neuromancer* (New York, 2000), with an afterword by Jack Womack. The hardcover "Twentieth Anniversary" edition (New York, 2004) also includes a new introduction by the author.

M. Keith Booker and Anne-Marie Thomas, *The Science Fiction Handbook* (Chichester, UK, 2009), pp. 257–263.

Sarah Brouillette, "Corporate Publishing and Canonization: *Neuromancer* and Science-Fiction Publishing in the 1970s and Early 1980s." *Book History* 5 (2002), 187–208.

Tatiani G. Rapatzikou, *Gothic Motifs in the Fiction of William Gibson* (Amsterdam, 2004).

George Slusser and Tom Shippey, eds., *Fiction 2000: Cyberpunk and the Future of Narrative* (Athens, GA, 1992).

Don DeLillo, *White Noise,* New York: Viking Penguin, 1985

Don DeLillo had published seven novels over a period of 11 years before the appearance of *White Noise*, the book that brought him a National Book Award and recognition as a major novelist. His subsequent fiction has gone on to confirm that status. The world of DeLillo's fiction generally, with *White Noise* no exception, is one of fragmented nuclear families, rampant consumerism, the infiltration into daily life of the mass media, real and imagined conspiracies, and a haunting, desperate fear of death.

The complicated family arrangements stemming from narrator Jack Gladney's record of five marriages, two of them to the same woman, results in none of his children living with a full sibling. In an ever-shifting pattern, children, ex-wives, and relatives appear and disappear within the narrative. Where visits are planned ahead, those plans rarely match what actually occurs, adding to the atmosphere of instability surrounding family life. When ex-wife Tweedy Browner disembarks from her flight she is met by Jack rather than, as expected, by daughter Bee. Current father-in-law Vernon's unannounced visit causes Jack to imagine that the shape sitting in the garden in the early dawn is the waiting figure of Death. Even the apparent stability of Jack's current marriage to Babette is clouded by the fear each holds of who will be the first to die, compounded by their ambivalent feelings about being the survivor. These instabilities and sudden shifts within the family are mirrored in the larger narrative by the intrusion of disasters that sometimes have direct narrative consequences, and sometimes do not – and in the case of Jack's exposure to the poison Nyodene D may have consequences at some

The Twentieth-Century American Fiction Handbook   By Christopher MacGowan
© 2011 Christopher MacGowan

time in the future. The test results are held by his doctor, but Jack would prefer not to know.

Jack recounts the disasters in a tone which tends to dissolve distinctions between them, a factor both of his anxiety about consequences and more generally part of the dislocation of conventional plot lines that *White Noise* has in common with such other post-modern fictions as *Catch-22* and *The Crying of Lot 49*. Only a few pages into his narrative Jack records: "The smoke alarm went off in the hallway upstairs, either to let us know the battery had just died or because the house was on fire" (8). No member of the family cares to check which of these alternatives is the case, and the family lunch continues in silence. Sometimes an event is described as if it did no more than mark the passage of time, or as if such events are so common that they deserve no particular emphasis. "This was the night the insane asylum burned down," Jack notes, and then he and son Heinrich exchange the two formulaic phrases that they acknowledge always accompany fires in buildings: "Faulty wiring" and "They die of smoke inhalation" (239). Elsewhere the distinction between actual and simulated disasters becomes blurred, with actual events at times serving as rehearsals for upcoming simulations. The final chapter opens by locating its events as happening on "the day Wilder got on his plastic tricycle" and rode into crowded freeway traffic (322). The two pages that follow are related in a deadpan tone that gives every detail an equally flat significance.

Disasters become part of the culture's "white noise" when filtered through the ever-present background of media. One of the novel's academics observes, "We need an occasional catastrophe to break up the incessant bombardment of information" (66). Jack, watching television news with the family, recognizes that "Every disaster made us wish for more, for something bigger, grander, more sweeping" (64). Such is the intrusion of the media that its presence or absence can dictate the significance of events. Daughter Bee's plane falls thousands of feet before recovering, but the media are not at the airport to record the plane's arrival. "They went through all that for nothing?" asks Bee (92). The tourist attraction billed as "THE MOST PHOTOGRAPHED BARN IN AMERICA" draws crowds armed with their cameras, but as instructor Murray Siskind points out, "No one sees the barn ... Once you've seen the signs about the barn, it becomes impossible to see the barn" (12). Such is the ubiquity of television – comforting, in this novel, when it allows the vicarious experiences of others' deaths, far away – that when Babette surprisingly appears on the screen in a live broadcast, Jack and the family are confused, disoriented by this "Babette of electrons and photons," and Jack fears momentarily that she has died, or that he has (105).

Jack sometimes has enough distance from the sounds coming from television, radio, supermarkets, and shopping malls that he can identify the source, but at other times sound bites and slogans take over his narrative voice. Babette becomes addicted to talk radio and it largely replaces discourse with real people for her. Appropriately, the automatic shut-off on the couple's bedroom radio malfunctions and takes on a will and pattern of its own. The town's "airborne toxic event" is a more immediately threatening version of this pollution. But the media misreports the accident that causes the leak, its experts incorrectly predict its direction, various euphemisms label what it is, and the predicted side effects keep changing, keeping overly-suggestive listeners a report or two behind on their imagined or actual symptoms.

The academic world's infiltration by the media also reflects the culture's anxieties about death. Jack invents "Hitler Studies in North America" as an attempt to submerge his anxieties about his own death within the enormity of the Holocaust, and in the image-driven academia of *White Noise* he can do this knowing no German. A program in Elvis Studies is in preparation, and the college chancellor advises Jack to change his appearance and invent an extra initial in his name if he wants to be taken seriously. On campus Jack's dark glasses ape the dress of a media star, providing both status and anonymity. Murray observes of the fascination with such figures as Hitler and Elvis, "Helpless and fearful people are drawn to magical figures, mythic figures, epic men who intimidate and darkly loom," an analysis that certainly applies to Jack, and that links academia to the comforts offered in this novel by the supermarket tabloids (287). The institution's name, "College-on-the-Hill," suggests an ironic distance from the world of faith behind John Winthrop's famous phrase "City upon a Hill" (from his "A Model of Christian Charity"). The college provides a hilltop refuge for displaced New Yorkers and others who like to argue over a comfortable lunch.

Jack tells his Hitler students, "All plots tend to move deathward ... We edge nearer death every time we plot" (26). Although he immediately wonders what he meant and why he said it, the particular plot that he narrates moves toward the planned death of his wife's seducer, Willie Mink. Jack's confrontation with Mink supports Murray's suggestion that killing another reinforces one's own sense of survival. As if to confirm the role of the media, Mink's television is on, its flickering screen lighting his room, and in his Dylar-drugged state he recites formulaic phrases from movies, advertisements, and weather reports. The murder plan that Jack recites to himself several times while in the room sounds like a parody of the mystery and detective stories that DeLillo has said in an interview allow readers to "play off their fears by encountering the death experience in a superficial way ... tightly in a plot ... containing it in a kind of game format." But throughout the novel, the emotions connected to fear of death finally drive events more than plans and plot, and Jack finds that once having shot his victim, helping him brings an even greater sense of comfortable well-being than the act of shooting does.

Unlike the plot-driven stories that it parodies, *White Noise* provides no closure to its various narratives, not even to the blood-soaked drama of the shooting. All the threats and anxieties remain. The spectacular sunsets, bringing a silent awe to the crowds of watchers, are probably the result of the toxic atmosphere. The men in Mylex suits still prowl the community, their purpose and findings unknown. Even the oasis of the supermarket, unchanging, Jack remarks earlier, "except for the better," and a measure that "Everything was fine, would continue to be fine," has rearranged its shelves "without warning," save for the generic products (170). However, within these confines the resulting anxiety, disorientation, and collisions among the consumers can be calmed. The scanners measure the secrets of price, not of impending mortality. And the tabloids at the check-out line fill the need of everything "that is not food or love" – offering miracle cures, tales of life after death, reports of extraterrestrial life, and of course the latest sightings of Elvis (326).

Bibliography

Don DeLillo, *White Noise* (New York, 1986). The Penguin Classics Deluxe Edition (New York, 2009) contains an introduction by Richard Powers. The printing in The Viking Critical Library series (New York, 1998), ed. Mark Osteen, includes a number of useful "Contexts," reviews, and critical essays.

Harold Bloom, ed., *Don DeLillo's White Noise* (Philadelphia, 2003).
Tim Engles and John N. Duvall, *Approaches to Teaching DeLillo's White Noise* (New York, 2006).
Frank Lentricchia, ed., *New Essays on White Noise* (New York, 1991).
Leonard Orr, *Don Delillo's White Noise: A Reader's Guide* (New York, 2003).

Toni Morrison, *Beloved*, New York: Alfred A. Knopf, 1987

The central event of Toni Morrison's Pulitzer Prize-winning novel – Sethe's act of infanticide rather than allow her daughter to be returned to slavery – is based upon an actual event that Morrison came across in her editorial work for Random House on a 1974 project titled *The Black Book*. Margaret Garner, upon whom Morrison's character is based, was returned to slavery after the murder, where she subsequently died of typhoid fever, but Morrison's Sethe returns to a home haunted by the event once she has served her prison sentence for the murder. (Garner's story is told in Steven Weisenburger's *Modern Medea: A Family Story of Slavery and Child-Murder from the Old South* [New York, 1998].) The murdered child remains a presence in the house for the almost 20 years that follow, manifested at different times as memory, spirit, and physically embodied ghost. The house itself, 124 Bluestone Road, is owned by sympathetic whites, the Bodwins. Because of the murder and subsequent haunting it is no longer the vibrant, lively crossroads of the community that it once was. The house and its inhabitants are largely avoided.

Set in the years just before and after emancipation, the novel tells Sethe's story within the broader context of the many individuals, families, and communities impacted by slavery – the "Sixty Million and more" to whom the novel is dedicated is one estimate of the deaths attributable to the slave trade. The story is told through the recollections of various characters, a process that illustrates the roles of both memory and forgetting in the ways in which a painful personal and cultural past is lived with. The legacy recalled by these memories of slavery is one of violence, exploitation, the ruthless

The Twentieth-Century American Fiction Handbook By Christopher MacGowan
© 2011 Christopher MacGowan

breaking up of families, and the insensitivity even of sympathetic white slave owners. Against this background Morrison explores the motives and morality of Sethe's act of murder, and the ideas of justice behind the personal, communal, and legal consequences that follow.

The community distances itself from Sethe and her family after the murder as one way of living with such an event. The communal action that does finally free the house of its predatory spirit visitor comes late, but the necessity of such communal support is illustrated in the novel's earlier examples of Negroes helping fellow Negroes either to escape, or to survive somehow the incidents of physical violence and emotional cruelty that are commonplace in the culture of slavery. Stamp Paid is a central figure behind Sethe's isolation but he later recognizes the error of his actions. Casual remarks by Nelson Lord bring pain to Denver, and only years later bring healing. Even the well-intentioned white family the Bodwins, who allow Sethe's family to stay in the house on Bluestone Road, and who find Sethe employment when she is released from prison, consider mostly the family's material rather than its emotional needs – as the coin holder in the form of a caricatured and kneeling black boy in their kitchen indicates. Sethe's murderous impulse to save Beloved by attacking Mr. Bodwin when he arrives to collect Denver is a resurgence of her desperate response years earlier to the appearance of the man called "schoolteacher" and the posse come to return her to slavery. The parallel suggests affinities between the actions of the whites despite all the differences between them, and further questions the well-intentioned but compromised and finally inadequate patrician governance of plantation owner Mr. Garner. Garner's benevolence takes little account of the future, depending upon a white male authority that, along with social pressure, leads his widow to feel obliged to bring in the pitiless schoolteacher to run the plantation upon her husband's death.

Paul D's memories of Sweet Home provide details of the personal traumas behind Sethe's infanticide, while his subsequent experiences after the attempted escape broaden the novel's picture of slavery. These experiences range from the dehumanizing chain gang in Alfred, Georgia, to the unexpected kindnesses of the Cherokee Indians and the "weaver lady" in Delaware (132–133). Emotionally scarred, Paul D is wary of making a full emotional commitment to Sethe, even though he is beginning to love her, a wariness that Beloved uses in her seduction of him. Although, once he knows of the murder, he condemns Sethe's actions and explanation – without articulating the alternative that he insists she could have taken – he is also the figure who at the close of the novel rescues her from the same self-destructive resignation with which Baby Suggs gave up living years earlier.

Sethe's character is defined in large part by the instincts and emotions of motherhood (a central issue in a number of critical discussions of the novel). Her own enslaved mother saves her, alone, of the babies produced by her violated body, since unlike her other pregnancies Sethe's conception results from an act of choice. But the mother is forced to return to field work, Sethe is nursed by a substitute, and later sees her mother's lynched and burned body. The pregnant Sethe is abused by schoolteacher's pupils on the night of the escape, and her desperate journey on the days following is marked by her awareness of the sweet, sticky milk oozing from her breasts. Ironically the maternal guilt connected to the spirit manifestation haunting the house eventually drives her two sons away, although the two women, Baby Suggs, and the baby who grows up to be Denver remain. When Beloved achieves a corporeal state, her predatory demands upon Sethe exploit the guilt of the infanticide, and Sethe is only able to extend the sense of herself and her emotional commitments beyond that guilt through some degree of release from the past. She is eventually allowed that opportunity by Denver's act of courageous independence in seeking outside help, and Paul D's healing love.

Beloved's status and identity is as much a product of individual states of mind, particularly of the three characters sharing the house with her, as of any supernatural powers. (For a few critics this aspect of Beloved detracts somewhat from the novel's achievement, since she lacks the vitality of the other main characters.) Beloved makes her appearance at the moment when Paul D, Sethe, and Denver return from their first significant outing together as a family. All three then reinforce her corporeality. She seduces Paul D. Denver's physical and emotional isolation leads her to nurse Beloved back to health with a kind of urgent desperation, and Denver later tries to ignore the increasing signs of the newcomer's malevolence. Maternal guilt, as noted above, gives Beloved substance for Sethe, although she only identifies Beloved as the spirit of her daughter after Paul D brings the full memory of the murder back to the surface once he hears of it from Stamp Paid. "To Sethe," the narrator comments at an earlier point in the novel, "the future was a matter of keeping the past at bay. The 'better life' she believed she and Denver were living was simply not that other one" (51).

Beloved's ambiguous status as spirit, projection, and physical presence, as legacy of a particular tragedy as well as of slavery itself, is reinforced by some of the attempts to understand the events that unfold. There is a range of responses among the community to the news that the murdered child has returned, from matter-of-fact acceptance to disbelief. Paul D tries to "make sense out of the stories he had been hearing" (315) reported by a crowd not always sure who or what they had witnessed in the yard of 124 Bluestone Road. Stamp Paid tells Paul D: "Was a girl locked up in the house with a whiteman over by Deer Creek. Found him dead last summer and the girl gone. Maybe that's her. Folks say he had her in there since she was a pup" (277). And "a little boy" claims to have seen, at the same time that Beloved disappeared, "down by the stream … cutting through the woods, a naked woman with fish for hair" (315). Paul D's task, like that of Sethe, Denver, and the community itself, is to try to understand something as inexplicable as the infanticide, and the equally inexplicable inhumanity that could produce slavery.

In its final pages the novel moves into the present tense, as Paul D tries to help Sethe prepare for a future that is more than "simply not that other one." More generally, the novel concludes with a summary of how time distances a story too painful "to pass on" (323–324), but a story whose significance, Morrison insists through its retelling and elaboration, must not be lost.

Bibliography

The Vintage International Edition (New York, 2004) includes a foreword by the author.

William L. Andrews and Nellie Y. McKay, eds., *Toni Morrison's Beloved: A Casebook* (New York, 1999).
Kathleen Marks, *Toni Morrison's Beloved and the Apotropaic Imagination* (Columbia, MO, 2002).
Carl Plasa, ed., *Toni Morrison: Beloved* (New York, 1998).
Barbara H. Solomon, ed., *Critical Essays on Toni Morrison's Beloved* (New York, 1998).

Amy Tan, *The Joy Luck Club,* New York: G. P. Putnam's Sons, 1989

Amy Tan's novel of four immigrant mothers and their American daughters was one of a number of works centered upon the Chinese American experience that received wide acclaim in the 1970s and 1980s. Two other prominent works of the same period were Maxine Hong Kingston's *The Woman Warrior* (1976) and David Hwang's Tony Award-winning play *M. Butterfly* (1988).

The Joy Luck Club is not a conventional novel. Its 16 stories and seven narrators are linked through a common immigrant heritage, some recurring narrative details, and the regular meetings around a game of mahjong of a Club that was first founded by Suyuan Woo at the time of the Japanese invasion of China. The four mothers who in 1949 began meeting regularly in San Francisco in the new version of the Club are all women who came to the United States from China in the late 1940s. Suyuan Woo has died shortly before the novel opens and her stories are told by her daughter, Jing-mei Woo. The four American daughters of these mothers grow up determined to free themselves from a heritage that they see as oppressive, one that handicaps their own efforts to assimilate into mainstream American culture. The stories, whether told by the transplanted mothers or by their daughters, share common themes of identity, communication, powerlessness, and hope.

Lindo Jong's daughter, Waverly, naïvely fears that if she visits China she may so blend in that "they don't let me come back to the United States" (253). This sense of heritage as entrapment is a characteristic attitude of all four daughters. Lindo Jong could be speaking for all four mothers when she asks herself: "It's my fault she is this way. I wanted my children to have the best combination: American circumstances and Chinese character. How could I know these two things do not mix?" (254). *The Joy Luck Club* suggests that mothers and daughters alike must find a way to transmit what the parable introducing the first of the book's four sections calls "the single swan feather"(17) – the potent reminder of the beautiful swan, carried away from China, but confiscated upon entering the United States.

A key difference between the childhood of the mothers in China (and also of *their* mothers, who are themselves an important presence in the stories) and the new generation lies in the matter of choice. An-mei's daughter, Rose, remembers setting her mother's views aside when she started going to school and learning "American opinions." But she adds, " it was only later that I discovered there was a serious flaw . . . There were too many choices, so it was easy to get confused and pick the wrong thing" (191). There are no such multiple choices for Lindo Jong when at the age of two a matchmaker arranges her marriage to a boy in a neighborhood family. Or for An-mei Hsu's mother, the victim of a rape that forces her to become the fourth wife of a rich businessman. Ying-ying St. Clair's marriage to her first, philandering, husband is inevitable, and Suyuan Woo loses her first husband as a result of the Japanese invasion of China. Thinking that she herself is dying, she abandons her twin baby daughters by the roadside hoping that they can be saved, an act that haunts her for the rest of her life.

The three married daughters use their freedom of choice to marry outside of the Chinese community. As economic circumstances improve they move to richer areas of the city, or out to the suburbs. All four daughters adopt American forms of their Chinese names, although Jing-mei, the only unmarried daughter, later returns to her Chinese name. As a child Jing-mei is oppressed by her mother's impossible hopes for her daughter to display a spectacular talent of some kind, and to achieve great success, expectations that led to Jing-mei's low sense of her self-worth and abilities, and her resignation that she could do little to change things.

Rose Hsu Jordan marries medical student Ted, who insists on making all of the important decisions for the couple. When the marriage begins to flounder and he does call upon Rose to give her views, she finds that her passivity has become an ingrained habit. In this respect Rose's situation is similar to that of Waverly Jong and Lena St. Clair. All three are trapped in an American version of their mothers' earlier fates. Rather than love, they tolerate, and even resent, their husbands.

Waverly's marriage is the result of an elopement, part of a pattern of rebelling against her mother's expectations. As a child she resents Lindo's demonstrative pride in her daughter's success at chess. After one argument she runs through the alleyways of Chinatown, only to find that they "contained no escape routes" (100). Later, as a mother herself, she is insensitive to the place of children in the older generation's cultural practices. Overly indulgent to a child whom she had originally intended to abort, she thoughtlessly treats her four-year-old daughter like one of the adults at Suyuan Woo's Chinese New Year dinner. She gives her daughter "the best crab" even though, as the girl protests shortly afterward, she doesn't even like the delicacy (202).

Lena St. Clair, sensing perhaps her mother's hidden past, and recognizing Clifford St. Clair's almost suffocating protectiveness of his wife, feels that her mother has "disappeared" and become "a ghost" (103). But she makes little effort to reach out to her. Her own emotional barriers lead her into a marriage in which nothing important is shared, as illustrated by the careful listing of separate and joint expenditures that she keeps with husband Harold, as well as in the disproportionate roles and responsibilities in their consulting company.

Despite such tensions and resentments, by the end of the 16 stories the mothers and daughters reach a point at which "the single swan feather" might be passed on. The last stories that Rose and her mother tell are both about finding a genuinely independent voice. Rose, still not fully recognizing what her mother has given her, begins to stand up to husband Ted's bullying, deception, and manipulations, and to recognize that the marriage is at an end. "Why do you not speak up for yourself," her mother asks of Rose's plans to confide in a psychiatrist. "Why can you not talk to your husband?" (193). A generation earlier An-mei had learned from her own mother to confront directly the deceptions of Wu Tsing's Second Wife.

Waverly Jong comes to acknowledge that her failed attempt to run away to "a safer place" in childhood has led to her erecting barriers against her mother, and telling untrue stories about her (183, 259). She now sees "in the brief instant that I had peered over the barriers" just "an old woman" who is waiting "patiently for her daughter to invite her in" (183–184). Part of this recognition comes from new fiancé Rich being so insensitive to her mother's culture and expectations that he does not notice his social missteps. Waverly's embarrassment serves, even if obliquely, to remind her of the heritage that she shares with her mother. She can even conclude, although still with ambivalence, that while the three of them going together to China for the couple's honeymoon "would be a disaster," at the same time "part of me also thinks the whole idea makes perfect sense" (184). Lindo Jong, meanwhile, determines that her daughter "must understand my real circumstances, how I arrived, how I married, how I lost my Chinese face, why you are the way you are" (259).

Ying-ying St. Clair is even more resolved to end the silence which has kept her true background and history in China from her daughter, a decision crystallized by seeing the emotional evasions in Lena's marriage to Harold. She deliberately breaks the unbalanced table and vase in the guest room in order to bring her daughter upstairs to talk, but the "spirit" that Ying-ying wants to pass on to her daughter starts to work in Lena even before this confrontation. Lena recalls that when she was only eight her mother predicted from the rice bowl, correctly as it turned out, that Lena "would marry a bad man" (151), and Lena has also begun to challenge the "balance sheet" (165) that is Harold's idea of emotional commitment in marriage.

In China the four mothers grew up in a culture in which relationships were hierarchical, and the most powerful figures were men. Living in the United States they find that respect for parents and elders does not govern the behavior of their children. In the book's earlier stories the daughters do not acknowledge that a mother could help a daughter in a culture within which, for all of the differences, men still claim more than an equal share of power. But in the Joy Luck Club the mothers have each other, sharing homes, displaying cooking skills, and even pooling their luck in the stock market. But when the generational insularity of the Club is broken by Jing-mei taking the seat of her deceased mother, the action is another important part of bringing mothers and daughters closer together. Sometime in the future all four daughters might inherit their mothers' places at the Joy Luck Club's mahjong table. "The single swan feather" (17) would then have been passed on, a continuity matched by the heritage, old and new, that Jing-mei brings to the meeting with her long-lost half-sisters in China – those two babies who years before her mother was forced to abandon by the roadside.

Bibliography

Amy Tan, *The Joy Luck Club* (New York, 2006).

Bella Adams, *Amy Tan* (Manchester and New York, 2005), pp. 35–71.
Harold Bloom, ed., *Amy Tan's The Joy Luck Club* (Philadelphia, 2009).
Robert C. Evans, ed., *Critical Insights: The Joy Luck Club* (Pasadena, 2009).
Gary Wiener, ed., *Women's Issues in Amy Tan's The Joy Luck Club* (Detroit, 2008).

Cormac McCarthy, *All the Pretty Horses,* New York: Alfred A. Knopf, 1992

All the Pretty Horses was Cormac McCarthy's sixth novel. His first four books had been set in the South, and the last of them, *Suttree* (1979), is considered by some critics to be his finest novel. Harold Bloom, among others, has made that claim for *Blood Meridian* (1985), the first of McCarthy's Western novels, the book immediately preceding *All the Pretty Horses*. But *All the Pretty Horses* was the first of McCarthy's books to win him a wide readership, and the novel won both the National Book Award and the National Book Critics Circle Award. This first of McCarthy's Border Trilogy novels was followed in 1994 by *The Crossing* and four years later by *Cities of the Plain*. In the last novel of the trilogy the central character of *All the Pretty Horses*, John Grady Cole, reappears along with Billy Parham from the second novel. The narrative takes place close in time to the first two books, but an epilogue brings the story up to the present.

The narrative of *All the Pretty Horses* is set in the spring of 1948, and centers around horses, their value, and the shared love for them that brings some of the characters together. Horses are central to some key events. Jimmy Blevins, frightened that God intends to kill him by lightning, loses his horse in a storm and initiates the series of events that lead to his death – and almost to the deaths of John Grady and Lacey Rawlins too. The Mexican officers see horses as a commodity to steal from their prisoners. John Grady sees the beautiful Alejandra on a black Arabian saddlehorse, and horses figure in the scene that brings them together as lovers. John Grady wins the respect of the *hacendado* Rocha through his knowledge of and love for horses. And the two boys share stories with ranch hand Luis, who tells them "no man who has

The Twentieth-Century American Fiction Handbook   By Christopher MacGowan
© 2011 Christopher MacGowan

not gone to war horseback can ever truly understand the horse," and that "if a person understood the soul of the horse then he would understand all horses that ever were" (111). John Grady talks to horses, whether to comfort a wild mountain horse that he is breaking in, to reassure his own horse Redbo, or to say farewell to Rawlins's grullo. When imprisoned in the cell in Encantada he dreams of running free with "the young mares and fillies over the plain" (161). Thinking of horses, "always the right thing to think about," brings him comfort as he recovers from his wounds in Saltillo (204). During the difficult trek with the three recaptured horses and the captain as hostage he dreams of "the order in the horse's heart," an order which he tries to find in his own relationship to the landscape (280).

In the early pages of the novel the narrator comments that what John Grady "loved in horses was what he loved in men, the blood and the heat of the blood that ran them" (6). But his journey into Mexico and back teaches him some of the ways in which horses, men, and women are very different. Bringing back the horses stolen by the Mexican officers, despite all the danger it puts him in, proves much easier than the task of trying to bring back Alejandra. He tells Rawlins, once the two are released from the Saltillo prison, that he is returning on account of "the girl and the horses" (211), but Alejandra's strongest ties, despite her love for him, are to her family, especially her godmother, and to a future that will be shaped by her family's wealth and political history. He learns the important difference between the unstinting loyalty that the horses provide to one who cares for and respects them, and the complex motivations behind human actions.

Such a contrast also underlies an important exchange between John Grady and Rawlins in Saltillo prison. "All over a goddamned horse," Rawlins says bitterly of their imprisonment, but John Grady replies, "Horse had nothing to do with it" (185). Blevins's horse is certainly at the center of the events that cost him his life, and cost John Grady and Rawlins their jobs at La Purisma. But Blevins's fear of lightning, and the actions and values of Duenna Alfonsa and Rocha, are equally if not more important causes, and both are products of history – the family history of sudden deaths from lightning in Blevins's case, and the violent history of Mexican politics in the case of the Duenna and Rocha. And history is behind the Duenna investing the hacienda "with oldworld ties and with antiquity and tradition" (132), while the flight that brings Blevins into the path of John Grady and Rawlins is flight from a violent stepfather. John Grady himself contributes to his expulsion from La Purisma by his relationship with Alejandra and by lying to Rocha when asked if he made the journey from Texas only with Rawlins. Thus, as John Grady realizes in his reply to Rawlins in the prison, human actions and human history, not the innocent horse, are the cause of events.

The question of whether these actions and forces of history amount to the operation of fate, and what, if any, actions and attitudes might have changed events, are issues that haunt John Grady once he returns to Texas. Both John Grady and Rawlins recognized from the beginning that riding with Blevins would inevitably bring trouble, but John Grady in particular feels a responsibility toward him, and they choose to let him stay. John Grady is disturbed by his reaction to the Mexican captain, and also to the killing of Blevins – even though "he wasnt nothin to me" (292), as he tells the judge who dismisses the three fraudulent claims for Blevins's horse. The Mexicans can rationalize a form of moral justice for killing Blevins, but John Grady cannot justify his own silence as he witnessed Blevins being taken away – despite the judge pointing out that no action or language could have made a difference. Grady is also concerned about the morality of his actions toward Rocha. Realizing such complexities is part of the initiation story that is John Grady's journey into Mexico, an initiation that includes, too, the possibility that to "the pain of the world ... there might be no limits" (257–258).

All the Pretty Horses has been seen by some critics as more romantic than the five novels that preceded it, and certainly large sections of the novel reflect John Grady's appreciation of the landscape and his love and respect for animals. But the novel has a bleakness even beyond the death of Blevins and the loss of Alejandra. As the Duenna tells John Grady with brutal directness, in refusing to allow his relationship with her goddaughter to continue, "The world is quite ruthless in selecting between the dream and the reality, even where we will not," and she adds shortly afterward, "We weep over the might have been, but there is no might have been. There never was" (238–239). Additionally, the story begins and ends with funerals – those of John Grady's grandfather, and of his childhood nurse, Abuela. His father also dies, and his actress mother is now a distant figure, on the stage or on the arm of a stranger, certainly not a part of the boy's life, and she is intent upon selling the ranch that had been his home. Lacking the ties that in her own world pulled Alejandra away from him, he responds to Rawlins's question "Where is your country?" with "I dont know ... I dont know where it is. I dont know what happens to country" (299). By the end of the novel Grady's only companions are his own horse, Redbo, and the horse belonging to the dead Blevins – man and horses, all three equally homeless.

Bibliography

All the Pretty Horses (New York, 1993), Vintage paperback edition.

Edwin T. Arnold and Dianne C. Luce, eds., *A Cormac McCarthy Companion: The Border Trilogy* (Jackson, MS, 2001).

Harold Bloom, ed., *Cormac McCarthy's All the Pretty Horses* (Philadephia, 2004).

Sara Spurgeon, ed., *Cormac McCarthy: All the Pretty Horses, No Country for Old Men, The Road* (New York, 2010).

Stephen Tatum, ed., *Cormac McCarthy's All the Pretty Horses: A Reader's Guide* (New York, 2002).

Part 4

Themes

Race and American Fiction

African slaves were transported to the Portuguese and Spanish colonies in the New World early in the sixteenth century, and the organized enslavement of Africans began in the English settlements when slaves were brought to Jamestown and to Massachusetts a hundred years later. Slavery was legalized in Massachusetts in 1641 and 20 years later in Virginia. By the end of the eighteenth century, by one count, 35 percent of the population of the southern states was African. The black population in the 1860 national census, just before the Civil War, was four and a half million, or 14 percent of the total population. The importation of slaves into the United States was banned by Congress in 1807, although the trade continued illegally until 1859, when the last known slave ship, the *Clotilde*, docked in Mobile Bay, Alabama. The first major step toward eradicating slavery occurred when Congress abolished slavery in the District of Columbia in 1862. Abraham Lincoln's Emancipation Proclamation, freeing all slaves in the rebellious southern states, came into effect on January 1, 1863. The Thirteenth Amendment to the Constitution, outlawing slavery in the United States, was passed by Congress in January 1865 and ratified by the states in December of that year. In 1866 Congress passed the Civil Rights Act that conferred citizenship upon black Americans, a decision that overrode President Andrew Johnson's veto and overturned the Supreme Court's Dred Scott decision of 1857, which had ruled that African Americans could have no rights of citizenship. A series of other amendments followed to grant voting rights and equal protection under the law, but these rights were gradually eroded in the following decades, particularly in the southern states, and sometimes by Supreme Court decisions. The Civil Rights movement that began in the 1950s with the work of Martin Luther King and others, and continued into sometimes violent confrontations of the 1960s, finally brought the equal opportunity laws that outlawed discrimination on the grounds of color in such areas as education, employment, and housing.

Some prominent novels by white writers in the nineteenth century had illustrated the cruelty of slavery. The most famous of these, *Uncle Tom's Cabin*, appeared in 1852. The raft scenes in Mark Twain's *Adventures of Huckleberry Finn* (1885) presented a small, fragile, and always threatened world, in which a black man and a white adolescent adventured together on more or less equal terms. Twain's *Pudd'nhead Wilson* (1894) explored the complexities of identity in a way that satirized racial categories – the "black" and "white" babies who are switched in the novel look exactly alike. Twain could be ambivalently sentimental in his fiction, however, about the pre-Civil War South. The triumph of Pudd'nhead in this novel amounts to restoring the status quo, for the black character returns to slavery, while that character's mother, who might have been cared for in old age by a paternalistic, slave-owning employer, suffers when released into the Darwinian ruthlessness of capitalism. Slavery is less overtly part of the Uncle Remus stories of Joel Chandler Harris, which were derived from the oral tradition of African folktales, tales that Harris heard in his youth from the slaves at Turnwold Plantation, Georgia. They first appeared in 1880, and although widely popular for decades, and a major influence on subsequent children's literature, have become controversial for what some see as their stereotypes and their romantic view of plantation life.

In twentieth-century writing by white writers, William Faulkner's novels stand out for their powerful, sympathetic treatment of black conditions in the post-Civil War South. To mention just a few examples, the black character Dilsey who serves the once slave-owning Compson family in *The Sound and the Fury* (1929) is herself worn down by many of the same family burdens that afflict the Compsons, but she has a genuine faith in Christianity that broadens her perspective beyond the past, present, and future of the haunted Compsons. In *Light in August* (1932) Joe Christmas sees his possible black heritage as a kind of original sin, and the white character Joanna Burden is treated as an outsider by the others in the town because she continues her family's history of supporting black emancipation. The complex narrative of *Absalom, Absalom!* (1936) explores the destructive effects of extreme and ingrained attitudes toward miscegenation.

Carl Van Vechten was a strong supporter and patron of black writing during the Harlem Renaissance, and his novel *Nigger Heaven* (1926) covers the broad spectrum of Harlem life, high and low, in its depiction of interracial relations. Reaction to the novel split the black literary community, with Countee Culleen and W. E. B. Du Bois considering it an "affront" while Nella

Larson, James Weldon Johnson, and Langston Hughes praised the book. For later printings Hughes contributed some poems to replace the song lyrics that Van Vechten had used without obtaining permission. Hughes was also supportive of DuBose Heyward's 1924 novel *Porgy*, set in South Carolina and the source of the now much better-known Gershwin opera *Porgy and Bess* (1935), for which Heyward wrote the libretto. Both novel and musical, while unarguably sympathetic toward their black characters, have been accused of using white stereotypes of blacks, and in the two or three decades following the first production of *Porgy and Bess* a number of prominent black artists refused to perform in the opera.

Waldo Frank received the guidance and friendship of African American writer Jean Toomer for his novel *Holiday* (1923), which depicted a southern lynching and the religious and sexual frenzy that led to it. But Toomer's friendship with Sherwood Anderson could not save the latter's patronizing novel *Dark Laughter* (1925). Anderson's only bestseller, the novel presents southern blacks as an alternative to the mainstream culture that the book condemns – leading to lyrical, sentimental passages on the supposed vibrant, primitive energy of "niggers" working in the docks and streets of New Orleans. The novel's prose style was mocked shortly afterward by Ernest Hemingway in his novella *The Torrents of Spring* (1926).

One of Flannery O'Connor's best-known short stories puts race ambiguously at the center of a spiritual revelation. "The Artificial Nigger" (1955) has produced a number of different interpretations of the racist garden ornament that gives the story its title. The two central characters, Mr. Head and Nelson, experience in Atlanta the equivalent of a journey into hell, a journey that results in their recognizing the importance of grace. They encounter a number of blacks during the day before coming upon "the artificial nigger." The battered and paint-chipped garden ornament serves symbolically for O'Connor's point that to consider the human condition without considering the fate of the soul is to live in a world of barren materialism, and to become oneself merely an inert, material thing. But the degree to which the black history and southern racist attitudes behind the ornament contribute specifically to the story's depiction of hell and mercy is ambiguous given O'Connor's insistence that an individual's spiritual condition is much more important than the fate of the body. O'Connor wrote of the story's central symbol, "What I had in mind to suggest with the artificial nigger was the redemptive quality of the Negro's suffering for us all," but the story has led one commentator to observe that, "Of the many stories that include overt white perspectives on race, 'The Artificial Nigger' is arguably the most complex and perplexing."

The most widely read twentieth-century novel by a white author on race is Harper Lee's *To Kill a Mockingbird* (1960). Although the book is set in the

1930s, it reflects the tensions in the South in the 1950s when demands for racial equality began to receive support at the federal level. The novel is widely taught in American schools, although some surveys have indicated that it is enjoyed more by its young white readers than its young black readers. There has also been some criticism that the novel does not explore the lives and thoughts of its black characters as much as it does the whites. This criticism could be countered by pointing to the limitations of the novel's child narrator, limitations which nonetheless allow Lee to make clear that the racial attitudes of most of the town's adult whites have been culturally formed and reinforced.

In the mid-nineteenth century the most prominent works by African Americans were slave narratives, the best known being the accounts by Frederick Douglass, William Wells Brown, and Harriet Jacobs. Brown is credited with being the first African American writer to publish a novel, *Clotel, or, The President's Daughter* (1853) – although the novel was published in England, not in the United States. The first novel published by an African American woman, and the first novel by a black writer published in the United States, was *Our Nig: or, Sketches from the Life of a Free Black* (1859) by Harriet E. Wilson, the story of a mulatto woman's life as a wage slave in New England. Following the Civil War, Charles W. Chesnutt published a number of realist short stories and novels that explored such issues as segregation, lynching, racial identity, "passing" as white, and southern racial and class attitudes. For William Dean Howells, Chesnutt's short stories invited comparison with those of Henry James, Guy de Maupassant, and Ivan Turgenev. Chesnutt's writing came to seem old-fashioned in the early years of the century and his literary reputation declined, but in 1928 the NAACP (National Association for the Advancement of Colored People) awarded him its prestigious Spingarn Medal for his "pioneer work as a literary artist depicting the life and struggles of Americans of Negro descent." His short story collections *The Conjure Woman* and *The Wife of His Youth and Other Stories of the Color Line* (both 1899), and his novels *The House Behind the Cedars* (1900) and the more political *The Marrow of Tradition* (1901), are now seen as important forerunners of modern African American fiction.

The Harlem Renaissance, usually dated as beginning after World War I and lasting into the early years of the 1930s, was the product of a number of factors: black migration from the South to urban centers in the North, a need for unskilled industrial workers during the war years when migration from Europe dwindled, an increasingly organized movement to improve living conditions for the black population – such as the founding of the National Association for the Advancement of Colored People in 1909, and Marcus

Garvey's Universal Improvement Association, which held its first convention in Harlem in 1920 – as well as the increasing interest in black culture by liberal whites. Never a coordinated movement, the period was one in which many forms of black artistic expression came to the fore, including jazz, photography, painting, dance, poetry, and fiction, with differences of opinion among the writers and artists about the best ways to take account of such issues as the heritage of slavery, the problems of fragmented identity, and the role of African folk traditions.

An important legacy of the decade was that African American art was no longer stereotypically seen as depicting rural life but became associated with more urban, sophisticated forms of expression – although in fiction by some white authors, and in many Hollywood films of the 1930s, this too produced its stereotypes. One of the foremost works of the Harlem Renaissance, Jean Toomer's *Cane* (1923), a mix of poetry and short fictional sketches, took the northward urban migration as its subject. Toomer's work illustrated the folk, community traditions of black Georgia farm laborers while also showing the passing of that culture as younger generations migrated to the cities. Other important fictional works to emerge in these years included Nella Larsen's two novels of mulatto women "passing" as white, *Quicksand* (1928) and *Passing* (1929). Larsen herself was of Danish and West Indian descent. The first novel is largely autobiographical, and the second particularly rich in its exploration of sexual and racial ambiguity. Langston Hughes published his novel *Not Without Laughter* in 1930, depicting an African American family's struggles to rise from poverty in Kansas, and a collection of stories, *The Ways of White Folks*, in 1934. Jessie Fauset, literary editor of the NAACP's journal *The Crisis* during the important years 1919–1926, published four novels treating the themes of passing and racial identity, two of which have received particular attention in recent years, *Plum Bun* (1929) and *The Chinaberry Tree* (1931).

Among the most important publications to come out of the Harlem Renaissance period was Alain Locke's anthology of and about African American writing, *The New Negro* (1925), which included a representative selection of poetry, short fiction, and essays. Locke's own influential essay, which gave the book its title, attempts a synthesis of the various attitudes held by its contributors on matters of heritage, form, identity, and the politics of activism. Two other important, shorter, texts that contain statements on the position of the black writer at this time are Langston Hughes's "The Negro Artist and the Racial Mountain" (1926) and Zora Neale Hurston's "How It Feels to Be Colored Me" (1928) – both writers who were included in Locke's anthology. Hughes noted the inexhaustible material available to the black writer who wanted to write about his own race or about relations with whites, but declared that many black writers lacked the will to explore this material: "this is the mountain standing in the way of any true Negro art in America – this urge within the race toward whiteness, the desire to pour racial individuality into the mold of American standardization, and to be as little Negro and as much American as possible." For Hughes, there was pressure from both races to compromise: "'Oh, be respectable, write about nice people, show how good we are,' say the Negroes. 'Be stereotyped, don't go too far, don't shatter our illusions about you, don't amuse us too seriously. We will pay you,' say the whites. Both would have told Jean Toomer not to write *Cane.*" Hurston declares firmly in her essay, "I have no separate feeling about being an American citizen and colored." For Hurston,

> Slavery is sixty years in the past. The operation was successful and the patient is doing well, thank you. The terrible struggle that made me an American out of a potential slave said "On the line!" The Reconstruction said "Get set!" and the generation before said "Go!" I am off to a flying start and I must not halt in the stretch to look behind and weep.

Thus, Hurston declares, "I am not tragically colored. There is no great sorrow dammed up in my soul, nor lurking behind my eyes. I do not mind at all. I do not belong to the sobbing school of Negrohood who hold that nature somehow has given them a lowdown dirty deal and whose feelings are all but about it." As for discrimination: "Sometimes, I feel discriminated against, but it does not make me angry. It merely astonishes me. How can any deny themselves the pleasure of my company? It's beyond me."

Hurston was a well-known and respected figure in the Harlem Renaissance both for her fiction and for her work in African American ethnography. But her reputation suffered one of the most precipitous declines of any writer of the period, in large part because her fiction mirrored the form of folklore narrative rather than exploring psychological motivation, and because the accurate recording of dialect, in Hurston's case the offspring of her fieldwork in anthropology, was seen by black critics as both demeaning and, by the late 1930s, old-fashioned. Thus her 1937 novel, *Their Eyes Were Watching God*, now arguably one of the most admired American novels of the century, was attacked by Alain Locke for its "pseudo-primitives," "over simplification," and its inability to present "the inner psychology of characterization or . . . sharp analysis of the social background." These latter qualities were paramount in African American fiction of the 1930s Depression years, and the premier black writer of such fiction, Richard Wright, accused the novel in his own review of having no "basic idea or theme that lends itself to significant interpretation," and charged Hurston with a "minstrel technique" that panders to the taste of a white audience for "that phase of Negro life which is 'quaint.'"

Wright's own politically charged novel of racial conflict, *Native Son* (1940), was itself accused of conforming to stereotypes by James Baldwin, in two essays reprinted in his *Notes of a Native Son* (1955). For Baldwin, Wright subordinated his characters and plot to the purposes of his protest, with the result that the novel was as reductive in its analysis of race as Harriet Beecher Stowe's *Uncle Tom's Cabin*. Baldwin's own essays, novels, and short fiction generally argue that racial intolerance is culturally grounded, and that with a fuller sense on the part of blacks and whites of their shared history – including that of slavery and racism – there could be some positive movement toward a multiracial community. A more pessimistic position was taken in Ralph Ellison's *Invisible Man* (1952), a novel which explored the limitations of Booker T. Washington's accommodationist policies and Marcus Garvey's "Back to Africa" movement, as well as the self-serving aspects of Communist Party support for racial equality.

Baldwin's support of the Civil Rights Movement was seen as naïve and ineffective by some black writers of the 1960s, who pointed to the continued violence and inequalities facing blacks in politics, employment, and education, despite the Civil Rights protections that had begun in the 1950s and accelerated during the presidency of Lyndon Johnson. The decade saw the assassination of Malcolm X in 1965 by a rival Muslim sect, and Martin Luther King (1968) and NAACP fieldworker Medgar Evers (1963) by white gunmen. Evers' assassin was early identified, but not imprisoned for his crime until 30 years later.

The Black Arts Movement (*c.*1965–1975) was a separatist movement that rejected integration as a goal. Much of its literary expression came through poetry and drama, but an important result of the movement was the setting up of independent presses so that black writers were no longer dependent on white establishment publishers. *Black Fire* (1968), edited by Amiri Baraka and Larry Neal, is an important anthology of black writing from the period and includes seven short stories, as well as essays, poems, and plays. *The Black Woman: An Anthology* (1970), edited by Toni Cade Bambara, which also emerged from the movement, is arguably the first important black feminist anthology. Alice Walker is among the writers represented.

By most accounts one of the main reasons for the splintering of the Black Arts Movement in the mid-1970s was the cooption by white establishment presses of the most marketable writers. As a result, fiction by more African American writers reached a larger readership, was regularly reviewed, and became integrated into the regular publishing schedules of the major publishers. This increased visibility contributed to the greater distribution of fiction by other minority writers, such as those from Spanish American and Asian backgrounds. As far as African American literature is concerned, the list of black writers who became prominent in the last quarter of the century includes some of the most important writers in contemporary American fiction – many of them women. These writers include Alice Walker, Toni Morrison, Maya Angelou, Paule Marshall, and the award-winning science fiction writer Octavia Butler. African American writing by the 1990s was less racially confrontational than 40 years earlier, although some of the writing centrally concerned with sexual identity and gender issues forcefully challenged what the authors saw as views still entrenched and prejudicial. But generally the fiction integrated African American folklore with realist techniques – as in the fiction of Morrison – or revisited cultural and personal history to bring to the fore stories that had not been fully told. Important examples of the latter include Margaret Walker's *Jubilee* (1966), Alex Haley's *Roots* (1976), and Charles Johnson's *Middle Passage* (1990).

The American Short Story

The short story, at least into the early 1950s and the advent of widespread television viewing, could often provide the American writer with an income to supplement what might be poor sales of a novel, or long stretches between the appearance of novels. Thomas Wolfe and F. Scott Fitzgerald are examples of writers whose stories provided such a crucial source of income. A collection of stories might then be put out by the publisher, as usually happened in Fitzgerald's case, to follow up on the publicity generated by a novel's appearance. On the other hand, some writers published almost exclusively in the short story form, as in the case of O. Henry, Ring Lardner, and Raymond Carver.

Short stories could provide such a source of income in the pre-television age because of the large readership of such mass-circulation and literary magazines as *McClure's Magazine*, *The Atlantic Monthly*, *The Smart Set*, *The Saturday Evening Post*, and *The New Yorker*. Some magazines became associated with a particular kind of story and a particular kind of writer, *The New Yorker* more prominently than any other, with J. D. Salinger and John Updike as two prominent examples of the writers associated with the magazine. And an editor with good judgment could have an important impact upon a writer's career. William Dean Howells at *The Atlantic* and in his later essays for *Harper's*, Willa Cather at *McClure's*, Jessie Fauset at *The Crisis*, and Marianne Moore at *The Dial* were all supportive of important writing.

Many of Henry James's best-known short stories – some of them, such as *The Aspern Papers* (1888), long enough to shade into the novella form – were published in the nineteenth century. Like *The Aspern Papers*, which first appeared in *The Atlantic Monthly*, many of James's later stories concern the nature of art itself, including its sources and the public and private aspects of its expression. "The Real Thing" (1892) explores the relationship of reality and illusion in art. Reality and illusion become more psychological themes in his well-known story "The Turn of the Screw" (1898), again long enough to be considered a novella, and extreme psychological conditions are explored further in two famous late short stories, "The Beast in the Jungle" (1903) and "The Jolly Corner" (1908).

Stephen Crane, a neighbor of James in Sussex, England, had published two of his best-known stories, "The Blue Hotel" and "The Open Boat," not long before his early death in 1900. Two other writers who published notable short stories in the earlier part of the century were Jack London and Willa Cather, two writers very different in their sensibilities. But in the first decade of the century the most popular short story writer in America was O. Henry, the pen name of William Sydney Porter. He authored around 300 stories after moving to New York in 1902, many of them centered on working-class city dwellers, such as shop girls, clerks, salesmen, policemen, and waitresses. The stories are characterized by witty narration and word play, but their most famous feature is the surprise, ironic endings, as happens, for example, in his most famous story "The Gift of the Magi" (1906).

O. Henry's stories were quickly collected in volumes such as *Cabbages and Kings* (1904), *Heart of the West* (1907), and *The Voice of the City* (1908), and the best of them have remained popular. But the reaction against their plot-driven structures is exemplified in the stories of Sherwood Anderson, in which the narrative centers upon a moment of epiphany rather than a surprise ending. In some of the stories in his *Winesburg, Ohio* (1919), for example, Anderson rehearses in the opening paragraph plot details that might serve for a novel or half a dozen stories, before taking the story in the direction of what he describes in "Loneliness" as "the essence of things." In *Winesburg, Ohio*'s format of the short story cycle Anderson found a way to preserve the individual epiphanies of the stories while linking them through a series of recurring themes. The possibilities of the short story cycle had been explored earlier by Sarah Orne Jewett in *The Country of the Pointed Firs* (1896), a book unified by its Maine setting and the residents of the fictional fishing village of Dunnet Landing, and would be explored later by many writers, including Jean Toomer in *Cane* (1923), John Steinbeck in *The Pastures of Heaven* (1932), and Eudora Welty in *The Golden Apples* (1949).

Anderson wrote a number of free-standing stories, and some of the best known mirror Mark Twain in featuring a first-person narrator who does not fully understand the significance of the event he is recounting. Anderson continued writing for 20 years after *Winesburg, Ohio*, but his reputation declined alongside the achievements of two writers he helped early in their careers, William Faulkner and Ernest Hemingway. Faulkner's stories reflect some of the powerful themes of race, obsession, and guilt that characterize his novels, but Hemingway's achievement in this form was more influential. Hemingway's early themes owe something to Anderson's; his Nick Adams bears some relationship to *Winesburg*'s George Willard, but a more lasting influence was imagist poetry with its emphasis upon "direct treatment of the thing" and the avoidance of abstractions. In the 1920s Hemingway crafted stories deceptively straightforward in their detail and narratives, but at the same time suggestive of deep-rooted anxiety and unresolved tensions. Such anxiety is behind the disciplined routine of Nick Adams in "Big Two Hearted River" (1925), keeping memories suppressed, making coffee, putting up his tent, and preparing to fish, as well as the understated emotional crises between the young married couples in such stories as "Hills Like White Elephants" (1927), "Cat in the Rain," and "Out of Season" (both 1925). The short story form was also perfect to describe such characters as Francis Macomber of "The Short Happy Life of Francis Macomber" (1936), who overcome years of defeat and compromise to live fully, courageously, and dangerously, even if only for a few moments. Hemingway was also capable of a caustic look at the cost of his own self-indulgence as a successful writer and public personality in "The Snows of Kilimanjaro" (1936).

F. Scott Fitzgerald claimed that he only wrote his short stories for money, and that before selling them he removed any sentences that seemed more worthy of a future novel. But despite this self-disparagement, the stories are notable for many qualities, not least Fitzgerald's ability to capture a heightened sense of youthful pleasure that carries with it the knowledge that such pleasure is doomed to pass even while being most enjoyed. Some of his stories are quite ambitious, such as the often-anthologized "May Day" (1920), and some fuse realism with the kind of fairytale quality that Nick Carraway ascribes to Jay Gatsby's fabulous parties. In one of the best known of such stories, "The Diamond as Big as the Ritz" (1922), Fitzgerald's own ambiguous fascination for the rich plays out in such a fairytale setting. Other stories provide glimpses of themes worked out more fully in his novels. Dexter Green in "Winter Dreams" (1922) shares some qualities with Jay Gatsby, while "Crazy Sunday" (1932) is an early indication of Fitzgerald's interest in Irving Thalberg that would be more developed in *The Last Tycoon*'s Monroe Stahr (1941). Many of Fitzgerald's stories of the 1930s deal with loss of one kind or another, one of the finest being "Babylon Revisited" (1931), in which widower Charlie Wales is haunted by his past even as he tries to make a possible future for himself and the daughter that he had neglected. The late story "Three Hours Between Planes" (1941) ends with the narrator commenting that "the second half of life is a long process of getting rid of things," but, as in this story, the "long process" is not one over which the central character has much control in Fitzgerald's later fiction.

In the 1930s Thomas Wolfe published as short stories a number of extracts from the piles of manuscript that would later be incorporated, with the help of his editors, into his massive autobiographical novels. One view of Wolfe is that his true talents lay with the short story and novella, and that in feeling the need to publish novels he was something of a victim of the commercial pressures and literary expectations of his time. Certainly such stories as "The Lost Boy" (1937) and "Only the Dead Know Brooklyn" (1935) make excellent use of the short story's organizational possibilities, the former in its evocation of loss and the latter in its focus upon the particular speech and character of a place. In this same decade Eudora Welty worked as a publicist for the Works Progress Administration, where the photographs and interviews she produced traveling through Mississippi gave her material for a highly regarded first collection of stories, *A Curtain of Green* (1941). The collection includes two of her best-known stories, "A Worn Path" and "Why I Live at the P.O." Two African American writers who were supported by the Federal Writers Project, Zora Neale Hurston and Richard Wright, are better known for their novels, but produced short stories that are often still read and taught. Hurston's anthropological studies of African American culture shape the language and detail of such stories as "Sweat" (1926) and "The Gilded Six-Bits" (1933), while Wright's short stories, like his fiction, usually concern more charged relationships between blacks and whites. Wright's first book was a collection of stories, *Uncle Tom's Children* (1938), while his posthumously published *Eight Men* (1961), containing stories completed some years earlier, includes the often discussed "The Man Who Was Almost a Man" and "The Man Who Lived Underground."

Katherine Anne Porter was sufficiently well established by 1941 to write a warm and perceptive introduction to accompany Welty's *A Curtain of Green* when it appeared. Porter (who claimed to be a cousin of O. Henry) published her best-known stories in the 1930s in the volumes *Flowering Judas* (1930) and *Pale Horse, Pale Rider* (1939). She went on to publish her only novel, *Ship of Fools*, 20 years later in 1962, and a book on Sacco and Vanzetti in 1977. Fellow southerner Flannery O'Connor, however, stricken with the degenerative disease lupus, had a much shorter career. O'Connor published her first short story in 1946, her first novel in 1952, and her first collection of stories, *A Good Man Is Hard to Find*, in 1955. But when her second collection, *Everything That Rises Must Converge*, appeared 10 years later it was published posthumously. O'Connor's stories are rich in description, comic in their dialogue and narrative voice, and fiercely committed to her Catholic vision of the importance of the spiritual over the secular. Both

Porter's *Collected Stories* (1965) and O'Connor's *Complete Stories* (1971) won the National Book Award for Fiction when they appeared, in O'Connor's case the judges making a rare exception to the rule that the award go to a living writer.

The moral imperatives in O'Connor's stories are matched by the urgency of James Baldwin's in his shorter fiction. Baldwin famously rejected Richard Wright's more confrontational narratives of race to explore instead ways in which, through remembering, confronting, and taking responsibility for their shared history, America's black and white populations might replace conflict with understanding. His "Going to Meet the Man" (1965), a story set in the Civil Rights era, is sympathetic to the racist white deputy sheriff, seeing him as an uncomprehending victim of a racism instilled when his father took him to a brutal lynching as a child. In this story prejudice is culturally instilled, and in the often-anthologized "Sonny's Blues" (1957) the fear and distrust it produces is shown working to the detriment of both blacks and whites.

The quiet tensions of suburban life in the middle decades of the century are exposed in the short fictions of John Cheever and later of John Updike. Cheever's writing tends more toward parable and surrealism, well illustrated in his most famous story, "The Swimmer" (1964), in which a journey home via the swimming pools of an affluent suburb slowly turns into a nightmare of loss and alienation. Cheever was long associated with *The New Yorker*, as was Updike, whose writing is generally more realist. Some of Updike's stories include recurring characters, such as the Maple family, or recurring settings such as Olinger and Tarbox, the former reflecting the town where Updike spent his childhood, and the latter the Massachusetts town of Ipswich to which he moved in 1957. A more brooding atmosphere covers the Glass family stories of J. D. Salinger, another writer associated with the magazine in the same period.

The realist mode was countered, particularly in the 1960s, by the self-reflexive stories of such writers as John Barth, Donald Barthelme, and William Gass. *Lost in the Funhouse* (1968) is Barth's most popular collection; its 14 stories, with titles that include "Frame-tale," "Title," "Autobiography," and "Life-Story," frequently draw attention to the assumptions of more conventional fiction. Barthelme is another writer often associated with *The New Yorker*. His well-known story "The Balloon" (1966) illustrates some characteristics of his fiction. The narrator inflates a giant balloon over Manhattan for personal reasons: children enjoy it, adults try to interpret it, and the authorities try to destroy it. All reactions appear equally valid. Barthelme's stories, often sometimes very short, might include illustrations or apparently random verbal references as part of undermining a reader's conventional expectations of narrative. William Gass's stories exist even more fully in the world of verbal constructions. The narrator of the title story in his *In the Heart of the Heart of the Country* (1968) is not permitted the imaginative escape undertaken by Yeats in his famous poem "Sailing to Byzantium" that this story's opening alludes to: "So I have sailed the seas and come ... to B." Not Byzantium but "B"; for Gass language can delight as it constructs its own reality – but as it comes "to be" it reveals a world within, not beyond, itself.

This kind of self-reflexivity was rejected by Raymond Carver, whose stories look back to Hemingway's kind of understatement, but are set in a much more working-class world – although the short story writer Carver most reverenced was Chekhov. Plot, character, and dialogue return in Carver's stories, the characters often dealing with hardship or stress. Only 12 years separate his first major press publication, the collection *Will You Please Be Quiet, Please?*, in 1976 and his death in 1988, but in that time he published four important collections of stories, the later stories some-what more expansive in their narratives than the earlier, some of which had apparently been subject to editorial decisions not fully meeting Carver's approval.

Realism is also often the prevailing mode in the stories by Native American, Asian American, and Spanish American writers which began to find more mainstream publication in the last quarter of the century. Ethnic identity and generational conflict are often important themes, along with racism, gender issues, and the abuse of drugs and alcohol – but important too is the celebration of difference and diversity, of hopes as well as disappointments. Some of the more prominent minority writers who have turned to the short story to express such themes are Native Americans Sherman Alexie and Louise Erdrich, Mexican American Sandra Cisneros, Dominican American Julia Alvarez, and Asian American writers Amy Tan and Ha Jin. Contem-porary African American writers who have enriched the form include Maya Angelou, Jamaica Kincaid, and Edward P. Jones. Other voices have become part of the discussion of the genre as commentators raise questions about canon selection and about certain genres being relegated to the status of "popular" literature. For example, some writers of fantasy and science fiction who have begun to receive more scholarly attention as masters of the short story include H. P. Lovecraft, Ray Bradbury, Arthur C. Clarke, Philip K. Dick, and Isaac Asimov.

The contemporary work of American writers of shorter fiction can be sampled in a number of annual anthologies. The *Pushcart Prize* annual, published since 1976, includes prize-winning stories from small presses. The *Pen/O. Henry Prize* anthologies date back to 1919, while the *Best American*

Short Stories series dates back even further, to 1915. Since 1978 this latter series has been edited annually by a leading practitioner of the form, a list that is itself a valuable reading guide to the contemporary short story. The editors of individual volumes have included such figures as John Updike, Raymond Carver, Amy Tan, John Gardner, and Joyce Carol Oates.

Hollywood and American Fiction

In the years between the coming of sound to Hollywood films – *The Jazz Singer* premiered in 1927 – and the late 1940s, when the studios were forced to divest themselves of their cinema holdings and widespread television ownership began to have an impact upon cinema attendance, the Hollywood studios offered a potentially lucrative additional income for American fiction writers. Sometimes, as in the case of Ernest Hemingway, the riches came from selling screen rights to the studios but not actually laboring on the screenplays themselves. But other writers, such as F. Scott Fitzgerald and Nathanael West, needing an income that their fiction couldn't provide, relocated to Los Angeles and became studio contract writers. Still others, such as John Steinbeck, Dorothy Parker, William Faulkner, and Raymond Chandler, worked occasionally for the studios on their own material or that of other writers.

The attitude of the writers toward what Hollywood represented was often an ambivalent one. Faulkner famously requested permission to work at home when he found difficulty working in his studio-assigned office, a request which his studio bosses evidently understood to mean Beverley Hills but which, after his extended absence, they realized meant Mississippi. This story and its many versions may be apocryphal, but it indicates something of Faulkner's attitude. Raymond Chandler, writing in the *Atlantic Magazine* in 1945, declared himself "pretty thoroughly bored" after two years of working in Hollywood. Screenplays, he had discovered, could be changed, cut, discarded, or altered beyond recognition at the whim of a producer ("in between telephone calls to his blondes and his booze-companions") or a director, with neither producer nor director feeling obliged to consult the writer. It was not only American writers who were attracted to and ambivalent about working in Hollywood. Aldous Huxley, P. G. Wodehouse, Christopher Isherwood, George Bernard Shaw, and Berthold Brecht all had something to say, usually critical, about their dealings with the studios. Michael Millgate, in his *American Social Fiction* (1964), has claimed as "the essential theme of all serious Hollywood novels" that "reality is distorted, human values are inverted or destroyed, and commercialism is always and everywhere the enemy."

F. Scott Fitzgerald was fascinated by the romance of Hollywood but resentful of the studios' treatment of his work, while Nathanael West adopted a very practical attitude toward what was required and what would sell. As a result, although Fitzgerald arrived in Hollywood with a high-paying contract, by the time he died in 1940 he was struggling to find freelance work; while West, who was killed in an automobile accident the day after the heart attack that had killed Fitzgerald, was becoming a success after some years of working for minor studios. Between them they wrote two of the finest novels about Hollywood. Appropriately, Fitzgerald's unfinished *The Love of the Last Tycoon* (1941) is based upon the life of legendary producer Irving Thalberg, while West's *The Day of the Locust* (1939) is centered upon the industry's marginal figures: the bit players, would-be stars, and hangers-on, as well as the crowds who feed on the illusions that films and film stars provide. Despite this difference of perspective, Fitzgerald was an admirer of West's novel, noting in a letter to S. J. Perelman in June 1939 its "scenes of extraordinary power" and its "vividly drawn grotesques."

One of the central figures in *The Day of the Locust* is Tod Hackett, a young east coast scenic artist who thinks that he can remain coolly objective about the desperation and resulting fantasies that bring people to California, but who gets caught up in a riot that in effect takes him into one of his own paintings. The other central figure is Homer Simpson, one of the novel's lonely mid-western dreamers who drift out to the west coast and fall victim to their unsatisfied illusions. Trying to return to the Midwest, Homer gets caught in the same riot that engulfs Tod.

Violence is just below the surface in both characters, and in the larger world of unsatisfied desire, rootlessness, and commercially driven fantasy that they inhabit. The movie industry's contribution to this violence includes the selling of vicarious sex, turning into costume drama some of history's most important and bloodiest events, and churning out clichéd plots that promise happy endings and magnificent rewards – while the movie magazines display the stars' world of glamour and excitement. Dreams of stardom drive a mother to hope that her child will be noticed by a film producer and come to rival Shirley Temple. Would-be cowboys dress like the stars of movie westerns, and when they are not employed as extras spend their days outside Tuttles Trading Post, purveyor of "Genuine Relics of the Old West." Such fantasies exist alongside a range of churches offering various kinds of religious comfort, including the "Church of Christ, Physical," the "Tabernacle of the Third Coming," and the "Temple Moderne" – under whose roof is taught "Brain Breathing, the Secret of the Aztecs."

Those inside and surrounding the movie industry become caught up in their own commercial perversions. In *The Day of the Locust* a decorative feature of screenwriter Claude Estee's swimming pool is a submerged model of a horse with a prominent hammerhead. A party of studio employees and friends visits a brothel in order to watch a pornographic film, staging their own mock riot when the film breaks down. Would-be actress Faye Greener keeps the attention of a room full of men by a series of gestures copied from performances on the screen, while her provocative dancing is framed by scenes of violence. Faye's ex-vaudevillian father pretends to be ill in order to hawk his silver polish, and dies calling out to his daughter – who thinks that he is just giving another performance. The novel finally suggests that the characters' inability to tell performance from reality is a state of mind reinforced and commercialized by Hollywood movies, and exploited by entrepreneurial religions – both enterprises founded on the American fantasy of a golden West and its resulting historical and cultural rootlessness.

F. Scott Fitzgerald used his Hollywood experience as the basis for some of his short stories as well as his unfinished novel. "Crazy Sunday" (1932) is based upon an incident at a party given in 1931 by Norma Shearer, Irving Thalberg's wife, at which Fitzgerald had embarrassed himself. And while he was writing his novel Fitzgerald was selling a series of short stories to *Esquire* centered on the once hugely successful, now washed-up, screenwriter Pat Hobby, a wry, self-mocking, and somewhat exaggerated version of the author's own literary reputation and financial straits.

When *The Last Tycoon* was published posthumously in 1941 it was edited by Fitzgerald's Princeton classmate Edmund Wilson. In 1993 the manuscript was re-edited by Matthew Bruccoli and the novel retitled *The Love of the Last Tycoon*. Monroe Stahr, the tycoon of the title, is based on producer Thalberg, the "boy wonder" of Metro-Goldwyn-Mayer, who had died in 1936, the year before Fitzgerald's third and final move to Hollywood. However, Stahr also shares a number of qualities with the title character of *The Great Gatsby* (1925), and there are similarities between the narrators of the two novels as well. Both Nick Carraway in the earlier novel and Cecilia Brady in *The Love of the Last Tycoon* are only peripherally involved in the central narratives. Cecilia is part of the studio world as the daughter of executive Pat Brady – a character partially based on Thalberg's rival at MGM, Louis B. Mayer – but she does not work in the industry and is in college at the time the narrative takes place. She is in love with Stahr, and has a short romance with him, but she is not the figure whom Stahr loves. That figure, Kathleen Moore, is based in part on Sheilah Graham, the future Hollywood gossip columnist, with whom Fitzgerald was having a relationship at the time of his death. Kathleen bears a striking similarity to Stahr's dead first wife and thus the relationship is rooted in the past in a way that recalls Gatsby's love for Daisy Buchanan. Stahr, as narrator Cecilia writes, wants "passionately to repeat yet not recapitulate the past," a goal which has affinities with Gatsby's claim to Nick Carraway that if one paid enough money one could turn back time.

The Hollywood of Fitzgerald's novel, unlike West's, includes east coast financiers, distinguished visitors to the studio, successful and faded actors, and a company of actresses, producers, directors, cameramen, and writers. One of the book's most famous scenes has Stahr trying to overcome the prejudices of a successful novelist imported to work on a screenplay, but disdainful of film, by getting him to think in cinematic terms. A typical day of Stahr's that Cecilia records shows him acting as nursemaid and therapist to his writers and players; being ruthless where necessary; reviewing, guiding, and editing the films in production as he looks at the day's rushes; restoring reputations or refusing to; making decisions on scripts; and carefully watching those who might prove dangerous to his power – such as Cecilia's father. He can exercise this power, including the authority to tell the financiers that occasionally a film should lose money in order to bring prestige to the studio, because he is usually right – and he projects the impression that there are reasons behind his choices, even if sometimes those choices are quite arbitrary. This is the power that he risks when Kathleen comes into his life, and Fitzgerald's manuscript ends as Stahr's power begins to crumble.

Stahr is doomed as was the stricken Thalberg – but in a broader sense the Hollywood in which one patrician tycoon can be involved in every facet of a studio, with the result that his particular human stamp is on all its productions, is also passing. As Stahr falls, the corporation figures take over: managers solely concerned with their own status, their hedonistic pleasures, and the bottom line. The last major scene that Fitzgerald completed has Stahr come up against a representative of the writers. The writers' attempts at collective power clashes with Stahr's sense of himself as nurturing patron. But Stahr is on the losing side. In the 1930s the studios were having to confront the writers organizing to seek protection against the kind of treatment described by Chandler in his 1945 article.

When an author sold a novel to a studio during the years of the studio system, the resulting film might present characters, even a narrative, quite different from the source. Once purchased, a writer's novel was usually as much at the mercy of a producer as was the work of an individual studio writer. Rare was the directive issued by David Selznick for *Gone With the Wind* (1939) that only the author's dialogue was to be used. In part this is inevitable given the different media, and sometimes the different audiences – for with the high costs of moviemaking the producers wanted a chance to get their money back. The censorship standards for films were stricter than for fiction, too. Thus the political edge of Steinbeck's *The Grapes of Wrath* (1939) was softened for the 1940 film, and Howard Hawks's version (1944) of Hemingway's *To Have and Have Not* (1937) is quite different in many ways from its source novel. Hawks's *The Big Sleep* (1946), from Raymond Chandler's 1939 novel, turns from noir to romance halfway through the film, in order to accommodate audience anticipation built up by the on- and off-screen relationship between Humphrey Bogart and Lauren Bacall. When Nathanael West sold his novel *Miss Lonelyhearts* (1933) to 20th Century Pictures, the resulting film, *Advice to the Lovelorn* (1933), used only the concept of an advice column from the novel, and was for the most part a screwball comedy. Even after the studio era closed authors could find themselves marginalized. Vladimir Nabokov's experience with Stanley Kubrick on *Lolita* (1962) serves as an example. Nabokov wrote a screenplay for Kubrick, who then kept Nabokov away from the set through various ruses, had Nabokov sign an agreement not to comment publically on the resulting film, gave the novelist the screen credit, but substantially rewrote the screenplay himself.

The novels by West and Fitzgerald are generally considered the finest about Hollywood. But other novels often discussed include Budd Schulberg's *What Makes Sammy Run?* (1941) and *The Disenchanted* (1950), Norman Mailer's *The Deer Park* (1955), and Joan Didion's *Play It as It Lays* (1970). Schulberg saw the industry from the inside, since his father was an executive at Paramount Pictures in the 1920s and 1930s, and a producer for Columbia in the 1940s. *What Makes Sammy Run?* narrates the rise through the studio world of the ruthlessly ambitious but finally isolated Sammy Glick. *The Disenchanted* is an account of the last week in the life of Manley Halliday, famously successful in the 1920s and now a drunken shadow of his former self. The portrait is widely recognized as based upon the career and last months of Scott Fitzgerald, with whom Schulberg worked briefly on the screenplay of *Winter Carnival* (1939), called "Love on Ice" in the novel. Schulberg went on to win an Academy Award for his screenplay of *On the Waterfront* (1954). His memoir, *Moving Pictures: Memories of a Hollywood Prince* (1981), is a candid account of growing up in the Hollywood of the 1920s and 1930s. Mailer's novel was the result of an unsuccessful sojourn in Hollywood following the runaway success of his novel *The Naked and the Dead* (1948). Mailer's Desert D'Or stands in for Palm Springs in a novel that sets the behavior of its starlets, directors, and producers within the context of the ruthless political witch hunts of the era.

Joan Didion and her late husband John Gregory Dunne spent more than 20 years working in Hollywood, writing a number of screenplays together. *Play It as It Lays* was her second novel. Film historian David Thomson has described the book as set "early on in the last great age" of Hollywood, although it is as much about Las Vegas and the desert culture spread out between the casinos and the coast as it is about the movie capital itself. But its central characters are all involved one way or another in making films. Set in the 1960s, the novel's spare prose and fragmented chapters record the disintegration of Maria, a successful model and would-be actress who is married to famous director Carter Lang. In her despair Maria is pulled back to memories of her childhood in a desert town that no longer exists, and is surrounded by film people who simultaneously try to help her, exploit her, and contribute to her despair – a despair that, given the world surrounding her, the novel suggests may be the only honest, if terrifying, response that she could have.

Women and Twentieth-Century American Fiction

As in many other fields of artistic endeavor, women have historically been denied many of the opportunities for a writing career that were available to men, in large part because of social and gender role expectations that saw the duties of women as primarily housekeeping, child rearing, cooking, and looking decorous. The exact priority of these expectations varied with a woman's particular economic class. Limited educational opportunities, limited travel possibilities, and sexual double standards, along with traditional expectations by publishers and readers of what a women writer should write about, have also restricted the experiences and subject matter available to women writers in the past. For a number of commentators, such restrictions were particularly pervasive in the United States because some of the underlying assumptions of a pioneer and colonial culture remained fundamentally unchanged as the nation moved into the early twentieth century.

Of course, there have been many women writers who overcame such limitations to a greater or lesser degree, helped perhaps by enlightened parents, a private income, patronage, commercial success, or just by a determined independence. Karen L. Kilcup's *Nineteenth Century American Women Writers: An Anthology* (1997) contains selections from almost 70 authors, including such figures as Louisa May Alcott, Kate Chopin, Margaret Fuller, Charlotte Perkins Gilman, Sara Orne Jewett, and Harriet Beecher Stowe. Elaine Showalter's *A Jury of her Peers: American Women Writers from Anne Bradstreet to Annie Proulx* (2009) devotes almost half of its extensive historical survey to pre-twentieth-century writing. Nevertheless, a number of the less well-known writers, and even some of those better

The Twentieth-Century American Fiction Handbook   By Christopher MacGowan
© 2011 Christopher MacGowan

known, had to be recovered in the extensive re-evaluation of canon formation and literary history that took place beginning in the 1970s. Showalter points out the almost exclusively male-dominated editorial boards behind the various histories of American literature which have appeared since the first in 1897. For example, the four editors of *The Cambridge History of American Literature* (1917) were male, and the *Literary History of the United States* (1948), considered a definitive account in its time, listed 54 male editors and one woman.

Some of the best-selling American popular novels of the century were written by women, but they usually delivered, in a very professional way, the material expected of a novel by a woman. Such material might include romance, history, sensitive heroines, or heroines exhibiting an energetic – but not too disruptive – independence, and perhaps some suggestion of decorous or historical – sometimes adulterous – sexual activity. Examples include Kate Douglas Wiggin's *Rebecca of Sunnybrook Farm* (1903), Eleanor H. Porter's *Pollyanna* (1913), Margaret Mitchell's *Gone With the Wind* (1936), Kathleen Winsor's *Forever Amber* (1944), and *Peyton Place* (1956) by Grace Metalious.

Charlotte Perkins Gilman had called for more complex narratives and characterizations of women in American fiction as early as 1911 in her *The Man-Made World*. When Kate Chopin published such a novel in 1899 the critical response effectively ended her writing career. Chopin was a well-regarded, local-color writer of short stories when she published *The Awakening*, which tells the story of a passionate woman rebelling against the constraints of her Creole society. The novel was condemned for what was seen as the indulgent sensuality of its heroine, and would not be rediscovered until the 1960s. Gilman herself had a writing career that extended well into the twentieth century, publishing both fiction and non-fiction, and was a prominent advocate of women's rights and social reform. Although the fiction for which she is best known, the short story "The Yellow Wallpaper," appeared in 1892, two utopian novels written more than 20 years later, *Herland* (1915) and *With Her in Ourland* (1916), have recently begun to receive attention. Women are completely self-sufficient in the all-female world of *Herland*, where socially constructed gender stereotypes of men and women do not exist. The 1916 sequel recounts the experiences of one of the inhabitants, Ellador, who married and left Herland with her husband, Vandyke Jennings, one of the three explorers who had come across the all-female world. Ellador's travels outside Herland include witnessing World War I, and observing with puzzlement the socially determined gender roles of the United States. Ellen Glasgow is another writer who began publishing in the nineteenth century and went on to a career lasting well into the twentieth.

Virginia is often the setting for her novels. The first, *The Descendant* (1897), was published anonymously. Glasgow gained critical attention in the mid-1920s with *Barren Ground* (1925), and won a Pulitzer Prize for her last novel, *In This Our Life* (1941).

Two writers whose work remained much more visible than that of Gilman and Chopin are Edith Wharton and Willa Cather. Wharton, despite a more determinist strain in her work than in that of her friend and contemporary Henry James, was sometimes seen as a writer in his shadow. Both James and Wharton explore in many of their novels the particularly vulnerable social position of American women; women with wealth who are potential victims of exploitation – as often in James – or women with too little money to be safely independent, as is the case with Lily Bart in Wharton's *The House of Mirth* (1905). Wharton's independence led her to resist being classified as a "woman writer," and there was the same resistance in Cather, who had a successful editorial and journalistic career in addition to the success of her fiction. She was sometimes discussed as a local colorist, a term – as with the judgments of Chopin – intended to suggest limitation of range, although since her death the complex thematic function of landscape in her novels is more fully recognized. The energetic, independent female characters of her novels are often obliged to make compromises with circumstances, in different novels having a greater or lesser degree of choice. Her fiction also at times takes up the issue of how men see women. *My Ántonia* (1918) arguably takes up such a theme, and it is the central subject of *A Lost Lady* (1923).

The 1920s brought a less restrictive sexual and social climate for many younger women, although the image and character of a "flapper" inevitably became another stereotype. The interest in African American writing that helped fuel the Harlem Renaissance brought opportunities to a number of women of black and mixed-race heritage, most prominently Zora Neale Hurston, Nella Larsen, and Jessie Fauset. Women were underrepresented in Alain Locke's important anthology *The New Negro* (1925), although the contents included a story by Hurston and an essay by Fauset. In a contribution on the problems faced by black women, titled "The Task of Negro Womanhood," Elise Johnson McDougald observed: "In the fields of literature and art, the Negro Woman's culture has once more begun to flower ... There is every prospect that the Negro woman will enrich American literature and art with stylistic portrayal of her experience and her problems." That prospect did show promise in the 1920s, but it would be some decades before it was more fully realized.

Out of the expatriate writing in Paris in the 1920s and 1930s came the genre and language experiments of Gertrude Stein, and the fiction of Djuna Barnes and Kay Boyle. Aside from her writing, Stein was also important for being at the center of a network of influential writers, artists, and critics. In that role she matched the important influence of expatriate editors Margaret Anderson and Jane Heap in their radical magazine *The Little Review*, Lola Ridge in *Others* and *Broom*, Ethel Moorhead in *This Quarter*, and – in Chicago – Harriet Monroe in *Poetry*.

Less well known than Barnes, Stein and Boyle are the radical women among the overwhelmingly male authors supported by the Federal Writers Project in the 1930s. Once a well-known figure, Josephine Herbst's Trexler family trilogy has recently begun to receive renewed attention, along with Herbst's other fiction and non-fiction. The three novels, *Pity Is Not Enough* (1933), *The Executioner Waits* (1934), and *Rope of Gold* (1939), follow three generations of the Trexler family from the Civil War through to the Depression. Meridel Le Sueur was well established for her proletarian short stories, essays, and radical journalism in the 1920s but could not find a publisher for her novel *The Girl*, written in the 1930s, until the revival of interest in her work in the 1970s. The novel, which describes the experiences of a farm girl who moves to the city of St. Paul and gets caught up in a world of political activism, crime, speakeasies, and prostitution, eventually appeared in 1978. Anzia Yezierska came to the United States from Eastern Europe with her family in 1915 and lived with them among New York's Lower East Side tenements. She had considerable success with stories and novels of immigrant experience in the 1920s, with the collections *Hungry Hearts* (1920) and *Children of Loneliness* (1923), and the novels *Salome of the Tenements* (1923), *Bread Givers* (1925), and *Arrogant Beggar* (1927). A number of her stories were filmed; she worked for a short period as a screenwriter, and reportedly turned down a lucrative contract from Samuel Goldwyn to remain in Hollywood. But following the publication of her novel *All I Could Never Be* in 1932, Yezierska had trouble finding a publisher for her fiction, although she continued to write articles, essays, and book reviews. She did not publish her next, and last, book for almost 20 years, the autobiographical *Red Ribbon on a White Horse* (1950). Yezierska's career suffered when stories of immigrant life went out of fashion, but the career of Nebraska-born Tillie Olsen was truncated by her own domestic circumstances. Olsen describes in *Silences* (1978) how the circumstances of class, gender, and race, particularly as they affect the lives of women, can limit the time to write and affect the reception of work that, despite the handicaps, does manage to get written and published. Olsen's own writing silence came after the birth of her children, and followed the significant early success that she experienced in the 1930s with her short stories, a success that brought her a contract for a novel from Random House. For the rest of her life Olsen continued the political activism that she had begun in her late teens, but she could not return to serious writing until her youngest child began school in 1953. When her first book, *Tell Me a Riddle*, a collection of short stories, appeared in 1961, the title story won the prestigious O. Henry Award. She published *Yonnondio*, the novel she had abandoned in the 1930s, in 1974. Once Olsen's career restarted she taught as a visiting writer at various institutions, including Amherst College, Stanford University, MIT, and Kenyon College, and was the recipient of a number of prestigious fellowships.

In contrast to these interrupted careers, Pearl S. Buck in 1938 became the first American woman writer to win the Nobel Prize in Literature. Her fiction and non-fiction writing on China, where she had been raised by her missionary parents and lived until her early forties, was very popular, particularly the first novel of her *House of Earth* trilogy (1931), which won a Pulitzer Prize. Buck was a prolific writer, publishing a novel almost every year until her death, in addition to collections of short stories and books of non-fiction. In order to escape the expectations raised by the fame of her writing on China, she published a few of her novels under the pseudonym John Sedges. Despite this extensive output, over 70 books by one count, she is probably better known since her death – aside from the Nobel achievement – for the legacy of her international work promoting the adoption of orphaned or abandoned interracial children.

Katherine Anne Porter, along with Carson McCullers, Flannery O'Connor, and Eudora Welty, is a writer often associated with the Southern Gothic tradition, a genre that includes among its features a reaction against stereotypes of the antebellum South, and characters who are exaggerated, grotesque, or deeply disturbed – often by elements associated with southern culture. The generalization has its value, but has been itself accused of being an externally imposed stereotype. Flannery O'Connor famously remarked, "I have found that anything that comes out of the South is going to be called grotesque by the northern reader, unless it is grotesque, in which case it is going to be called realistic."

Texas-born Porter spent time in the early 1920s in Mexico, and some of her earliest stories stem from her time there and her interest in the country's revolutionary politics. Her reputation rests mainly on three volumes of finely crafted short stories, *Flowering Judas* (1930, expanded 1935), *Pale Horse, Pale Rider* (1939), and *The Leaning Tower and Other Stories* (1944), which when published in 1965 (with four additional stories) as *Collected Stories* won both a Pulitzer Prize and a National Book Award. The "pale rider" of the 1939 volume is a reference to the many deaths caused by the devastating 1918 influenza outbreak, an epidemic from which Porter herself nearly died while living in Denver. Porter spent many years working and reworking her one novel, *Ship of Fools* (1962), which was a commercial success but viewed by some critics as a somewhat overly schematic allegory. The novel is set in 1931 aboard the German passenger ship *Vera* as it returns to Germany from Mexico with passengers from various nationalities. Porter wrote little after the appearance of the novel, although well into her eighties she published *The Never-Ending Wrong* (1977), an account of the Sacco and Vanzetti trial held 50 years earlier.

Carson McCullers, born in Columbus, Georgia, studied creative writing in New York at both Columbia and New York Universities. Her four major novels were all published within a period of six years, during which time she was involved in a tempestuous relationship, marrying, divorcing, and remarrying James Reeves McCullers Jr. – who eventually killed himself in Paris in 1953, having earlier tried to talk the novelist into a suicide pact. Something of the complications in the marriage is behind the love triangle in her third novel, *The Ballad of the Sad Café* (1943). Her first novel, *The Heart Is a Lonely Hunter* (1940), was received with much more universal approval than her second, *Reflections in a Golden Eye* (1941), with its more daring themes of infidelity, voyeurism, and homosexuality. Racial and sexual identity and adolescent alienation are central issues in *The Member of the Wedding* (1946). At the suggestion of her friend Tennessee Williams, McCullers adapted the novel for the stage and the resulting prize-winning play had a very successful run on Broadway from 1950 to 1951. Stanley Kramer produced the successful film versions of both *The Member of the Wedding* (1952) and Porter's *Ship of Fools* (1965), and directed the latter.

McCullers and O'Connor both suffered from debilitating health problems. When McCullers died at age 50, a recent biography notes, she had been an invalid for over 25 years. O'Connor died even younger, and unlike McCullers was still at the height of her powers. She was diagnosed with lupus at 26, the year before her first novel, *Wise Blood* (1952), was published, and died 13 years later having published a collection of stories, *A Good Man Is Hard to Find* (1955), and a second novel, *The Violent Bear It Away* (1960). A posthumous collection, *Everything That Rises Must Converge* (1965), appeared the year after she died. O'Connor's fiction is characterized by narratives that follow through ruthlessly on the logic of her Catholicism: that the fate of the body is of trivial importance compared to the fate of the soul and the necessity to welcome grace. Her characters will sometimes go to extreme lengths to deny their recognition of that truth, while others are so fixed upon earthly values, and upon substituting well-worn clichés for serious thought, that only violence and the immediate threat of oblivion can challenge their stubbornness.

Eudora Welty, in contrast to the shortened lives of McCullers and O'Connor, lived to see her ninety-second birthday. In the introduction to her *Collected Stories* (1980) she wrote of the early encouragement that she received from Katherine Anne Porter, and of the support from editors at *The Southern Review*, *The Atlantic Monthly*, and *Harper's Bazaar* who accepted her first short stories, opening the way for publication of her first book, the collection *A Curtain of Green* (1941). Porter wrote a warm introduction, and 31 years later would present Welty with the Gold Medal for Fiction from the National Institute of Arts and Letters. Welty published her first novel, *The Robber Bridegroom*, in 1942, and another collection of stories, *The Wide Net and Other Stories*, the following year. While living in New York in 1944–1945 and writing for the *New York Times Book Review*, she wrote the reviews that dealt with war topics under the pseudonym "Michael Ravenna," since one of the editors felt that a southern woman writer would not be expected to know much about the subject. According to an article in the *Book Review* 30 years later, "Michael Ravenna's sage judgments came to be quoted prominently in publishers' ads and invitations from radio networks for Mr. Ravenna to appear on their programs had to be politely declined on grounds that he had been called away to the battlefronts."

In her productive career Welty went on to publish two further collections of stories, and four more novels. The novels include *Delta Wedding* (1946), which some consider her finest, and *The Optimist's Daughter* (1972). In the latter, which won Welty a Pulitzer Prize, she displays the humor, the ear for regional speech, and the juxtaposition of deeply sensitive characters with those more boorish and self-centered that is a feature of much of her fiction. Welty was awarded the highest honors that the nation bestows upon its artists, the Presidential Medal of Freedom in 1981, and the National Medal of the Arts in 1986. In 1984 Welty brought Harvard University Press its first bestseller with *One Writer's Beginnings*, a version of the Massey Lectures that she had delivered at the university the year before, and in 1998 she became the first living author to be included in the Library of America series.

Gothic elements are even more central to the work of Shirley Jackson, born in California but living in Vermont in the most productive years of her career, the 1950s and early 1960s. She had become famous for a story since much anthologized, "The Lottery," published in *The New Yorker* in 1948 and producing more mail from readers than the magazine had ever received. Its bleak vision of the dark side of humanity continued to be part of her later novels and stories. Her last two novels have been particularly influential on a number of contemporary gothic writers, *The Haunting of Hill House* (1959) and *We Have Always Lived in the Castle* (1962). In the latter the unreliable narrator is possibly a mass murderer. The genre has more recently been explored by Joyce Carol Oates in such novels as *Bellefleur* (1980), *A Bloodsmoor Romance* (1982), and *Mysteries of Winterthurn* (1984). Oates makes some distinctions between the "grotesque" and "horror" in "Reflections on the Grotesque," an Afterword to her collection *Haunted: Tales of the Grotesque* (1994), and she surveys the history of the genre in the introduction to her selections for the anthology *American Gothic Tales* (1996). Appropriately, Oates edited and introduced the Library of America volume of Jackson's *Novels and Stories* (2010).

African American writing in the mid-century was largely dominated by male writers, with Richard Wright, Ralph Ellison, James Baldwin, and Langston Hughes particularly prominent. With the exception of the latter, women in their male-centered fictions were usually marginal, often victims. Although Wright was dismissive of Zora Neale Hurston's work, he was particularly helpful to poet Gwendolyn Brooks early in her career. In Brooks's one novel, *Maud Martha* (1953), the title character moves from childhood to the life of a middle-aged housewife and mother, always having to deal with the anxieties of the daily, quiet, undramatic incidents of racism that stem from her color. The novel is all the more powerful, and angry, for its understatement. Brooks's novel was the forerunner of the remarkable array of fiction by African American women in the decades to come, including works by Maya Angelou, Alice Walker, Gloria Naylor, and Toni Morrison – whose Nobel Prize in 1993 was the second awarded to an American woman writer. In addition, the century's store of writing by African American women was enriched by the rediscovery of a number of forgotten writers, including Hurston and Larsen from the Harlem Renaissance.

The emergence of these African American voices coincided with the publication in the 1970s of a number of groundbreaking feminist studies that insisted upon new ways of looking at writing by and about American women. These works not only helped prepare the way for the African American novelists, but also other women minority writers whose voices would move from the margins to the mainstream in the 1970s and later. Any list of these groundbreaking feminist studies would include Betty Friedan's *The Feminine Mystique* (1963), Kate Millett's *Sexual Politics* (1970), Patricia Meyer Spacks's *The Female Imagination* (1975), Ellen Moers's *A Literature of Their Own* (1977), Sandra M. Gilbert and Susan Gubar's *The Madwoman in the Attic* (1979), and their *Norton Anthology of Literature by Women: The Tradition in English* (1985). Important, too, were two books which expanded the concept of genre, Erica Jong's *Fear of Flying* (1973) and Maxine Hong Kingston's *The Woman Warrior* (1976).

Some of the genres and subjects formerly deemed most masculine have recently been enriched by contributions from women writers. Annie Proulx moved from Vermont to Wyoming in the mid-1990s and has contributed to the contemporary western with her collections of Wyoming stories, *Close*

Range (1999), *Bad Dirt* (2004), and *Fine Just the Way It Is* (2008), and her novel *That Old Ace in the Hole* (2002). Women have been writing science fiction since Mary Shelley's *Frankenstein* (1818), but Pamela Sargent describes the difficulty women have had in gaining recognition in the genre in the introduction to her two-volume anthology *Women of Wonder* (1995). The selections cover 50 years of science fiction by women, from the 1940s to the 1990s. Ursula K. Le Guin is one of the most honored of contemporary science fiction writers, having first come to prominence with her novel *The Left Hand of Darkness* (1969). Octavia Butler, who died in 2006, is probably the most prominent of the few African American women writers to write science fiction, and used the imaginative possibilities of the genre to powerful effect. In *Kindred* (1979), for example, a young African American woman living in contemporary California is taken back in time to antebellum eastern Maryland, where she has to survive as a slave while engineering the events that will ensure her existence in the following century. And Joyce Carol Oates published a series of essays titled *On Boxing* (1987, expanded 1995, 2006) that has earned the respect of fighters and ringside commentators alike. Clearly, by the end of the century the old assumptions about the language, subjects, narratives, characters, and genres deemed appropriate for a woman writer had become part of literary history.

Guide to Further Reading

Thematic and Historical Studies Ranging across Periods

Phillip Barrish, *American Literary Realism, Critical Theory, and Intellectual Prestige, 1880–1995* (Cambridge, 2001). Discusses the cultural prestige associated with turn-of-the-century literary realism and offers an extended reading of *The Wings of the Dove*.

Bert Bender, *Evolution and "the Sex Problem": American Narratives During the Eclipse of Darwinism* (Kent, OH, 2004). Looks at a number of writers' treatment of sexuality in the context of evolutionary thought, including Dreiser, Stein, Cather, Anderson, and Fitzgerald.

Bruce L. Chipman, *Into America's Dream-Dump: A Postmodern Study of the Hollywood Novel* (Lanham, MD, 1999). Discusses Hollywood novels in terms of the century's move from utopian promise to spiritual deprivation. Gives particular attention to Fitzgerald, West, Schulberg, Mailer, and Didion.

Thomas J. Ferraro, *Ethnic Passages: Literary Immigrants in Twentieth-Century America* (Chicago, 1993). Ferraro's discussion of ethnic heritage in five "up-from-the-ghetto" narratives focuses on five writers, including Henry Miller and Maxine Hong Kingston.

James Goodwin, *Modern American Grotesque: Literature and Photography* (Columbus, OH, 2009). Sees the grotesque as a central visual and literary tradition in the century's fiction and photography. With chapters on Anderson, West, and O'Connor.

Robert Jackson, *Seeking the Region in American Literature and Culture: Modernity, Dissidence, Innovation* (Baton Rouge, 2005). Argues that while regionalism is often associated with provinciality and minor genres, it is central to the issues in work by Twain, Faulkner, O'Connor, and Morrison.

J. Gerald Kennedy, ed., *Modern Short Story Sequences: Composite Fictions and Fictive Communities* (New York, 1995). Discusses definitions of the genre, and includes useful essays on James, Hemingway, Wright, Faulkner, Welty, Salinger, Updike, and Erdrich.

Andrew Levy, *The Culture and Commerce of the American Short Story* (New York, 1993). Discusses the politics, markets, and writers behind the history of the American short story back to Poe. Includes a chapter on Wharton.

Thomas J. Lyon, ed., *Updating the Literary West* (Fort Worth, TX, 1997). A comprehensive set of essays focusing mainly on the 1980s and 1990s, updating an earlier edition. Includes essays on Carver, Didion, Cormac McCarthy, and Silko.

Susan Garland Mann, *The Short Story Cycle: A Genre Companion and Reference Guide* (New York, 2009). A useful reference book, with sections on *Winesburg, Ohio, In Our Time*, and Updike's Maples stories.

David Minter, *A Cultural History of the American Novel: Henry James to William Faulkner* (Cambridge, 1994). A well-argued synthesis of literary and cultural history from the 1880s to the early 1940s from a leading Faulkner scholar.

Chip Rhodes, *Politics, Desire, and the Hollywood Novel* (Iowa City, 2008). Contrasts the Hollywood novel of the 1930s and 1940s studio era with novels reflecting the deregulated film industry of the 1960s. Includes essays on West, Chandler, and Didion.

Susan L. Roberson, ed., *Women, America, and Movement: Narratives of Relocation* (Columbia, MO, 1998). Essays that explore narratives of displacement in women's lives and writing, including Cisneros, Erdrich, Hurston, and Stein.

Elaine Showalter, *Sister's Choice: Tradition and Change in American Women's Writing* (Oxford, 1991). Argues against monolithic national and gender stereotypes; includes an extended discussion of *The House of Mirth*.

Elaine Showalter, *A Jury of Her Peers* (New York, 2009). A wide-ranging history of writing by women from a major scholar. Half of its more than 500 pages cover the twentieth century.

Studies of Fiction in the First Two Decades of the Century

Elizabeth Ammons, *Conflicting Stories: American Women Writers at the Turn into the Twentieth Century* (New York, 1991). Explores the relationship of a number of women writers from 1890 to 1930 in terms of shared cultural and formal interests. The 17 writers discussed include Stein, Cather, and Wharton.

Donna M. Campbell, *Resisting Regionalism: Gender and Naturalism in American Fiction, 1885–1915* (Athens, OH, 1997). Argues the gendered nature of the conflict between 1890s local color writing and the rise of naturalism.

Susan V. Donaldson, *Competing Voices: The American Novel, 1865–1914* (New York, 1998). A clear, balanced account focused on the issues of realism, local color, race, the "New Woman," and naturalism.

Amy Kaplan, *The Social Construction of American Realism* (Chicago, 1988). Explores concepts of realism within the context of social change, class, and mass culture. Includes extended discussions of *The House of Mirth and Sister Carrie*.

Elsa Nettels, *Language and Gender in American Fiction: Howells, James, Wharton, and Cather* (Charlottesville, VA, 1997). Looks at the gendered language of the four novelists as it is contextualized by the articles and essays in the magazines that published their work. A final chapter looks at utopian fiction.

Studies Focused upon Modernism, the 1920s Expatriates, or the 1930s

Shari Benstock, *Women of the Left Bank: Paris 1900–1940* (Austin, 1986). Gertrude Stein and Djuna Barnes are among the women whose contributions to expatriate Paris are documented.

Janet Galligani Casey, ed., *The Novel and the American Left: Critical Essays on Depression-Era Fiction* (Iowa City, 2004). Essays that look at the aesthetic aims as well as the politics of several 1930s writers, including Josephine Herbst and Tillie Olsen.

David Fine, *Los Angeles in Fiction: A Collection of Essays,* revised edition (Albuquerque, 1995). Includes useful essays on West and Chandler.

Barbara Foley, *Radical Representations: Politics and Form in U.S. Proletarian Fiction, 1929–1941* (Durham, NC, 1993). Looks at four kinds of proletarian novel: the Fictional Autobiography, the Bildungsroman Novel, the Social Novel, and the Collective Novel.

J. Gerald Kennedy, *Imagining Paris: Exile, Writing, and American Identity* (New Haven, 1993). Offers fresh perspectives on Stein, Hemingway, Miller, Fitzgerald, and Barnes.

Walter Benn Michaels, *Our America: Nativism, Modernism, and Pluralism* (Durham, NC, 1995). Sees the issues of race and collective identity usually associated with later multicultural debates as a central issue in modernist writing, with extended discussion of Faulkner, Cather, and Hurston.

Craig Monk, *Writing the Lost Generation: Expatriate Autobiography and American Modernism* (Iowa City, 2008). Looks at autobiographies of some of the 1920s expatriates, including Hemingway, Stein, and some lesser-known figures.

Michael North, *Camera Works: Photography and the Twentieth Century Word* (New York, 2005). Argues that the impact of photography and film bring a new kind of "sensory enjoyment" to modern fiction. Includes chapters on Fitzgerald, Dos Passos, and Hemingway.

Monty Noam Penkower, *The Federal Writers' Project: A Study in Government Patronage of the Arts* (Urbana, 1977). A well-researched history, particularly useful on the State Guides.

Paula Rabinowitz, *Labor and Desire: Women's Revolutionary Fiction in Depression America* (Chapel Hill, 1991). A wide-ranging study that includes extended discussion of Herbst, Olsen, and Le Sueur among others.

Walter B. Rideout, *The Radical Novel in the United States, 1900–1954* (New York, 1992). An early and still essential study of 1930s fiction and its contexts. First published in 1956, the 1992 edition has a new preface by the author.

Nora Ruth Roberts, *Three Radical Women Writers: Class and Gender in Meridel Le Sueur, Tillie Olsen, and Josephine Herbst* (New York, 1996). Extensive treatment of the three writers, with particular attention to their careers in the 1930s.

John Parris Springer, *Hollywood Fictions: The Dream factory in American Popular Literature* (Norman, OK, 2000). Versions of Hollywood in popular literature of the 1920s and 1930s.

Michael Szalay, *New Deal Modernism: American Literature and the Invention of the Welfare State* (Durham, NC, 2000). Examines the relationship of literature and the state in light of New Deal reforms in a discussion that includes work by Wright, Steinbeck, Hemingway, and Stein.

David A. Taylor, *Soul of a People: The WPA Writers' Project Uncovers Depression America* (Hoboken, NJ, 2009). Highly readable account that accompanied the television documentary with the same title.

Catherine Turner, *Marketing Modernism between the Two World Wars* (Amherst, 2003). A well-researched, highly readable account of the major publishers of modernist work in the period: Huebsch, Knopf, Harcourt, and Scribner's.

Studies Focused upon Post–World War II Fiction

Carl Abbott, *Frontiers Past and Future: Science Fiction and the American West* (Lawrence, KS, 2006). Argues that visions of the future in contemporary American science fiction are often based on themes in earlier novels of the western frontier. Includes discussion of William Gibson, Ursula K. Le Guin, and Octavia Butler.

David Brauner, *Post-War Jewish Fiction: Ambivalence, Self-Explanation, and Trans-Atlantic Connections* (New York, 2001). Sees a common sensibility in post-war British and American Jewish writers that includes a desire to explain themselves and their heritage. Extended discussions of Bellow and Roth.

Abigail Cheever, *Real Phonies: Cultures of Authenticity in Post-World War II America* (Athens, GA, 2010). Using the concept of the "authentic self," looks at the treatment of identity, alienation, and social norms in fiction from the 1950s to the 1990s. Discussion includes Salinger and Walker Percy.

Marc Chénetier, trans. Elizabeth A. Houlding, *Beyond Suspicion: New American Fiction since 1960* (Philadelphia, 1996). One of the essential surveys. First published in France in 1989.

Marcel Cornis-Pope, *Narrative Innovation and Cultural Rewriting in the Cold War and After* (New York, 2001). Sees innovative fiction as responding to and redefining some of the "polarized ideologies of the postwar period." Gives particular attention to Robert Coover, Pynchon, and Morrison.

Morris Dickstein, *Leopards in the Temple: The Transformation of American Fiction, 1945–1970* (Harvard, 2002). Argues that innovative post-war American fiction was sustained largely by outsiders to mainstream culture. Discussion includes Roth, Salinger, Kerouac, and Mailer.

Jeremy Green, *Late Postmodernism: American Fiction at the Millennium* (New York, 2005). Green sees the threat to literature posed by the new media producing a response by various contemporary writers, including Roth and DeLillo.

Kathryn Hume, *American Dream, American Nightmare: Fiction since 1960* (Champaign, 2000). Reads much contemporary American fiction as exhibiting disillusionment and "spiritual recoil."

Suzanne W. Jones, *Race Mixing: Southern Fiction since the Sixties* (Baltimore, 2004). An overview of contemporary southern fiction and its treatment of integration, racial violence, and racial identity.

Frederick R. Karl, *American Fictions, 1940–1980: A Comprehensive History and Critical Evaluation* (New York, 1983). Lives up to its title, ambitious and comprehensive in scope.

Catherine Morley, *The Quest for Epic in Contemporary American Fiction: John Updike, Philip Roth and Don DeLillo* (New York, 2009). Sees the three authors as influenced by Joyce in their attempts to write contemporary epic.

James Nagel, *The Contemporary American Short-Story Cycle: The Ethnic Resonance of Genre* (Baton Rouge, 2001). Reads *The Joy Luck Club, The House on Mango Street,* and Erdrich's *Love Medicine* as short story cycles, and the genre as particularly suited to themes of ethnic assimilation.

Patrick O'Donnell, *The American Novel Now: Reading Contemporary American Fiction since 1980* (Chichester, UK, 2010). A useful guide to some major strands of contemporary fiction, looking at such issues as realism, linguistic experiment, ethnicity, gender, and history.

Thomas Hill Schaub, *American Fiction in the Cold War* (Madison, WI, 1991). Discusses Ellison, O'Connor, Mailer, and Barth in terms of what Schaub terms a post-war "discourse of revisionist liberalism."

Tony Tanner, *City of Words: American Fiction 1950–1970* (New York, 1971). Important essays on more than a dozen major novelists.

Studies Focused upon African American, Native American, and Ethnic Writers

Houston Baker, Jr., *Modernism and the Harlem Renaissance* (Chicago, 1987). Argues that African American writers, artists, and musicians produced work just as modern on its own terms as the figures usually associated with high modernism such as Eliot, Pound, and Joyce.

Bernard W. Bell, *The Contemporary African American Novel: Its Folk Roots and Modern Literary Branches* (Amherst, 2004). An updating and expansion of the author's *The Afro-American Novel and Its Tradition* (1987). Begins with mid-nineteenth-century novels, but gives most space to 1983–2001.

Mary Pat Brady, *Extinct Lands, Temporal Geographies, Chicana Literature and the Urgency of Space* (Durham, NC, 2002). Uses the concept of a culture's spatial transformations and the relationship to language to read various Chicana writers, including Cisneros.

James W. Coleman, *Faithful Vision: Treatments of the Sacred, Spiritual and Supernatural in Twentieth-Century African American Fiction* (Baton Rouge, 2006). Argues the importance of a combined Judeo-Christian and West African voodoo/hoodoo spiritual tradition in African American novels. Looks mainly at novels since 1950, including *The Color Purple* and *Beloved*.

Martha J. Cutter, *Lost and Found in Translation: Contemporary Ethnic American Writing and the Politics of Language Diversity* (Chapel Hill, 2005). In arguing that America's post-modern identity lies in its diverse languages, dialects, and cultures, looks at a range of writers including Alexie, Morrison, and Kingston.

Henry Louis Gates, Jr., *The Signifying Monkey: A Theory of African American Literary Criticism* (New York, 1988). A major study that identifies important vernacular traditions in African American writing; includes discussion of novels by Hurston, Ellison, and Alice Walker.

George Hutchinson, *The Harlem Renaissance in Black and White* (Cambridge, 1995). An influential study that argues for the importance of an interracial context in discussions of the Harlem Renaissance.

Gene Andrew Jarrett, *Deans and Truants: Race and Realism in African American Literature* (Philadelphia, 2007). Looks at changing definitions of African American literature from the turn of the century to the late 1960s. The Deans are Howells, Locke, Wright, and Amiri Baraka, and the Truants include Toni Morrison.

Elaine H. Kim, *Asian American Literature: An Introduction to the Writings and Their Social Context* (Philadelphia, 1982). A pioneering study that covers the nineteenth as well as the twentieth century.

Arnold Krupat, *Red Matters: Native American Studies* (Philadelphia, 2002). A valuable survey of current critical approaches to Native American literature. Includes an extended discussion of Alexie's *Indian Killer*.

David Levering Lewis, *When Harlem Was in Vogue* (New York, 1997). Originally published in 1981, an important pioneering study of Harlem in the 1920s. With a new preface by the author.

David Leiwei Li, *Imagining the Nation: Asian American Literature and Cultural Consent* (Stanford, 1998). Li's analysis of the tensions between ethnic and national identities includes discussion of *The Joy Luck Club* and the work of Maxine Hong Kingston.

Kenneth Lincoln, *Native American Renaissance* (Berkeley, 1983). An early and influential review, includes discussion on Momaday and Silko.

Deborah L. Madsen, *Understanding Contemporary Chicana Literature* (Columbia, SC, 2002). The six authors who form the focus of this useful study include Sandra Cisneros.

William J. Maxwell, *New Negro, Old Left: African American Writing and Communism between the Wars* (New York, 1999). Explores the influence of communism on African American writing in the 1920s and 1930s, including the work of Hurston and Wright.

Robert Dale Parker, *The Invention of Native American Literature* (Ithaca, 2003). Puts contemporary Native American literature into the context of central themes in Native American writing of earlier generations.

Joy Porter and Kenneth M Roemer, eds., *The Cambridge Companion to Native American Literature* (Cambridge, 2005). The wide-ranging subjects include individual essays on the work of Silko, Erdrich, and Alexie.

Ross Posnock, *Color and Culture: Black Writers and the Making of the Modern Intellectual* (Cambridge, 1998). In arguing against a "tribal conception of politics founded on a romance of identity" it offers provocative readings of Ellison, Hurston, and Baldwin.

Catherine Rainwater, *Dreams of Fiery Stars: The Transformation of Native American Fiction* (Philadelphia, 1999). Looks at the way Native American writers have to counter some of the storytelling strategies of their own traditions in writing a novel. Includes discussion of Silko and Erdrich.

A. LaVonne Brown Ruoff, *American Indian Literatures* (New York, 1990). Although ending with the 1980s, a particularly valuable resource for earlier Native American writing, in particular oral and written histories going back to the eighteenth century.

Sonia Saldivar-Hull, *Feminism on the Border: Chicana Gender Politics and Literature* (Berkeley, 2000). This argument for a "feminism on the border" that transcends national borders and ethnic identities includes an extended discussion of Cisneros.

Gerald Vizenor, ed., *Narrative Chance: Postmodern Discourse on Native American Indian Literatures* (Albuquerque, 1989). Includes useful essays on Silko and Erdrich.

Cheryl A. Wall, *Women of the Harlem Renaissance* (Bloomington, IA, 1995). Surveys the period with particular emphasis on Fauset, Larsen, and Hurston.

Index

Note: The dates assigned to individual texts are those of the first United States publication.

slavery
African American narratives 342
history in the USA 339
in Morrison 324–7
white writers on 340–2
Smoke Signals (film) (1998) 192
Southern Gothic tradition 364
Southern Review, The (journal) 366
Spanish Americans 346, 352
Spanish Civil War 4, 20, 23, 83, 94
Stedman, Edmund Clarence 1
Stein, Gertrude (1874–1946) 58–61,
362–3
influence 228
lectures 60
Paris salon 19, 59
The Autobiography of Alice B. Toklas
(1933) 58
Everybody's Autobiography (1937)
60
Lucy Church Amiably (1930) 60
The Making of Americans (1925)
59–60
Tender Buttons (1914) 59
Three Lives (1909) 59
Stein, Leo 58–9
Steinbeck, John (1902–1968) 107–11
awards 107, 109
criticized 250
Cannery Row (1945) 110
Cup of Gold (1929) 107, 108
East of Eden (1952) 110
The Grapes of Wrath (1939) 6, 109,
246–50, 358
In Dubious Battle (1936) 108
Of Mice and Men (1937) (also a play)
108–9
The Pastures of Heaven
(1932) 107–8, 348
The Pearl (1947) 110
Pipe Dream (musical) (1955) 111
Sea of Cortez (1941) 109–10
*The Short Reign of Pippin IV: A
Fabrication* (1957) 110–11
Sweet Thursday (1954) 110–11
Tortilla Flat (1935) 108
The Winter of Our Discontent (1961)
110–11

Stone, Phil 85, 86
Story (magazine) 118, 133
Stowe, Harriet Beecher, *Uncle Tom's
Cabin* (1852) 340

Tan, Amy 35, 352
The Joy Luck Club (1989) 35,
328–31
Tanner, Tony, *City of Words* (1971)
298
Tarnished Angels, The (film) (1958) 88
Thalberg, Irving (producer) 355, 356,
357
Thirteenth Amendment 15, 339
Thomas, Dylan 242
Three Mountains Press 92
Tobacco Road (film) (1941) 25–6
Toklas, Alice B. 19, 58, 59, 60
Toomer, Jean 341
Cane (1923) 343, 348
Toyon (magazine) 179
Transatlantic Review 2, 19, 59, 95
Twain, Mark 1, 17
Adventures of Huckleberry Finn
(1885) 340
The Mysterious Stranger
(unfinished) 1–2, 11–12
Pudd'nhead Wilson (1894) 340

Updike, John (1932–2009) 29, 152–6,
347
awards 154, 155
influenced by Hawthorne 155
short stories 153, 351
Bech series 154
The Centaur (1963) 155
The Coup (1978) 155–6
Couples (1968) 155
A Month of Sundays (1975) 154,
155
The Poorhouse Fair (1959) 153
Rabbit series (1960, 1971, 1981,
1990) 153, 154
Roger's Version (1986) 154, 155
S (1988) 154, 155
The Widows of Eastwick (2008) 155
The Witches of Eastwick (1984)
155